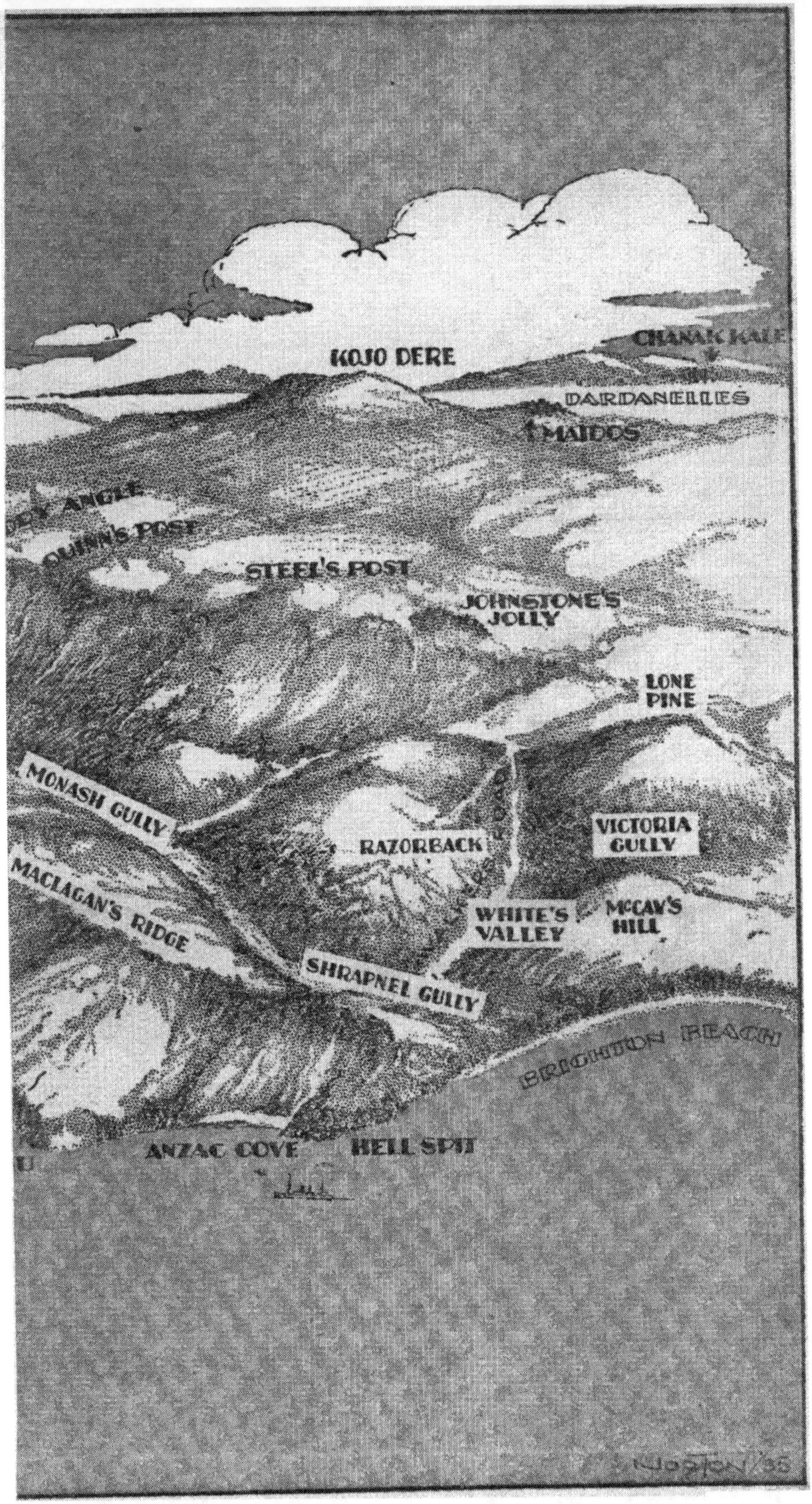
CHANAK KALE
KOJO DERE
DARDANELLES
MAIDOS
ANGLE
QUINN'S POST
STEEL'S POST
JOHNSTONE'S
JOLLY
LONE
PINE
MONASH GULLY
RAZORBACK
VICTORIA
GULLY
MACLAGAN'S RIDGE
WHITE'S
VALLEY
McCAY'S
HILL
SHRAPNEL GULLY
BRIGHTON BEACH
ANZAC COVE
HELL SPIT

RANDWICK TO HARGICOURT

LIEUT.-COL. R. H. OWEN, C.M.G.

RANDWICK TO HARGICOURT

HISTORY OF THE 3RD BATTALION, A.I.F.

By
ERIC WREN

Foreword by
MAJOR-GENERAL SIR NEVILL M. SMYTH, V.C., K.C.B.

The Naval & Military Press Ltd

Published by
The Naval & Military Press Ltd
5 Riverside, Brambleside, Bellbrook
Industrial Estate, Uckfield, East Sussex,
TN22 1QQ England
Tel: +44 (0) 1825 749494
Fax: +44 (0) 1825 765701
www.naval-military-press.com
www.military-genealogy.com

In reprinting in facsimile from the original, any imperfections are inevitably reproduced and the quality may fall short of modern type and cartographic standards.

*Dedicated to the memory of officers,
N.C.Os and men of the 3rd Battalion,
A.I.F., who fell during the war.*

FOREWORD

Major-General Sir Nevill M. Smyth,
V.C., K.C.B.,
In command of the 1st Australian Infantry Brigade from May, 1915 to December, 1916.

THE valour, endurance and intelligence of the Australian soldier shone conspicuously under the most trying conditions of the war of 1914 to 1919, and the authentic record of the 3rd Australian Battalion reveals deeds so heroic and so prodigious that I commend its perusal to every Australian and to every person who reveres the noble deeds of our forebears, and draws inspiration from the pictures which fill the imagination when we read the actions of such men as Abercromby, Lord Nelson, Broke, Livingstone, General Gordon, and others too whose noble characters, unheard of by the world, are only known to a few.

I feel confident that the labours of those who have contributed to this memoir will be crowned with great usefulness.

The 3rd Battalion exemplifying the proverb of the Romans, *Fortis cadere, cedere non potest*—"the brave man may fall, he cannot yield," lost more men killed in action than any other Australian regiment, but it played a leading part in every epic victory of the Infantry of the Commonwealth.

"Always do what you are afraid to do" might have been the high counsel of those stalwart soldiers of the Third had we not often doubted whether they knew what fear was.

It is a coincidence that the figure three seems to be associated with immutable resolution. Our thoughts naturally turn to the old Third Foot, The Buffs, which is the Allied Regiment of the old Regular Army to the Third Australians, and we recall their part in 1811 at Albuera. They entered the battle with 24 officers and 750 other ranks, and on the morrow 5 officers and 35 men answered the roll-call. Again the 3rd Dragoon Guards in the last war lost more in killed than any other cavalry regiment, but they never lost a trench or a prisoner to the enemy.

As I have the privilege of referring to the illustrious victories of my brother officers and comrades of the 3rd Battalion, I wish to dispel a fallacy which may still prevail that the Australian soldier owed his supremacy in action to sudden bursts of undisciplined valour, and I venture to state definitely that the victories of the brigade could never have been won without a high sense of battle discipline, and in the 3rd Battalion precision, skill, steadiness and co-ordination were unsurpassed. In proof of this statement I may mention that the troops of the 1st Australian Infantry Brigade practised an irresistible combined attack on enemy trenches, which involved the co-ordination of a laterally rolling barrage by field artillery; of trench mortars and cross-fire of machine-guns, covering a progressive advance from bay to bay of men armed with rifle grenades and hand grenades and bayonets. Only the most highly drilled troops could carry out such complex tactics successfully.

As one of the innumerable examples of the stubborn courage of the men of the battalion, whose whole being was concentrated on devotion to duty, I remember Sergeant Foley received no less than seven wounds in the war, and on 6 August 1915, after he had been wounded three times in the Capture of Lone Pine, he and four others were waiting for their wounds to be dressed, when at a call for reinforcements one of them exclaimed, "I'll go." Foley said, "If you can go, I shall, too," and they pushed back into the thick of the fray. Foley then received a fourth wound which necessitated his being reluctantly borne off the field.

The "boys" carried their sunshine with them, and many were the gleams of humour which brought gaiety in the sinister surroundings. They fulfilled Wordsworth's ideal of

> The happy warrior . . . .
> Whose high endeavours are an inward light
> That makes the path before him always bright.

And those high endeavours were not for themselves but for others, and for the cause of justice which is eternal.

We feel a thrill when we see the young soldiers to-day who inherit the glorious tradition of the battalion. Guardians of the Commonwealth, you are trusted and honoured!

> Abroad in arms, at home in studious kind
> Who seeks with painful toil shall soonest honour find
> In woods, in waves, in wars, she wonts to dwell
> And will be found with peril and with pain.
> He can, the man that moulds in idle cell,
> Unto her happy mansion attain.

Nevill M. Smyth

"Kongbool,"
   Hamilton,
      Victoria.
         21st March, 1934.

MESSAGE FROM
Lieutenant-General Sir H. B. Walker,
K.C.B., K.C.M.G., D.S.O.,
In command of the 1st Brigade and subsequently the 1st Division.
To Lieutenant-Colonel D. T. Moore, Officers, N.C.Os and men
of the 3rd Battalion, A.I.F.

I greatly appreciate having been asked by your historian to add a message to you on the publication of your Regimental History.

I had the honour to have the battalion under my command as G.O.C. 1st Brigade on Gallipoli, and subsequently as the divisional commander till 30 June 1918.

I am very grateful at having this opportunity of paying tribute to your consistent gallantry and high standard of efficiency during those trying times. Space does not permit my saying all I should like, and my Gallipoli diaries, which recorded so much of the doings of your battalion there, were lost when I was evacuated for wounds in October 1915. But I have vivid recollections of my close association with your original battalion commander, Colonel Owen—of his friendship and charming personality—and then the capture of Lone Pine in which your battalion participated and where, if my memory serves me right, you lost 70 per cent of your officers, including one of my warmest friends, Colonel E. S. Brown—whose body, I fear, was never recovered—with his death and the loss of so many officers, the possibility of having someone able to speak on behalf of so much individual gallantry on the part of survivors, was lost.

And then in France when I lost a personal friend in

McConaghy, and Howell-Price—the first of three gallant brothers to give their lives.

Your battalion with its accustomed gallantry and sang-froid took part in the costly though successful attacks at Pozières.

Colonel Moore must look back with pride and satisfaction on the prominent part he and his battalion played in the complicated but entirely successful attack on Hermies in April in 1917, which was one of the most important operations carried out that year in front of the Hindenburg Line. A few days later the battalion again demonstrated its high standard of training and gallantry, in successfully resisting the German attack on the 1st Brigade front. Here the division held a front of over 12,000 yards.

In no case was the battalion front penetrated, whereas the German dead lay thick before them.

In the Second Battle of Bullecourt, in the following month, your battalion was taken to reinforce the 2nd Division—and I learnt afterwards that Colonel Moore's cool-headed tactics and the gallantry of his battalion contributed largely to success.

Through the long drawn out Third Battle of Ypres, your battalion added to its reputation for unflinching bravery, losing some 20 officers and over 400 other ranks.

In 1918 on the Hazebrouck front your battalion heavily defeated a German attack on your line, and again later it operated on a strong raid on Meteren, thus helping to prepare the way for a next forward advance of the 1st Division if required. Here my lengthy association with you and the A.I.F. terminated. But I have been able to follow your career through *Reveille* to some extent, and your doings in Lord Rawlinson's Army during the closing scenes of the War in France. Here the capture of "Big Bertha" at the Battle of Chuignes by your battalion appeals to me as one of your crowning achievements in the war.

New South Wales has reason to be proud of its battalions, but of none more so than yours.

Harold Walker

Palace Lodge,
  Crediton,
    Devon.
      5th February, 1934.

TO MY COMRADES OF THE 3RD BATTALION, A.I.F.
Brigadier-General W. B. Lesslie,
C.B., C.M.G., R.E.,
Commanded 1st Infantry Brigade, A.I.F., 1917-18.

This record of the service of the battalion throughout the Great War must commend itself to you, and to all others who had the good fortune to be associated with you.

It is fitting that the foreword has been written by Sir Nevill Smyth, V.C., who was your brigade commander in much of your hard fighting in Gallipoli and in France, and who is still with you as a resident in the Commonwealth.

I had the honour to succeed him as your brigade commander in France, and I am now accorded a further distinction in that I am asked to add these few lines to what he has written. I must, of necessity, be brief, and as well, perhaps, because no amount of writing could adequately express my appreciation of the service of the battalion from January 1917 to June 1918, the period of my command of the 1st Australian Infantry Brigade.

I had many opportunities of judging its work in the line. This was characterized by gallantry, determination, and a spirit of exploitation beyond all praise.

I feel sure that there can have been few brigade commanders in France whose charges gave as great a feeling of security and freedom from anxiety as did mine.

What a record, too, that throughout the whole of this period it was not found necessary to make a single raid to obtain identification. This record was in peril near Strazeele in May 1918, but was saved by the gallantry of a sergeant of the battalion, whose name I withhold because he was but one of many who distinguished themselves.

If when out of the line there was an occasional individual break away from the bonds of discipline, we must realize that the circumstances were exceptional, and we must forgive the happy warrior who, freed from his responsibilities in contact with the enemy, gave way to the temptations of more peaceful surroundings. Whatever his lapses when out of the line he invariably did all that was asked, and more, when the situation was critical and called for special effort.

Yours was a cheerful and a happy battalion—a sure sign that it was an efficient one. My visit to you was never an inspection—it was a friendly call on comrades for whom I had a great regard, and whose companionship I valued.

When I parted with you it was with very great regret, but I had the consolation that I was handing over my much treasured charge to the officer whom I most wished to succeed me, Brigadier-General I. G. Mackay.

Sixteen years have passed—the happy memory of my association with you continues, and I realize now more than ever how fortunate I was in my command.

I offer a tribute to the many gallant lads who gave their lives to build up the reputation of this fine fighting battalion, and a greeting to the survivors who maintained and strengthened it.

"King's Furlong,"
  Basingstoke, Hants,
    England.
      6th March, 1934.

PREFACE

THE production of the 3rd Battalion history is rather belated, and for that reason it has been somewhat difficult to give to the narrative the treatment it deserves. Nevertheless the author trusts that readers of the following pages, particularly members of the old battalion, will be satisfied with the story of its share in the Great War that he has been able to reconstruct from various sources.

In collecting the data from which this history has been written, the author received assistance from many members of the battalion, but he would like to mention that he is especially indebted to Lieut-Col B. V Stacy, who lent him a copy of the war diary of the 1st Infantry Brigade; to Colonel A. J. Bennett, for his notes on the formation of the battalion; to Lieut-Col D. T. Moore, for various personal records and reports; to Major J. W. B. Bean, for his stirring narrative of the early days of the unit; to Lieut-Col A. F Burrett, for his vivid notes of Lone Pine, Strazeele, Proyart and Hargicourt; to Mr W. H. Nicholson, who also played a prominent part in the writing of the book; to Major J. R. O. Harris, for his account of Pozières; to Mr C. M. Geddes, in connection with the Turkish counter-attack of 19th May, 1915; to Major P. Goldenstedt and Messrs E. N. Litchfield and Keith Martyn, for assistance on several aspects of the Gallipoli campaign; to Mr E. R. Shelley, for notes on Hermies and Passchendaele; and to Captain A. McDermid and Messrs L. W. S. Loveday, G. H. Leslie, C. O. Clark, P. Kinchington, C. J. Clifton, H. D. Robb, A. J. S. Croll, L. F. Cook, L. Jones, W. Brett, W. C. Vandenbergh, and others for various interesting records.

For several years after the war the Defence Department was able to furnish unit history committees with nominal rolls, lists of killed and wounded and of officers and men who were decorated or mentioned in dispatches, but eventually, as the staff of the Base Records Office dwindled, this assistance had to be withdrawn. In these important matters, therefore, the committee of the 3rd Battalion was to a great extent thrown upon its own resources. Mr W. H. Nicholson took over the colossal task of compiling the nominal roll, and the fact that he got together approximately 5200 names from various sources is a tribute to his zeal and energy. If there are any errors or omissions, it is hoped that readers will be generous in their criticism.

The maps reproduced in this history were compiled mainly by Mr A. S. McKenzie. That of Gallipoli at the beginning and end of the volume is the work of Mr C. B. Norton of the *Sun* newspaper. Many of the photographs were taken by the late Lieut M. McL. Keshan, who was killed at Proyart. His sister, Miss A. A. Keshan, kindly made the negatives available to the author, and Mr H. Hanlon took prints from them.

Dr C. E. W. Bean, the official historian, and his secretary, Mr A. W. Bazley, have been untiring in their efforts to assist in the production of the history. Major J. L. Treloar and Mr L. J. R. Bain of the Australian War Memorial have kindly rendered assistance from time to time; and throughout the work of compilation Captain Q. S. Spedding of the 38th Battalion has given much help.

Major-General Sir N. M. Smyth, V.C., has taken a personal interest in the work and made many useful suggestions.

E. W.

"*Therma*,"
  Cooper Street,
    Strathfield.
      30th March 1935.

CONTENTS

FOREWORD		vii
AN APPRECIATION		xi
TO MY COMRADES		xv
PREFACE		xvii
TRAVEL DIARY		xxv
I.	REMEMBERING BACK	1
II.	RECRUITING BEGINS	7
III.	BATTALION OFFICERS AND MEN	13
IV.	EARLY EVENTS	19
V.	IT IS GOOD-BYE	22
VI.	THE LAND OF THE PHARAOHS	28
VII.	"FIT FOR WAR"	38
VIII.	THE LANDING	44
IX.	THE SECOND DAY	61
X.	THE THIRD DAY	66
XI.	THE MARINES ARRIVE	70
XII.	THE TURKISH ATTACK	77
XIII.	ARMISTICE	84
XIV.	TRENCH WARFARE	88
XV.	LONE PINE	97
XVI.	HAMILTON WINS THE VICTORIA CROSS	108
XVII.	LONE PINE AGAIN	112
XVIII.	THE EVACUATION	121
XIX.	THE RETURN TO EGYPT	126
XX.	IT IS FRANCE!	135
XXI.	INTO THE LINE	145
XXII.	THE CAPTURE OF POZIÈRES	155
XXIII.	THE SECOND POZIÈRES	175
XXIV.	TO BELGIUM	186
XXV.	FLERS	192
XXVI.	WINTER WARFARE	205
XXVII.	GERMAN WITHDRAWAL—BATTLE OF HERMIES	222

CONTENTS

XXVIII.	THE SECOND BULLECOURT	238
XXIX.	THE THIRD BATTLE OF YPRES	247
XXX.	THE WINTER OF 1917-1918	270
XXXI.	THE DEFENCE OF HAZEBROUCK	277
XXXII.	THE ADVANCE TO VICTORY	302
XXXIII.	THE BATTLE OF PROYART	316
XXIV.	THE BATTLE OF HARGICOURT	322
XXV.	THE ARMISTICE AND AFTERWARDS	329
BATTLE HONOURS		333
LIST OF DECORATIONS		335
NOMINAL ROLL: OFFICERS; N.C.Os AND MEN		339
APPENDIX		423

LIST OF ILLUSTRATIONS

LIEUT.-COL. R. H. OWEN, C.M.G.	*Frontispiece*
LIEUT.-COL. A. J. BENNETT, C.M.G., D.S.O., V.D.	16
ORIGINAL OFFICERS, 3RD BATTALION, KENSINGTON, N.S.W., 1914	17
3RD BATTALION BAND, MENA, FEBRUARY, 1915	32
3RD BATTALION, MENA, FEBRUARY, 1915	33
THREE VIEWS OF MENA CAMP, EGYPT	48
1ST INFANTRY BRIGADE ON ITS WAY BACK TO MENA, IN THE EARLY MORNING, AFTER AN ALL-NIGHT FIELD PRACTICE IN THE DESERT NEAR THE PYRAMIDS	49
3RD BATTALION LINES AT MENA	64
COLONEL MacLAURIN, MAJOR IRVINE, AND CAPTAIN D. M. KING	64
GENERAL SIR IAN HAMILTON, WITH HIS STAFF, LEAVING MENA CAMP	65
3RD BATTALION BOARDING THE *DERFFLINGER* AT ALEXANDRIA, APRIL, 1915	65
PRACTISING BOAT DRILL AND LANDING OPERATIONS AT LEMNOS, APRIL, 1915	80
LIEUT.-COL. OWEN ADDRESSING THE MEN ON THE EVE OF THE LANDING	81
3RD BATTALION MEN LEAVING THE *DERFFLINGER* ON A DESTROYER TO TAKE PART IN THE LANDING	96
BEFORE "REVEILLE" ON THE MORNING PRIOR TO THE LANDING	97
3RD BATTALION MEN ON A DESTROYER PROCEEDING INSHORE FOR THE LANDING	97
SHRAPNEL GULLY	112
SICK AND WOUNDED GOING ABOARD A BARGE AT ANZAC	112
STRETCHER-BEARERS ON THE WAY DOWN TO THE BEACH	113
ANZAC COVE	128
SCENE IN COMMUNICATION TRENCH, GALLIPOLI	129
THE FAMOUS NEW ZEALAND WATER TAPS, GALLIPOLI	144
CONSTRUCTING NEW HEADQUARTERS FOR THE 3RD BATTALION, ANZAC, JUNE, 1915	144
THE GRAVE OF SGT. JONES, B COMPANY	145

ILLUSTRATIONS

THE GRAVES OF 3RD BATTALION MEN IN SHRAPNEL GULLY	145
LIEUT. MEAGER WITH HIS PERISCOPIC RIFLE	160
WHILE THE BILLY BOILS. (LIEUT. E. C. H. RITCHIE, PTE BAILEY AND PTE TIMOTHY NOLAN.)	160
A TYPICAL "POSSIE," 3RD BATTALION TRENCHES, ANZAC	161
PTE FREDERICKS SNIPING WHILE THE OBSERVER WATCHES THE EFFECT	161
LIEUT.-COL. D. M. McCONAGHY, C.M.G., D.S.O.	176
LIEUT.-COL. E. S. BROWN	176
LIEUT. J. HAMILTON, V.C.	177
LIEUT.-COL. O. G. HOWELL-PRICE, D.S.O., M.C.	192
3RD BATTALION GOING INTO RESERVE TRENCHES, ZONNEBEKE, 5TH NOVEMBER, 1917, FOR PASSCHENDAELE	193
HARBONNIERES. 3RD BATTALION FOLLOWING UP AFTER ATTACK BY A.I.F., 8TH AUGUST, 1918	208
3RD BATTALION N.C.Os, TAKEN AT METEREN, 1918	209
3RD BATTALION OFFICERS, AT METEREN, 1918	224
VIEW FROM OBSERVATION POST, RAVINE WOOD	225
STRONG POINT, 20TH SEPTEMBER, 1917	225
YPRES-BRUSSELS RAILWAY CUTTING, NEAR HILL 60	225
VERBRANDENMOLEN ROAD	225
COMMUNICATION TRENCH, BULGAR WOOD	240
DRAINING IRON ALLEY	240
HEAD OF COMMUNICATION TRENCH, HILL 60	240
IRON ALLEY, ZILLEBEKE, HILL 60	240
THE CLOTH HALL, YPRES	241
THE LACE SCHOOL, YPRES	241
INTERIOR ST PIERRE CHURCH, YPRES	241
EXTERIOR, ST PIERRE CHURCH, YPRES	241
BILLETS, SEC BOIS	256
LA BREARDE. WINDMILL	256
RAILWAY CROSSING, STRAZEELE	256
BILLETS, STEENVORDE	256
GERMAN OBSERVATION POST, RAVINE WOOD	257
RAVINE WOOD, HOLLEBEKE	257
A FINAL RESTING-PLACE NEAR WYTCHAETE	257
THE RAVINE, HOLLEBEKE	257
RUINS OF CAESTRE	272
FLETRE	272
RUINS OF FLETRE	272
RUINS OF CAESTRE	272
DESERTED STRAZEELE	273
R.C. CHURCH, PRADELLES	273

ILLUSTRATIONS

D COMPANY HEADQUARTERS, STRAZEELE	273
SUPPORTS, SHREWSBURY FOREST	273
TRENCH AT MERRIS, ROUND A DUD MINENWERFER	288
STRONG POINTS, 20TH SEPTEMBER, 1917	288
SWAN CHATEAU, DICKEBUSCH	288
DUG-OUTS, SPOIL BANK	288
LIEUT.-COL. D. T. MOORE, C.M.G., D.S.O., V.D.	289
MAJOR A. F. BURRETT, D.S.O.	304
PROMINENT OFFICERS	305
PROMINENT OFFICERS	320
BATTLE OF MENIN ROAD. 3RD BATTALION GARRISONING THE LINE AT CLAPHAM JUNCTION	321
SOME N.C.Os AND MEN	336
A GROUP OF OFFICERS	337
DECORATED OFFICERS	352
OUTSTANDING MEMBERS OF THE BATTALION	353
OFFICERS DECORATED WITH THE MILITARY CROSS	368
SOME OFFICERS AND N.C.Os	369
DECORATED N.C.Os AND MEN	384
14 IN. GUN CAPTURED BY 3RD BATTALION AT ARCY WOOD	385

LIST OF MAPS

FROM AUSTRALIA TO EGYPT	24
LEMNOS, IMBROS, TENEDOS, AND THE DARDANELLES	40
TURKISH ATTACK, 19TH MAY, 1915	79
ALEXANDRIA TO MARSEILLES	133
ACROSS FRANCE	137
BATTLE OF POZIÈRES, MAP No. 1	161
BATTLE OF POZIÈRES, MAP No. 2	164
THE SECOND BATTLE OF BULLECOURT	242
THE ATTACK ON BROODSEINDE RIDGE	258
THE DEFENCE OF HAZEBROUCK	283
THE BATTLE OF PROYART AND CHUIGNES	318
THE BATTLE OF HARGICOURT	325

TRAVEL DIARY OF THE 3RD BATTALION

1914.
Aug. 13—Major A. J. Bennett, D.S.O., instructed to form 3rd Battalion.
 ,, 17—First batch of recruits marched to Randwick Racecourse camp.
 ,, 24—Moved to Kensington Racecourse.
 ,, 31—Returned to Randwick Racecourse.
Sept. 10—Camp transferred to Paton's Paddock, Randwick.
 ,, 19—Camp shifted to new site at Kensington.
Oct. 19—Embarked on troopship *Euripides*.
 ,, 20—Departed from Sydney.
 ,, 26—Arrived at Albany.
Nov. 1—Departed from Albany.
 ,, 9—*Emden* destroyed by *Sydney*.
 ,, 15—Arrived at Colombo.
 ,, 17—Departed from Colombo.
 ,, 25—Arrived at Aden.
 ,, 26—Departed from Aden.
Dec. 1—Suez.
 ,, 2—Port Said.
 ,, 3—Alexandria.
 ,, 4—Arrived at Mena camp.

1915.
April 3—Marched out of Mena camp. Entrained at Cairo for Alexandria.
 ,, 4—Embarked on the *Derfflinger*.
 ,, 5—Departed from Alexandria.
 ,, 8—Arrived at Mudros Harbour.
 ,, 24—Departed from Lemnos Harbour. Took up position outside.
 ,, 25—Sailed for Gallipoli. The Landing effected.
 ,, 29—Relieved in trenches by R.M.L.I.

May   1—Took over from R.M.L.I. front line trenches.
  „   19—Heavy Turkish attack.
  „   24—Armistice to bury dead.
Aug.   6—Battle of Lone Pine.
Sept. 15—Left for Lemnos.
Oct. 29—Returned to Gallipoli.
Dec. 19—Evacuation of Gallipoli. Then to Lemnos.
  „   24—Departed for Alexandria.
  „   28—Arrived at Alexandria.
  „   29—Tel-el-Kebir.

1916.
Feb. 29—Entrained for Serapeum.
March 19—Inspected by H.R.H. The Prince of Wales.
  „   21—Entrained for Alexandria.
  „   22—Embarked on troopship *Grampian*.
  „   27—Arrived at Toulon.
  „   28—Marseilles. Entrained for north.
  „   31—Detrained at Steenbecque. Marched to Wallon-Capel and Ebblinghem.
April 10—Marched to Moolenacker.
  „   20—Marched to Sailly-sur-la-Lys.
May   3—Moved into firing line for first time in France—Levantie-Fleurbaix sector.
  „   19—Relieved by 9th Battalion. Moved into billets, Croix du Bac.
June   9—Fleurbaix.
  „   23—Took over firing line from 1st Battalion.
  „   28—1st Battalion raid from C Company trenches.
July   4—Relieved by 45th Battalion. Moved to Sailly.
  „   9—Marched to Oultersteene.
  „   10—Entrained at Bailleul for south.
  „   11—Detrained at Candas. Marched to St Ouen. Billets.
  „   12—Marched to Vignacourt.
  „   13—Marched to Allonville.
  „   16—Marched to Warloy-Baillon.
  „   19—Albert. Relieved 13th K.R.R. in supports near Pozières.
  „   23—First battle of Pozières.
  „   26—Relieved by 2nd Brigade. Moved to bivouac west of Albert.

TRAVEL DIARY

,, 27—Marched to Vadencourt. Visited by G.O.C. and Lord Northcliffe.
,, 28—La Vicogne.
,, 29—Bonneville.
,, 30—Pernois.
Aug. 9—La Vicogne.
,, 10—Hérissart.
,, 14—Marched to Vadencourt.
,, 15—In bivouacs near Albert.
,, 16—Relieved 49th Battalion. Pozières—Mouquet Farm trenches.
,, 18—Relieved by 1st Battalion. Attack on German trenches.
,, 19—Relieved 10th Battalion. Billets in Albert.
,, 21—Marched to Warloy.
,, 22—Val-de-Maison.
,, 23—Marched to Gezaincourt.
,, 26—Marched to Doullens. Entrained for Poperinghe. Toronto camp.
,, 31—Entrained at Brandhoek for Ypres.
Sept. 1—Relieved 2nd Royal Dublin Fusiliers. Ypres to Menin railway sector (Hill 60).
,, 7—Relieved by 1st Battalion. Moved to railway dug-outs, Zillebeke.
,, 12—Relieved by 11th Battalion. Entrained at Ypres Asylum for Brandhoek Siding. Detrained and marched to Dominion camp.
,, 13—Poperinghe. Dominion camp.
,, 25—Marched to Brandhoek Siding. Entrained for Ypres Asylum Siding.
,, 26—In supports at The Bluff tunnels and Swan Château.
Oct. 7—Relieved 1st Battalion trenches at Swan Château.
,, 12—Raid by Lieut C. L. L. Burrett.
,, 13—Relieved by 14th Battalion.
,, 14—Marched from Dominion camp to Steenvoorde.
,, 15—Marched from Steenvoorde to Arneke.
,, 16—Marched from Arneke to Questmont.
,, 21—Entrained at St Omer. Detrained at Longpré. Marched to L'Etoile.
,, 23—Embussed at Mouflers. Debussed at Fricourt.
,, 25—Mametz Wood (bivouac).
,, 29—Marched to Trones Wood. Relieved 16th Middlesex.

TRAVEL DIARY

Nov. 1—Relieved 1st Battalion in trenches at Flers.
,, 2—Lieut-Col O. G. Howell-Price mortally wounded.
,, 5—Raid by Lieut L. W. S. Loveday.
,, 7—Relieved by 11th Battalion. Moved back to supports.
,, 13—Relieved by 49th Battalion. Moved to Bernafay Wood.
,, 14—Marched to Fricourt.
,, 15—Marched to Buire.
,, 17—Embussed for Flesselles.
,, 25—Moved by motor lorries to Buire.
Dec. 20—Relieved by 6th Battalion. Marched to Mametz.
,, 21—Marched to Bernafay Wood.
,, 22—Relieved 8th Battalion in trenches at Gueudecourt.
,, 31—Relieved by 4th Battalion. Marched to Gap and Switch trenches in support.

1917

Jan. 6—Relieved by 46th Battalion. Marched to Bendigo Camp.
,, 7—Entrained at Quarry Siding. Detrained at Méaulte. March to Ribemont.
,, 13—Marched to Baizieux.
,, 23—Marched to Bécourt.
,, 26—Marched to Bazentin Camp.
,, 27—Relieved 4th Yorks and 4th East Yorks in Eaucourt-l'Abbaye sector.
Feb. 8—Relieved by 1st Battalion. Marched to Bazentin Camp—Site 5.
,, 27—Relieved 11th Battalion outposts at Ligny-Thilloy.
March 6—Relieved by 18th Battalion. Marched to Bazentin.
,, 7—Mametz Camp.
,, 16—Marched to Dernancourt.
,, 22—Marched to Ribemont.
April 3—Marched to Montauban.
,, 5—Frémicourt.
,, 6—Vélu.
,, 9—Attack on Hermies.
,, 15—German attack at Hermies.
,, 16—Relieved by 2nd Battalion. Moved to Beaumetz-lez-Cambrai.
,, 21—Relieved 4th Battalion in front line Demicourt.

TRAVEL DIARY

",, 25—Relieved by 6th Yorks and Lancaster Regiment. Moved to Vélu Wood, then to Riencourt-les-Bapaume.
,, 26—Took over Beaumetz-Morchies-Vaulx-Vraucourt line from 18th Battalion.
,, 27—Relieved by 18th Battalion. Marched to Riencourt.
,, 29—Took over from 18th Battalion.
May 3—Moved into line at O.G.2—Vaulx.
,, 4—German attack at Bullecourt.
,, 6—Relieved by 2nd Battalion.
,, 7—Vaulx.
,, 9—Relieved by 29th Battalion. Moved to Riencourt.
,, 13—Marched to Bazentin.
,, 21—Buire.
June 28—Marched to Englebelmer.
July 2—Mailly-Maillet.
,, 6—Buire.
,, 13—Bray-sur-Somme.
,, 24—Buire.
,, 27—Le Nieppe.
Aug. 9—Marched to Petit Sec Bois.
Sept. 13—Meteren.
,, 14—Ottawa Camp. Ouderdom.
,, 16—Dickebusch.
,, 19—Forward to Château Segard area.
,, 20—Trenches. Menin Road.
,, 24—Ottawa Camp. Ouderdom.
,, 25—Embussed at Ottawa Camp for Steenvoorde.
,, 30—Embussed for Château Segard area.
Oct. 2—Relieved the 10th Battalion at Anzac Ridge.
,, 4—Attack on Broodseinde Ridge.
,, 5—Relieved by 10th Battalion. Moved to Anzac Ridge.
,, 8—Relieved by 4th Battalion. Moved to Dickebusch huts.
,, 9—Embussed to Wippenhoek Area.
,, 16—Embussed for Ypres.
Nov. 1—Canal dugouts near Ypres.
,, 5—Took up left support position. 1st Division Ypres area.
,, 10—Relieved by 2nd/7th Lancashire Fusiliers.
,, 11—Halifax Camp. Ouderdom.

" 13—Berthen.
" 14—Wallon-Capel.
" 15—Henringhem.
" 16—Assinghem.
" 18—Senlecques.
" 19—Halinghem.
Dec. 14—Marched to Enquin.
" 15—Ledinghem.
" 16—Assinghem.
" 17—Marched to Wizernes. Entrained for d'Kennebak. Detrained and marched to Ramilles Camp (Kemmel).
" 31—Relieved 6th Battalion in line.

1918

Jan. 1—Oosttaverne sector.
" 15—Relieved by 6th Battalion.
" 16—Wytschaete Area.
" 22—Relieved 1st Battalion in line.
" 30—Relieved by the 56th Battalion.
" 31—Ramilles Camp (Kemmel). Embussed and moved to Meteren. (Training).
Feb. 27—Moved to Murrumbidgee Camp.
" 28—Moved to Ridge Wood Camp. Relieved 50th Battalion.
March 22—Relieved 2nd Battalion in front line—Verbrandenmolen sector.
" 26—Relieved by 8th Lincoln Regiment. Moved to Ridge Wood Camp.
April 2—Moved to Reninghelst.
" 5—Moved by route march to Godewaersvelde. Entrained for Amiens.
" 6—Detrained at Amiens and marched to Cardonnette.
" 9—Marched to Frechencourt.
" 11—Montigny. Billets.
" 12—Amiens. Entrained to Hondeghem. Moved by motor buses to Strazeele.
" 13—Strazeele. Front line trenches.
" 17—Relieved by 2nd Battalion.
" 18—Sec Bois (supports).

TRAVEL DIARY

,,	21—Relieved by 18th Battalion, Durham Light Infantry.
,,	22—Borre-Pradelles area. Billets.
,,	28—Relieved 9th Battalion in front line. Meteren.
May	4—Relieved by 4th Battalion.
,,	5—Meteren. In reserve.
,,	9—Marched at Caestre. Embussed for Wallon-Capel.
,,	10—Wallon-Capel.
,,	19—Front line at Strazeele.
,,	27—Relieved by 12th Battalion.
,,	28—Strazeele. In support.
,,	29—La Kreule.
June	3—Relieved by 6th Battalion. Moved to Sercus.
,,	4—Sercus.
,,	7—La Kreule.
,,	9—Strazeele. In support.
,,	17—Relieved 4th Battalion in front line.
,,	27—Relieved by 8th Battalion.
,,	28—La Kreule.
July	5—Moved forward to Strazeele sector. Relieved 9th Battalion. In reserve.
,,	12—Relieved 1st Battalion in front line.
,,	15—Relieved by 2nd Battalion, South Wales Borderers.
,,	16—In support.
,,	22—Relieved 2nd Battalion. In reserve.
,,	29—Racquinghem.
Aug.	5—Moved by route march to Wizernes.
,,	6—Entrained at Wizernes for Pont Remy. Detrained, marched to Liercourt. Embussed for Daours via Amiens.
,,	7—Aubigny.
,,	8—Big attack. Morcourt—Chipilly.
,,	9—Relieved by 49th Battalion. Moved to Harbonnières.
,,	10—Rosières.
,,	12—Lihons. Front line.
,,	17—Relieved by 45th and 46th Battalions. Marched back to Vaux-sur-Somme.
,,	18—Vaux.
,,	23—Attack on Proyart.
,,	27—Relieved by 24th Battalion. Bivouac in Morcourt area.

Sept. 6—Hem.
  „ 8—Doingt area.
  „ 9—Tincourt-Boucly area.
  „ 10—Relieved 38th Battalion in supports.
  „ 14—Relieved by 5th Battalion.
  „ 18—Front line—Hargicourt.
  „ 22—Relieved by 5th Battalion. Moved to Roisel area.
  „ 26—Biaches area. Marched to La Chapellette and entrained. Detrained at Longpré. Marched to Bellancourt.
  „ 27—Bellancourt. Billets.
Oct. 6—Marched to Villers-sous-Ailly.
  „ 10—Marched to Epagne.
Nov. 8—Marched to Pont Remy and entrained.
  „ 9—Detrained at Tincourt.
  „ 10—Embussed at Tincourt. Debussed at Bazuel.
  „ 11—Armistice.
  „ 13—Marched to Busigny.
  „ 21—Marched to Mazinghien.
  „ 22—Prisches.
  „ 23—Flaumont-Waudrechies.
  „ 25—Solre-le-Château.
Dec. 15—Barbencon.
  „ 16—Pry.
  „ 17—Gerpinnes.

CHAPTER I

REMEMBERING BACK

THE history of the 3rd Battalion A.I.F. might have been written sixteen years ago, but it was not—and for a variety of reasons. They are considered good reasons and sufficient reasons. Experience has taught that time mellows perspective in a way that is most desirable.

Back in 1918, after four long years of war, we did not see things quite as we see them to-day. What then we might have been inclined to dismiss or disregard as unimportant, to-day, perhaps, has a more vital or a different significance. What then we might have imagined the incidents vital to our history, to-day might be considered only incidental and have little prominence in our memories. By comparison the years have made them to appear trivial.

Any history that has ever really been of consequence has always considerably ante-dated the events that are chronicled and perpetuated; and it is significant that as yet only a fraction of the official stories of Australian units in the Great War have been written. However, to celebrate the twentieth anniversary of our birth as a distinct entity during the greatest crisis in the world's history, it is felt that our plain and unvarnished tale should be told to become a permanent record in the archives of war.

In the long years since the first man—it has, of course, been impossible to identify him because all recruits were drafted more or less indiscriminately in those far-off 1914 days to a dozen units all in the process of formation—to enlist in our old unit marched, perhaps diffidently, perhaps somewhat shyly, in under the shabbily-sombre, freestone archway to the unknown that had as its starting-point Victoria Barracks, Paddington, Sydney; since those far-away days, when we had Randwick Racecourse as a home; since Mena and the Pyramids and those training days of near torture upon Egypt's blistering sands; since we dropped from the blood-specked and missile-splintered tows into the Aegean Sea and scrambled wet, anxious, and grimly determined across that narrow strip of sand that was Anzac, to climb those death-haunted hills that were Gallipoli; since we charged across the bullet and bomb-swept plateau of Lone Pine; since we knew shell-hell of Pozières, war as it was at Mouquet Farm, Gueudecourt, Thilloy, Lagnicourt, Bullecourt, the Menin Road, Merris, Lihons, Chuignes, and Hargicourt; since we knew the miseries of snow, of ice, and mud, without shelter and without release, the terror of the box barrage, and annihilating efforts of machine-guns with determined brave thumbs on the buttons, the stubbornness of the enemy strong-post; since we choked in the gas, and walked rifle at hip close upon the flame and roar of the wall barrage; since we knew that so strange and indescribable feeling that comes when first bayonet stabs into warm human flesh and checks upon human bone —the years have helped us to a much greater appreciation of what should be remembered and what should be chronicled in the 3rd Battalion history.

In those years we have not been idle. We have not forgotten—could we ever forget? We have not neglected to preserve the important official data, and those so vital personal records essential to an accurate recounting of our four years of existence in war. Rather have we added to the storehouse of our knowledge of us, and salved material that originally was not at our disposal.

And now we are able to set down in detail the experiences, the vicissitudes, the triumphs of our unit, and permanently record the deeds of men who were proud to wear the brown-green colour-patch in rectangle. Accuracy has been the first consideration and aim of those who for years have never lost sight of the fact that the history of the 3rd Battalion must be written. And those upon whom the heavy task of compiling this record, without thought of any reward or recompense beyond the satisfaction of a duty done honestly, has been loaded, feel that this record is as comprehensive and as accurate as it is possible to make it.

If this history does no more than to draw together in the old spirit of comradeship the now so widely scattered survivors of the 3rd Battalion, and help to perpetuate cherished wartime memories—sad or gay—the work will not have been in vain. And perhaps our story will give, to the younger generation who read, the inspiration that is to be found in unselfish, unswerving loyalty to ideals, in duty cheerfully done with death and mutilation ever at hand, in sufferings nobly borne and sacrifice even of life itself.

Loyalty, suffering and sacrifice for our own country, for our ideals and for the pride of our unit and of our race.

This history is not written by an individual. It is written *in the spirit* of us all who were the 3rd Battalion.

Remembering back now to the events immediately preceding the outbreak of the Great War, those who offered for service—those who were of the original 3rd Battalion—will surely gather as their strongest impression that the crisis was precipitated with the greatest suddenness —that so far as they were concerned it was almost unheralded.

To Australians in any walk of life, then as now with a plethora of interests—sporting, business, and social— and a great variety of rural, industrial and commercial pursuits, the assassination at Sarajevo in Serbia on June 28th, 1914, of the Archduke Franz Ferdinand of Austria and his royal consort the Duchess of Hohenburg, was just a tragic incident overseas to be quickly forgotten in the hurly-burly of local football premierships, industrial disputes, surfing on sunny beaches, and party politics.

The possible outcome of this murder was not appreciated here, the far-reaching consequences were not grasped —were not even considered. It was just an episode of remote overseas. Came occasional veiled hints of trouble brewing in the brief cabled messages to the Australian Press which were scanned with more or less disinterestedness and unconcern. Those with a general interest in affairs overseas were more intrigued by happenings in troubled Ireland and what the King had had to say in this connection. The Caillaux trial in Paris, too, was a topic. Also, the position of certain Hindu immigrants in Vancouver was a matter of passing interest.

In Sydney, we had been interested in the Farmers' Conference just concluded, were arguing the pros and cons of double dissolutions and the possibilities of a forthcoming Federal election, had begun to notice the fact that the British Association for the Advancement of Science would be shortly holding conferences in the various Australian capitals—quite an event in our then not particularly colourful history.

These things might interest the more serious minded! The Rugby competitions were at an interesting stage. There were cricket and swimming prospects in the coming summer to be enlarged upon; and, the ubiquitous industrial tussles, big and small.

It was on July 28th that we gathered from the local Press a first serious hint that real trouble was brewing on the other side of the world. And we felt sympathetic for those troubled unfortunates who lived over there— those of us who read anything beyond the captions.

The cables told of feverish warlike activities, not only in Serbia and Austria, but in Russia and Germany. On July 30th realization of the crisis was complete, and from then on the Press was crowded with war news and rumours of war. Austria startled the world by declaring war on Serbia. In rapid succession Germany declared war on Russia and on France, and then on August 4th Germany invaded Belgium. And so Great Britain, which had been making every effort to remain aloof, was embroiled. The motherland declared war on Germany.

In those very eventful days preceding Great Britain's declaration of war, Australian parliamentarians, though many of them with a by no means complete appreciation of all that was happening, had been more or less closely following developments, and, just before the decision of Britain, the Prime Minister, Mr (now Sir) Joseph Cook, announced that the Commonwealth Government had decided, in the event of war, to place the Australian Navy under the immediate control of the British Admiralty. And—more significantly—to offer the Imperial Government "an expeditionary force of 20,000 men of any suggested composition (to be sent) to any destination desired by the Home Government . . . the cost of despatch and maintenance will be borne by this (i.e. the Commonwealth) Government."

This announcement was contemporary with the stirring declaration of the then leader of the Federal Labour Party, Mr Andrew Fisher: "Should honour demand that the mother country should take part in hostilities, Australia will stand behind her to the last man and the last shilling." On August 6th Great Britain accepted Australia's offer of 20,000 troops. On August 10th, the day after the first "Old Contemptibles" landed in France, recruiting began in the capital cities of the Commonwealth.

It was war. Out of the blue—war!

The wave of enthusiasm which swept our country will not be forgotten by the generation of that day. We had not expected—we had not desired—we scarcely understood—war. But the homeland was in difficulties—was calling. The "iron heel was grinding," the "sabre" which had "rattled" for so long was "unsheathed"—we remember well the phrases of those days—militarism in its most objectionable form was loose. Our freedom, the freedom of our kith and kin overseas was imperilled.

Twenty thousand men! A mighty host! Who foresaw then that thrice that number of the flower of Australian youth would give their lives before the world's guns had been silenced and the world's bayonets had been sheathed.

And so. . . .

The A.I.F. came into being.

The 3rd Battalion was born.

CHAPTER II

RECRUITING BEGINS

IT has been necessary to review the events leading up to a state of war to emphasize how suddenly—and, in most places in Australia, how unexpectedly—the call came. Within a week men who ultimately served in the 3rd Battalion had deserted desk and farm, football and tennis, for the greatest adventure.

The duty of raising the 1st Infantry Brigade quite naturally devolved upon New South Wales as the senior State of the Commonwealth. Four battalions were required, each to be of a strength of 1200 men distributed in eight companies with the full complement of auxiliary services—administrative, medical, machine-gun, signalling, transport, etc.*

It was on August 13th, exactly a week after the acceptance by Britain of Australia's offer of an expeditionary force that Major A. J. Bennett, D.S.O., was commissioned by Colonel H. N. MacLaurin, commanding the 1st Infantry Brigade, to form the 3rd Battalion. Major Bennett was a thoroughly experienced officer who had served with distinction in the Egyptian and South African campaigns.

His first action was to select a medical officer (Captain J. W. B. Bean), a regimental sergeant-major (R.S.M. A. McAskill), a quartermaster-sergeant (Q.M.S. A. Stronach), and an efficient orderly-room staff. Also he chose

---

* Shortly after arrival in Egypt the original battalion formation was scrapped for the more modern "four companies, four platoons, four sections" system of battalion organization. This reduced the effective strength in the field of each battalion nominally to 1023 all ranks.

several officers with experience gained in the British Army at home and on imperial service (in some instances in South Africa with the Australian contingents) and in the Citizen Forces and cadet units. In the main their knowledge of the military sciences was sufficient to enable them to commence immediately the training of raw recruits.

Recruiting, especially for the 3rd Battalion, began seriously on Monday, August 17th, at Victoria Barracks. On that day twenty acting-officers and 310 other ranks were allotted to the battalion provisionally. Next day three skeleton companies were formed, and by the 20th there were five. On August 23rd the battalion consisted of 18 acting-officers and 533 other ranks.

Who will forget that first day, August 17th, at Victoria Barracks, at 9 a.m.? What a scene of confusion it was! Crowds of men in mufti jostled each other, talking and laughing excitedly. Tall men, short men, youngsters just left school, men in the prime and full maturity of manhood, even a sprinkling of grey heads. Mostly their faces were bright, attentive, and eager.

Here and there in the crowd stood men with quiet, resolute faces, and trim bodies—men with an air of respect and self-control. These were not excited—they waited patiently, not speaking for the most part unless spoken to—they were scholars of a grand school for character, the British Army. Steady, solid, reliable men to form the nucleus of the regiment's N.C.Os—and the regiment always is so emphatically what its N.C.Os make it.

A few there were with the unmistakable stamp of "soldier," but with, alas! faces on which certain excesses had plainly writ their signature. The dissolute ex-Imperial man—called technically "The Old Soldier"—a clever shirker and a skilled malingerer. Not usually a weak man, but rather one with strength uncontrolled and misdirected who, in the hour of battle, often shone out splendidly, and proved himself a magnificent fighter.

"At length the sorting, shuffling and list-taking ceases," wrote Captain J. W. B. Bean. "The men have all presented themselves before the second-in-command—a major of long service, old and wise in war, with the ribbons of Egypt, South Africa, and the D.S.O. on his breast. His keen eyes have swept them over and summed them up. He has seen each medical certificate of fitness, and jerked out to each a few short queries. He turns to the knot of officers who represent our regimental staff so far, and gives them a few orders, and they depart to sort out the men. Markers are called out of the regiment—so far about 300 strong—eight squads are told off —the skeleton of a battalion. They are 'shunned,' dressed, numbered, formed into fours, formed two deep, proved, and stood at ease. Then steps forward a young militia captain who is to take charge, and march them to lunch and quarters at Randwick Racecourse.

"'The battalion will move to the right in fours. A Company, shun! Form fours, right! By the left, quick march!' snaps out the company commander, leading. The others in turn take up the cry, and the 3rd Battalion of Infantry, no longer a name, but a living entity, moves off in column of fours—a long, sinuous serpent, to lunch and glory.

"I stand and watch it for a while. So does the major. Then turning to me, with a twinkle in his eye, he says, 'Always look after the inner man, Bean; I'm off to feed. You'd better do the same. We'll join them over there directly. But a good feed first. What say you?'"

Thus the 3rd Battalion had its genesis. Quarters in those early days were pretty rough for the men. Two battalions camped on the Randwick Racecourse, and two on the Kensington Racecourse, both very handy to Sydney. The grandstands were the men's dormitories. They had no tents at first, but just slept in their clothes on the wooden terraced steps; a blanket over them, and their civilian greatcoat, perhaps, to cover them.

Who fully realizes what a tremendous job it is raising a battalion of infantry? One thousand and twenty-three men (1200 in 1914), bodily and mentally fit to a high degree, have to be sorted out from a still greater number of applicants. Once accepted, the would-be soldier is, as it were, re-born into the army. He brings nothing with him into his military world save the "mufti" he stands in.* And that, as soon as possible, is shed. He has to be clothed, fed, supplied with all toilet necessaries, with blankets, waterproof sheet, eating and cooking utensils, firearms, entrenching tool, spade and pick, and divers other things. Then, too, he has to be sworn in and, finally, paid.

What an enormous amount of work has to be done in the orderly-room by the adjutant and his two orderly-room sergeants! And the quartermaster and his clerks —they are required to be as much business men as soldiers. Piles of accounts, requisitions, receipts, supply lists, statistics, etc. have to be kept and checked. The medical officer and his staff of five A.M.C. men, again, have an immense amount of clerical work to do. There are the morning and evening sick-reports, to begin with. Medical history sheets of all men have to be handed in if they are to be discharged; requisitions made for drugs and dressings; and divers reports rendered to the C.O. and to brigade headquarters. Attestations have to be signed; and many other things too numerous to mention here.

---

* A widely-published statement to the effect that no kit whatever was required by intending recruits was responsible for the condition, with regard to clothing, of many men arriving from the country being most unsatisfactory. The prompt response to a request for 800 shirts, made by Major Bennett to Messrs Denison and Le Maistre Walker, of the executive of the Soldiers' War Chest—then newly formed, and later to become the most practical of all soldiers' "comfort" organizations—was the occasion for great joy.

It was an extraordinarily busy time those first long days—examining men from morning to night. Administrative officers and N.C.Os were up at 6 a.m. and often not to bed until 1 o'clock the next morning, sitting up gruelling over, and preparing, interminable lists.

"Funny fellows, these men, dare-devils many of them, but for the most part now quivering all over with nervousness in my extremely mild presence," wrote Captain Bean with reference to early medical examinations. "They are all secretly terrified that they will be rejected, and they look at you with a pathetic, feeble smile and twitching lips, and heave a huge sigh of relief when it is over and they are safely in.

"Many of them have thrown up jobs of three or four pounds a week, and have travelled hundreds of miles to join us. They have been fêted as heroes before leaving their native villages, and they would rather die than go back there rejected. Some I have to refuse, and they plead with me and almost break down. In fact, some do go away, poor chaps, gulping down their feelings, and with tears of disappointment in their eyes. We do the best we can for the rejects—write them a certificate to say they have been rejected, and why, and pay their railway fare home. This helps them to get taken on again at their work. But it does seem so awfully hard.

"Poor beggars. They were regular heroes right from the start. Such awful mouths the Australians have, many of them. You couldn't fail them for teeth too rigidly, or you'd never have made up your battalion.* They

---

* Major Bennett set such a high standard of fitness, especially in relation to teeth, that of the first fifty men examined, only four satisfied requirements. Thereupon it was arranged that these men, otherwise physically fit, should be passed conditionally on their teeth being treated. The 3rd Battalion also had the advantage of expert treatment of feet by a skilled chiropodist, Pte (afterwards Sgt) Wolsey, from Utah, U.S.A. Both at Kensington and Mena the 3rd had comparatively fewer casualties than other units, due to this very critical first selection and subsequent treatment of teeth and feet.

used to come to me in squads of forty at a time for black draught and Condy's or chlorate of potash as a mouthwash. Up they would stalk with a grin, toss off their portion with a shudder and a wry face, give me an involuntary wink, and march off cheerfully with their lozenges to the Chamber of Horrors—in this case a dental pavilion at the Agricultural Grounds. There shoals of victims were lined up awaiting their turn. In the afternoon they would turn up with swollen faces and bleeding, lacerated gums, having had a dozen or more roots dug out. Still cheerful, for the most part, though unable to manage their "solid tack" for some days. The men had to be vaccinated, and inoculated for typhoid, too. Altogether they went through a lot with the utmost cheerfulness—just like a lot of happy-go-lucky schoolboys."

CHAPTER III

BATTALION OFFICERS AND MEN

On August 19th Lieut-Col R. H. Owen was given command of the battalion. Recalling the incident, Major Bennett, the first C.O., said: "In August, 1914, I was ordered to raise the 3rd Battalion, A.I.F., and expected to have the command, but one morning the brigadier informed me, over the telephone, that an imperial officer of great ability and distinction was to take over from me. Wonderingly I awaited the newcomer, and judge my surprise and joy when in stalked 'Bob' Owen to announce himself as the new C.O. I say 'joy,' for I was not too happy with many of the amateurs who at that time were giving a wholesale supply of 'order, counter-order, and disorder.'"

Lieut-Col Owen had been a member of the historic Sudan contingent from Australia (1885). Afterwards he joined the Regular Army. When the South African War broke out he became chief staff officer of the New Zealand forces, and was responsible for organizing the whole of that dominion's contingents for this campaign.

No better description of the battalion's new C.O. could be quoted than that supplied by Captain Bean: "Owen had a slight, medium-height figure. He was always spotlessly clean and neat. So upright and so well knit, and so thoroughly soldierly. He had a clear, healthy, tanned face, a close-cut, white moustache, rather prominent cheek-bones, and a firm though kindly mouth. His eyes were alert and bright—in their way perfect reflections of the colonel himself, now bubbling over with fun, now thoughtful and grave, and so often sympathetic and tender, if occasionally very stern. There were times, too, when they looked worried and anxious. Colonel Owen felt his responsibilities very deeply, and he sympathized very much with his men. He could feel their troubles and difficulties acutely."

Because of his paternal appearance, and his habit, quickly developed, of personally looking into and after the individual welfare of his men—especially at meal time—the new C.O. soon became known as "Dad." The name stuck to him throughout—"Dad" Owen.

Major A. J. Bennett thus became second-in-command, and very loyal he proved to his old comrade "Bob" Owen. Major Bennett's war record also included service with the New South Wales contingent to the Sudan, for which he was awarded the Egyptian medal and clasp, Suakim and Khedive's Star. In the South African War he won the D.S.O. and gained the Queen's medal with three clasps, and the King's medal with two clasps. He had the distinction of attending King Edward VII's coronation, representing Australian soldiers in the field.

Over six feet in height, loose limbed, a school-teacher by profession and a strict disciplinarian, Bennett had absolutely no use for the shirker and malingerer.

While the battalion was training in Egypt, contiguous to Cairo with its manifold attractions and distractions, naturally it was to be expected that the orderly-room parades of defaulters should be governed largely by the severity of the penalty as compared with the pleasure. The increasing number of defaulters worried the kind-hearted Colonel Owen, who, hating to see his men in trouble, greatly disliked punishing them if reform by other methods was possible. Happening at this stage to come into temporary command of the battalion for a few days, Major Bennett issued instructions to company officers to maintain their own discipline, and not to refer trivial cases to the C.O. An indication was given of what an energetic provost sergeant could do by a systematically inconvenient sounding of the "Angel's Whisper" (defaulters' parade), rousing pack drill parades under an impost of only three days' "C.B.," with stoppage of leave. In addition, a transfer of half a dozen "bad hats" to Cairo detention barracks sobered up others wonderfully. Five days later the C.O. returned to find not one case listed for orderly-room. This provoked the delightful remark from "Dad" Owen: "I knew the battalion would settle down; the men were just a little excited at first."

This drastic change made for great good, though Major Bennett earned for himself the title "Defaulters' Waterloo." Confinees in the guard tent subsequently would inquire anxiously, "Who's taking orderly-room today?"

Captain E. S. Brown, of the permanent Instructional Staff, a soldier by profession, was appointed adjutant. His uncanny judgment in sizing men up will always be remembered by those who knew him. He rarely, if ever, made a mistake.

Warrant-Officer A. McAskill, formerly a sergeant in the Scots Guards, also of the Instructional Staff, was gazetted regimental sergeant-major. He proved to be an excellent drill-master.

The chaplain attached to the battalion was the Dean of Sydney, the Very Rev. A. E. Talbot, M.A.

The original officers of the battalion were in the main drawn from the militia. Many had already seen active service. Besides the colonel and second-in-command,

Captain C. W. H. Coulter (H Company) had soldiered in the South African campaign, being awarded both the King's and Queen's medals with clasps.

Lieut G. Wall, the quartermaster, had been through the Egyptian and South African campaigns.

Captain J. C. Wilson (D Company), an Englishman, also had seen service in the South African War, with the 2nd Loyal North Lancaster Regiment and been awarded the Queen's medal with five clasps.

Other officers who had seen service on the African veldt were: Captain C. D. Austin (C Company), with the 5th Queensland Imperial Bushmen; awarded the Queen's medal with five clasps; Captains M. St J. Lamb (A Company) and C. E. Leer (B Company), with the 2nd Regiment, N.S.W. Mounted Rifles, the former as a trooper, the latter as a sergeant, and both receiving the Queen's medal with four clasps. Lieutenant W. B. Carter (F Company) was a trooper in the special squadron of New South Wales Lancers which was in England at the time of the outbreak of the war. Proceeding direct to the scene of hostilities, he was subsequently awarded the Queen's medal with four clasps and the King's medal with two clasps. He later attended King Edward's coronation.

The militia also supplied the majority of the battalion's non-commissioned officers. A number of militia officers, eager to leave with the first contingent, handed in their commissions and reverted to the ranks to earn speedily, in most cases, the chevrons of non-commissioned rank.

Many of the original N.C.Os, too, had active service to their credit, having served with British regular regiments. Also among the N.C.Os was a sprinkling of "Coronation" cadets—that is, the detachment which trav-

LIEUT.-COL. A. J. BENNETT, C.M.G., D.S.O., V.D.

ORIGINAL OFFICERS, 3RD BATTALION, KENSINGTON, N.S.W., 1914

PREPARATION

elled to England in 1911 for the coronation of King George V.*

In the ranks were men representing almost every profession, trade, and calling. The occupations actually given by the first dozen on the original battalion roll were: teacher, soldier, railway clerk, commercial traveller, medical practitioner, civil servant, miner, police constable, bricklayer, factory manager, tramway employee, labourer.

Intermingled with the Australian-born soldiers were recruits from all parts of the Empire. There were an American, several Greeks, a Belgian, and a Russian. The men from the British Isles were mostly British ex-soldiers who had served with the colours in India and Africa. The vari-coloured ribbons worn by some of them denoted active service in many countries of the world. Many of these recruits had served in some of the finest regiments in the British Army. Quite naturally their influence played no small part in the making of the battalion.

There were seasoned campaigners like Corporal Harry Allen, who received his baptism of fire on the Indian frontier, later took part in Buller's heroic dash for Ladysmith, participated in the ill-fated reverse at Spion Kop.

---

* The Coronation Cadets were: D. T. Moore (Lieutenant), T. D. McLeod (Sgt), J. Manning (Cpl), J. H. Matthews (Cpl), S. A. Pinkstone (Cpl), M. H. Stewart (Sgt), W. H. C. Rose (Cpl), J. T. Philpot (Sgt), R. Rosser, H. G. Howes (Sgt), and W. B. Phipps (Colour-Sgt Instructor). Moore afterwards commanded the battalion. McLeod, who attained commissioned rank, was a brilliant and daring officer, and was killed at Lone Pine. Manning and Howes accepted commissions with the Indian Army, the former becoming a major and being killed in India after the war, the latter being killed in Mesopotamia. Matthews and Pinkstone became captains in the 55th Battalion. The latter won the M.C.; Matthews was taken prisoner in the ill-starred Battle of Fromelles in July 1916. Stewart, injured badly at Lone Pine, returned to Australia. Rose, also given his commission in the 55th Battalion, was killed during the Fromelles "stunt." Philpot, as a lieutenant, lost his life at Pozières, and Rosser made the great sacrifice in the same action. Phipps, who went to the Coronation as drill instructor to the lads, was given his commission at the beginning of 1916.

And "Jock" Towers from the Gordon Highlanders, another Indian frontiersman who, like Allen, had fought with the "Regulars" in South Africa. Dick Humberstone from Duke Edward's Rifles was another notable.

Perhaps the most romantic figure of all was Corporal Bob Graham, a veritable human fighting-machine, whose active service career included the Spanish-American War, service with the revolutionary forces in Nicaragua and Guatemala in 1905-1906, with the Government forces in the Mexican rebellion in 1910, and with Lord Strathcona's Horse in the South African campaign.

CHAPTER IV

EARLY EVENTS

ON Monday, August 24th, the battalion moved to Randwick Racecourse. Three days later five officers and five N.C.Os were sent to Randwick rifle range for a course of instruction in musketry, the intention being that they should then impart their knowledge to the remainder of the battalion.

By Friday, August 28th, recruiting in the country districts was well in hand. Very early it was decided that the 3rd and 4th battalions should basically be country formations, the 3rd being allotted the southern and western railway systems. Major Bennett visited the southern centres—Goulburn, Cootamundra, Wagga Wagga (his native town), and Albury, addressing public meetings at each, and sending forward batches of recruits to Sydney. A recruiting officer was detailed on the 29th to meet country trains, and conduct new arrivals to Kensington racecourse.

Monday, August 31st, found the battalion rapidly getting into its stride at Randwick Racecourse. The parade state on September 2nd read: 32 officers, 966 other ranks; 961 rifles issued.

By the following day the battalion was complete—32 officers and 991 other ranks. Permission was then given to recruit 5 per cent over establishment in order that unsuitable men might be discharged. On September 4th two Maxim guns were received. By the next day 624 men had been fully clothed and equipped. A full kit inspection was held on the 9th to ascertain deficiencies.

Thursday, September 10th, saw the battalion move to a new location at the Randwick Asylum grounds, Barker Street, better known as "Payten's Paddock." There training operations continued. On the 12th this camp was completely flooded out by heavy rain. Many men had to take refuge under the verandah roofs of neighbouring cottages, and in the horse-boxes of Payten's stables. Mr Payten proved himself very considerate and a wonderful help, placing all his resources at the disposal of the men of the unit.

A brigade route march was held on September 14th in the direction of Long Bay and Maroubra. A similar march was carried out on the 17th, this time to the vicinity of the South Head Lighthouse.

The battalion band held its first daily practice on September 16th. The band instruments were generously donated by Miss (now Dame) Eadith Walker.* The first appearance of the band on parade was, in its way, unique. With few preliminaries, instruments had been issued to those claiming some knowledge of their use. In precisely half an hour the band was playing a march while the battalion was stepping out proudly in honour of the donor.

On September 19th camp was struck and the unit moved to a new site at Kensington. There it remained until its departure for overseas. On arrival at Kensington the Governor-General carried out an inspection. The parade state on September 24th read: 32 officers, 1015 other ranks, 58 horses, 22 vehicles.

In the meantime the public had been clamouring for a view of the troops in full war equipment, so on October 6th the whole 1st Brigade marched through the city of Sydney to enthusiastic and continuous acclamation.

On Thursday, October 15th, news came that the bat-

---
* This lady also supplied the battalion officers with their sleeping-bags.

talion would embark in the *Euripides* on the 19th. The next few days were occupied in making up deficiencies of equipment and allotting mess decks on board ship. Sunday the 18th saw the troops far dispersed, bidding relations and friends good-bye.

On Monday, 19th October, the battalion paraded at 8.30 a.m. in full marching order. It left shortly afterwards by tram for Fort Macquarie, where the *Euripides* (H.M.T. A14) was boarded. Later the 4th Battalion, 1st Field Ambulance, the Headquarters Staff of the 1st Infantry Brigade, and a party of nursing sisters also embarked on the A14.

All the horses and mounted details of the brigade, with Major Bennett in command, embarked in H.M.T. *Clan Maccorquodale*.

It was 5.30 p.m. when the troopship *Euripides* moved downstream, to an anchorage off Bradley's Head.

CHAPTER V

IT IS GOOD-BYE

THE *Euripides* slipped away from Bradley's Head at 6.30 a.m. on October 20th, 1914, and passed through the Heads to the accompaniment of shrieking siren calls from the early ferry steamers. Small gatherings of friends and relations dotted the harbour foreshores to wave their last sad farewells. Once outside Sydney Heads the *Euripides* —under the command of Captain A. H. H. G. Douglas, a fine old Scots skipper—turned south. The great adventure had begun.

The sea was very rough and choppy the first day out, and soon men began to stagger to the ship's side. Those who proved themselves immune from sea-sickness found much amusement at the expense of their less fortunate comrades. But this state of affairs did not continue for long. That first day was the only rough day encountered during the whole of the voyage.

It is surprising how many men can be stowed away on a troopship. There were fully 2300 on board the *Euripides*, which, at the outbreak of war, was the second largest ship trading to Australia. The once luxurious liner had been stripped of her finery, but the cabins on the upper decks were allowed to remain and here the officers were quartered. Cabins on the lower decks had been demolished, and only open spaces remained. These became the mess decks where the men took their meals. Stout deal tables had been erected, with forms on either side. Each table accommodated sixteen men.

The "other ranks" slept in canvas hammocks swung from stout hooks attached to the deck ceiling. Each morning the hammocks were taken down, and, together with the men's blankets, were folded and stacked neatly in receptacles made specially for the purpose. All hammocks had to be down and stowed by 6 a.m., this being necessary in order to allow the troops to sit at the tables for breakfast.

The day began with "Reveille," sounded at 6 a.m. Breakfast was at 7 a.m., dinner at noon, and tea at 5 p.m. "Lights out" sounded mournfully at 9 p.m.

The daily routine consisted principally of physical exercises, which kept the troops very fit during the voyage. Musketry instruction and lectures on various warlike topics also played a big part in the daily proceedings. With the limited deck space, the carrying out of ordinary military drill evolutions was quite out of the question.

During the voyage examinations were held for N.C.Os. Colour-sergeants were first on parade, their examination being a comparatively easy one. Then followed the sergeants, with a much stiffer questionnaire. The corporals, who came next, had to submit to a test the standard of which was higher again than that of the sergeants. The climax was reached when the lance-corporals faced the music. The first question on their examination paper read: "What are the badges of rank worn by a field-marshal?" How many of the officers could have answered that question then?

At noon on October 26th the *Euripides* steamed slowly to an anchorage in King George's Sound, the picturesque harbour of Albany. This was the rendezvous of a great armada of Australian and New Zealand troopships. The voyage was continued on November 1st, the *Euripides* being an important unit and a "division" leader in the convoy of thirty-eight troopships carrying the Australian and New Zealand contingents to the front.

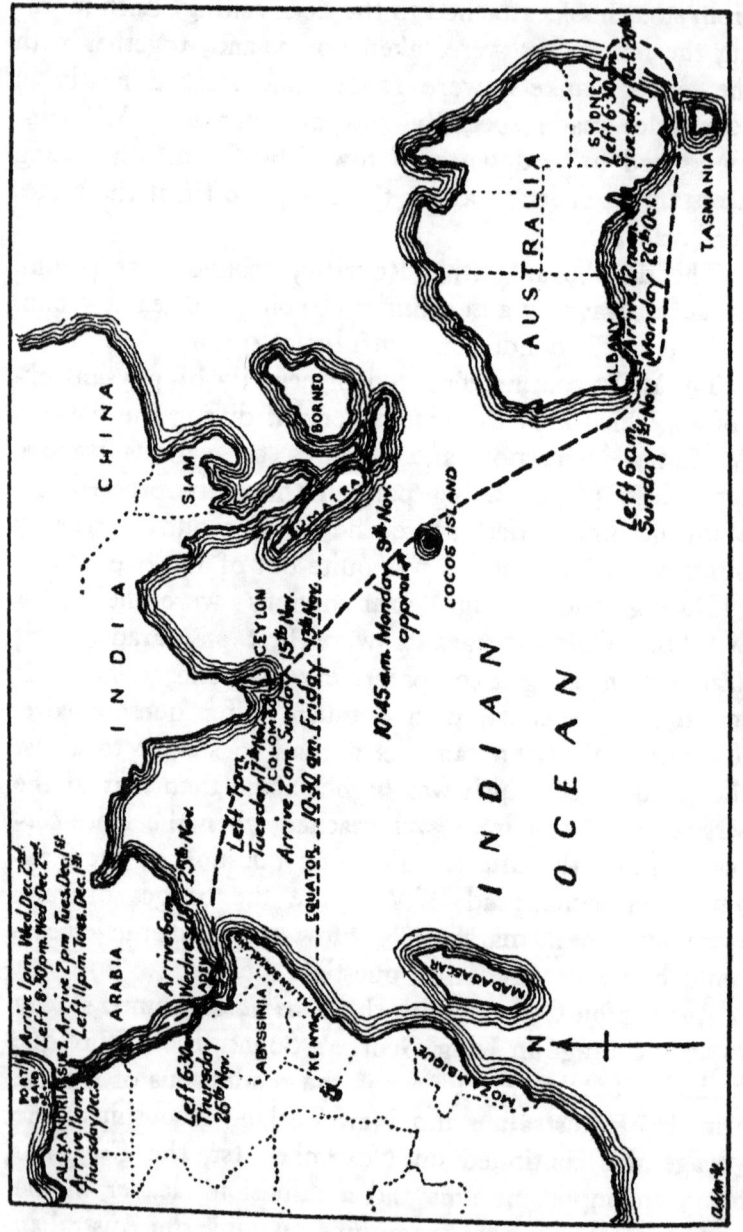

FROM AUSTRALIA TO EGYPT

Outside the heads of King George's Sound the troopships at once took up allotted positions and were flanked by warships. One officer wrote at that time: "Looking aft I see the long line of ships, each behind each—a cable length—keeping their distance wonderfully. We lead the starboard division in the *Euripides*. The flagship *Orvieto* is away on our port side, leading her line. On her port side, again, is a third long line, with men-of-war, faint smudges on the sky-line, scouting for us in the van and on each quarter. On we go slowly over a huge desert of ocean—day after day, week after week, at about ten knots—the fastest speed of the slowest boat. Each morning as I awake I gaze out of my porthole and see the *Orvieto* ploughing slowly forward—and the other line beyond that one—each ship exactly in her appointed place, where I had left her the night before. It gives a curious sense of inevitable destiny—a mysterious background to the dull routine. Drifting, drifting, always drifting forward—to that unknown something—war."

On November 2nd only three of the escort could be seen—the Japanese warship *Ibuki*, H.M.S. *Minotaur*, and H.M.A.S. *Sydney*. The weather was perfect, with scarcely a ripple on the water. A little diversion was caused on November 6th, when the Orient mail steamer *Osterley* passed close to the starboard line. The following day the battalion had its first casualty. Private V. H. Kendall of A Company passed away. He was buried at sea at 10.15 a.m. on Sunday, November 8th, with full military honours. The service was impressive. Naturally there was a gloom throughout the whole ship.

November 9th was the most exciting day of the voyage. The morning's work was well under way and groups of men scattered over the troop decks were busily engaged in their various tasks and exercises when suddenly, as if drawn by a magnet, all eyes turned to the Japanese warship *Ibuki*, at this time not far distant on the starboard side. The flashing of helio messages and the clearing of the decks for action signified beyond doubt that something out of the ordinary was happening. All ranks paused in their work to watch the business-like methods of the Japs. The *Ibuki*, with dramatic swiftness, left her position in the line and ran straight across our bows, only to be suddenly recalled to her post—an order which, we learned later, caused great chagrin to the officers and men on our gallant ally. The cruiser on the port side of the convoy, H.M.A.S. *Sydney*, had previously disappeared over the western horizon. About 11 a.m. the message came through that the German raider *Emden*, in an engagement with the *Sydney* off Cocos Island, had been beached and was done for. There was great excitement on board. All work was suddenly forgotten, and the remainder of the day was declared a holiday.

While the news of the *Emden's* fate was filtering through, Private Jack S. Lowe, a signaller in B Company, lay dying of illness. He was buried at 3 p.m. the same day.

Regarding the health of the troops, in those early days an interesting statement is contributed by the battalion medical officer, Captain J. W. B. Bean:

We had a great deal of sickness on board. The men were very crowded, and the heat of the tropics was stifling. We had quite a lot of pneumonia, and two of our poor chaps died of it. Just as we got to Egypt there was a tremendous epidemic of colic, hundreds suffering. Many were brought to the hospital in a state of collapse. We made them very sick with soda, gave injections of morphia and atropine, lots of hot water bottles and abdominal massage, and nobody died though some looked rather near it. It was a mystery. The steam cooker was found in a very dirty state, much food refuse having silted between the inner and outer jacket. This may have had something to do with it. One of the horses, too, had strangles, and sprayed his nasal discharges over the lines of mess orderlies as they waited by the kitchens with their dixies. This was looked on as a possible cause, and the third idea was arsenical poisoning by a spy. But we never knew for certain. I shall never forget the hospital deck, strewn thick with writhing, groaning men—for all the world like a battlefield.

The Equator was crossed on November 13th, and the usual "crossing-the-line" ceremony was held. One platoon took the opportunity of showing appreciation of their cook, tieing one of his alleged plum puddings round his neck, tossing him head-first into the big canvas bath that had been rigged on deck, and leaving him to the tender mercies of Father Neptune and his not too gentle court.

Two days later Colombo was reached. All hands naturally were on the look-out for the *Sydney*. From members of the crew we obtained first hand information regarding the engagement with the *Emden*. At 7.15 p.m. on November 17th, the *Euripides* left Colombo. The barren, desolate-looking island of Socotra was passed on the 23rd, and Aden was reached two days later. The troops were informed that Aden was a punishment station for the British Army, and because of the most forbidding appearance of the place were quite prepared to believe the story.

The heat had now become almost unbearable. The convoy departed from Aden on November 26th, bound for Suez, whence it arrived on December 1st and continued its journey through the Suez Canal. There was much interest in the Indian troops, who lined the eastern bank and continually enquired as to our identity. On December 2nd the *Euripides* arrived at Port Said. We were at Alexandria at 11 a.m. on the following day.

CHAPTER VI

THE LAND OF THE PHARAOHS

DISEMBARKATION began at 9 p.m. on December 3rd, when B and C Companies entrained for Cairo. On arrival at the railway station of that city, the troops were supplied with very welcome refreshments—tea, cocoa, and cakes—the gift of one of the voluntary aid organizations. Later the journey was resumed by tram and the two companies arrived at Mena, in the shadow of the Pyramids, at 4 a.m. on the 4th of December, 1914, being followed by the remainder of the battalion at intervals during the following day.

It had been confidently expected on leaving Sydney that our destination was England and then—France. To find themselves in a land so rich in romance, traditional and Biblical history, carried the memories of many of the men back to the stories learnt in early childhood. The unchanging Sphinx, the towering pyramids, contrasted very greatly with the so cosmopolitan city of Cairo, distant only 7 miles and connected with the terminus at Mena by an electric tramway. Those were the days of intense interest in an utterly strange world.

Just a breath of Australia was provided by the homely eucalypts bordering the Mena-Cairo roadway. Egypt and Kitchener, Egypt and Napoleon, Egypt and the Mamelukes, Egypt and Gordon; the country of Cleopatra, of the great Pharaohs. All seemed so strange, so wonderful, a land of kaleidoscopic changes!

But such musings were of short duration. The monotony of sand—sand—sand—everywhere sand, quickly vanquished all romantic dreams of other picturesque days and historic peoples. No camp had been prepared, so fatigue duty became the order of the day. One of the first tasks was the marking of the boundaries of the various battalions. This was carried out in an unusual manner. All troops were marched up a hill covered with large stones. Long lines of men spread out from the top to the bottom—each man about three yards distant from his neighbour, and that hill quickly became quite stone-bare. Finally the stones were neatly placed between the tents of the 3rd and 2nd Battalions on one side, and the 3rd and 4th Battalions on the other. The boundaries of all units of the 1st Australian Division were thus clearly distinguished. The method was an instance of the aptness of the proverb "many hands make light work."

The camp—situated on the fringe of the Sahara Desert—was within easy walking distance of the tram terminus at Mena House and of the Pyramids and the Sphinx. For the first few days tents were not made available, and it became necessary for the battalion to bivouac. The days were hot, but the nights being cold the tents were very welcome when they did arrive. Although it rains very rarely in Egypt, December 8th was an exception, the troops of the divisions in the open and without shelter receiving a severe drenching.

Now began the task of training. The training ground proper was situated at a distance of from two to three miles' march from the Mena camp. To the man in the ranks it seemed that the higher command had no thoughts other than of—route marches. Day after day the troops were marched over the scorching desert. Private C. M. Geddes wrote:

Breakfast at 7 a.m. and the battalion moves off at 8.15 a.m. It does not get back till 2 p.m. for dinner. Talk about tired and hungry! On the return journey each man trudges along with his head down, treading in the footsteps in the soft sand of the man in front of him. The chattering and whistling of the march "at ease" on the way out is sadly missing on the way back. The universal thought is "how much further before I can get rid of this rifle and equipment, and out of the dust and heat."

Seven hours between breakfast and dinner. It is amazing how one just falls into one's tent on returning, quite worn out. Yet after a short rest, cooling off, and dinner one feels as fit as a fiddle again. No wonder the whole world writes of the magnificent physique of the 1st Australian Division. None but the most physically fit could stand up to the strenuous months of drilling and marching. Will any 3rd Battalion man ever forget the White House? Until you pass the White House on the way back to camp, you don't feel that you are really marching home.

As the battalion became tougher and more enduring, so the hours of training were increased, until every man in the regiment became as hard and fit as a navvy. The elementary practices of soldiering were performed with such monotonous regularity, that there came a time when the men handled their rifles, which came to be almost part of them, with the same confidence and precision as the British Regular. Squad, section, platoon, company, and battalion drills were practised till the whole battalion moved like a well-oiled machine. In musketry instruction remarkable progress was made. On February 4th, in the brigade field firing competition, the battalion was triumphantly victorious.

A post examination of the training syllabus shows that considerable time was devoted to practising saluting—so much indeed, that the impression was left on many minds that the successful issue of the war depended solely on the ability of the Australian soldier to swing his hand snappily to that point just above the eyebrows and pivot the head and eyes like an automaton.

The 3rd Battalion was honoured in being chosen by the brigadier to represent the 1st Brigade on Sunday, December 20th, at the ceremony of the installation, under British protection, of the first Sultan of Egypt. Reveille was at 5 a.m. and breakfast at 5.15. It was dark and there was a wild rush upon the mess orderlies. Everybody was growling. Each member of the battalion was issued with 20 rounds of ball ammunition—a most significant action —and went into barracks at Cairo. A march through the city streets followed, and what a gay scene it was that day! The red fezzes of the Egyptians who lined the pavements; the vari-coloured robes of the natives; overhead the flags, as it seemed, of all the nations—English, French, Belgian, Russian, Italian, Greek, and the new Egyptian flag—scarlet with three crescents and three stars, altogether a most colourful and stirring sight. The Turkish flag—scarlet with one crescent and star—was, of course, missing.

Australian troops with rifles loaded and bayonets fixed, the officers with swords drawn and revolvers loaded, lined both sides of the street; prepared for any disturbance which may have taken place during the official "progress," each rank watched the crowd behind the other rank. The troops thoroughly enjoyed the spectacle they were privileged to witness. First some splendidly mounted troops rode by. Then came a detachment of the 5th Lancashire Fusiliers, marching proudly, to be followed by Egyptian troopers of the new Sultan's bodyguard, riding perfectly-shaped spirited grey Arabs of about 14.2 hands. The graceful greys, snapping at the bit, were succeeded by troops of chestnuts and then troops of bays, ridden by Egyptian lancers, attired in gaudy blue uniforms with gold facings, and equipped with gay fluttering lance pennants. A really thrilling martial sight.

Followed two natives in white robes with bare legs and feet. They ran along the street followed by the carriage containing the new Sultan. Driver and footman were in red and gold livery. The carriage was drawn by four brown horses of immense proportions, truly magnificent and exactly matched. Then a carriage with three British potentates, frock-coated and silk-hatted, and another carriage with General Sir John Maxwell, Commander-in-Chief of the Forces in Egypt.

It had been an interlude of absorbing interest to the troops, but the arduous tour of duty and the long march back to Mena camp—seven miles—left the troops very weary. On the following day, the battalion was granted one day's holiday, in recognition of its excellent bearing during the ceremony.

On December 30th, Sir George Reid, then High Commissioner for Australia in London, reviewed the troops. He opened his address with a characteristic remark, "Well you Australians are the b——y limit!" He went on to remark, among other things, "The youngest of these august pyramids was built 2000 years before our Saviour was born. They have been silent witnesses to many strange events, but I do not think they have ever looked down upon so unique a spectacle as this splendid array of Australian soldiers massed to defend them. . . ."

Next day the rectangular regimental colour patches, brown above green, were issued—green to distinguish the 1st Brigade and brown the 3rd Battalion. Many an "A.W.L." subsequently regretted the ease with which he was identified.

Life at Mena was not all hard training. It offered compensations. The food was good, and could always be supplemented by the purchase of ready-boiled eggs, tomatoes, dates, and oranges. These were readily procurable from native vendors who fairly swarmed about the camp. Some were undoubtedly enemy spies, easily camouflaged in the guise of itinerant and clamorous vendors.

For the first few weeks meals were taken in the open—picnic style; later, fine mess huts were erected. Leave

3RD BATTALION BAND, MENA, FEBRUARY, 1915

3RD BATTALION, MENA, FEBRUARY, 1915

was given freely—first, within the precincts of the camp, when the men scrambled over the Pyramids and the Sphinx, probably the most historic and among the most ancient piles of masonry in the world. As time went on, permission to visit Cairo was given just as generously. A hard day's work was soon forgotten when Cairo leave was announced, and the men and lads trooped off like happy schoolboys. Much could be written concerning the various ways in which leisure hours were spent. The native bazaars, the Ezebekiah Gardens, the Kursaal, the famous mosques, the citadel, and a legion pleasure resorts all had their special patrons. Also the notorious "wazzer." For a few piastres the services of a guide could be had. What cheerful liars these chaps were! They knew everyone from Moses to the Prince of Wales. They could answer all questions with the greatest ease. Their English was perfect, but as historians they were deplorable.

The temptations of an Eastern city claimed not a few and some thus early became casualties and were returned to Australia without firing a shot. Cairo's backwaters were responsible for one of the minor tragedies that came upon the A.I.F. The two leading hotels, Shepheard's and the Grand Continental, were more or less reserved for officers. Woe to the ranker who had the temerity to trespass within the portals of these hallowed sanctuaries.

The pranks of some of the wilder spirits were many and varied. It was quite a common occurrence for some of the men—under the influence of native liquor—to arrive back at camp with all manner of purchases, including donkeys and monkeys. The most artful were the leave breakers—those away from the camp without leave, or returning to camp after hours. Crowds of these offenders would gather outside the picquet lines, form themselves into squads, number off, form fours, right turn, and then, one of their number placing himself at the head of the column, would give the order "quick march," and head them straight into camp. Naturally the guards would turn out to salute and pass these men, little dreaming that they were defaulters. It is doubtful whether the officers ever worried seriously about this trick, not considering it objectionably "prejudicial to good order and military discipline." Another favourite means of deception practised by the homing troops was to return in native *gharris*, dressed as Gyppos. Once inside the lines the rest was easy.

Picture shows made their appearance at the camp—first of all with French titles, but later translated into English. Still later the camp was to witness the erection of drinking saloons, where the men could obtain beer of reputable brews. This was a good tactical move on the part of the Administration, because it had the effect of keeping a big percentage of the men in camp. For those with a perpetual thirst there was subsequently no great incentive to visit Cairo.

Christmas Day, 1914, was a wonderful day. In addition to the ordinary bill of fare, plum puddings, preserved fruit, wine, nuts, and dates were supplied. Queen Mary's gift of chocolate was a much treasured souvenir of the occasion. It was probably the one and only day in the history of the battalion when, in answer to the orderly officer's query "Any complaints?" the reply came from all sides, "Yes, sir, we've had too much to eat." To make the day even more enjoyable, there were no parades.

Concert parties and sports meetings were held occasionally to relieve the monotony of camp life. The spiritual side of the men's welfare was not forgotten. There were four padres to the brigade. Dean Talbot represented the Church of England and Father McAullife the Roman Catholics, while Chaplains Green and

McKenzie looked after the Methodists and Presbyterians respectively.

It was rather humorous how quickly the men could change their religion. On one occasion the church parade under Dean Talbot was wonderfully attended. Thousands turned out. The brigadier and his staff were also in attendance, and in their honour everybody had to stand throughout the service. The news soon got round that at the service conducted by Padre McKenzie (shortly to become known far and wide as "Fighting Mac," now Salvation Army Commissioner for Eastern Australia), the men were allowed to sit down and smoke. The following Sunday all hands became Salvationists and turned out in thousands for the service conducted by McKenzie. Just as the service was about to commence, who should put in an appearance but the brigadier. Again everyone had to stand. There was nothing left for it but to turn Roman Catholic, and the following Sunday was notable for the magnitude of the Roman Catholic parade. But alas! There was to be no Roman Catholic service that day. Instead there had been arranged an extra large fatigue party, and the unhappy "converts" under the Papal banner spent the morning cursing as they had never cursed before. Such was the religion of the 3rd Battalion.

On January 1st, 1915, the double company and platoon system was introduced into the 3rd Battalion. A Company was placed under the command of Major E. S. Brown, B was allotted to Major M. St. J. Lamb, C to Captain C. E. Leer, D to Captain C. W. H. Coulter. As we passed from the kindergarten to the secondary stage of training, field operations were arranged. The battalion carried out the advance in open order, the advance in artillery formation, and fought imaginary advance and rear-guard actions—till such time as it attained the proficiency necessary to participate in a brigade action.

Dr C. E. W. Bean, the Official Historian, has put it on record:

> In order to give the 1st Infantry Brigade a thorough exercise in night attacks—which were continually practised on a smaller scale—Colonel MacLaurin marched it, on February 8th, eight miles from Mena to the village of Beni Yusef, higher up the Nile on the edge of the desert. The brigade camped for a midday meal, posted outposts, theoretically attacked a position in the desert in the afternoon, spent the night in entrenching itself, and marched back to camp next day. The remainder of that day, and the night which followed, the brigade rested. Then it marched again to Beni Yusef, and went through four days and nights of almost continuous sham-fighting and entrenching. In the short rushes of the final night attack the men, when they flung themselves down to fire at the end of each advance, dropped fast asleep. In some cases the next line found them in this state when it came up, and nudged them to go on again.

It was during this operation that the following episode, recalled by Lieut-Colonel A. F. Burrett (a name is necessarily omitted), occurred. The programme, briefly, was to march to a certain place, dig in, and be ready to hold up the enemy who were advancing on us. Members of the 3rd Battalion had dug a trench in accordance with the platoon commander's plans and specifications, and when the divisional staff came along, this exceedingly junior officer could not resist butting in to air his knowledge. Singling out Colonel White (later Major-General Sir Brudenell), and looking at the men and the trenches with undue satisfaction, the 2nd "Loot" remarked, "Good job that, sir."

"Yes," said Colonel White, looking critically at the job. "Splendid job! Splendid! But let me see—facing in the wrong direction entirely, is it not?"

He moved on. The appalled junior remained staring into the night until dear old "Dad" Owen, who had nearly ridden over him, remarked sadly something about "the war still being on."

During these manoeuvres our old colonel was a familiar figure. Seated on his pony—a sturdy little animal named "Tommy"—he would watch the progress of his "boys." They were all boys to the "old man." He could never look on them as anything else. Returning to camp after a heavy day in the desert, Owen would insist that his officers should first of all look after the welfare of the men before attending to their own requirements.

CHAPTER VII

"FIT FOR WAR"

On February 16th, at the conclusion of the brigade's manœuvres, the brigadier, Colonel MacLaurin, addressed the troops and told them they were "fit for war." Colonel A. F. Burrett recalls the incident:

"It is peculiar how memory of an expression or habit lives longer than famous deeds. Just prior to going aboard the troopships for Mudros, the 1st Brigade was taken out on the desert for a couple of days and nights of manœuvres to complete training. At the finish the four battalions were formed up in mass, and our brigadier, Colonel MacLaurin, made a wonderful speech, finishing up dramatically with, 'Men, you are now fit for war.' And in the years that followed, I heard that sentence repeated in many places in strange times and in curious ways. I heard one Digger shout to his pal at the Landing, 'Men—you are now fit for war.' I saw a badly wounded Digger, at Lone Pine, grin and tell his pals who were trying to help, 'Men, you are now fit for war.' I've heard many a Digger up to his eyes in mud and slush in France dramatically affirm, 'Men, you are now fit for war.'

"Most of us have forgotten what our first young brigadier looked like. We might even remember only dimly the circumstances of his gallant death at the Landing. But I do not think 'Men, you are now fit for war' will be forgotten so long as an original 1st Brigade Digger has both his identity disks round his neck."

On March 30th Sir Ian Hamilton inspected the whole of the Australian troops and expressed entire satisfaction, thus confirming the opinion of the brigadier that we were "fit for war."

Two days later the battalion paraded at 5.55 a.m. and left camp shortly after to take part in a divisional operation, returning to camp again at 4 p.m. April 2nd was Good Friday, and an early church parade was held. The day was unusually quiet. Rumours were flying about everywhere. The 3rd Brigade had already left Egypt, and the immediate destination of our battalion was the sole topic of conversation. It was like the prelude to a storm.

The following day marching orders were received, and preparations were made for an early departure. At 7 a.m. Captain J. L. Chester and six men of B Company left for Alexandria as an advance guard. The remainder of the battalion spent the day in cleaning up camp. Tents were struck and handed into store, and great bonfires were lighted to burn rubbish. When night came a camp-fire concert was held which lasted till it was time to pack up and move off.

The right-half of the battalion—the "hold party" (*i.e.*, party for unloading ships) and the first-line transport—marched out of Mena at 7.30 p.m. *en route* for Cairo. The remainder of the 3rd left camp at 11 p.m. Portion of the battalion entrained at Madbouli station, and the balance at Cairo, in the early hours of the 4th. Alexandria was reached the same day. By 1 p.m. the battalion—with the exception of the hold party, which had embarked on the *City of Benares*—was crowded expectantly on board the *Derfflinger*.

Thus ended the days of training of the 3rd Battalion, which had been welded into a potentially magnificent fighting unit, each man inordinately proud of his brown-

and-green colour patches, and each having unbounded confidence in himself and in his mates. Alas! Many fine young men who answered their names that day are now sleeping on the rugged slopes of Gallipoli, or where the once blood-sodden fields are green again in France and Flanders, awaiting the Great Captain's final roll-call.

On April 5th, the *Derfflinger*, a captured German liner, with the 2nd and 3rd Battalions on board, left Alexandria Harbour and put out to sea. Although the conditions were fairly calm, many men were sea-sick.

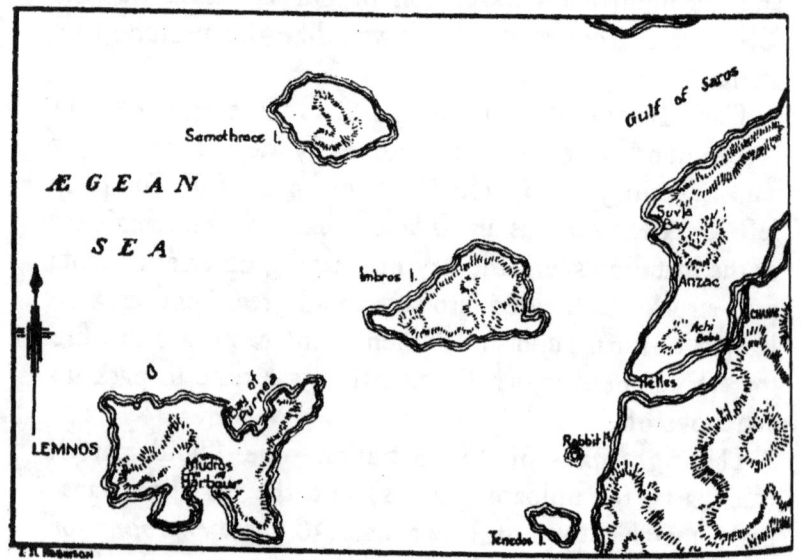

LEMNOS, IMBROS, TENEDOS AND THE DARDANELLES

The crowded state of the troopship prevented much activity, and so there was little in the way of drill. However the men were given plenty of physical exercises to keep them fit.

The journey through the beautiful Aegean Sea, studded with numerous small islands, was all too short. It seemed then more like a specially conducted tourist trip than a serious war venture. Of the many islands passed, one showed to particular advantage the bright sunshine burnishing its snow-capped peak and lending to the seascape a unique grandeur. There was quite a stir on the ship when Patmos was passed. Standing out in bold relief on its rocky heights was a beautiful old monastery. According to traditional history, it was here that the Apostle John wrote the Book of Revelations.

Our destination—Lemnos Island—was sighted during the early hours of April 8th, and by 10.15 a.m. the *Derfflinger* was riding at anchor in Mudros Harbour. The sloping green hills of the island were in marked contrast to the sun-scorched plains of Egypt, which had been our world for so long. Patches of highly coloured poppies gave the landscape a very necessary relief. To us Lemnos was a veritable Garden of Eden. What wonderful sunsets, and how we were to remember them! The harbour reminded us of Sydney. But there are no sharks at Lemnos, and the men were allowed to enjoy their swimming parades in absolute safety.

Mudros Harbour was literally alive with craft of all descriptions—from the mighty *Queen Elizabeth*, with 15-inch guns, to the frail little row-boats of island traders who peddled wares from ship to ship.

It had now become well known to the troops that an attempt would be made to storm the heights of Gallipoli —news, whatever the source or the reliability, always spread with great rapidity in the A.I.F.—and the syllabus of training was modelled to meet the occasion. Landing operations were practised on several occasions. Down rope ladders strapped to the sides of the *Derfflinger*, the men were sent as fast as they could go. These rehearsals were not without incident. More than one man missed his foothold and went headlong into the sea to the delight of his companions. These full dress rehearsals were carried out in co-operation with the navy. A warm friendship thus sprang up between the Australians and the senior arm of the service. If confidence were needed, the British sea dogs were the men to supply it. We all knew at the time that the covering fire for our landing would be provided by the fleet.

During manœuvres our eyes instinctively were on the "middies"—lads not yet out of their teens. What wonderful little chaps they were, too. To the Australian soldier it was a novelty to hear full-grown men being ordered about by these youngsters. Nevertheless, Australians have never stinted their praise of the able manner in which these young sailormen performed their duties during the trial landings.

On the 16th and the 17th, disembarkation practise was carried to the harbour foreshores, and the battalion was given an opportunity of stretching its legs on a route march through the village of Mudros. On the second day, the programme was varied slightly to allow the men to wash their garments in the local village. Disembarkation rehearsals took place again on the 19th and 23rd. Then on the 24th sailing orders came. During the afternoon the old colonel assembled the men in the well deck and addressed them.

"I feel," he said, "very confident of the manner in which you will acquit yourselves in the task that lies before you." Just a few brief words—a few last instructions.

The sergeants' mess that night was the scene of the wildest enthusiasm. The N.C.Os sang, danced, and behaved like schoolboys on the eve of a "breaking-up" at a boarding school. A visitor from the 2nd Battalion gave the star turn of the evening's entertainment, demonstrating his alleged hypnotic powers. His most humorous victim proved to be the regimental sergeant-major, a staid old British soldier.

At 12.30 on the following morning, April 25th, the *Derfflinger* left her anchorage off Lemnos Island and steamed for the shores of Gallipoli. A few hours later we were within swimming distance of the Peninsula. The great moment had arrived. No more foot slogging. Good-bye to sham fighting—and all that. It was war! At last!

CHAPTER VIII

THE LANDING

On historic April 25th Reveille was set forward for 4 a.m., but there was not the slightest necessity to waken any man of the 3rd Battalion. All ranks had lain down to sleep, or to attempt to sleep, in their clothes the previous evening. The first faint streaks of dawn found the troops climbing to all possible vantage points on the ship and straining their eyes in a vain endeavour to catch a glimpse of the terrain and—the fighting. *

It was a very hurried breakfast at 5 a.m. "The destroyer was to be alongside at 6 a.m.," wrote Captain Bean, the medical officer, "to take us in as close as possible, and the last 200 yards was to be travelled in open boats. At dawn I was up and saw that we were lying a couple of miles or so off shore, in company with other boats. Closer in were several men-of-war already shelling the indistinct shore hills. You could hear the boom of the guns after the flashes—followed by other little flashes on shore and puffs of smoke, and little scatters of dust where the shells burst. I watched for a minute or two—intensely interested.

---

* It should be noted at this stage of the narrative that the Turks had received a thorough warning of the pending attack. The warning had begun with the naval attack on March 18, when the fleet vainly endeavoured to force the Narrows. Further warnings were in the form of air reconnaissances by British observers on April 14 and 15. Then again, commanding and staff officers were taken along the coast for observation purposes in patrolling warships under the very eyes of the enemy. The departure of troops from Egypt and the huge gathering of ships in Mudros Harbour could scarcely have escaped the notice of the Turks, who had many active spies on the mainland, and small trading boats were allowed to come in and out of Mudros Harbour at will during the period that the fleet of troopships was anchored there.

"Punctually to time the destroyer came alongside, and at once the lieutenant in command called to me. He had wounded on board. So I was the first to board her, and immediately went below—though not before I had noticed a tarpaulin spread over something lying very still on the deck, and with little red trickles running away to the waterway along the ship's side. It was at that moment I fully realized that the war had begun for us. Down below I found a few slight flesh wound cases, and, with my men, attended to them. I just got up again in time to get into a shore-going boat. There were several, and we bundled in anyhow and in no particular order. A couple of sailors rowed and another fine breezy old salt took the helm—grand chaps those tars were—as cheery as if we were setting out on a pleasure cruise. A shell or two whistled by, none very close. There were no bullets. We couldn't beach right up, we had to wade ashore. I got a wetting up to my hips."

The other boats did not have such an easy passage. Lieut E. N. Litchfield, then a platoon sergeant, relates his experience: "No. 9 Platoon filled one boat and half-filled another. Lieut O. G. Howell-Price, my officer, told me to fill the second boat with No. 10 Platoon men. The Turks by this time were peppering away at the boats. Two shells hit one of the destroyer's funnels. At the same moment a little midshipman, facing the bridge beside the funnel, without so much as turning a hair, called out in a drawling voice, 'You chaps want to keep down there or you will be hit.' Several more shells hit the destroyer in that few minutes. As we were towed in by a pinnace we had a hot time. When we cast off and rowed from the pinnace, each boat independently, Lieut Howell-Price's boat was just on the right of mine. He was sitting high up in the stern. The shell that hit our boat under the water line must have just missed his head.

"My boat started to fill rapidly. Luckily, the lads put

their backs into the hole, and we landed on a reef about 20 or 30 feet from the shore, with the boat settling down to the gunwale. Men started to scramble ashore in full kit, and the two Jack Tars who were with us to take the boat back were diving about grabbing men heavily loaded with equipment, and helping them into shallow water when they fell into the deep holes of the reef."

Private C. M. Geddes and his companions had a unique experience. Geddes wrote: "For a while our boat was rowed along safely. Then suddenly there was a crash, and a piece of shell passed through the bottom. Nobody was hit, but the boat began to fill, and we felt she'd go down. An old sailor, wearing a cap-band H.M.S. *Ocean* —he had been on that ship when she was sunk in the Narrows—was in charge. He called out, 'Keep on rowing, lads, she can't sink, she's a lifeboat.' The oars were getting difficult to pull, as the water rose higher and higher in the boat. The old sailor said, 'Keep on, boys, I can see the bottom.' I could, too, but it was a mighty long way down, as the Aegean is nice and clear. He then yelled out, 'Hi, picket-boat, hi!' to an empty boat returning from shore. Luckily she saw our plight and steamed towards us.

"The water in the boat had now risen to the level of that outside, and we all just stepped into the sea. As I left the boat she was three feet under, and I carried my rifle, full pack, three days' rations, and 120 rounds of ammunition. Down I went, and the thought flashed into my mind, 'What a rotten way to die in the dark, and without having fired a shot, too.' When I came up again, my cap, which had been fixed tightly on my head with the chin strap, was gone, and my beloved rifle, which I had been taught to look after and treat as my best friend, had gone also, to a watery grave in the Aegean. The picket-boat hauled the sailor in with a boat hook, and I tried to reach his legs as they hauled him in, but couldn't reach him. Finally they threw me a lifebuoy on a line and dragged me in when I was almost done.

"Soon after we got on the picket-boat, a little pink-faced middy in charge asked us each to move up one place to trim the boat. We moved just as a huge shell threw a column of water in the air, half-way between us and another boat. We felt nothing, but the chap near me, Bill Logan, who was sitting in the place I had just moved from, swooned back and was caught by the sailor who had thrown the lifebuoy. A fragment of the shell had entered his side, and he lived only a few minutes.

"The middy then said, 'Are we making water?' and the Jack Tar replied, 'I think we are, sir'; I thought 'Great Scott, we're out of one shipwrecked boat into another.' The picket-boat steamed hard for the *Galeka* and reached the gangway just as she began to sink. We stripped off our wet clothes and were given hot tea, and blankets to wrap in. There were thirteen of us, and poor Bill Logan belonged to No. 13 section."

Despite the fact that the 1st Brigade landed in full daylight, while the 3rd Brigade—the covering troops—set foot on Gallipoli just before dawn, the battalion had a comparatively easy passage ashore. As the men stepped or jumped from the tows to the beach they were speedily marshalled and formed up in platoons and companies by their officers under the shelter of that great physical prominence which subsequently came to be known as "Plugge's Plateau."

The instructions which had been issued to all ranks in the division the night before the Landing were explicit. In them was nothing that could possibly be misunderstood. In effect, they were the orders given to the 3rd Brigade—"push on at all costs."

The result of the battalion's strenuous and most effective training at Mena was immediately apparent. Delays and indecisions there were none. Colonel Owen at once found himself supported by an orderly force eager to carry out his first commands. The sound of incessant rifle and machine-gun fire was wafted down from the hills, and it was apparent that there was fierce skirmishing. The covering force had, it was clear, already made considerable headway. Men of the 3rd Battalion were straining to be away.

B Company, under Major M. St. J. Lamb, was first to move. Officers and men scrambled willingly up the steep sea-face of Plugge's Plateau, and, making their way through the scrub at the summit in orderly military fashion, filed down into Monash Gully. The remaining companies either followed the same route, or proceeded with all haste to the fighting by way of Shrapnel Gully, to become at once absorbed into the struggling firing line that had by this time been formed by widely dispersed units of the 3rd Brigade.

The platoons which worked along the track in Monash Gully had a particularly strenuous time scrambling up the farther side of that valley, where men of the "dawn" battalions were bravely and frantically endeavouring to establish a line. Unlike those in the first wild rush, the men of the 3rd Battalion carried full packs; in addition, each was weighted down with 250 rounds of ammunition, to say nothing of picks and shovels supplementary to the ordinary entrenching equipment.

Among the earliest casualties was Sergeant Walter Cavill, one of the most popular non-commissioned officers in the battalion. He had seen service in the South African War, with the New South Wales Lancers, but his soldiering experience was not destined to benefit the men of A Company for very long on that eventful day.

By approximately 10 a.m. every man of the battalion was in action reinforcing the 3rd Brigade wherever a junction could be effected. Major E. S. Brown with the

THREE VIEWS OF MENA CAMP, EGYPT

1st INFANTRY BRIGADE ON ITS WAY BACK TO MENA, IN THE EARLY MORNING, AFTER AN ALL-NIGHT FIELD PRACTICE IN THE DESERT NEAR THE PYRAMIDS
Photo: Aust. War Memorial Museum.

majority of A Company worked to a position just beyond MacLaurin's Hill, and Lieutenants G. E. McDonald and W. B. Carter began a fierce action a little to the right at Wire Gully. On Major Brown's left, at Courtney's Post, Captain J. C. Wilson had reinforced the 11th Battalion. Near by were Captain Ronald Burns, Lieutenants L. W. Street, Eric Goldring, and O. G. Howell-Price. Captain D. McF. McConaghy and the major portion of B Company settled down to serious work facing the position afterwards known as German Officer's Trench.

Perhaps the most vital phase of the early fighting was on the left of the Australian line up near Russell's Top, directly fronting the Turkish counter-attack which was rapidly developed on Baby 700. There the Turkish position dominated nearly every section of the Australian line, and men began to fall with cruel frequency until the toll was bewildering.

C Company, under Captain C. E. Leer, lost many men before it was able to make any progress in establishing itself at the head of Monash Gully near the Bloody Angle. This company was fortunate to have, in addition to its commanding officer, the services of two very fine leaders in the persons of Lieut R. O. Cowey and Sergeant-Major W. B. Phipps, the latter an old African campaigner who had seen long service with a British regiment.

Machine-gun and rifle bullets were now pouring into the Australian line from all directions, and the slaughter was appalling. Turkish machine-guns were operated from the hidden recesses of Baby 700, while snipers carried on their deadly work with ghastly precision from the shelter of innumerable "hide outs" in the scrub. This most spirited opposition, added to the fact that the Turks had all the advantage of position, made it extremely difficult for Captain Leer and his men to come into holts with the enemy.

"No. 9 Platoon manœuvred to a point about in rear of the Bloody Angle," wrote Lieut R. O. Cowey. "The platoon was skirmished for perhaps 300 or 400 yards towards Baby 700, with the right flank just touching Mule Valley. On the way over, some tents came into view at the head of Mule Valley, and some anxious moments were experienced, while rifle fire was poured into this locality in case the tents and environs were being used as an ambush.

"On attaining the advanced position, it was considered advisable to take stock of the country in front and to the flanks before moving forward, because we did not know where any other troops were. Sergeant Palmer was instructed to fire at bare patches of ground while I observed with field-glasses, endeavouring to pick up the ranges of various positions. I did not observe any hits, as the sergeant's shots were, apparently, masked by bushes. So we changed over, and in this way established the fact that the Turkish trenches near Scrubby Knoll were between 900 and 1200 yards distant, and that a concealed enemy trench, at about the junction of Owen's Gully and Mule Valley, was about 600 yards distant.

"Turks could be seen advancing in open order from Scrubby Knoll towards the 400 Plateau. A few shots were fired at them, but the range was too great to be effective. It was considered, too, to be bad tactics to cause the enemy to be put too much on their guard before they approached our troops who, we believed, were waiting for them at the 400 Plateau.

"As we watched, about half a battalion of Turks were skirmished to a trench near Owen's Gully, and others were moved similarly to the valley on the far side of Mortar Ridge, from No. 9 Platoon, and up re-entrants giving covered approaches to the Battleship Hill locality.

"Captain Leer, about this time, brought up men who extended our line towards Baby 700. I asked him for covering fire while No. 9 Platoon raced the Turks for possession of Mortar Ridge, but the request was not granted. The Turks finally occupied Mortar Ridge, and commenced to pour a deadly fire upon us, from there as well as from the plateau to the north of Owen's Gully, and from the east flank of Baby 700. Many of our men were killed. The wounded, as well as some others towards Baby 700, commenced retiring. Captain Leer ordered them back to the line, but the majority retired. A steady retirement of individuals from the locality meant that at the end of an hour no men were left on Captain Leer's extreme left.

"Captain Leer was sitting down smoking a pipe in full view of my position, where I was among my men who were lying down. Once he stood up in full view of Mortar Ridge, during a burst of heavy firing, and gazed towards it. A bullet struck his cap and twisted it round so that the peak was at the back of his head. He put up his hand to touch the right-hand side of his head, as if he were feeling for blood. Then he sat down again."

At the end of an hour's fighting Captain Leer was shot through the neck and chest, and died almost immediately. Lieut Cowey, who was about ten yards away, took charge. While in command Leer had displayed the utmost disregard for his own safety, and shown the greatest coolness. He was a fine example to his men.

"Private Glasgow just previously was shot dead within a yard of me," continues Lieut Cowey, "and on the other side Private Carr was killed by a bullet which must have only just missed me. I now made a sketch of the locality, addressed it to Colonel Owen, wrapped it round a stone, and threw it to the rear. This sketch was subsequently delivered to Major A. J. Bennett. It was made with a view to showing Colonel Owen how advantageous a machine-gun would have been in firing at moving Turkish troops from where I was.

"Ammunition commenced to run short. I tried to get word to the rear, but could not. I turned Private Carr's dead body over, and distributed his unused ammunition. My men cried out that they were being fired on from the rear, and asked what they should do. I told them to hang on and continue firing. Several times they called to me that our reinforcements were firing upon them, and we endeavoured to make those to the rear understand that we were not Turks.

"Late in the afternoon, about 5 p.m., several men rushed to the rear. They had not previously been able to move, owing to the intensity of the Turkish fire. As these men were not immediately shot down, I ordered the survivors to retire, and followed as soon as I saw them on their way.

"The reverse fire alone was what made me decide to retire, as it appeared that reinforcements had mistaken us for Turks, and could not be convinced by our shouting that we were not. When I had gone back about 100 yards, I found all my men rallied under a slight eminence by Lieut Heugh, of the 2nd Battalion A.I.F. Lieut Heugh and I then held a consultation, with the result that I gave him covering fire while he took half my men back to an empty Turkish trench at the Bloody Angle. He then covered my retirement."

Some hours after this retirement, under cover of darkness, Company Quartermaster-Sergeant Dargin went out alone in search of Captain Leer's body. He was never seen or heard of again. On Tuesday a similar attempt was made by Private Aubrey Farmer. He, too, was never heard of again.

Farmer was one of the most extraordinary men in the battalion. He made no secret of the fact at Mena, when the battalion was training, that everything that savoured of war was abhorrent to him, and he elected to remain in the Q.M.'s store during that period. But during those first days on the Peninsula he proved himself to be a man of quite unexpected calibre—the great crisis developed another man, and Farmer's work throughout those first three days was of such a nature that he was awarded a posthumous D.C.M.—an honour probably unique in A.I.F. history.

As the darkness and rain set in on the Sunday night (April 25th), Lieut Cowey set his men to digging trenches. The work was not only difficult but dangerous, as, by this time, the Turks had concentrated a continuous rifle and machine-gun fire along the edge of the cliffs to which Cowey's men were clinging. This fire in some instances was at ranges as short as 100-125 yards. Actually the Turkish infantry frequently came much closer, but always they were thrust back by the sheer ferocity of Cowey's defence. At about 10 p.m. a company of the 15th Battalion reinforced Cowey's right. The newcomers were placed on neighbouring high ground, thus prolonging the line thereabouts and helping to give Cowey's flank an urgently-needed greater measure of security. Lieut Heugh, of the 2nd Battalion, joined Cowey in strengthening the position, and splendid use was made of the picks and shovels the men had carried with them from the beach in the early morning.

But the trench-digging was rudely interrupted. The greater portion of Sunday night till the dawn was spent in meeting a rapid succession of Turkish attacks, which aimed at dislodging the defending troops from the position they so precariously occupied. There was fierce hand-to-hand fighting during the awful night watches. At times the Turks approached so closely and so boldly that it was impossible to distinguish friend and foe. There were occasions when the defenders were actually firing at each other. Such was the nature of the greatly confused and uncertain conflict on the left flank.

While Captain Leer and Lieut Cowey were in the thick of it there, the remainder of the battalion were experiencing very severe trials and having a most hazardous time generally in other parts of the line. Early on the Sunday morning, Captain Ronald Burns, adjutant of the battalion, hearing that the 10th Battalion badly needed reinforcements, took a party of men across MacLaurin's Hill to Courtney's Post. Here they occupied a shallow trench which had been hastily scooped out by the Turks.

Captain Burns had just settled down to the task of directing the fire of the men about him, when a Turkish bullet ended his life. The loss to the 3rd Battalion was a severe one. Burns had many special qualifications, and, in addition to his knowledge of infantry work, he was one of the select few who then held an air pilot's certificate.

Captain J. C. Wilson now assumed command at Courtney's, and Lieut O. G. Howell-Price took over the duties of adjutant. Howell-Price was a brilliant young subaltern who afterwards commanded the battalion. The enemy fire in this particular locality was most deadly, and there were many casualties. Next day, Captain Wilson was wounded in the head; subsequently he died in hospital at Alexandria. Lieut C. E. M. Brodziak was badly shot while in the same trench.

Two 3rd Battalion men, Private A. Mullins and H. W. Minter, who helped to garrison this post, must be specially mentioned for their gallantry in carrying messages under heavy fire to and from headquarters. For several days they kept Colonel Owen posted with news from Courtney's. Rather than return empty-handed, each man regularly carried back supplies of ammunition and water.

On MacLaurin's Hill, early on Sunday morning, Sergeant-Major D. N. McGregor of A Company, formerly a master at Newington College and a splendid athlete, lost his life while attempting to get his men safely under cover. About the same time Lieut G. E. McDonald, who had taken most of his platoon (No. 3) down to Wire Gully, returned to an old Turkish trench behind the same hill to pick up a section of his men who had lost touch. Crossing the hill he was greeted with a terrific burst of fire, and the section he led back passed through a regular hail of bullets. A sergeant was shot in the neck, the man on one side of him had his water-bottle pierced, while another on the other side had his puttees riddled. It is on record that shortly afterwards the same section burst into loud spontaneous laughter when a young lance-corporal, receiving the full impact of a spent bullet on his shin, exploded in a series of shrieks. "Listen to him," said one man, "yelling like a stuck pig."

But such humours were few and short lived. The crescendo of rifle and machine-gun fire, the moan and sharp crack or thud of Turkish bullets as they struck the ground or human flesh, the screech and crash of Turkish shrapnel, the bark and whip of spiteful machine-guns, and the whine and roar of the heavy shells from the battleships—all this made it a nerve- and soul-racking ordeal for new and till then unblooded troops. The ear-splitting detonations of great guns and huge shells were echoed and re-echoed from cliff to cliff, until they seemed to shake the whole countryside. The only cover available, in the main, was low scrub and slight folds in the ground; real shelter there was none. Throughout the whole of that fateful Sunday the troops sniped whenever a target offered, and scraped anxiously with their entrenching tools the protection for their aching bodies that even shallow holes offered.

Opposite MacLaurin's Hill on Sunday afternoon a file of men was seen proceeding along the front at a range of about 150 yards. Immediately they came into view the cry passed along the line, "Don't shoot; they are

Indians." Fire was withheld for a few minutes, but Major Brown decided to renew the attack. It was known to him that there were no Indians with the Australian troops.

Early in the night a verbal message passed along the line to the effect that British troops were now behind the Turks, and warning the Australians to refrain from firing. This message created a great deal of enthusiasm among some, but a feeling only of distrust in others, because the Turkish fire never slackened. Soon it was quite obvious that the message was false, and the belief spread in the firing line that the message was merely a ruse on the part of the enemy, who had been clever enough to make contact somewhere and cause it to be relayed. Similar messages were received in other parts of the line. At Courtney's Post at about 9 p.m. a message was passed along purporting to come from the commanding officer, Colonel Owen. This was to the effect: "Indian scouts are going out in front. Do not fire at them."

Sergeant Keith Martyn recalled this particular incident: "Shortly afterwards," he said, "a line of men in extended order rose in front of us and an order came from the left not to fire. The leader, a few paces in front of the others, happened to be directly in front of my position, and turned, to wave on the others. As he did so, the manner in which his greatcoat was fastened to his pack gave me the clue to the identity of these troops. I called on those in my vicinity for rapid fire, and this was commenced all along the line. Most of those advancing were shot down. Needless to say we kept the ground in front of us well sprayed with rifle fire during the remainder of the night.

"Shortly after, I heard a commotion in the pit on our right flank. Going to investigate, I found several Turks in the pit with their arms thrown down, and about 20 or 30 just below the pit, evidently similarly intentioned. As our garrison was very small I gave the corporal in charge instructions to keep the Turks covered while I went back to battalion headquarters to get a party to take charge of the prisoners. I passed Sergeant Bob McLelland, who was among those dug in between the lines and the cliff. On my telling him what was going on he said he would go down and keep an eye on things."

At battalion headquarters, Sergeant Martyn was directed to apply to brigade headquarters. Failing to locate brigade headquarters, he returned to his original position to find that as a result of the delay the Turks had become restive. Several of our men in the rear had opened fire on the party, whereupon the Turks had returned the fire and bolted. In the confusion several Australians were hit, including Sergeant Bob McLelland, who was shot through the stomach, the wound proving fatal.

At Wire Gully Lieut G. E. McDonald succeeded in capturing a Turkish officer who was endeavouring to approach his post on the pretence of being an Indian. Corporal Harry Allen, Private J. Towers, and a few others—men who had served with the "regulars" in India—were of great assistance during the "Indian" scare. Able to speak Hindustani, they were in a position to challenge the bona fides of those out in front.

The fighting near Wire Gully was of a particularly desperate nature. As Lieut McDonald scrambled through the bushes below MacLaurin's Hill, he first caught sight of the Turks through his glasses from the little dip between what ultimately came to be known as Steele's Post and Johnston's Jolly. This officer was quick to size up the situation. Major Brown and Captain McConaghy with the men under their command were crowded on the hilltop to McDonald's left, and, anticipating that his platoon would not be required there, McDonald dived down Wire Gully, ensconced himself in a little watercourse, and established a post that was destined to play one of the most important parts in the fight that was to follow.

This little post in Wire Gully was peopled throughout its short but all-important existence by men of all brigades. Perhaps no other isolated position on the whole of the Peninsula suffered more, or put up a more heroic defence. Exhausted and isolated parties of all brigades were lying out in the scrub, and there appeared to be little hope of their hanging on. Behind, and to the left of McDonald's Post in Wire Gully, towered the heights of MacLaurin's Hill, packed with men of the 1st, 3rd, and 4th Brigades, all in the state of anxiety induced by the uncertainty of the immediate future. Just as twilight came to the Gallipoli scrub, there was a great movement of troops in the gullies below where McDonald with his handful of men lay hidden. As indicated previously, the spirits of the assaulting troops in places had been raised during the day by whispers of help from Indian regiments presumed to have landed with the 29th Division farther south.

Now from out of the approaching darkness came voices shouting: "For God's sake don't shoot: we are Indians." It was a critical moment. All that could be seen were shadows moving in the scrub. McDonald and his men lay with bayonets fixed, sceptical but not daring to fire. Crouching low, the better to get a silhouette against the now fading light, McDonald saw a tall officer undoubtedly in the uniform of a Turk. Quick to realize the significance, he grabbed a rifle, and, by a gentle persuasion of the bayonet, brought the Turk in, but unfortunately not before his prisoner had given some rapid monosyllable instructions to the figures moving about in the scrub behind him. Then did McDonald realize that his suspicions had been well-grounded. The Turks had planned a counter-attack through Wire Gully, in the guise of Indian troops.

As his little company poured volley after volley into

the scrub at short range, there came frantic cries from the Australian line above, exhorting him to stop firing. "You are firing on Indian troops." Shouting back the information that the supposed Indians were Turks, the by now more slender garrison rapidly slipped and slammed the bolts of their almost red-hot rifles.

It was indeed a stroke of fortune for the precariously placed Australian invaders that this tiny "battle out-post" stood in the way of the advancing pseudo-Indians. Had it not been there, and had not Lieut McDonald acted with promptitude, the odds are that some hundreds of Turks—who could guess the number?—would have penetrated unobserved through Wire Gully, and by morning the Australians would have been fighting both to their front and rear. It was a cruel circumstance that, after sticking so tenaciously and bravely to his key-post until Tuesday, McDonald should have his arm badly shattered by Turkish bullets.

On the left flank, in the vicinity of the Bloody Angle, Private Markovitch relates that he went out to ascertain what the troops were to the front. Another rumour had gained currency that the French were approaching. Arriving at a spot where he could discern a semi-circle of men in a prone position, he called out in French, "Who are you?" "Troops of the Ottoman," came the answer. Markovitch dashed back to his own lines, and the order was "rapid fire."

Throughout the first night there was much confusion as a result of the multitude of false orders and baseless rumours of the nature that has been indicated being passed along and discussed in the line. *

---

* Some men were seen out in front who said they were Indian scouts. I was told by Captain Wilson to investigate and was about to go and see who the men were when one turned and ran. At once a fusillade of bullets swept them all over. We roared "Cease fire," but all had been shot. One man, Foley, went out and brought in a body to satisfy me that they were Turks. There was no doubt.—Extract from the diary of Lieut-Col. O. G. Howell-Price.

The battalion machine-gunners had their full share of the fighting. On the Sunday the section, consisting of two guns, operated from Plugge's Plateau, where Lance-Corporal Thomas Wilson was shot through the head. He was carried into an enclosure, formerly used as a sheep-pen by the Turks, where he was given every aid, but his wound proved fatal.

When night fell both guns were pushed out in front of Steele's Post, in anticipation of an attack at dawn on the Monday. As the attack did not materialize, the guns were withdrawn just before daylight.

During the process of digging in, three gunners of A section and five of B were wounded. Lieut T. H. Evans displayed great gallantry in effecting the rescue of several of these men. A score or so of bullets found a billet in the water-jacket of one of the guns, and it was rendered useless. However, repairs were speedily effected, and the gun was back in service again at 4 p.m. on the first day.

CHAPTER IX

THE SECOND DAY

It was a very tired battalion that faced the Turks on the Monday morning (April 26th). The night had been without rest, physical or mental. There had been trenches to dig, posts to construct, and wounded to evacuate, and a ceaseless vigil to maintain throughout. The men were thoroughly exhausted.

Overnight, more enemy artillery was placed in position, and throughout the second day raked the battalion lines with shrapnel. It became impossible to see the bottom of Shrapnel Valley because of the haze of smoke from bursting shells. This continual shell-fire had the effect of greatly harassing the gallant stretcher-bearers in their endeavours to reach the beach. At this time the trenches had not been deepened sufficiently to be proof against either shrapnel or enfilade fire, and casualties in the firing line were again heavy as a consequence.

During the day the Turks pressed Lieut Cowey's position so closely that he formed up a few reserves, told them that it was impossible to retire, and that they must kill every Turk they could before they themselves were killed. The Turks actually charged the position about 50 yards on Cowey's right from Mule Valley, but all except one were immediately killed. This man jumped into Cowey's trench, and was then killed—a shovel crashing on his head.

Cowey, when digging his trenches, sited them to cover approximately the sector between Mortar Ridge and Owen's Gully. The left flank was mostly dead ground.

In his narrative he says he was determined to construct a trench after dark, facing north from the position; but first he arranged for the relief of men actually in the trenches. As far as possible he withdrew the men who were most tired.

"This," he says, "occupied till about 10 p.m., when I lay down and slept till midnight, in the rear of the trenches. At midnight I went into the trenches and attempted to get the new trench dug, but the Turks watched us, and fired at the men each time they appeared silhouetted in the bright moonlight against the skyline, and to such purpose that eventually the men were afraid to work. I took a pick and shovel and showed them how sapping could be done on the hands and knees. But this was slow work, and moreover the Turks fired at every shovelful of earth as it was thrown up. Soon I had every man wakened, and I wanted my own men—particularly Sergeants Palmer and A. J. B. Hamilton, Corporals F. Barlow, A. B. Symons, W. J. Ryan, and Walsh, and Privates W. L. Chambers and F. Leighton, who had supported me so bravely and vigorously—to continue resting while the reinforcements who had come up during the day did the work. However, they one and all refused to rest while I wanted work done, so I had them all gather branches and bushes in the rear of the trench and then we piled these bushes breast high for some distance on the Turkish side of where I wanted the trench dug. I then loosened the top of the earth behind this concealment and the men readily followed with pick and shovel.

"The Turks at frequent intervals poured a withering fire in our direction, and each time we were compelled to go back into the completed portion of the trench until the fire had ceased. As day was breaking on April 27th the trench was almost completed, and I ordered the men who were working to put their tools away, as I wanted to

THE LANDING

relieve them with fresh men. They asked to be allowed to stay, and I consented.

"In this position we had a clear field of fire extending from Walker's Ridge to Baby 700, with about 200 of our troops hanging on to the face of the cliff at the Chessboard, at a much lower elevation than we were. They were faced by entrenched Turks visible to me, along a waterway on the S.E. flank of Baby 700. My men accounted for most of the Turks they hit, by firing over the heads of the troops at the Chessboard, who, not being able to see what we were doing, protested at our action. When the light became strong enough to see dimly, the men in the trench with me—they numbered about eight—put some rapid fire into about 50 Turks who were travelling down the waterway from Hill 971. I had planned to catch them at this moment, and it is significant that the Turks avoided the waterway for the remainder of the day. The fire evidently nonplussed the Turks for half-an-hour, and I started to ascertain the exact range to some trenches between Walker's Ridge and Baby 700. The men did not seem to be able to fire steadily enough, so I took a rifle and found out the exact range to each trench.

"As I completed this work, many Turks started to dribble over the skyline, and attempted to occupy these trenches. As they did so I fired on them and encouraged the men who were with me to deliver rapid fire, pointing out that we must maintain superiority of fire by preventing the Turks from aiming at us. The Turks would run over the skyline and hide behind bushes. If we did not hit them as they ran, we fired at the bushes behind which they were lying. A few tried to escape by running to the flanks of their position, but we shot them.

"Later the Turks attempted to carry two machine-guns over the hill and place them close to Pope's Hill, apparently with a view to wiping out by reverse fire the 200 men who were at the Chessboard. However, we shot these Turks while they were attempting to get into position.

"Still later about 300 Turks from the S.E. flank of Baby 700, an officer leading with sword flashing in his hand, charged the troops at the Chessboard. This was the most critical moment of the day. The Turks approached within about 200 yards of our position, and within 10 yards of the troops at the Chessboard (the latter were too far down the cliff to see them until the Turks were right upon them). My men steadily poured aimed rapid fire into the Turks, killed most of them, broke up the charge, and maintained such superiority of fire that though fresh Turks were massed at several points with a view to again charging the Chessboard, we shot them.

"I had been firing so rapidly up till 2 p.m. that I had to use two rifles, allowing one to cool while I used the other. This may seem strange, but the oil actually bubbled between the stock and the barrel, and the shells jammed in the expanded barrel. This made it compulsory to change to a cool rifle.

"Private Leighton I kept in my rear loading clips with ammunition from the out-of-date brown paper packets of ten. I particularly remember Private Fabian, standing on my left, with his eyes blood shot for the want of proper rest, and firing continuously from daylight until about 2 p.m., when all Turkish movement ceased to the north of our position. He turned a deaf ear to all suggestions that he be relieved by a man less in need of rest, and stated that he would not leave while I was there. He was one of about eight men who, from the concealed trench we had constructed the previous night, frustrated the Turkish designs on the head of Monash Valley that day."

It was on Monday, April 26th, that Lieut Evans, then in command of the machine-gun section, met his death.

3RD BATTALION LINES AT MENA
Photo: Aust. War Memorial Museum.

LEFT TO RIGHT: COLONEL McLAURIN, MAJOR IRVINE, CAPTAIN D. M. KING
Photo: Aust. War Memorial Museum.

GENERAL SIR IAN HAMILTON, WITH HIS STAFF, LEAVING MENA CAMP
Photo: Aust. War Memorial Museum.

3RD BATTALION BOARDING THE *DERFFLINGER* AT ALEXANDRIA
APRIL 1915
Photo: Aust. War Memorial Museum.

A gunner from the 3rd Brigade, suffering badly from shell-shock and the strain of the continuous fighting, commenced firing into the position held by Captain J. C. Wilson and others, in the belief that the men in front were Turks. Evans went back and succeeded in silencing the gun, handing the latter over to his own section. On the return trip he stopped to pick up a wounded man, only to fall riddled with bullets. His exploit was carried out with such daring and under such circumstances that eye-witnesses fully expected a recommendation for the Victoria Cross. Evans had acted with just the same coolness and bravery on several occasions previously. The confiscated machine-gun was put to good use by Lance-Corporal J. Wilson and Private G. Preston, both of whom had been trained as emergency gunners. The machine-gunners generally experienced a most torrid time. During the same afternoon Private J. J. Jagoe was wounded. Then a few minutes later Private Perkins was wounded, and died before the stretcher-bearers could reach him. There were other casualties, too, among the gunners.

CHAPTER X

THE THIRD DAY

TUESDAY was a day full of incident. The Turks opened up at 4.30 a.m. with a heavy barrage of shrapnel. At times throughout the day the head of Monash Valley, where B Company was stationed, was hard pressed, and on several occasions it looked as though the men there would give way. Yet when darkness fell the line was still intact.

The day was a most disastrous one for the brigade. At about 3 p.m. the gallant brigadier, Colonel H. N. Mac-Laurin, lost his life. He was reconnoitring in the vicinity of Steele's Post, close to where Lieut-Colonel Owen had established his headquarters. Major F. D. Irvine, the brigade major, had been warned by both Major Brown and Corporal Malone not to expose himself, but he disregarded the warning and met the same fate as his brigadier. The command of the 1st Brigade was given to Colonel Owen, and Major A. J. Bennett took over the 3rd Battalion.

On Wednesday, April 28th, the fighting continued with unabated vigour and fury. The men were completely worn out, but the timely arrival of reinforcements and the assistance of the guns of the fleet prevented the Turks from pushing home their advantage.

Four days and nights of fierce fighting were beginning to tell their tale. Malone, the gallant medical corporal attached to the battalion, recalls that some of the men were at breaking point, and that the relief by the Marines on the night of the 28th was not a minute too soon.

THE LANDING

The first four days' fighting left many gaps in the ranks of the officers. Captains Leer and Burns were killed, while Captains J. C. Wilson and W. B. Douglas and Lieut Hinde died as a result of their wounds. There were very few who were not wounded: Major E. S. Brown, Major M. St J. Lamb, Captain J. W. B. Bean, Lieuts G. E. McDonald, R. O. Cowey, W. B. Carter, T. L. Cadell, and the Goldring brothers, were all included in the casualty list, and, with the exception of Major E. S. Brown, all were evacuated.

Sergeant Holdaway, militia sergeant, 24th Infantry Regiment, had his leg blown off and died on a hospital ship. Corporal Roberts, whose cartoons kept the battalion amused at Mena; Reynolds, the gallant lifesaver from Manly Beach; young Bernays, son of Queensland's Clerk of Parliament; Bourne, the sergeant cook, and Bill Henry, a tall lad hailing from Cootamundra, were among those who fell during those anxious days.

At the start of the fight the medical officer, Captain J. W. B. Bean, after consultation with the C.O., had decided to establish a dressing station near Plugge's Plateau. The spot chosen was adjacent to a square pit, about 6 yards by 6 yards and about 4 feet deep. "Here we were quite comfortable," writes Captain Bean, "and I had my three men, Carruthers, Lance-Corporal Duncombe, and Wolsey—the little corn doctor who was afterwards a sergeant. We stayed here some time while the colonel with the adjutant and signalling officer and his men (these constituted headquarters) directed things, despatching company after company into the firing line and to positions on the heights in front. We lay down in this pit and waited for wounded, but very few came. So I planted a 'red cross' flag in a cairn of stones just above the pit.

"We were far away behind the firing line, but many bullets kept flying around—like bumble bees for all the world—and which gave little cracks, too, at times like a whip—this I think when a bullet hit something and flicked off with a sharp change of direction.

"I was lying well concealed in my pit when bang! I felt a sharp tap on my head and said 'Hullo.' I took off my cap and found it punctured just at the crown and a spot or so of blood on the head. I went forward a bit and found one of our officers, Carter, hit in the arm. I got a message from one of my men, Moore, to come along forward. He had about 10 men badly hit he wanted me to see. So I left the rest there and went forward with my stretcher-bearers to quite close behind the firing line at Steele's Post—in a very safe position, it seemed.

"Gordon, later a sergeant, was one of the wounded, lying shot through the lung. Colonel Owen, with Lieut Brodziak, was quite close by, I think in a shallow hole or pit. I looked about a bit and started Cavanough and the stretcher-bearers to evacuate the wounded down to the regimental aid post. Like an idiot, I didn't think to notice the sniper to our left, though occasionally a bullet would sing by fairly close. He, evidently, was having several tries for me, as I was exposing myself too much. One of my men, Moore, noticed a bullet hit the rock close by me, and was just coming forward to warn me, when 'crack!' I felt a blow like a sledge-hammer on the left buttock. I put my hand to the spot and said 'Damn.' My knees seemed to slip away from me, and I was just sinking to the ground when one of the men rushed up and caught me. Brodziak, happy and gallant young daredevil, only saw the comic side of it. He slapped his side and burst into a guffaw: 'Old Bean's got it in the bottom. My God that's funny.' 'Shut up,' said the colonel, hotly, 'it's nothing to laugh at.'"

With Captain Bean out of action, Corporal J. B. Malone took over the duties of R.M.O. If there is one memory which original 3rd Battalion men revere above others, it is the work of this man at the Landing. For three days and three nights Malone moved freely about the front line rendering first aid to the wounded. Very often his duties took him to some of the very hottest parts. But Malone modestly asserted that the Turks never once attempted to fire at him during his errands of mercy. However, the following reference to him appears in Dr C. E. W. Bean's *Australia in the War*: "Malone, medical corporal of the 3rd Battalion, when going his rounds after his officer was wounded, had to hop from shelter to shelter. On April 26th a machine-gun put three bullets through his cap, one through puttee and boot, one through his coat, and ripped the bottom out of the bucket which he carried."

The A.M.C. section was a particularly well-trained one. Captain Bean spent a lot of his own money on medical goods, consequently the battalion was better equipped in this direction than most units. All his men had been trained in the use of the hypodermic, and supplied with a mixture of camphor, olive oil, and ether in equal parts, used by the Japanese in the Russo-Japanese War, with so much success, as a prophylactic against shock.

The distance from the firing line to the beach dressing station was two and a half miles, down steep dangerous mountainous tracks; and for three days and nights the gallant 3rd Battalion stretcher-bearers carried big heavy men back to the safety of the dressing station.

CHAPTER XI

THE MARINES ARRIVE

THE battalion had had four days' continuous fighting on an unknown and hostile littoral, under terrific nerve strain and without rest, when reinforcements of Royal Marine Light Infantry arrived. The completely exhausted men of the 3rd Battalion were moved down in small parties to the beach. Not till then had it been possible to form a correct estimate of the casualties. The strain of those terrible four days was deeply ingrained on the faces of the survivors. A muster parade revealed that the casualties had been:

Officers—killed 3, wounded 13;

Other ranks—killed 36, wounded 180, missing 69.

To make up the deficiency of officers, the following N.C.Os were promoted to the rank of second-lieutenant because of "meritorious service in the field":

Warrant Officer A. McAskill, C.Q.M.S. A. M. D. Blaydes, C.S.M. H. R. W. Meager, Sergeant "Tully" McLeod, Sergeant Stan Garnham, Sergeant C. H. O. White, Sergeant Norman Gibbins, and Sergeant L. D. Sheppard. *

The Marines commenced the relief of the battalion at 4 a.m. on April 29th, but because of the difficulties asso-

---

* A few months later Blaydes, Meager, McLeod, Garnham, and White were all killed in the Lone Pine fighting, and Gibbins gave his life in the disastrous attack at Fromelles on 19th July, 1916; for his work during this action he *was recommended for the V.C.* Sheppard subsequently transferred to the artillery. McAskill left the battalion just before the attack on Lone Pine and did not rejoin it.

ciated with ingress and egress in the trenches, the operation was not completed until late in the day. On April 29th and 30th, the battalion rested at the beach, but on May 1st, orders were received to relieve the Marines, who obviously were in a bad way. At 9 p.m. the relief began. The change-over was not finalized until 4 o'clock the following morning.

Some idea of the plight of the Marines was supplied by Private W. Ward, who wrote: "I was one of a squad who were detailed to go out and reinforce the Royal Marine Light Infantry at No. 1 Battle Outpost in Wire Gully. We went over at daybreak, and only five of us gained the trench. To reach our objective it was necessary to cross a very steep-sided gully. This we accomplished by sliding down the hillside. Then, under the cover of the opposite side, we crawled along to the trench.

"When I reached it I could see things were in a bad way. There were many dead lying in the trench, also a few wounded. It appeared that the Turks had invaded and overwhelmed the defenders.

"This outpost trench was approximately 50 yards from our lines and about 150 yards from the Turks, with a ridge between its right flank and the Turkish lines. The trench was occupied mostly by the R.M.L.I., and as soon as we arrived they began to retire. I tried to persuade them to stay, but they were not having any. I don't know why, but I think they had had enough.

"We had not been there very long before one of our chaps, Pritchard, was wounded. A pal of mine, Bill Downer, carried him back to our lines. That left only three of us, Bill Hatton, Bill Beal, and myself, and we settled down to make the best of things, and to look after the trench and the wounded. The dead, including an English officer, were thrown over the back of the trench and covered with dirt. . . .

"We fared all right for a while in the matter of food and water. When the Marines retired they left behind their water-bottles, packs, rifles, and ammunition. There was a little muddy pool at the end of the trench near the gully, and this cleared sufficiently to allow of drinking. Food we obtained from our lines during the night.

"There were three wounded Marines in the trench, so we set to work to make them comfortable and feed them. Luckily we had candles which we had brought from Mena Camp. These came in handy for boiling the bully-beef and biscuits in our mess-tins. One of the wounded men had been shot in the head. Another had had his leg fractured and it was tied up with puttees with a couple of rifles as splints. The third chap died shortly after our arrival. The Marine wounded in the head had to be fed with a spoon. He could not talk or do anything for himself. After a while he began to knock himself about. So, with the aid of a couple of bayonets driven into the ground, one each side of him, we fastened him down to the bottom of the trench with puttees. Although our lines were within call, stretcher-bearers, they told us, were not procurable. So we had to be satisfied with things as they were.

"While we were in this trench the Turks made an attack on our lines, but we, being in the corner near the gully, could not see them coming from the left. We were told afterwards that they had been very close to our trench. They were repulsed and driven back to their own lines with machine-gun and rifle fire by the 3rd Battalion on the right, and by the 4th on the hill at the back.

"While in occupation of the trench we made it deeper and generally improved it for defence, while a strict watch was maintained night and day. On the third night a stretcher-bearer, 'Jumbo' Blackburn, was sent over to help get the wounded back to our lines. When we took

THE LANDING

them back we were told to remain with the battalion. So we left the outpost trench unoccupied."

Private Ward, who was wounded while defending this outpost, subsequently lost his leg.

The trenches generally were in a bad state and open to and harassed by enfilade fire. Consequently the first night was occupied in deepening and improving them in various ways, and in addition to this work there was the gruesome task of clearing out the dead. The Marines had suffered very heavy losses. They had vacated some of the forward positions, and were, for the most part, occupying trenches right on the rim of the gully.

"We were kept busy that night passing out their wounded and dead, as well as their rifles and equipment," relates Lieut E. N. Litchfield; "and what a huge pile these made down the slope near the communication trench. Portion of the cliff fell down and caused a landslide, which temporarily buried most of the heap and a few of the lads who were digging just below."

The battalion was now operating for the first time as a distinct and intact unit, with a definite frontage. Fortunately the Turks' activities quietened considerably when the battalion reoccupied the line, although Lieut Blaydes and his men had a slight skirmish with the enemy. On the second night Sergeants Litchfield and Dick Irving were taking it in turns to sleep, with Private Tom Middleton posted at the other end of the trench, when Litchfield was surprised to see a Turk walking straight to the spot where Middleton was standing. Recalling the incident, Litchfield says: "I gave Irving a kick and he sprang up. We fired together. Middleton grabbed his rifle and looked in our direction as I yelled. The Turk, still holding his own rifle, and with our two shots in him, fell on Middleton's bayonet."

Although badly wounded this Turk would not allow the stretcher-bearers to touch him, so Captain Moore sent him to the rear with Private Lilley. Peter Rados, a Greek with the battalion, who had lived in Constantinople for some years, asked the Turk in the absence of the official interpreter why he had come in. "Jacko" replied that he was on his way to surrender, as his non-coms, Germans, had been very severe on the Turkish rankers. He was very badly wounded, and everyone was touched when the poor fellow handed Lilley a baby's sock containing some trinkets. The A.M.C. took charge of him, but he died at daybreak the next morning.

"On May 3rd," writes Private C. M. Geddes, " a party was detailed to erect barbed-wire defences along a gully near our trench, and while working we were surprised to see Captain T. O Smith coming up the slope. He was the second-in-command of D Company, and one of the best-liked and finest officers. Much to his disgust, he had been left behind on the *Derfflinger*, to return later to Egypt with stores and baggage. He had taken advantage of a barge carrying rations to come ashore and see how the boys were faring. The contrast of his appearance with that of the officers and men on the Peninsula was very great. He looked fat, well groomed, and clean, while the others, with practically no rest and eight days on bully-beef and no fresh bread or meat, had fallen away greatly.

"We were pleased to see the captain, and he said he hoped to be with us soon. He went into the trench, and being a deadly rifle shot, asked one of the boys to lend him a rifle. As I went down the slope as N.C.O. in charge of the wiring party, I heard Captain Smith laugh and say, 'I got him with that shot.' Evidently he had spotted a Turk in the bushes. A little while later, when we were still at work, one of our chaps said, 'Captain Smith is dead.' I told him not to be silly, as I had just seen him firing through a loop-hole. As I spoke, two men came along carrying a body on a stretcher. One glance showed me that it was Captain Smith. And he had 'just taken a run ashore to see how the boys were getting on!'"

During the next fortnight, hard work was the order, day and night. It was dig, dig, dig, until the collective bones of the battalion ached, and hands were blistered and calloused. But it was a case of digging for dear life, as the Turk constantly shelled the parapets, and it was essential that the trenches should be deeper and more secure.

All this time the heat was intense. The flies became unbearable, and the "chats" almost invincible. The flies were of all sizes and hues, and, as many of the dead still remained unburied since the Landing, it was inevitable that sickness should ally itself with the Turkish bullets in adding to the casualties. It was, then, quite impossible to bury the dead who lay out in No-Man's land, and they lay there until an armistice was arranged later. The "chats" got into the seams of tunics, shirts, trousers, and even into the socks of the troops, and each day were slaughtered unmercifully. Yet they were just as plentiful next day. Heaven alone knows how the men could have survived had they not been able occasionally to swim off the beach, in the blue Aegean, even though "Beachy Bill" daily sprayed the water with shrapnel.

Not knowing what to expect next, the battalion's whole efforts were directed night and day towards improving its positions. Individual men and junior officers were all the time so busily engaged that very little was known concerning the activities of other units.

Beach and water parties cultivated the habit of bringing back from their contact with other troops all sorts of weird tales, popularly known as "furphies" or "latrine wires." These parties, returning to the trenches, would be greeted with the enquiry, "What's the latest latrine?" Information gathered on the beach was generally of a startling nature: as, "Greece has declared war, and is sending

50,000 men to Gallipoli"—"The Russians have begun their offensive, and have already captured 100,000 prisoners."

How eagerly the men of the battalion absorbed news of any description! With rumours like these, how could there be depression or loss of morale, and again out at the back of the firing line great battleships and stolid transports could be seen, still standing by, so staunch and dependable—links with the past and the future and the world. The ships of war fired sometimes at the Narrows or burst their great lyddite shells on the hills in front of the trenched fighting line. The firing was directed occasionally by a solitary plane which the Turks tried desperately to hit. That plane the troops came to worship as a sort of guardian angel. They came to know that it was sometimes piloted by the redoubtable Commander Samson, an air ace supreme in those early days of war— one whose exploits on the Western and other fronts the troops had read about while in training in Australia and Egypt—a dare-devil Britisher upon whose head the Kaiser himself had put a price, so the reports went. What daring antics, what aerial gymnastics he performed. With shells bursting all around, Samson's machine would stagger and flutter and begin to fall. The Turks would cease firing. Then, when the gallant commander had swooped and stalled drunkenly to within a few hundred feet from the ground, the engine would roar and off he would fly, to the great chagrin of the enemy.

CHAPTER XII

THE TURKISH ATTACK

BETWEEN the 3rd Battalion and the 2nd Battalion on its right, there existed a re-entrant of something like 250 yards, and strenuous efforts were now made to straighten out the line, the two battalions sapping towards each other. By midnight on May 18th the gap had been reduced to something like 100 yards. Meanwhile the territory between the two points was protected by the converging machine-gun fire of the two battalions. It was towards this opening that the spearhead of a formidable Turkish attack was now directed.

"On May 18th I had No. 10 Platoon in the sap," relates E. N. Litchfield (then a sergeant). "In the afternoon the Turks seemed to concentrate the fire of most of their guns into the horse-shoe bend positions, and they knocked our parapet to pieces in no time. I heard a commotion down on the right and went to investigate. One of the lookout 'possies' had been hit by a salvo of no fewer than five twelve-pounder shells, and the whole outfit—sandbags, roof, and all—was blocking the main trench. Embedded in the back wall of the trench were the five shell-cases.

"Someone called out 'Old General (meaning Private George Gordon) is underneath.' We dug him out. He only had a few scratches on his face. Major (later Brigadier-General) Brand was commanding the battalion at the time. He came down the sap late in the afternoon to see what damage had been done. I said to him, 'It looks as though something will happen to-night.' He said, 'Yes, the Turks have a big concentration of troops behind them, and have sent a message saying they will drive us into the sea if we do not capitulate within six hours.' I mentioned to him that the sap was getting longer, that the platoons could not occupy all the "possies" made, and that we were now in front of B Company's sector in the old line. I suggested that a communication trench should be dug back in case we needed assistance. To this proposal he agreed. Four of the men, Dick Irving, Cess Tutill, Herb Minter, and another, undertook to do this work, two at each end. Those chaps *did* work.

"At 6 p.m. No. 9 Platoon came into the sap and Sgt Leo Palmer took charge of the watch till midnight. He had plenty to do rebuilding the parapets, with No. 10 Platoon sleeping as best they could. The Turks kept up a sweeping fire all night with machine-guns and rifles, trying to prevent the rebuilding of our parapets. With the greatest expedition the communication trench back to B Company was completed and occupied by a platoon under Lieut L. W. Street. At midnight No. 10 Platoon took over from No. 9, and we found everything in order again, despite the sweeping fire of the Turks which had not abated."

In graphic manner, Private C. M. Geddes, describes the Turkish attack on May 19th: "Notices were posted in the trenches in which General Birdwood entreated everybody to keep a strict lookout, and not to allow weariness and fatigue to affect them. 'Keep awake, men,' said Birdy, 'and I have no fear of the result of any Turkish attack.'

"We were told that the festival known as Ramadan was approaching, when the Mohammedan religious belief, that any Turkish soldier dying for his country in battle receives an eternal reward from Allah, was likely to be emphasized. It was expected that a fierce attack would be made. It was explained that at Ramadan the Turk, always a brave foe, would fight with added religious frenzy.

"At this time our platoon spells consisted of four hours 'in support.' 'Supports' referred to a trench about 20

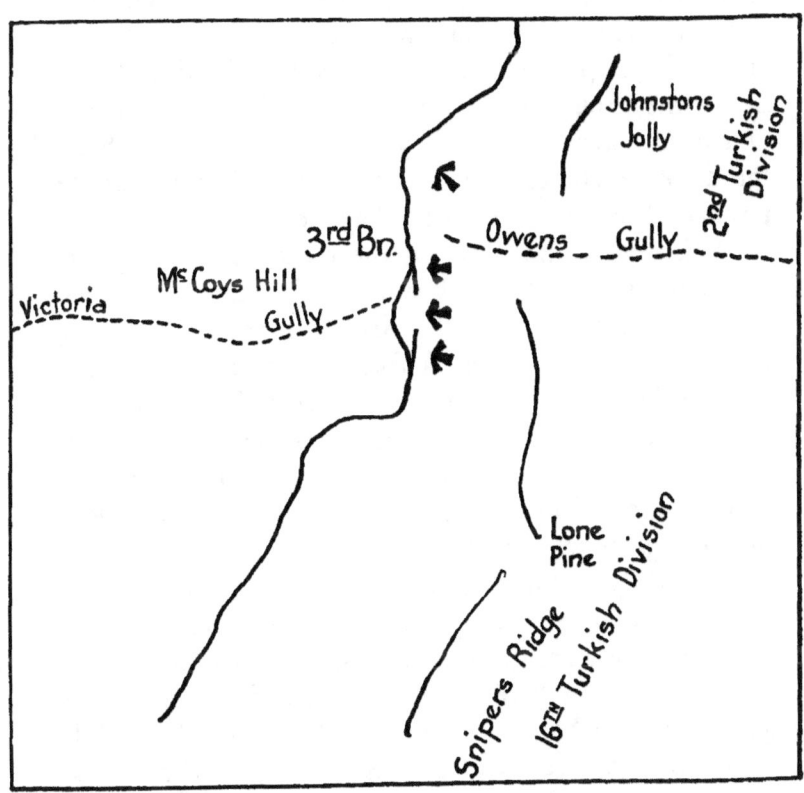

TURKISH ATTACK 19TH MAY, 1915

yards behind the front line, where one might snatch a little sleep, in full kit, of course, with one's rifle at one's side, and not even the heavy military boots unlaced. The moon feast was now at hand.

"At midnight on May 18th, our platoon came out of the front line and passed along to the support trench, to try and get a little sleep. We were soon afterwards awakened by heavy fire and the order came 'stand to.' After standing-to for 20 minutes, the order was passed along to 'stand down.' We again lay on the floor of the trench, later to be awakened by such terrific fire that no stand-to was necessary to bring us to our feet.

"Word came for every man, for whom there was room, to line the front trench, and we stood shoulder to shoulder on the fire-step. Captain Austin ordered a party of us to lie on the ground above the trench behind the parados. Our orders were—not on any account to fire, but, should the Turks reach our trenches, we were to jump across the top and charge them with the bayonet.

"When we climbed out of the trench a startling sight met our eyes. The darkness of No-Man's Land was literally illuminated by the fire of many rifles blazing from the grass, and many Turks were within 25 yards of our trenches. We were again told from the trench below not to fire, and thus expose our presence to the enemy. So our party had the unique experience of viewing at first hand, and from the 'dress circle,' as it were, the most thrilling game ever played.

"Our chaps were magnificent. Every man for whom there was room was firing, across the trench at the line of fire from the dark ground, as fast as he could press the trigger and draw back the bolt to reload. When a rifle got too hot to hold, or jammed, the man below on the trench floor would hand up his weapon with additional cartridges. The machine-guns, too, poured back at the enemy a hail of lead. Many of our fine chaps died that morning shot through the head. But immediately there would be another man to jump up on the step and take the place of him who fell. Every man knew full well that, if the Turks broke through, the 3rd Battalion would be wiped out to a man. We had no reserves; only the steep dangerous hillsides and the Aegean Sea lay behind us.

PRACTISING BOAT DRILL AND LANDING OPERATIONS AT LEMNOS, APRIL, 1915

Photo: *Aust. War Memorial Museum.*

LIEUT.-COL. R. H. OWEN ADDRESSING THE MEN ON THE EVE OF THE LANDING

Photo: Aust. War Memorial Museum.

"The dawn now began to show. And what a sight before our eyes. It seemed as though an army was asleep out in front in the grass. So confident had the Turks been of the result that they had attacked with blankets strapped to their backs, anticipating that they would sleep the next night in our trenches. But the majority were fated to sleep their long last sleep out in No-Man's Land. Those remaining alive could now not stand the even deadlier fire poured on them after the dawn, and they raced back towards the safety of their own trenches.

"I remember so well the great running of one of the Turks. He sped like a deer in the direction of his own trenches, despite the treacherous torn up ground. Bullets threw up the dirt all round him and whipped at his flying feet. But on he sped unharmed. It was a most thrilling race. I really hoped that he might reach his goal—he was such a magnificent runner. Then just as he reached his own line, and was about to make a last leap into the trench, an Australian bullet ended his great dash for safety. He fell and rolled helplessly, horribly—he who had been so alive—back down the banked slope in front of the Turkish parapet.

"Now we were called back into our trench, and my first concern was to dive round the corner, and see how my particular friend, Edgar Hamonet, had fared. He was in charge of a machine-gun pointing down a nasty gully, up which the Turks had poured. When I saw him he was cleaning his gun, and laughing with excitement. 'I had a lovely target,' he said, 'and mowed them down in dozens—have a look over the top.' The mass of still forms in the gully bore out the truth of his statement. The dead body of Lieut L. W. Street lay on the bottom of the trench beside him. He told me how bravely this officer had fought and died.

"We learned later that the flower of the Turkish Regular Army—the 'Nizam'—had withered in the face of our defence. The Nizam had been transferred to the Australian front with strict orders from Enver Pasha to 'drive the Australians into the sea.' They had been fresh troops, too, against very weary Australians.

"The Turks in that attack lost 3000 men killed out in front; and looking back now, as one writes of this day—a great day for Australian arms—it seems to me that this battle has not been given the prominence it deserves.* Had the Australian line wavered then, the 1st Division, that magnificent body of men which left our shores in 1914, would have been completely annihilated.

"I would like to mention a lad of 19 named Sherman —he was Captain Austin's runner. This youth exposed himself above the trench parapet in many places that morning to ascertain just how close the Turks were winning. A Turkish bullet got him in the head, and so passed a most gallant soldier."

Lieut E. N. Litchfield, already quoted, says that at about 3.45 a.m. on the morning of the 19th the heavy firing ceased and everything seemed unnaturally quiet. "I kicked Leo Palmer, who was dozing at my feet, and told him to get all his men up. I was peering over the top straining to pierce the darkness. Just as Leo came back, I saw the Turks. I beckoned Palmer up alongside me, whispering 'Look at them—hundreds running up to the first trench and hundreds crawling out of the first trench.' He laughed. At that I pulled a sand-bag down and stood up higher. Then I was astounded to see the enemy not ten yards out in front, in the dip known as Owen's Gully. I screamed out 'Rapid fire' just as the ghostly shapes rose to their feet to charge.

"My own rifle was red hot in no time. Line after line rose and fell. My rifle-bolt jammed. I had the butt on the ground kicking the bolt, could not get it to slide, so

---

* The 3rd Battalion casualties on May 19 were: 1 officer killed, 1 died of wounds, and 1 wounded; other ranks, 41 killed, 49 wounded.

grabbed another rifle near by. Then I realized suddenly that the look-out post on my right was not manned, and that Turks were crawling in front of it. It projected a yard in front of the line. I climbed up on top and a lad named Chadwick did likewise. He was down, shot through the head after we had accounted for about half-a-dozen Turks, who were about to get in. I stayed up too long, and just at daylight, when exchanging shots with Turks playing 'possum' among the dead out in front, I got a crack on the side of the head and fell back into the trench like a bag of coal."

CHAPTER XIII

ARMISTICE

THE next day everybody was amazed to see a flag appear—white with red crescent—out in the Turks' trenches. Three Turks climbed out and approached the Australian line slowly but determinedly carrying this flag. A party from our side carrying a red cross flag almost immediately advanced to meet the strangers, when the Turks expressed a wish to bury their dead.

The order "cease fire" was passed along the line, and the Turkish stretcher-bearers began to collect their wounded. However, the Australians' suspicions being aroused, they were fired on. Again came orders to "cease fire," and the enemy came out again. The orders now were not to resume hostilities until 7 p.m. unless precipitated by the enemy. The watching Australians noticed that some of the Turks not bothering about the wounded were collecting rifles and ammunition. This action was quickly checked by firing shots over the heads of every Turk who touched a rifle or ammunition.

Suddenly the Turks withdrew and the Australians also went back to their trenches. It was the general conclusion now that the armistice was a mere ruse. Following the withdrawal, heavy artillery and rifle fire was immediately poured on the Anzac trenches. Next morning an enemy aeroplane came over, and in the afternoon an 8-inch gun dropped six high-explosive shells near battalion headquarters. One shell buried three men and wounded four others.

The unburied dead now became a real menace to health and of the gravest concern to both combatants, and as a consequence another unusual happening is recorded on May 24th. This again served to show how unlike any other campaign in British military history was the great Gallipoli adventure. An armistice was now formally arranged. This embraced the daylight hours between 7.30 a.m. and 4 p.m., and both armies contracted to bury their own dead. Fifty men from the 3rd Battalion went out as one of the burying parties, and worked strenuously throughout the day. The Turks, too, were very active burying their dead.

It was all so uncanny, so unreal and disturbing after the hectic days that had gone before. The roar and rattle and crash of war were stilled. Not a single rifle spoke all that day. The hush was almost unnerving after 29 days of almost continuous rifle, machine-gun, and artillery fire, which had come to be regarded as inevitable in the new so-cramped world which was Anzac.

But it was a silence which to the sorely tried troops was really heavenly. Those men who were not actually on fatigue or other duty lazed and slept or cleaned and oiled their rifles, looked to their equipment generally or scrambled down to the beach to swim and wash their sweat-clogged shirts and foul socks in the limpid sea, a molten Gallipoli sun drying these garments as the men, sockless but booted and clad only in breeches, scrambled back up the slopes to the trenches, shirts flapping on bare backs with sleeves knotted loosely about the neck.

During the afternoon, with nothing else to do, men of the battalion climbed out of the trenches and endeavoured to get into conversation with the dark visaged Turks, and shouting across No-Man's Land, "Hello, Johnnie"—"Saida Johnnie"—"Give it baksheesh"—and the various "bon mots" that had come to grace the Australian vocabulary during Cairo days. Generally, however, Abdul was unresponsive. An occasional grin and a glimpse of white teeth—somewhere a hesitant exchange of cigarettes or souvenirs—but no fraternizing in the real sense.*

At 4 p.m. the burial parties vacated No-Man's Land and returned to their respective trenches. Men of the 3rd Battalion "jollying" the Turks from out on top of the parapet were ordered to come down, but they lingered enjoying each other's quips or too pointed compliments shouted across at the Turks. The enemy were voted to be poor linguists—they showed no inclination to enter into chaffing arguments in Cairo Arabic with the Australians.† "Jacko" was anxious to get on with the war. He appeared above the trenches and signalled the Australians to get down. But the latter were in good humour and reluctant. They stood their ground. However, a warning volley just over their heads from the opposite trenches was the signal for a scramble for shelter. The war was on again.

That night at 9 p.m. and again at 11 the enemy made slight attacks from the nullah. Several bombs were thrown into that section of our trenches. The next day, May 25th, the new sap-trench leading to the 2nd Bat-

---

* Captain Leslie Dunlop, Battalion Medical Officer and A.M.C. Corporal Malone, went across to the Turkish trenches, spoke to a couple of Turkish doctors, and exchanged English for Turkish sovereigns. They searched for and found the bodies of some of our own men and attended to their burial, collecting the identity disks. The burial parties plugged their nostrils with medicated wool. Father McAullife read the burial service.

† H. C. Armstrong, in his book *Grey Wolf*, which actually is the story of the life of Mustafa Kemal Pasha, who commanded the Turks on Gallipoli, on page 72 says: "He (Mustafa Kemal) was constantly in the line talking with the company officers and the men (Turks), and so getting first hand information. Often he was up in the sap-heads, or even in the danger zone beyond with the advanced snipers, studying the ground. During an armistice in May he worked as a sergeant in one of the burial parties so as to be able to spy out the Australian trenches himself."

talion lines was completed and the 3rd Battalion occupied 25 yards of this new trench, its frontage now taking in the head of the gully. Days immediately following were occupied in deepening trenches and contriving disguised loop-holes. A constant look-out was maintained through periscopes. But there were few signs of movement from the enemy trenches.

CHAPTER XIV

TRENCH WARFARE

D COMPANY—on the extreme right of the battalion—was at this time exactly in front of the Lone Pine, a small isolated pine tree, by then quite devoid of leaves. It stood like a bare pole, sprouting branches, on dry ground and above and beyond the Turkish trenches directly opposite.

On May 28th the battalion was subjected to heavy shrapnel fire. Two days later our artillery heavily bombarded the enemy trenches, to assist an attack away on the left. Reinforcements reached the battalion about this time. As their training had been rather hurried, they were exercised in musketry and fire discipline behind the lines. This training was a source of much amusement to the "old hands" who had been on the Peninsula a month. But this amusement was forgivable, for the first month in the front line trenches on Gallipoli under fire day and night did make "old soldiers" in every sense of the term. Going down the hill to fill their water-bottles at the well, they found delight in good naturedly chaffing the new arrivals occupied in firing blank cartridges at imaginary targets; this, while just up above in the trenches a man daren't look over the top even momentarily without grave risk of a bullet spattering his brains on the parapet.

On June 1st, two tunnels leading forward were begun from D Company. Picked sections of miners worked in groups to push on this work quickly. It was known perfectly well that the enemy too was sapping forward towards our line.

On the 8th a "traction engine" was reported to have been seen at Lone Pine ridge, and a Japanese mortar brought up by us fired five shots, with what results we did not know. During that night very strong wire-entanglements were erected by the Turks at the place where the traction engine had been seen. The enemy showed further considerable activity there on the following night with bursts of fire.

On June 12th, the enemy bombarded the firing line with heavy artillery from a close range. A machine-gun position was destroyed and the gun tripod wrecked. The Japanese mortar was returned to our trenches, and fired two shots at the suspected gun position. The Turks now showed great activity in sniping during the day. The next day they fired again from the same position, and the Japanese mortar returned the fire. About this time observation posts were constructed in our parados. They were a decided advantage.

On June 14th, 134 reinforcements joined the battalion. They, too, were given further training in musketry. Meanwhile the enemy was busy pushing on with new saps and tunnels on the battalion's left front. The Japanese mortar fired four shots at the Turkish sap-head and the trenches near Johnston's Jolly. Three bombs actually burst in the Turk trenches. How we wished then that our artillery could fire heavy shells by the hour instead of just one or two now and again.

With the Turk on high ground, and great hills before us, it was indeed a gruelling task to ensure defence with the men and guns at our disposal, but the troops never complained nor lost their saving sense of humour, even though the dreaded dysentery, caused by the hordes of awful flies, was now beginning to thin the ranks. The men who remained to fight were visibly falling away in weight in alarming fashion. The flies, big, black-and-green, fat brutes, were nauseating in the extreme. The troops carried food to the mouth with one hand, using the other strenuously to ward off their ubiquitous and irritatingly persistent attacks. It was a common happening to hear a man say, "Who pinched my bread and jam?" when, having put the food down for a moment, he would not immediately sight it again. It would be there all the time, the white bread and jam completely hidden by a swarm of cloying black flies. No wonder dysentery exacted its toll!

On the evening of June 20th instructions were received from divisional headquarters to prepare to take part in a ruse to draw the enemy's fire. This ruse consisted of the firing of two red lights at the extreme left of the corps' front and two white lights at the extreme right five minutes later. The firing of two shots by a destroyer out at sea five minutes after that would be the signal for short rapid bursts of rifle- and machine-gun fire by the infantry. This plan was very successful in drawing the enemy's fire, and disclosed that his trenches were held strongly. Also we were able to locate his machine-guns.

On June 21st Lieut T. L. Cadell was mortally wounded. Because of his youth Cadell was always referred to as "the baby of the battalion." Nevertheless, he carried out his duties with the dignity and assurance of a veteran, and his death was a distinct loss to us.

Colonel Owen was wounded in the foot the same day, the wound proving sufficiently serious to put him out of action for the remainder of the war. Some members of the battalion were under the impression that the old soldier had been sent back because of his age. Very emphatically this was not the case, and the rumour naturally upset the gallant old colonel very much. That was the last the battalion saw of the fine old gentleman, affectionately known as "Dad." With him went the good wishes of every member of the unit. Although the battalion had several commanding officers after Colonel

Owen departed, it was he who had made the regimental spirit, and it continued always the same, a fine tribute to his systematic and sympathetic early training. His services were officially recognized by the bestowal of the C.M.G.

The command of the battalion now passed temporarily into the hands of Major D. McF. McConaghy, who acted thus to within a few days of the Lone Pine engagement, when Lieut-Colonel E. S. Brown took over.

On June 25th the enemy did considerable damage to the 4th Battalion lines with his trench-mortar, and the 4th requested the 3rd Battalion to open fire with the Japanese mortar. The second shot silenced the Turk.

At daylight on the 27th heavy rifle and machine-gun fire broke out all along the enemy's line. The rifle fire was wild, the Turks being observed simply thrusting their rifles above the parapet and firing into the air without any pretence of aiming. Our troops sat tight and made no sign, and very soon the demonstration died down. Two nights later rapid machine-gun and rifle fire again crackled all along the line. This time the aiming was more accurate, and bullets whistled over and thudded into the parapets. Again the Australians "lay low and said nuthin," and the enemy fire quickly slackened. It was apparent that the Turks were nervous and suspected an attack. On July 5th they fired about 20 rounds from an 11-inch gun. This gun was located and the artillery informed.

About this time D Company was subjected to a severe gruelling. Its members were directly enfiladed on several successive days by a French 75-millimetre gun which tossed over high-explosive shells at a great rate. "The speed of the shells was astounding," writes a member of D Company. "Almost before we heard the report in the distance indicating that a shell had been fired, and before we could dive for shelter, the missile seemed to crash above our heads to scatter the sandbags on our parapet."

On July 12th, the battalion received instructions relating to a projected ruse to distract the enemy's attention, and prevent his reserves from going south to Achi Baba, where the British were to attack. These theatricals began at 8.15 a.m. and continued periodically throughout the day. Whistles were blown and words of command shouted. Bayonets were shown here and there "over the top," and dummy figures were thrust into view at various points. But little fire was drawn on our front by these gestures. At night we fired star-shells, and our artillery heavily bombarded the enemy.

During all these days tunnelling had proceeded with a view to forming a new firing line ahead of the existing one. This was now all ready. It remained only to break through a thin crust of earth overhead. On the night of July 15th five recesses on the right, joining the existing firing line at C Company's front, were opened up. But the work could only be done slowly because of the heavy outside fatigues, and the run-down state of the men's health.

The Turks and ourselves suddenly became very desirous of possessing a crater caused by the explosion of mines just in front of our left flank. Our gun-fire was concentrated on this spot during the night, as the Turks were reported to be in occupation.

A section of the new firing line having been opened up, it was manned for defence on July 18th, and the work of improvement was pushed on. The old firing line, however, continued to be strongly held as it was still the main line of resistance. Heavy artillery bombardments by the enemy occurred now, which disclosed the possession of a new large trench-mortar. But the expected attack did not develop. All bombs and flares had been moved to the new line in preparation. The battalion's left flank was very vulnerable, as the adjoining battalion had not opened up its recesses to junction with us. The flank rested almost on a mine crater.

Digging and improving did not slacken. The men worked vigorously, as the enemy was reported to be very active on our front. And Turks were seen moving in behind Johnston's Jolly. By July 19th all precautions against the expected attack had been completed, and wire-entanglements and a small quantity of barbed-wire had been set in position out in front. However, at 9.30 p.m. that night work on the new firing line was suspended. The order came from brigade headquarters.

On the morning of July 21st, a conference of commanding officers was called by the brigadier, and orders were issued that the new firing line was to be converted into a wire-entanglement as the enemy was expected to attack in force on the 23rd. We held the new line that day, but withdrew at 9 p.m. to the old fire-trenches. At this hour the work of throwing up wire-entanglements began, and was carried on all night. Then began the work of renovating the now somewhat neglected old firing line. This task was pushed ahead for the expected attack. Weary men worked as strenuously and as rapidly as their exhausted physical condition would allow.

Daylight on July 22nd showed the new and deserted firing line as a high and tangled mass of wire, which would serve as a very effective obstacle to attacking troops. All recesses were blocked with bags taken from the parapet. The parados was razed. During the day the work of remaking the old firing line was pushed ahead, and by evening a good fire parapet had been completed along its whole length. Our artillery was very active during the day, shelling Johnston's Jolly and Lone Pine with 5-inch howitzers. However, the expected attack did not eventuate. There was no perceptible movement by the enemy.

On the following evenings the usual heavy bombardments occurred. A Taube flew over the lines on July

29th and again on the 30th. Several bombs were dropped on the beach. On August 2nd Captain E. M. MacFarlane, an original officer, and one of the most daring and fearless leaders in the brigade, was killed.

Throughout the months of June and July the monotony of trench-warfare was relieved somewhat by unofficial rifle competitions. Each morning at "stand-to" the troops saw shovel blades tossing earth appear above the Turkish parapet at Lone Pine. For the want of something better to do, it became the habit to take pot shots at the shovels. The Turks, whom we looked upon as "good sports" in those days, and who, no doubt, found trench life just as irksome as we did, demonstrated their interest and good-naturedly signalled the hits and the misses.

We returned the compliment by exhibiting targets also in the shape of shovels and hats. The Turks, who fancied themselves as marksmen, were intrigued, and we signalled their scores. When occasionally some of the lads—in mischievous mood—would deliberately signal a series of misses, the Turkish machine-guns would "spit" a burst or two as a gentle reminder to "play the game." A few "bulls-eyes," indicated by holding the shovels in a perpendicular position, always put the Turk in good humour. And so the war continued.

One morning while these competitions were in full swing a huge flock of ibis flew over our lines towards the Turks. Machine-gun and rifle fire from both sides was suddenly diverted towards these unfortunate birds. There was much agitation in "brass hat" circles for a time, the staff being at a loss to understand the unexpected disturbance. Despite the combined fire of both sides, only one or two birds fell—and they fell into the Turkish trenches.

Preparations were now well advanced for our impending attack on Lone Pine. And, in connection with that engagement, it is well to remember the health and general condition of the troops at that time. Major J. W. B. Bean, who was now back with the battalion as medical officer, comments: "The men were in a very bad way from constant work and strain, and no sleep worthy of the name. It was all trench work and one heavy fatigue after another. It was bad enough, dragging up those steep hills with slippery fine white dust underfoot—it was clay soil, and the moment there was rain the paths became slippery and cloddy and the soil clung to one more tenaciously than the mud of a ploughed field. The sun was absolutely broiling—quite tropical—beating down fiercely on the back of one's neck, making all feel sick and dizzy.

"Imagine under these conditions carrying up great iron loop-hole plates, ammunition boxes weighted with cartridges, or heavy cans of water. And remember, the food was very 'samey' for tired digestions. There was too much onion, so very indigestible when washed down unmasticated with gulps of tea. The tea was a terrible brew, nearly ink-black. Often the men lived on nothing but this inky tea. They couldn't keep anything else down. They became so exhausted that often they could not even keep the tea down.

"What with this, no rest worthy of the name, pestered by flies and walked over by various people as they lay in the trenches, their condition can be imagined. Add to this the constant digging, digging, digging. Pick and shovel work that had to be done.

"Well, it was not according to regulations, but Colonel Brown determined that each day one platoon should have 24 hours off, which they could spend as they liked. It was a bold thing to do—it was not complying with orders, but it was just the salvation of our boys. They went down to the beach in turns, and bathed and lazed and slept. Sometimes one or two were hit by a shell-burst, but that was the risk wherever one was. In the evening they would come back and have a jolly good 'sing-song' within a quarter of a mile of the Turks' trenches—and then go for some more sleep.

"They would feel quite fresh when they came on at 7 o'clock next morning. It made all the difference, and it was a very keen lot who rushed the Turkish trenches at Lonesome Pine, so very different from the exhausted men of a week or two before.

"Those water cans. We got our water-supply by sinking bores and pumping—the engineer's job—and some off the ships, from their tanks. The water was stored in big black iron tanks ashore. Latest of all, great plants were sent to condense sea water. The allowance was very scanty—a water-bottle filled for drinking, and half-a-gallon per head per day for washing and cooking. In an intensely thirsty land like Gallipoli this is very scanty."

3RD BATTALION MEN LEAVING THE *DERFFLINGER* ON A DESTROYER TO TAKE PART IN THE LANDING

Photo: *Aust. War Memorial Museum.*

BEFORE "REVEILLE" ON THE MORNING PRIOR TO THE LANDING
Photo: Aust. War Memorial Museum.

3RD BATTALION MEN ON A DESTROYER PROCEEDING INSHORE FOR THE LANDING
Photo: Aust. War Memorial Museum.

CHAPTER XV

LONE PINE

DURING the closing days of July the battalion received particulars of the proposed British landing at Suvla Bay, on the left flank of the Anzac position. As part of this programme, the 1st Brigade was selected to make an attack on Lone Pine, with the object of drawing all Turkish reserves away from the Suvla area, and to prepare a breaking-through point should the Suvla thrust be successful. The area for the Australian attack was approximately in the centre of the Turkish lines at Anzac.

Lone Pine, so named by reason of the solitary pine tree, already mentioned, which stood gauntly just behind the plateau at the top of White's Gully, was a strongly-fortified position, enclosed by rows and rows of barbed-wire, and reputed to be one of the strongest positions on the Australian front.

As a preparation, 383 shells were fired into the position at various times on the day of the attack and during the three preceding days. The engineers, too, had assisted by constructing an underground line of trenches which brought the brigade 50 yards closer to the enemy. This row of trenches was "unlidded" by the removal of the surface of the ground overhead—about a foot thick—on the night preceding the attack.

From this new line a sap was driven out towards the Turkish position, and at its extremity a mine was laid which was exploded three and a half hours before the attack. This sap and mine-crater later greatly expedited the work of digging the first communication trench to the captured position.

"Zero" hour was fixed for 5.30 p.m. on Friday, August 6th, the attack to be preceded by an "intensive bombardment of one hour." The 1st Brigade attacked with three battalions in line—the 2nd on the right, the 3rd in the centre, and the 4th on the left, with the 1st Battalion in reserve.

The 3rd Battalion officers for the attack were:—

COMMANDING OFFICER	Lieut-Col E. S. Brown
SECOND-IN-COMMAND	Major D. McF. McConaghy
ADJUTANT	Captain O. G. Howell-Price
A COMPANY	Lieut T. D. McLeod (O.C.), Second Lieuts P. W. Woods, H. Allen, E. W. G. Wren, R. I. Moore
B COMPANY	Captain W. C. Beeken (O.C.), Second Lieuts A. McDermid, T. E. McGowan, A. M. D. Blaydes, and G. W. Greyson
C COMPANY	Captain D. T. Moore (O.C.), Captain E. Dawson, Second Lieuts S. M. Garnham, C. H. O. White, J. H. Harrison and E. N. Litchfield
D COMPANY	Major C. D. Austin (O.C.), Lieut J. E. Barlow, Second Lieuts H. R. W. Meager, S. A. Pinkstone, and A. F. Burrett
MEDICAL OFFICER	Captain J. W. B. Bean
SIGNALLING OFFICER	Second Lieut V. E. Smythe
MACHINE-GUN OFFICER	Lieut C. J. A. White
CHAPLAIN	Dean Talbot

The early part of the day was given over wholly to final preparations. Many devoted the morning to oiling and furbishing their rifles, sharpening their bayonets, and adjusting their equipment. Others went to the beach for a quiet refreshing swim. The more serious minded spent busy hours writing and arranging for the despatch of letters to their home-folk. In this latter connection, special mention should be made of a very touching letter written that morning by Second Lieut Hubert Meager to his mother:* "During the next few days," he wrote, "we shall be facing death every minute. If I am taken, do as did the Roman Matrons of old . . . keep your tears for privacy, steel your heart, and get a dozen recruits to fill my place."

There was spiritual preparation also. For the Roman Catholic members of the brigade, Father McAullife celebrated Mass. A special service had been conducted for the Anglicans the previous evening in the dug-out church behind the lines at the head of Shrapnel Valley.

"The Church had been an ammunition dump," writes Dean Talbot, "and, though improvised, it possessed a holy table on which rested a wooden cross made by one of the pioneers. The Church was circular in shape, like a miniature amphitheatre, and the seats rose one above the other. The roof was the sky overhead, and we looked down the gully to the Aegean. That Thursday evening we knew, or we guessed, that a move was imminent. So we celebrated the Holy Communion, the Church being crowded. Would that our churches here were similarly packed. About 100 received the sacrament, and I still treasure the chalice that I used on that memorable occasion."

Shortly after midday, companies moved to the battalion "parade ground"—a ledge close behind the line—where packs were stacked, rifles and equipment examined by officers, rolls called, and last vital instructions issued. To distinguish friend from foe, each man wore a white arm-band and a piece of white cloth sewn on the back of his tunic.

At 2 p.m. the battalion marched round to Brown's Dip, the rendezvous for the attack. Then followed the

---

* After the attack and when the companies had checked up their nominal rolls, it was found that Meager was among those who had made the supreme sacrifice.

suspense of the last hour or so while the officers and men made their way to the camouflaged front line and the support line, fixed bayonets, crowded shoulder to shoulder on the fire-steps and waited patiently, almost silently, for the signal to charge.

Watches were synchronized several times that day, and at 5.30 p.m. the signal for the charge was given by Major D. M. King, the brigade major. The signal was a whistle blast. This was taken up in turn by company officers, who each shrilled three blasts. And the men, scrambling quickly behind their glittering bayonets, were on the parapet—on their way—running—charging—madly—resolutely.

During those last few minutes Lieut-Col E. S. Brown moved rapidly along the line of tense waiting figures crouched behind the sand-bags, giving an order here, a little friendly advice there, and cheering newly-arrived reinforcements with words of encouragement. Brown, it is known now, had a feeling that it would be his last fight. But he appeared quite happy and cheerful and confident. He certainly inspired the men. His last effort was a particularly fine one.

"I was standing with Colonel Brown, Dr Bean, and his brother—the Official Australian War Correspondent —and other officers," writes Colonel (then Lieut) A. F. Burrett. "I remember Colonel Brown laughing and saying, 'There won't be a chat alive over there'; throughout the whole bombardment, he kept us amused. I can see vividly that almost cynical little smile of his when he said, 'Now Bean—tell us a funny story.'

"As I was climbing out of the trench with my platoon Colonel Brown gave me a push and, still smiling, said, 'Go on, give it to them.' It was the last time I saw that exceptionally gallant and brilliant officer alive."

At the head of one of the underground tunnels stood the tall figure of Major D. McF. McConaghy, his eyes fixed upon his wristlet watch. Then we heard his deep voice—"Three minutes to go"—"two minutes to go." And then—"over you go."

Everywhere whistles were blowing. The covering artillery-fire had ceased. We were scrambling, hands and knees, up the trench side—we were kneeling—we were walking—we were running. . . . The Lone Pine was out there—in front.

As we scrambled over the parapet or emerged from the underground line there came immediately from the Turkish lines opposite the roar of continuous, rapid rifle-fire and the just-distinguishable staccato note of angry machine-gun, tap-tap-tapping, it seemed, in furious rage. Here—there—men staggered, crumpled, pitched forward, sagged sideways. Men shouted, men laughed. Men groaned.

Shells came shrieking. One came to decapitate a bugler—the headless body ran on for several yards before it stopped and dropped. In front khaki-clad figures struggling on the parapet of the first Turkish trench. The glint of steel. Red flashes from a thousand rifle-barrels. Khaki figures that were not moving. Men lying huddled together as if awaiting another signal to move forward.

Yes, some were moving—twitching. Others—crawling away—or trying to—maimed—dying. All were perfectly still—a spent wave of dead men.*

But there were others—they ran—they stumbled—

---

* "The slaughter commenced from the second we emerged from our trenches. Machine-gun and rifle fire came from the direct front and enfilade fire from both flanks. Men fell thickly on the way over. Imagine our surprise when instead of finding open trenches we saw only holes in the ground at intervals of 10 yards or so. The Turks had sheltered their front line—and to a minor degree their rear trenches—with logs about one foot in diameter and covered these with a foot or so of earth. Each hole spat fire. However, a few men managed to get down through these holes into the trench. Many of us just rushed over the front line and got into the rear trenches right among the Turks. Then started probably the most gruesome, bloody, and fierce hand-to-hand fighting of the whole war."—Lieut-Col A. F. Burrett.

always going forward. The Turkish defence weakened. The khaki figures were at the parapet. They were on the roofs of the covered trenches. They were tearing at beams and sand-bags with bleeding hands. They were in the enemy stronghold and their bayonets were bloody—reeking.

So rapid, so persistent was the advance of those who were at the heels of their faster-flying comrades across to the Pine—those, at least, who survived that first terrible slaughter—that they caught the Turkish garrison as it attempted to vacate its covered trench-shelters.*

"Much has been written of the surprise of the Australian troops in finding the whole of the Turkish front line a covered fortress," wrote a correspondent in the *Sydney Morning Herald*. "But with traditional initiative they quickly saw the necessity of pushing on to the rear communication trenches, which afforded an opportunity for gaining an entry to the maze the position was found to be. Some men, indeed, dived through the loop-holes of the Turkish front lines, to be shot or bayoneted by the enemy waiting below. For a full hour isolated sections of the line conducted little fights of their own. In every sap, in every dugout, fights of this nature took place."

A typical example was that of Lieut Blaydes, whose body was found in the Turkish support line. His revolver was empty, and Turkish dead were heaped all about him. It required little imagination to visualize the terrible struggle that had taken place there before the gallant Blaydes met his death.

---

* "Half-way down the sap, his face upturned to the heavens, lay a splendid specimen of Turkish manhood. He was an officer, and had been shot in the back while trying to escape, after being dislodged from the forward position. His appearance bore ample evidence that the attack had been a surprise. As well as being unshod, his toe-nails had been newly-trimmed. His general appearance suggested that he had just about completed his afternoon's ablutions when the attack came."—Lieut C. O. Clark, M.C., M.M.

Lieut S. A. Pinkstone, pushing through to the Turkish support line, nearly jumped on top of a big Turk, who ran for his life. "I had two or three pot shots at him with my rifle," writes Pinkstone, "but he always beat me round a traverse. Then suddenly coming round a bend, I found him nicely spitted on the end of a digger's bayonet. The digger had come in the opposite direction. It was a lucky thing for me that the Turk got there first. Otherwise I might have decorated that bayonet."

Pinkstone's younger brother, Victor, met a tragic fate. At the Landing he was wounded during the first hour. He was evacuated to Egypt. The wound became septic and he did not return until the day of the Pine attack. Before going over the top, a rifle fell on him and cut his forehead. The injury was bound up. Then going over to the Turkish lines he was hit by a bomb. While this wound was being dressed a shell killed him. Sergeant Norman Pinkstone, another brother, became a casualty through a shell bursting near him. He suffered from shell-shock for some time afterwards.

The problem of removing the wounded was a difficult and serious one. Captain Bean, the medical officer, was hit shortly after the start, while dressing wounded in a temporary aid-post in the old front line, and the A.M.C. details were forced to "carry on"—as they had done at the Landing—without his assistance. To add to their difficulties, the communication trench leading back to the vacated lines was not finally driven through until late that night; and even when the saps were completely through they were used immediately for reinforcements and the sending forward of supplies—ammunition, picks, shovels etc. The needs of the battle line were the first consideration, and thus the evacuation of the wounded was considerably delayed. The only course left open to the stretcher-bearers was to carry their broken and suffering comrades across No-Man's Land. This they did as soon as darkness fell.

But in the meantime the gallant medical section worked feverishly, taking every risk in the open and elsewhere in the bravest endeavour to alleviate the sufferings of the badly injured. The plight of many of the men was pathetic. Wounded were lying in all variety of postures, on the floors of the captured and congested trenches. They were trampled upon time and again by the garrison as the defenders moved hurriedly from point to point to meet and repulse successive and most determined bombing attacks. The victims displayed the greatest fortitude while waiting for their wounds to be dressed. But, as always, there were instances where the torture was quite beyond human endurance.

From Corporal A. C. Haua came a screaming, sobbing request, "Christ, won't someone finish me off." And Private Dougherty appealed to his officer, Lieut Allen—"As long as I've known you, Mr Allen, you've been a gentleman; for God's sake continue to be one and put a bullet through me."

Poor Dougherty's death was a lingering agony. He sank lower and lower, to expire finally supported by the arms of his officer. And Allen, too, lost his life a day or so later while attempting, single-handed, to recapture a section of trench that had been lost.

Captain D. T. Moore, O.C. of C Company, had his thigh badly shattered. He lay for a long period forgotten among a heap of dead. He was discovered and rescued by Lieut P. W. Woods, who saw him safely into the hands of stretcher-bearers.

Seventeen minutes after the signal to charge, brigade H.Q. reported to division that the 3rd and 4th Battalions were well advanced in the centre of the Lone Pine position; in 35 minutes the 3rd Battalion had reached its objective.

The work of consolidation—mainly the erection of

sand-bag barricades—began soon after the Pine was taken, and was not completed till after dark. In many instances only a single stack of sand-bags separated the opposing forces. With the advent of daylight on the Saturday morning the Turks launched a very heavy counter-attack. This was preceded by showers of "cricket ball" bombs. Up to this time the 1st Brigade had had little or no experience of bombing, beyond the throwing occasionally of a few "jam tin" grenades, the employment of which generally was regarded as a huge joke. But the initiative of the Australians stood to them on this occasion, and the bombing menace was met in a daring and novel manner. The more enterprising spirits of the battalion quickly conceived the plan of catching the Turkish bombs and hurling them back at the enemy before they had time to explode. The plan worked well, but occasionally a man had his arm blown off. Bombs which found their way to the floor of the trench were promptly smothered with blankets, overcoats, or half-filled sand-bags. Thus the explosion was strictly localized.

Lieut C. O. Clark, M.C., M.M., who at this time was a sergeant, and took a prominent part in bombing duels, writes: "It was soon perceived that a couple of seconds elapsed between the landing of the cricket ball bombs and the explosion. So the policy of returning the bombs was adopted with most satisfactory results, although the practice occasionally led to casualties in our own ranks. To give credit where credit is due, it must be related that the Turk was not slow to follow suit, and he returned our jam tins to us.

"This meant a further adaptation to local conditions. Our fuses were cut a little less than half-way, so reducing the time elapsing between the lighting and the explosion to about three seconds. Results quite justified the extra risk, although an occasional 'premature' reduced our ranks. One gallant chap was so highly incensed at having his bombs returned that he decided to make the feat impossible with his next. But he cut too low. At the zenith of his swing the bomb exploded and his hand up to the wrist went over with the bomb. Grasping the stump with his left hand he jumped from the fire step, and with a cheery 'That's the end of this business for me,' set out for the beach."

Colonel A. F. Burrett recalls the following incident: "Two of my bombers—Norton and Hamilton—the latter won his V.C. there—were up on the parapet throwing bombs as fast as they could light them. One burst prematurely in Norton's hands, and blew both of them to fragments. We sent him back to the dressing station. Next morning a doctor said to me: 'Good God! It's wonderful. That man Norton is the gamest thing that ever breathed. After I had finished fixing him up for the beach he said—"Good-bye Doc., old sport. Sorry I can't shake hands." ' "

There were intermittent attacks throughout Saturday, and during the night; also on Sunday. Details of one of the most thrilling episodes connected with these engagements are supplied by Colonel Burrett: "On Sunday morning I was with Captain O. G. Howell-Price, when suddenly a digger rushed along the trench and shouted, 'The Turks are in behind us.' The trench we were in ran in a straight line about 50 yards from the old Turkish firing line. Then it swung back in a semicircle to the old Turkish firing line again. It was the semicircular section that was in the hands of the enemy. The situation looked desperate. We were guarding the saps, now absolutely vital to us—a handful of done up men. Every second man faced about—we felt that we were there to make a last stand—fighting front and rear in our long straight trench. Every man there was, in the ordinary course of events, due to die in a few minutes. But none hesitated—a long silent line of almost statue-like soldiers waiting—waiting—to fire their last shots.

"One man—Baker—standing close to me, said, as he grabbed my hand and shook it—'Good-bye, Mafeesh.' After a few minutes when the Turks did not come on, Howell-Price sent me to see what had happened. Taking Shannon (a runner who afterwards got a commission in the 1st Battalion) I pushed along the trench to find only the dead bodies of our men who had been holding it. The Turks for some unaccountable reason had retired. Lone Pine had been theirs for the taking, and they had failed to push their advantage."

By Sunday night the 3rd Battalion had been reduced to half its original strength, and the losses included the commanding officer, Lieut-Col E. S. Brown, who was killed by shell-fire. Also dead were Lieut T. D. McLeod, O. C. of A Company; Captain W. C. Beeken, O.C. of B Company; and Major C. D. Austin, in charge of D Company.

Captain D. T. Moore, O.C. of C Company, had been seriously wounded in the first phase of the attack, while his second-in-command, Captain Dawson, had been killed. Lieut C. J. A. White, the machine-gun officer, was put out of action before the attack had been properly launched. Of the junior officers, Garnham, Allen, C. H. O. White, Blaydes, Meager, and Barlow had all been killed, while McGowan and Harrison subsequently died in hospital as the result of their wounds.

"Lieut Harrison saved my life," writes Colonel Burrett, "when a bomb fell at our feet in the trench where Hamilton won his V.C. We were standing together and I did not notice the bomb when it landed. He shouted, 'Look out,' and pushed me out of the way. Doing so, he got the full force of the explosion himself."

Second-Lieuts S. A. Pinkstone, Greyson, R. I. Moore, McDermid, and Litchfield were all wounded and evacuated. Litchfield eventually lost his right arm as a result of his wounds.

CHAPTER XVI

HAMILTON WINS THE VICTORIA CROSS

At dawn on the Monday morning the Turks launched a very determined attack, but for some unknown reason the effort petered out. The situation at the time was so serious that General Smyth ordered the men to leave the fire-steps and await the attack on the floors of the trenches. In the course of this attack the Turks advanced up a trench separating the 3rd and 4th Battalions, but rifle fire by the battalion snipers posted on the parados prevented them from pushing home their thrust.*

It was at this stage of the fighting that young Hamilton won his V.C. The official citation reads:—

For most conspicuous bravery on August 9, 1915, on the Gallipoli Peninsula. During a heavy bomb attack by the enemy on the newly-captured position at Lone Pine, Private Hamilton, with utter disregard of personal safety, exposed himself under heavy fire on the parados in order to secure a better fire position against enemy's bomb throwers. His coolness and daring example had an immediate effect. The defence was encouraged and the enemy driven off with heavy loss.

Also prominent in the frustration of the Turkish attack was Private Dunn, a veteran of the South African campaign, who, like Hamilton, mounted the parados and helped to drive the Turks back.

---

* According to Private P. W. Ward, the actual discovery that the Turks were massing for attack was made by Captain O. G. Howell-Price. Pushing his periscope over the sand-bags at the junction of the 3rd and 4th Battalions, just as the first streaks of daylight made their appearance, Howell-Price saw the Turks coming. He leaned over the parapet and emptied his revolver into them, while his batman (Ward), following his officer's example, did good work with his rifle.

On Monday at 10 a.m. the 3rd Battalion was relieved by the 7th, and moved back into the reserve trenches behind Brown's Dip.*

"And what a show it was," writes Major (then C.S.M.) P. Goldenstedt. "I shall never forget the sight of the unclaimed packs lying piled up on the little parade ground below battalion headquarters and overlooking the track down Shrapnel Gully. On Tuesday morning we held a muster parade. I have to this day my Field Service Pocket Book with the carbon copies of the B Company parade state before the hop-over on the Friday; the 'present' on that afternoon—when the men crammed in behind the Pimple, just facing the Pine, and made ribald jokes about all manner of things—numbered five officers and 166 other ranks. B Company came out of the Pine without a single officer, and with only 49 men. My Field Service Pocket Book puts the losses at one officer and 16 other ranks killed, 52 wounded, four officers and 49 other ranks missing. Subsequently three of the four wounded officers died, including Captain Beeken, who commanded the company, and that beloved-of-all the original men of the 3rd—big Eddie McGowan. He was wounded in fifteen places as he lay out between the Turkish and our lines for 36 hours or more. He died during October at Mudros."

The fighting strength of the 3rd Battalion on the day of the attack was 27 officers and 856 other ranks. One officer was hit before leaving the trench. Of the remainder, 13 were killed outright, or subsequently died

---

* "We went back to our old trenches. Many of us had not closed our eyes since Thursday night. We had a muster parade in a little gully behind the old trenches. Major McConaghy tried to speak to us, but almost broke down. We were dismissed for a meal—and sleep. I remember the Dean of Sydney, quite proud of his grazed 'little Mary' —a really miraculous escape as he was saved by his abdominal belt deflecting the bullet—but very overcome, shaking hands with us officers and saying:—'Bravo—the thin red line.' And I think as we stood there and looked at each other we all saw big tears in the other chap's eyes."
—Lieut-Col A. F. Burrett.

of their wounds. At the end of the three days' fighting Major D. McF. McConaghy, Captain O. G. Howell-Price, Second Lieuts P. W. Woods, A. F. Burrett, V. E. Smythe, and E. W. G. Wren were the sole survivors. Of 856 "other ranks," 277 were all that remained. The losses in N.C.Os, especially those who had landed with the battalion on April 25th, were equally heavy. The 6th reinforcements, who had joined up only a day or so before the attack, were wiped out almost to a man.

During training in Egypt the battalion boasted a splendid brass band. At the Landing many of the bandsmen were killed. After Lone Pine only a few remained.

Privates Bell, Gurney, Fawley, Foote, and several others, an exclusive little band of Englishmen who enlisted together at the outbreak of war and had been drafted to A Company, were all killed. Privates Val Deane, Reg Humphreys, Joe Charlton, Bugler Page—a dapper little youngster with a perpetual smile—were also among those who failed to answer their names at the subsequent muster roll call.

One of the most striking personalities to fall in the attack was Private Smalley, a stretcher-bearer, the "Gunga Din" of the battalion. Concerning this soldier, Colonel Burrett writes:

"He was unassuming—a square-faced, determined-looking chap, practically unknown outside his own company during those strenuous months at Mena. He worked for weeks on the Peninsula as never human being worked before. The cry of a wounded man would bring Smalley to his side. The call for men for fatigue always found Smalley. His strength and energy were superhuman. Everyone knew him. Everyone admired and wondered at him. I saw him on many occasions going round quickly cleaning the rifles of the men who were sleeping, after coming off post. 'What about a sleep yourself, Smalley?'

I used to ask him; but his only reply was, 'I'm all right, sir, these poor fellows are tired.'

"I remember him before the charge at Lone Pine, covered all over with field dressings, 'to fix up some of the poor chaps,' as he put it. He was hit in the stomach going over, and died almost immediately, saying only, 'Leave me, leave me, I'm done.' And so passed one of the most self-sacrificing, noble, and courageous men who ever wore the Australian uniform."

The following decorations were won by members of the 3rd Battalion at Lone Pine:

V.C.
Private J. Hamilton.

C.M.G.
Major D. McF. McConaghy.

M.C.
Captain O. G. Howell-Price.
Second-Lieut R. I. Moore, D.C.M.

D.C.M.
Sergeant R. L. Graham.
Sergeant A. G. Edwards.
Private P. W. Ward.

M.M.
Sergeant C. O. Clark.
Lance-Cpl J. T. Flynn.

Those mentioned in despatches were:

Lieut-Col E. S. Brown; Major D. McF. McConaghy; Major C. D. Austin; Captain O. G. Howell-Price; Captain D. T. Moore; Lieuts T. D. McLeod, V. E. Smythe, P. W. Woods, R. I. Moore; C.S.M. P. Goldenstedt; 2133, Sergeant C. O. Clark; 1088, Sergeant A. G. Edwards; 1364, Corporal M. M. McGrath; 20, Sergeant R. L. Graham; 1390, Private E. Thomas; 168, Corporal E. Powell; 2360, Private G. C. Green; 2174, Private P. Morgan, and 941, Private C. T. Horan.

CHAPTER XVII

LONE PINE AGAIN

THE battalion commenced a further tour of duty in the Lone Pine salient on August 11th. From that date, until September 12th, it was the practice to garrison the front line for 48 hours and then to return to the reserve trenches for a similar period. On August 12th, the battalion pioneers continued the gruesome task of clearing the dead from the trenches. As a result of the one day's work no fewer than 137 bodies were removed. The following day burial services were conducted at the new graves by Dean Talbot, chaplain to the 3rd Battalion, and Father McAullife from the 2nd.

The diary of Colonel Burrett gives some idea of the appalling condition of the trenches: "Dead are lying on top of each other—fifty-seven of them in one small section of trench. They had been dead for four or five days: we had to walk over them. I was sick and so were the men."

Lieut-Col D. McF. McConaghy was invalided from the Peninsula on September 5th, suffering a nervous breakdown. He joined the battalion again after the evacuation, but subsequently took command of, and organized, the new 55th Battalion. He held that appointment until he fell in April, 1918.

Dave McConaghy was a most likeable and amusing man, with a ready wit and always cheerful personality. On one occasion, when he was in command of the 3rd Battalion during the absence of Colonel Brown, his

SHRAPNEL GULLY

Photo: *Major H. Jacobs*

SICK AND WOUNDED GOING ABOARD A BARGE AT ANZAC
See Appendix
Photo: *Aust. War Memorial Museum.*

STRETCHER-BEARERS ON THE WAY DOWN TO THE BEACH
Photo: Aust. War Memorial Museum. *See Appendix*

batman rushed into his dugout and shouted excitedly "Sir! the cook and Pat are having a fight!"

"Well! I'll have two bob on the cook," was the unexpected reply. It was typical of the man.

Captain O. G. Howell-Price now assumed command, and was immediately promoted to the rank of major. He was at this date the only "original" officer left with the battalion.

Relieved at Lone Pine for the last time at 8 a.m. on September 12th, the battalion went to the bivouac area in Shrapnel Valley. There the welcome news of a transfer to and a spell on Lemnos Island was received.

So ended our connection with Lone Pine. "The object of the attack on Lone Pine is twofold," Colonel Brown explained to battalion officers before the charge. "Firstly, the attack will draw the Turkish reserve, and so make the Suvla landing easier. Secondly, should that operation be successful, a further push through the broken Turkish line at Lone Pine will split their army in two, and give us a magnificent victory."

How faithfully the 1st Brigade, with assisting units, subsequently pursued the first object, may be measured by the appalling slaughter in this epic battle. Not only was the Turkish garrison—a fresh brigade, just in the line after a spell—beaten, but counter-attack after counter-attack, by fresh troops and still more fresh troops, was withstood by the gallant remnants of the Anzac brigade, until in the end those few acres of Turkish soil were saturated with the life-blood of thousands, and Lone Pine became the tomb of most gallant memory. Suvla failed, but Lone Pine—one of the bloodiest battles in the history of the British arms—was a glorious victory, and a noble sacrifice.

By 11 p.m. on September 14th the battalion had been embarked on the troopship *Osmanieh*. At 5 a.m. the

I

voyage began, and within a few hours Lemnos was reached. Disembarkation was completed by 10.30. At 1 o'clock the 3rd was on the site of its new camp at West Mudros, and two hours later was under canvas; but it was not destined to remain there long. Before the day was through, rain came down in torrents, and the camp was completely flooded. On the 16th tents were hauled down and packed preparatory to a move to a better site. But again the rain intervened. It was not till 3 p.m. the following day that the move was completed.

The battalion parade-state on September 22nd gives an indication of the losses sustained during the brief five months of front-line service on the Peninsula. It read:

	Officers.	Other ranks.
Strength on Landing, 25/4/15	29	880
Reinforcements (a)	9	677
Transport Section (which remained in Egypt)	1	48
Officers promoted from the ranks (b)	22	—
Left on the *Derfflinger*	—	18
	61	1623
Killed	21	212
Wounded	19	608
Missing	1	140
In hospital	10	390
Transport Section	1	48
Present on Sept. 22, 1915	9	225
	61	1623

(a) Officer reinforcements: Captain A. Tarleton, Captain E. Dawson, Lieuts J. J. Marshall, G. W. Greyson, E. W. Stutchbury, G. F. Barber, L. J. Burley, J. H. Harrison, and K. J. Hinde.

(b) Officers promoted from the ranks: A. McAskill, T. D. McLeod, A. M. D. Blaydes, S. M. Garnham, H. R. W. Meager, C. H. O. White, N. Gibbins, L. S. Sheppard, A. F. Burrett, A. McDermid, J. H. Matthews, S. A. Pinkstone, T. E. McGowan, P. W. Woods, E. W. G. Wren, R. I. Moore, H. Allen, E. N. Litchfield, P. Goldenstedt, V. E. Smythe, A. Stronach, and A. J. Dayas.

And what of those nine officers and 225 other ranks left with the battalion? Some had fought through from the Landing; others had been wounded and had returned; others again were reinforcements with battle experience for varying periods. But on the faces of all those 234 bronzed, gaunt men with their so grave eyes, and their lean, shabby, faded khaki-clad figures and tired movements, there was written indelibly the story of great stresses. This handful left over from the battalion's 1700 who had braved the Gallipoli tempest had, in a period of a few months, been transplanted from an atmosphere not less balmy and peaceful than anywhere in the world—from the safety and security of comfortable homes—where food is good and ample and the surroundings pleasant and joyous, where there was seldom a cloud in the zenith's blue—to toil and dwell in the grime and filth of corpse-befouled trenches—to sweat and freeze in the stench of war—to endure the agonies that inevitably sprang from their daily diet of tinned salty beef, biscuits which broke many a sound tooth, and that were associated with foul vermin-infested garments, dysentery, barcoo rot, and scurvy and fly-blown wounds—a transition to a fearful new world where an evil death grinned round every trench corner or reached over every sand-bag with clawing greedy hands—a world where day after day men went longing in vain for one good sleep, although to sleep meant perhaps never to awaken.

While there remains one Anzac of the 3rd Battalion, the Gallipoli nightmare can never be forgotten. Bad as were the conditions in the mud of Flanders and on the Somme, there were always the compensations of good wholesome food, occasional clothing changes, and a refreshing rest in more or less comfortable billets behind the line. But for men on Anzac, cut off completely from the world, living like rats in holes, clinging, precariously, to a mere foothold on enemy territory with only death out in front and with the only retreat the Aegean waters that washed into Anzac Cove—there was never security, never rest, never respite.

But that brief spell at Lemnos worked wonders. The men were kept hard at work, and were allowed no time or opportunity to brood. Route marches, squad, platoon, company and battalion drills, night manœuvres, and bomb-throwing kept them fully occupied. Regular hours, regular rest, reasonably good food, plenty of relaxation, swimming parades, concert parties, and a new-won freedom from body vermin and the dreaded dysentery, soon had everyone in good spirits and physically trim again. The battalion morale jumped by leaps and bounds. So much for the wisdom of army training.

It was during this period of rest and training that the real worth of O. G. Howell-Price as a battalion commander came to be realized and appreciated. Profiting by the lessons taught at Lone Pine, where many men were lost as a result of inexperience in bomb fighting, the C.O. concentrated on individual efficiency in the use of bombs and experimented with other schemes aiming to lessen casualties when the battalion was in the line.

Many picturesque "soldiers of fortune" fought with the A.I.F. Perhaps the most remarkable among many remarkable soldiers in the 3rd Battalion was Private Williams—at least, that is the name by which he was known in the Australian unit—of whom mention may be made at this stage. Williams originally landed at Helles on April 28th with the French Foreign Legion, but shortly afterwards deserted the Legion, and by some means, which were never made known and are quite inexplainable, found his way to Anzac where he cheerfully and unofficially attached himself to the 3rd Battalion. He was tall, lean and sinewy, with a rigid military carriage and soldierly bearing, and a personality that was just so mysteriously romantic as are all the stories of the world famous Régiment de Marche. The only echo that came to the battalion of his past, apart from the knowledge of his desertion from the Legion, was that at one time he had served with the Coldstream Guards.

Anzac was no place to query any man's past, and so, with some natural caution at first, but later with implicit confidence, this adventurous character was allowed to serve with the 3rd Battalion. And very soon he proved himself to be a most valuable asset in the fighting line. On Lemnos, however, Williams was placed under arrest for attempting to stir up strife among the other ranks of the battalion, and was handed over to the French.

A court-martial summarily sentenced him to be shot for desertion. Actually he was being marched off to his execution when he was recognized by a former officer of the Coldstreams. This officer interviewed his commander and obtained his reprieve, subject to the 3rd Battalion agreeing to again take him on strength. This it was decided should be done, and Williams, instead of ending his vivid career against a wall, looking along the barrels of French rifles, continued to serve with the 3rd Battalion until the formation of the 55th Battalion at Tel-el-Kebir. He was transferred to the new unit and was killed in action in France long after—lean, sinewy, and romantic to the last.

It was a splendid sight to see Williams, who was promoted to sergeant's rank at Tel-el-Kebir, drilling his platoon. Combining the cold, calculating efficiency of Coldstream methods with the magnetic fire of the Legion, he was almost hypnotic, inspiring those under his command to parade-ground manœuvres that had perhaps no parallel in the A.I.F.

On October 19th, the battalion was called upon to perform a very sad duty, providing a firing party for the burial of Lieut T. E. McGowan, who died at No. 3 Australian General Hospital. Thirty-five years of age,

6 ft 6 in. in height, McGowan, affectionately known in the battalion as "Willy-Grow," had been a popular N.C.O. His promotion to commissioned rank came early on Anzac. Later he was wounded out in front of one of the Lone Pine trenches, where he lay fully exposed for more than 24 hours before being discovered and rescued. In that time he received no fewer than fifteen separate bullet wounds, but his death two months later was actually the result of dysentery with pneumonia supervening.

Lieut J. H. Harrison, also a victim of the Lone Pine fighting, was buried on the island about the same time.

The sojourn at Lemnos Island ended on October 27th, when the battalion embarked once more on the *Osmanieh*. The weather being rough and squally, departure was delayed until 1.30 p.m. on the 29th, when the vessel steamed for Gallipoli again, arriving off Anzac at 7 o'clock that night. By 5 o'clock the following morning it had been disembarked—a much more peaceful landing than on the first occasion—and gone into bivouac at Green Gully. Next day a move was made into trenches immediately in the rear of those occupied by the 1st Battalion.

On November 2nd, the battalion took over the trenches on Bolton's Ridge, one of the quietest sectors of the line, and previously occupied by the 9th Battalion. Immediately opposite was a ridge known as Knife Edge, with the Valley of Despair intervening as No-Man's Land. From these trenches a grandstand view could be had of the Olive Grove, Gaba Tepe, and Achi Baba, and the troops were able to watch from time to time the shelling of these strongholds by the navy. The 3rd remained in this position till the evacuation.

The casualties at Lone Pine had left the battalion with very few officers. To make up the deficiency, Company Sergeant-Major P. L. Goldenstedt, Sergeant Leo Palmer and Sergeant Norman Giblett were promoted to commissioned rank. From the light horse came Second Lieuts G. F. Plunkett, G. E. Blake, D. V. Mulholland, W. Cotterill, and W. L. Lamrock. From the 1st Battalion came Second Lieut W. Denoon. Lieut J. J. Marshall joined up from hospital, while Captain A. C. S. Holland and Second Lieuts J. G. Tyson, H. L. Wilson, and A. L. Hewish came as reinforcement officers.

As the battalion was in need of senior officers, Captain A. R. Edwards was transferred from the 4th Battalion, and Captain G. F. Wootten—a Duntroon graduate—from the brigade staff.

During the sojourn at Lemnos, Captain S. C. Fitzpatrick—a dapper little graduate from Melbourne—joined the battalion as Medical Officer. His predecessors, Captain J. W. B. Bean and Captain Leslie Dunlop, were exceptionally good men, keen about their job, tireless in their efforts to help the wounded, and, what appealed to the troops most of all, very cool under fire. Captain Fitzpatrick proved himself a worthy successor.

During the last days of the Gallipoli campaign—at a time when padres were not at all popular—Chaplain B. C. Wilson joined the battalion. As most of his time was spent in the firing line, he soon became a popular figure. Subsequently he came to be regarded as one of the stalwarts of the regiment.

What came to be known as "the silent ruse" began at 6 p.m. on November 24th. Strict instructions were issued that there were not to be any exposed movements by the troops, that the men must refrain from firing at the enemy. Indeed the garrison was ordered to do everything possible, by stealthy silence and by remaining under cover, to make the Turks believe that Anzac had been evacuated. It was all part of the enemy's education prior to the masterly actual retirement.

At midnight on the 27th this ordered method of fooling the Turk came to an end, and the usual routine was resumed. That same night came a heavy snow-storm, and the following day the landscape looked like the Kosciusko country in the depth of winter. Blankets left out in the open or used for overhead cover were frozen stiff and, when handled, fell to pieces like mouldy cardboard. For several days this cold weather continued, and the machine-gunners spent very anxious hours. If once the water-jackets of their weapons became frozen, the guns would have been useless. Thanks to the high elevation of our particular trenches, sickness in the battalion at this time was not great. Other sectors, however, were not so fortunate. From Anzac no fewer than 2700 men were evacuated with frost-bite. So serious were many of the cases that amputations became necessary.

CHAPTER XVIII

THE EVACUATION

ORDERS concerning, and full details of, the plan of evacuation were received on December 14th, and preparations in accordance with the letter of the instructions were made immediately. All tools and kit likely to be of service to the Turks were systematically destroyed and buried, and all sick men were sent off shore. Chaplain B. C. Wilson took away the first batch of men—16 all told—on December 15th.

There was a good deal of "grouching" in the unit as to which men should be selected to comprise the last parties to leave the Peninsula, as it was generally anticipated that there would be some sort of a fight at the end. The ultimate choice fell upon original members of the battalion with the greatest fighting experience. None begrudged these veterans their special honour.

To help ensure a safe "getaway," orders were issued for all troops to bind sand-bags and strips of blankets around their boots to deaden the sounds of marching. To prevent the rattling of accoutrements such as mess-tins, bayonets, and entrenching tools, the men in the rear held firmly the loose equipment of those marching in front. For several nights the rear-guard sections rehearsed their very important individual parts, so that on the final night they knew to the second how long it would take them to reach the point of embarkation—Watson's Pier.

At points where there was a possible danger of men being side-tracked, lights were placed to guide them during their dangerous nocturnal flit. At point "X" a white light was placed. At point "Y" a green light was shown, while the cemetery was marked by a red lamp. Dangerous steps cut out of the hillsides were whitewashed so that they showed up clearly in the dark.

At 4.30 p.m. on the 18th word was received that the evacuation of Anzac would begin that night, and be completed on the following night. The machine-gun captured from the Turks at Lone Pine, and since used by the battalion, and its crew of six men left the lines for embarkation at 6 o'clock on the night of the 18th. They were followed by three officers—Lieuts P. W. Woods, L. S. Sheppard, and P. L. Goldenstedt—and 82 other ranks, including a second machine-gun, at 9.30 p.m.

The 19th was an exceptionally quiet day. General Birdwood inspected the trenches at 1 p.m. and generally had a final look round. At 5 p.m. ten officers—Captain A. C. S. Holland, Lieut N. Gibbins, Second Lieuts J. J. Marshall, H. L. Wilson, C. F. Elliot, W. L. Lamrock, W. Denoon, J. G. Tyson, G. E. Blake, A. G. Hewish—and 238 other ranks and a machine-gun left the trenches. By 7 o'clock they had safely boarded the *Abbassieh*.

At 9.40 p.m. seven officers—Captains A. R. Edwards and S. C. Fitzpatrick, Lieuts S. A. Pinkstone and A. F. Burrett, Second Lieuts L. Palmer, G. F. Plunkett and W. Cotterill—and 49 other ranks, accompanied by another machine-gun, left for the beach.

There now remained in the 3rd Battalion firing-line sector only five officers and sixty-one other ranks, with one machine-gun. To maintain the illusion of a well-manned firing line, this weapon was fired in short bursts from various parts of the line, while bombers helped the bluff by walking up and down the trenches throwing bombs from numerous points. At 2.20 a.m. on the morning of the 20th, Lieut D. V. Mulholland and 20 other ranks left the lines, followed 20 minutes later by Lieut

E. W. G. Wren and Second Lieut S. F. P. White and 29 other ranks.

At 2.50 a.m. the final remnant of the battalion—Major O. G. Howell-Price, Captain G. F. Wootten, and 12 other ranks—left the trenches and hurried along Anzac Gully to the beach where they were safely embarked.*

The departure of the last party of the 3rd Battalion from the front line synchronized with the withdrawal of last parties of somewhat similar strength by other battalions from the other sections of the Anzac front line. From all points of those bloody, battle-scarred hills the rear-guard marched silently, if sadly, away into the night, converging on the beach. Material possession was left to the Turks, but the spiritual possession of Anzac will forever be Australia's.

Quietly, quickly, but in an atmosphere of inexpressible sadness, those last men filtered through the mazy trench systems to the beach to pass through that last cordon of gallant fellows, commanded by Captain Phil Howell-Price, of the 1st Battalion, who were in position as a rear-guard, 300-400 yards from the embarkation point. This rear-guard was to stand its ground at all costs, should the Turks attack, until the last of the front-line parties were reported in. For the front-line troops the orders that night were, that in the event of an attack they were not to stand, but were to fight a hurried rear-guard action to the beach, and if possible, embark.

And so, on that calm, still, and solemn morning of December 20th, the daring and brilliant feat of evacuation was carried out without the loss of one man—and under the very noses of a well-trained and intelligent army. A seemingly impossible task.

Who can adequately describe the thoughts of the men of the rear-guard who in the darkness marched so silently,

---

* No. 290, Corporal E. L. Richardson, was mentioned in despatches in connection with the evacuation.

so anxiously, along the treacherous pathways and down those hallowed slopes for the last time? Everywhere were rough, drab little crosses looming out of the night to divert memory to eight thousand comrades who would never give up Anzac.

"Good-bye, 'Blue'—'Snow'—Tom—Bill—'Darkie'— old cobbers. Forgive us, we don't want to desert you." And from the silent ghostly hills and valleys seemed to come the whisper—"So long, mates! Buck up and fight on—no matter where. We will be watching to cheer and urge you on."

And so Anzac was left to "Jacko" the Turk—after eight months of one of the most tragic yet most glorious efforts in military history, an effort that placed Australia and the Australian soldier in a high place among the soldiers of the world, and gave Australia a glorious heritage. The spirit of Anzac is exemplified in the fact that a detachment of A.M.C. details had volunteered, should fighting occur at the last, to stay on at Anzac under the white flag, and then surrender and care for our wounded. They waited to the last moment, those brave men, but fortunately their heroic and self-sacrificing mission was not necessary, and they were brought away with the rest.

On December 20th the various evacuation parties were re-united at Sarpi camp on Lemnos Island, where Christmas mail, Christmas billies, and gifts from the Comforts' Fund were delivered. And how they were appreciated!

At 9.20 a.m. on December 24th the battalion, with a strength of 25 officers and 456 men, marched out of camp for West Mudros pier and was conveyed by lighters to the transport *Simla*, which sailed for Egypt about midday. The *Simla* was well-stocked with good food, and —with champagne at 6s. and whisky at 2s. 6d. a bottle respectively, and beer at that price the dozen—it was in every sense a very "Happy Xmas."

The ship's captain put on a really wonderful dinner. For those who had served throughout the campaign it was the first "civilized" meal for eight months.

That day was one occasion in the life of the 3rd Battalion when military discipline and the army routine were quite forgotten—for a few hours, at least—when officers and N.C.Os threw off their crowns, stars, and chevrons, and mingled with the men and each other in the truest sense of comradeship.

CHAPTER XIX

THE RETURN TO EGYPT

AT midday on the 28th of December, 1915, the *Simla* arrived at Alexandria and berthed at 6 o'clock. In the early hours of the next day the battalion disembarked and entrained for Tel-el-Kebir, arriving at 10.30 p.m. As tents were not available, the troops bivouacked and continued to do so for four days. Tents then arrived and camp was pitched.

Egypt once again! Egypt—but with vivid, overwhelming memories of those nine tempestuous months since the battalion had gone forth so virile and confident from Mena Camp! Only the skeleton of the original regiment came out of the Gallipoli holocaust—just a leavening of the "old originals." The ranks had been built up time and again by anxious, eager reinforcements. Men, who had been just rankers at Mena, were commissioned and non-commissioned officers now; they had been trained in a terrible school, and very earnestly they accepted their responsibilities.

So the 3rd Battalion, tired physically and weary mentally, came back to Egypt—"back home," it seemed. Egypt was friendly, companionable—an oasis in the war. The unit morale was splendidly mature—stronger than ever it had been; its *esprit-de-corps* was now built upon the permanent foundations of common suffering and sacrifice cemented with blood and agony.

Tel-el-Kebir—in Arabic "The Great Sand-Hill"—is not distinguished by any outstanding physical features. It comprises just a tract of sandy and hard gravelly hillocks, but it is a place of strategical value, lying as it does between Cairo and Ismailia, Ismailia being midway between the extremities of the Suez Canal. Tel-el-Kebir was a railway station, connected by a bridge to a village of mud huts sprawling among date palms to the southwest. It lay on the fresh water canal which runs from Cairo to Ismailia, and thence along the western bank of the Suez Canal to Port Said in the north and Suez in the south.

It was here, on September 13th, 1882, that Lord Wolseley's British force, numbering 17,000 men with 61 guns and six machine-guns, defeated the Egyptian Army, which was in rebellion under its leader Arabi. This battle had the effect of reinstating the Khedive, securing the safety of the Suez Canal, and saving Europeans throughout Egypt from almost certain massacre. The Egyptian earthworks two miles long, facing E.S.E. with diagonal works in rear, were observed to be still in good preservation, and members of the battalion spent many of their leisure hours wandering over the old battlefield and unearthing mementos of the historic battle.

Tel-el-Kebir protects the populous city of Zag-a-zig, 15 miles to the west, and capital of the province of Eastern Egypt. Zag-a-zig is an important railway junction on a waterway of the Nile delta. It is believed that it was in this locality that the infant Moses was found concealed in the bull-rushes. The concentration of Australian troops at Tel-el-Kebir was of great strategical value in the defence of the Suez Canal, which was still threatened by the Turks.

The battalion transport section, which had remained in Egypt while the battalion was on Anzac, now rejoined, and a period of reorganization and training was begun. Whereas at Mena the daily routine of training had been carried on in a somewhat carefree and impatient atmosphere, at Tel-el-Kebir a very deliberate, serious, and determined bearing distinguished all ranks. Realization had come—been earned. Those who had served on Anzac quickly infused into new arrivals something of the spirit of Anzac. There had been no scars at Mena, no notches on the rifle-butts. But men had since looked into the eyes of desperate enemy and lunged into the heart of hostile machine-gun and rifle nests. They had lived in a hell of shell-bursts and watched the still living, fly-blown wounded out in front—die—and blacken—and other horrors—and those realities were the beacon at Tel-el-Kebir. Thus early had Anzac, of reverent and fearful memory, become the pattern upon which all newcomers were modelled and fashioned in battalion spirit and ideals. It was the Anzac spirit which dominated the 3rd in all its later cruel fighting on the Western Front. It was memory of Anzac which stiffened its resolution in adversity and extremity. To the end the men of the 3rd Battalion were dominated by memory of Anzac. Old-timers and newcomers to a man were inordinately jealous of the reputation won in the face of the Turks. Anzac won many victories in France and Flanders.

A comprehensive programme of training was prepared and carried out, and very soon the battalion reached a state of high efficiency. Particular attention was given to "close order" work and ceremonial drills. Later there were daily manœuvres in attack and flank and rear-guard actions and musketry. Night marches and night attack practices were also carried out by compass bearing and the stars, fitting the battalion for any possible thrust on the Canal necessitating movement by night.

On January 6th, 1916, the 9th reinforcements joined the battalion, but on February 13th these men were all transferred to the 55th Battalion. Two days later we took part in a ceremonial parade and inspection of the 1st Australian Division by Lieut-General Sir Archibald

ANZAC COVE

SCENE IN COMMUNICATION TRENCH, GALLIPOLI.
Photo: Aust. War Memorial Museum.   See Appendix

Murray, the new G.O.C. of the Egyptian Expeditionary Force.

Major D. McF. McConaghy rejoined us on January 26th, and assumed command of the battalion vice Major O. G. Howell-Price. About this time, Lieut P. Goldenstedt, Sergeant Williams, and a number of others transferred to the Camel Corps.

At 6 p.m. on February 11th, word was received that the battalion was to be split up, one half to form the nucleus of a new battalion—the 55th. The transport section and all headquarters details were to remain with the 3rd Battalion. Next day a grand parade of the battalion was held, and the difficult and unpleasant work of subdividing the personnel was carried out.

At 6 p.m. on Sunday, February 13th, the separation of the 3rd and 55th Battalions had been completed. Major McConaghy was gazetted to command the 55th. He took as his officers:

CAPTAINS.—R. O. Cowey, A. C. S. Holland.
LIEUTS.—P. W. Woods, N. Gibbins, J. J. Marshall, E. W. Stutchbury, J. H. Matthews, S. A. Pinkstone, H. L. Palmer, W. Denoon, L. D. Sheppard.
SECOND LIEUTS.—H. L. Wilson, J. S. E. McCarthy, W. N. Giblett, F. J. Cotterill, N. E. F. Pinkstone, P. W. Chapman.

The 55th Battalion remained at the old camp site. The 3rd moved to a new area about a mile away, with Major O. G. Howell-Price once more in command.

This separation of old comrades was not carried out without deep regrets on both sides. Those who were drafted out felt very keenly the wrench at parting with the battalion and old comrades. Life friendships had been made while hardships were being suffered together. Those who remained mourned the loss of most loyal pals. However, discipline restrained or suppressed any serious display of feeling, and the remnant of the old 3rd marched out, carrying with them the good wishes of the new 55th and connected with it by a bond of the kindliest feelings of comradeship and good-will. The subsequent triumphs of the 55th Battalion in France are history. It was always a matter of great satisfaction and a source of pride to the 3rd to witness the offspring battalion taking its place on an equal footing with the parent units of the A.I.F.

The work of reorganization and training was continued systematically. A quota of the 10th and 11th reinforcements, totalling two officers and 455 other ranks, joined the battalion on February 14th. The balance of those reinforcements was diverted to the 55th Battalion.

Lieut-General Sir William Birdwood inspected the camp site on the 15th, on which day, as it happened, sixteen members of the battalion were isolated following an outbreak of cerebro-spinal meningitis. On February 23rd, Major D. T. Moore rejoined the battalion, having recovered from his severe wounding at Lone Pine. He became second-in-command. The company commanders now were:

A COMPANY	Captain A. R. Edwards
B COMPANY	Lieut F. C. Kemp
C COMPANY	Lieut E. W. G. Wren
D COMPANY	Captain I. R. O. Harris
ADJUTANT	Lieut A. F. Burrett
QUARTERMASTER	Lieut A. Stronach
TRANSPORT OFFICER	Lieut G. F. Plunkett
SIGNALLING OFFICER	Lieut H. S. Chapman

During the period February 16th-29th, the 1st Brigade was commanded by Lieut-Col H. E. ("Pompey") Elliott. On the latter date Brigadier-General N. M. Smyth, V.C., returned to the command.

At 10 a.m. on February 29th, the battalion (now 16 officers and 920 other ranks) entrained at Tel-el-Kebir, arriving at Serapeum at 3.30. The transport section proceeded by road, and all tents and stores were taken to the new destination.

Prior to the evacuation of Gallipoli, a plan for the formation of a defensive line in the desert east of the Suez Canal had been laid down. This involved the construction of a main line of defence 12,000 yards east of the Canal. Isolated positions, ten miles apart, were occupied by small bodies of infantry. One of these posts, at Gebel Habeita, eight miles from Serapeum, was formed on December 19th, 1915, by a company of the newly-arrived 31st Battalion, A.I.F.

When Sir Archibald Murray arrived in Egypt on January 11th, 1916, as Commander-in-Chief, his first attention was given to the problem of the defence of the Canal. His anxiety was increased about January 19th by receipt of reports indicating increased activity by the Turks in preparation for an invasion of Egypt. The 1st and 2nd Australian Divisions were chosen to take up part of the front line in the desert. The area further to the east was patrolled by the Bikanir Camel Corps.

The 1st Infantry Brigade was allotted the defence of the "inner line" portion of the general defence scheme, which consisted of the posts of Tussum, Serapeum East, North Post, South Post, and Deversoir. The defence of the bridge-head at Serapeum remained the responsibility of divisional headquarters.

The 3rd Battalion pitched camp at Serapeum East, about two and a half miles east of the Canal. The other battalions of the 1st Brigade were also in the locality. Garrisons were allotted to the various posts. The principal duty of these troops—apart from actual defence in case of attack—was to guard against the possibility of enemy patrols getting through and placing mines in the Canal. The sinking of a single boat might have meant grave consequences, as it would have blocked the Canal, temporarily at least, and the possible results were not to be contemplated.

A system of outposts guarding the camp at Serapeum East was placed in position at night. These troops were supplied by each battalion of the 1st Brigade in rotation. Almost daily, huge camel trains were seen taking stores and materials forward to the outer zone of defence. As far as possible, the training of the troops not on duty was continued. Bathing parades went to the Canal as frequently as could be arranged.

On March 5th, one officer (Second Lieut G. W. Greyson) and 56 other ranks were detailed as the battalion's quota to form the 1st Pioneer Battalion; on the 12th the battalion Maxim gun section, consisting of two officers (Lieuts A. L. Hewish and D. V. Mulholland) and 31 other ranks, together with the guns, were transferred to help form the 1st Brigade Machine-gun Company. In its place the battalion formed a Lewis gun section, consisting of one officer (Lieut J. G. Tyson) and 30 other ranks with an equipment of four guns.

On March 15th the 1st Brigade was inspected by Major-General H. G. Chauvel, who addressed the troops prior to his departure to the new Anzac Mounted Division. He had been in temporary command of the 1st Division. At 10.30 a.m. on the 19th, His Royal Highness the Prince of Wales, quite informally, rode along the front of the battalion's lines, and he received a lusty cheer. The Prince also attended the 1st Brigade church parade.

That day word was received that the battalion would shortly embark for another theatre of war, and the arrangements connected with the move were rapidly put into operation. The transport section, complete with horses and waggons entrained at Serapeum on the 20th. Next day tents were struck and returned to ordnance, and the battalion, 27 officers and 970 other ranks, marched out at 4.30 p.m. At 9.45 p.m. we moved from Serapeum

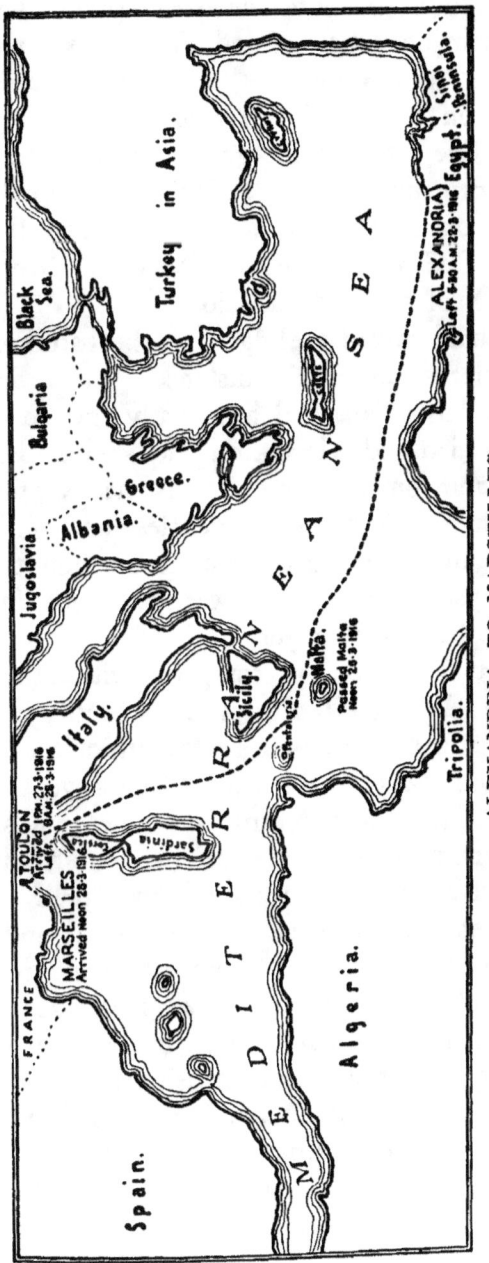

ALEXANDRIA TO MARSEILLES

Siding by train *en route* for Alexandria. The journey was made in open trucks, and the troops arrived at the seaport at 7.30 a.m. on the 22nd. At noon the battalion embarked on the H.M.T. *Grampian*, which put to sea at 5.30. The 1st Machine-gun Company, the 2nd Field Artillery Brigade, and the 1st Divisional Signal Company were also on board. Major O. G. Howell-Price was appointed O.C. troops, and Major D. T. Moore became acting C.O. of the 3rd Battalion.

It was with mixed feelings that the battalion watched Egypt's shores fade in the distance. In the land of the Pharaohs, Australians had been truly trained in the arts of war. Cairo and Alexandria had sheltered Australian wounded and, on happier occasions, had supplied varied and delightful pleasures. Relentless and pitiless sands, sun, dust, and desert had brought the unit to a superb state of physical fitness. The weak had gone under. The strong had become stronger.

The 3rd Battalion, in company with other original units of the A.I.F., will always retain fond and delightful memories of the country of greatest antiquity. The words of "Fighting Mac's" old song, "Good-bye Cairo-Cairo, Good-bye Cairo-Cairo," came into the minds of those who were now steaming out over the blue Mediterranean to new adventures. The usual boat drill and alarm station assemblies were at once rehearsed and practised daily. Enemy submarines were active in the Mediterranean. The food on the *Grampian* was very poor. The ship had just returned from the Persian Gulf after discharging a contingent of British troops, and had not had time to revictual. Malta was passed at 2 p.m. on the 25th, and at 1 p.m. on the 27th the *Grampian* anchored off Toulon.

CHAPTER XX

IT IS FRANCE!

THE approach to the French coast was made in beautifully clear weather. In the far distance could be seen the snow-capped Alps, and at the foot of the rugged coast line, like tiny white smudges, were the towns of the famous Riviera. Padre B. C. Wilson recorded the arrival in his diary: "As we looked at the ancient seaport of Toulon and saw it rising terrace on terrace from the water's edge, we thought we had never seen anything more beautiful in our lives. It was amusing to hear the comments passed from lip to lip as the men chose 'possies' for themselves among the dignified homes on the foreshore."

A ferry boat passed close to the *Grampian*. There were many women among the passengers, and it was observed that everyone appeared to be in black. It gave a first impression of France, "a nation in mourning."

At Toulon word came that the battalion would be disembarked at Marseilles the next day.

The *Grampian** sidled into the pier at the "Gateway of Europe"—Marseilles—at noon on 28th March, 1916. The 3rd Australian Battalion set foot in France—that France which they had only known in imagination! France of delightful romance, of beautiful legends! France so rich in relics and the arts! France of great chivalries, of tempestuous, valorous history!

---

* The *Grampian* was torpedoed and sunk on her next trip. The *Simla* had met the same fate after landing the battalion at Alexandria.

There, in the shadow almost of the Château d'If, about which Dumas wove his grim story of Monte Cristo—which many had read—the drab, sun-bronzed, khaki-clad strangers from the newest continent "formed fours" and carried out their regimental and disembarkation chores, steeped in a world of enchantment that never will be explored. They knew that far away in the north, the same France they now stood upon was rocking to its foundations with the thunder of thousands of cannon. Up north were Mons and Ypres and the Marne and the Somme and Verdun—a score of bloody fields, and every minute of the day and night was counting its dead and maimed.

Perhaps it was the thought of what was happening "up there" in the heart of the conflict, and what might happen "up there," that came quickly to overwhelm all other thoughts in those first few precious moments. Would the old battalion—it seemed so insignificant now in the strange land where all wore uniform or mourning; a place of white-faced women and anxious men and unsmiling children—would the old battalion stand up in face of the German hordes and meet the picked troops of the Kaiser as they had met the Turk? Could the battalion hold its own with the crack regiments of Britain and France?

The doubt was only momentary. In the Australian soldier was always an inherent confidence and optimism. No one really doubted the battalion's ability to add to its laurels when the time came. Yet, there was an overpowering feeling that eventful midday, of the nearness of something big—a crisis—a feeling that here the battalion would either perish or conquer—that now it meant a fight to a finish—that, whoever the victor, the consequences would be decisive.

Clemenceau—"the Tiger of France"—later said to the Australian troops, after the Battle of Hamel: "When the Australians came to France we expected a great deal of them.... We knew that you would fight a real fight. But we did not know that from the very beginning you would astonish the whole continent."

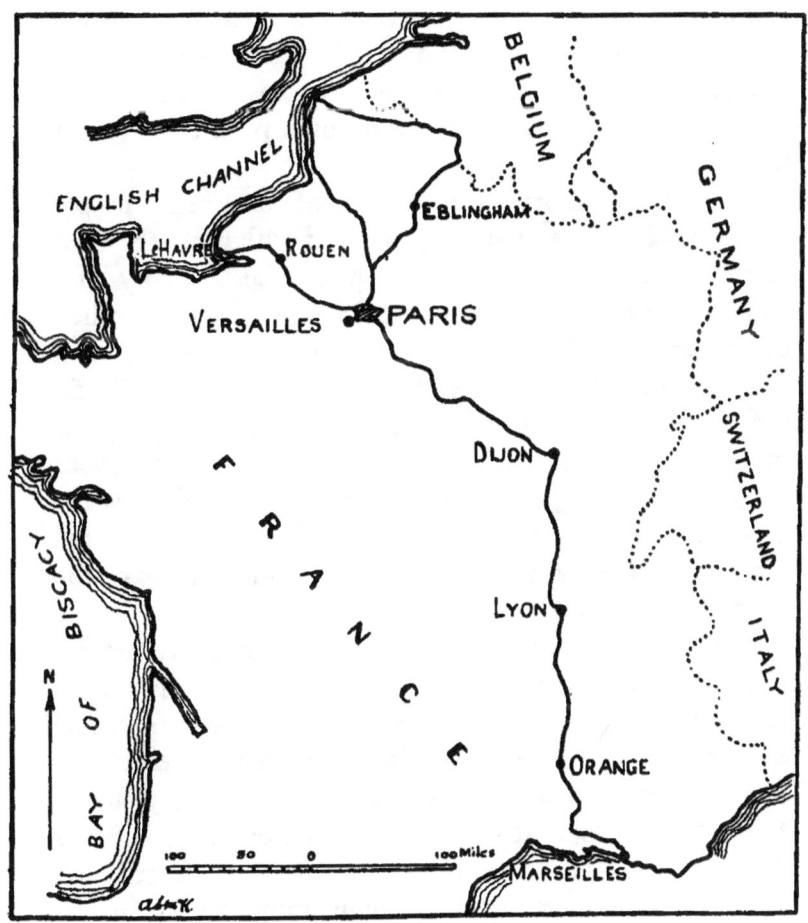

TRAIN JOURNEY ACROSS FRANCE

The battalion entrained for the north at 9.30 p.m. in a drizzling rain, and commenced that wonderful journey through the Rhone Valley—seen at its best in the glorious spring weather. "It would be hard to overestimate the impression of that three days' train journey," wrote Padre Wilson, "the wonderful Rhone Valley looked unreal in its beauty to our desert-weary eyes, and we spent our days watching the panorama as it changed from smiling fertile valley to wide sweeping vista of mountains rising tier upon tier in the distance. To the impressionable man of the A.I.F. that journey will always take pride of place, not only because of the matchless scenery, but because the heart of a people welcomed us."

A vivid memory are the cheers of the French people as we passed through the towns and villages—the cries of the French children for "bis-queets" and "booly-bif," and the inglorious efforts of members of the battalion to converse in French. Generally their vocabulary then consisted of *"bon-jour, mademoiselle," "tres bon,"* and a few other elementary words, given with an atrocious pronunciation. As the battalion passed through Lyons at 8 p.m. on the 29th, thoughts flew back a hundred years, and the ghosts of Napoleon's army, recruited along the same route for his march on Paris, seemed to wave the battalion on.

Every four hours a halt was made when refreshments were provided by the French authorities. Throughout the journey—a route that traversed almost the whole expanse of France—the battalion everywhere received a welcome that was entirely spontaneous. At every station at which the train stopped, crowds flocked to greet *"les Australiens,"* and the troops were much affected and somewhat embarrassed by the temperamental Latin displays of friendship. It seemed as if the Australians had been seized upon as representing a new element of hope to this war-stricken people. On any other grounds it would have been difficult to account for the enthusiastic completeness of the welcome. But what made an instant appeal to all were the signs of universal mourning. Everyone seemed to be in black. In those days the A.I.F.

did not know that it was the custom, in the event of death, for all members of a French family close and distant, to go into mourning. Consequently the new arrivals pictured every house saddened by a personal bereavement. The effects of war upon a people were now seen and appreciated for the first time. The first glimpses of the long trails of sorrow which marked the operations in the field most certainly stiffened the men of the Australian units in their determination to do their very best to help fling the invader back from this fair land, where the people smiled bravely through their tears and met us so cordially.

The long sixty-hour train journey came to an end on the afternoon of March 31st when the battalion detrained at Steenbecque and billeting orders were received. Tea was provided in the Steenbecque station yard. After an hour's wait, when the men were glad to be able to stretch their cramped and weary limbs, the battalion moved off to find its quarters in the billeting areas. A and B Companies, under Major D. T. Moore, were billeted at Wallon-Capel, and battalion headquarters, with C and D Companies, at Ebblinghem.

Ebblinghem was a delightful little village, undisturbed and, up to that time, very little used by British troops for billeting purposes. It knew its war by the rumble of guns in the distance—by the motor traffic which swept continually through its quiet streets, but most directly through the dwindling ranks of its own menfolk in the trenches in the south.

All our previous ideas of billets had now to go through a violent process of revision. The men had all believed that billets meant houses—and that they would be the guests of the people among whom they were quartered. Many had been worrying over the fact that they did not feel clean enough—the fault was not their own really—to enter a house and sleep in a bed. Some had decided to ask for a bath before they accepted the hospitality of the home. It came, therefore, as a rude shock to face the naked truth. At 2 a.m., after a strenuous route march, the anticipated cosy homes dissolved into barns or stables or any old place with a roof on it, and the clean white sheets and feather mattresses into floor or bare ground. Fortunately these particular billets were clean, and an abundance of straw was available. A sense of humour covers a multitude of disappointments. It came to the rescue on this occasion.

In 1916, the late Private C. V. Walters, well-known in the battalion, wrote: "Many were the mental pictures we had painted of our billets-to-be. But they were only kalsomined, and the French rain quickly washed it away. While travelling on that glorious three days' train trip from Marseilles, a cobber of mine—who is still going strong—confided in me what he was going to do on arrival at his French 'home.' 'I'm going to tell the woman straight that I'm chatty,' he said. 'You're not!' I exclaimed. 'Yes, I am,' he persisted, 'I'm going to ask her to give me a hot bath to drown the cows; I'm not going between her clean sheets like this; it's not fair.' And that night we left the train, and I slept beside him in an old barn with an ice-cold draught whistling through it. And all night long his hand was in the opening in his shirt—moving them on here, arresting them there, like a policeman on beat. White sheets! Chateaux! Mademoiselles! Breakfast in bed! Champagne! Cripes! How I do smile when . . . Well, how many times have we seen the pigs chased out of their styes to let us in. Poor pigs!"

April 1st was practically a holiday. Everyone took steps to display a tourist's interest in the surrounding countryside and its inhabitants. No time was lost in making the acquaintance of the French folk in the villages of Wallon-Capel and Ebblinghem. The people of

Ebblinghem soon became very attached to the Australians, who lost no opportunity of helping them in the house, in the field, and on the farm.

"Some of us went back to Ebblinghem two years after we had been billeted there," wrote one officer. "We had never been close enough in the intervening period to renew our acquaintance. It was astonishing to find that the first impression still held. The people remembered our lads by name, and wanted to know how they were." This was the more astonishing, as during those two years the village had never been free of troops coming and going continually. On hearing of some of our losses, the residents could not have been more genuinely distressed had the Australians been men of their own families.

The stay in this neighbourhood was all too short. A week was spent in general training and short practice marches along the hedge-lined lanes that were just beginning to show the first green tints of spring.

On April 5th, Second-Lieuts Lemon and F. E. Page left for Meteren to attend a school of instruction in trench-mortar work. On the 7th, the battalion was issued with gas helmets, and lectured by special gas officers. This was in the grounds of the château near Ebblinghem. After donning their gas helmets, all ranks of the battalion were conducted through a trench filled with poison gas. This test was calculated to serve the dual purpose of, first, proving to the authorities that each gas mask was serviceable, and, second, convincing the somewhat dubious troops that the simple-looking flannel helmet was entirely trustworthy. All ranks were also made acquainted with "tear gas," a chemical concoction with a peculiar odour resembling pineapples, and with the power of irritating the eyes in a most distressing manner. This diversion into chemical warfare occupied a whole day.

Two days later a scout platoon, under the command of

Second-Lieut C. Howie, was formed. This new form of battalion intelligence organization was founded on very comprehensive lines, and in a manner designed to meet the requirements of the fighting that was now approaching. Company commanders were particularly requested to supply suitable men for training in observation, reconnaissance, scouting, and patrol work. The battalion was well served by the volunteers for this important work, as was afterwards proved. The same day orders were received for a move by route march to another area.

At 7.30 a.m. on April 10th, the left half of the battalion left Ebblinghem and made rendezvous with A and B Companies at Wallon-Capel. From there the whole of the 1st Infantry Brigade moved off at 8.30 a.m. The march was a particularly severe one. After the soft sands of Egypt the rough cobbled roads of France played havoc with the feet of the troops. By the time the 12-mile march was finished, no fewer than 50 men had fallen out of the ranks of the 3rd Battalion to be attended by the medical officer, Captain Fitzpatrick, for foot trouble. The villagers everywhere lined the roadsides to cheer the marching troops.

On arrival at Strazeele, each battalion split up and moved off to its own billeting area. Two years later, during April 1918, Strazeele was destined to figure prominently in 3rd Battalion history. It was then successfully defended by the battalion against the German onslaught for the Channel ports, a thrust which the 3rd helped to bring to a standstill.

The billeting advance party met the battalion at Strazeele and led the companies to their respective billets in the Moolenacker area. The billets were in every way similar to those at Ebblinghem, except that headquarters and details were accommodated in collapsible army huts. The battalion, however, was now much nearer the firing line. Evidence of this was always present in the muffled sound of gun-fire, and occasional shooting by anti-aircraft guns.

The people at Moolenacker were less French and less attractive from every point of view. But now, for the first time, we were where there was real obtrusive evidence of the struggle. Between Moolenacker and Meteren, men of the battalion saw the farthest point reached by the Germans in their early endeavour to overrun France. Out in the fields, by the wayside, in little gardens, were scattered the lonely graves of British troops, isolated for the most part. All were carefully tended, and the local peasantry and villagers had very apparently made these graves their special care. Flowers and bushes had been planted on the mounds and, daily, women could be seen tenderly promoting the growth and jealously preserving the flowers. In some cases the people here had actually watched the outpost skirmishes and seen the casualties occur. From their accounts, the Australians were able to visualize the vivid scenes of those other days, and see again the stealthy approach of "Tommy" outposts along the ditches, with fatal results whenever the Britishers came into the line of fire from a house in which a watchful German patrol lay concealed. The graves of four German Uhlans in the farmyard where C Company was billeted were grim reminders of the work now close at hand.

Hot water baths were a welcome interlude at Moolenacker. There were facilities also for the fumigation of clothing—the troops were comfortable and clean again.

On April 16th, after Church Parade which General Birdwood attended, the battalion was inspected by Major-General H. B. Walker, G.O.C., 1st Australian Division. On the 18th the battalion transport, under Second-Lieut E. Clark, arrived from Egypt with 22 other ranks, 53 horses, 1 G.S. waggon, 1 Maltese cart, 4 travelling kitchens, 1 officers' mess cart, 9 limbers, and 2 water carts. The battalion was now up to full strength.

It was about this time that a further addition to the regimental equipment was made by an issue of steel helmets. The arrival of these strange and, it then seemed, unwieldy and impossible samples of headgear was responsible for certain derisive comment and grumbling. But all ranks shortly learned the many uses to which the "tin hat" could be put. It was afterwards used for cooking, for washing and many other illegal purposes; and in battle came to be regarded as a real friend.

THE FAMOUS NEW ZEALAND WATERTAPS, GALLIPOLI
Photo: Aust. War Memorial Museum.   See Appendix

CONSTRUCTING NEW HEADQUARTERS FOR THE 3RD BATTALION, ANZAC, JUNE, 1915

THE GRAVE OF SGT. JONES OF B COY.
Photo: *Aust. War Memorial Museum.*   See *Appendix*

THE GRAVES OF 3RD BATTALION MEN IN SHRAPNEL GULLY
Photo: *Aust. War Memorial Museum.*

CHAPTER XXI

INTO THE LINE

THE respite at Moolenacker came to an end on April 20th when A Company and the scout platoon began the forward movement, marching to billets at Sailly-sur-la-Lys, where they took over the advanced reserve-line posts from the 9th Australian Battalion. During the whole of this preparatory period, much specialist training had been indulged in, and many officers and N.C.Os had been trained in specialist and, to the battalion, new arts of war at British Army schools of instruction in the field.

The battalion strength was now 28 officers and 930 other ranks, and the morale was never higher. On April 21st it moved forward by companies towards the firing line, through the low-lying Lys valley to the town of Sailly in the Laventie sector. As the "brigade reserve battalion," the battalion hereabouts occupied a defensive line in Windy and Charred Posts (2 platoons in each place), while the remainder of the men were billeted in barns, stables, and lofts, in and around the township of Sailly. Headquarters were at Rouge de Bout, less than three miles from the firing line. A Company was already in possession of the following posts—Laventie, Nouveau Monde, Rouge, Maison, and Granny.

This plan of defence was something new to the battalion. At this time the Germans, notwithstanding their heavy commitments at Verdun, were still overwhelmingly strong and quite capable of delivering an attack at any point of the far flung battle-line. The scheme, therefore, was to hold the forward trenches with as few men as possible, while the majority of the troops garrisoned the back areas to a considerable depth. These mobile reserves were stationed in a series of fortified strong-points. Nevertheless this plan was a source of great uneasiness to the Australian commanders who had been trained in the elaborate trench-systems of Gallipoli.

The front line trenches in France, and the communication trenches leading to them, had been allowed to fall into what the Australians regarded as an alarming state of disrepair. The troops were not surprised to learn that they were now among the authentic originals of Captain Bruce Bairnsfather's "Fragments from France." But the defences were not allowed to remain in a dilapidated condition. However admirable they might have been from the point of view of that talented artist, they were quite unsuitable for the purposes of defence, as our 3rd Brigade had already found to its cost. Energetic preparations were put in hand immediately to make them fit for war. For a fortnight the whole battalion laboured strenuously at the task, and an astonishing change for the better was soon manifest. Strong trenches, with comfortable shelters, soon took shape where previously all was chaos and wreckage.

The front admittedly was a quiet one—little more than a nursery for new and untried divisions. But it was all the more dangerous on that account. Carelessness of movement and indifference to enemy observation soon brought ominous warnings. On May 3rd, a sharp lesson was taught when an enemy battery of "5.9s" opened suddenly on Weathercock House, in which C Company and the scout platoon were billeted. It fired 50 shells into the building within the space of half-an-hour. This sudden shelling was attributed by most to the action of two British artillery officers who used the high, square tower of the building as an observation post. But many also thought that it was intended to stop open movement along the paths and roads that were at all times visible around Sailly. Whatever the reason, the shelling was the direct cause of the battalion's first casualties in France. Lieut L. S. Elliott and Private Denis O'Sullivan were killed, and Private Tim Horn had his arm blown off. Elliott was a promising officer. A veteran of the South African campaign, he joined the battalion at Tel-el-Kebir, having previously served with the light horse. O'Sullivan had rendered good service during the Gallipoli operations.

On the night of May 3rd, the battalion continued its forward move to the firing line, and by the following day the whole section from Bond Street to Devon Avenue, in the Petillon sector, had been taken over from the 1st Battalion. Thus began the 3rd's first tour of duty in the firing line in France. The section occupied consisted of breastworks some eight feet high, built along the eastern side of a small stream known as the Laies. This was the stream or ditch which two months later ran red with Australian blood in the Battle of Fromelles.

Quiet was the most notable feature of the battalion's first tour of duty on this front. The most exciting work was that of the patrols and scouts, who prowled nightly in No-Man's Land. Occasionally the working parties engaged out in front, wiring or on trench construction, came in for "strafes."

Sniping was general, and all ranks found much that was interesting in the trench garrison life. Enemy action was confined to trench-mortar and rifle-grenade fire which, because of the width of No-Man's Land—in this section some 350 yards—was not very accurate, and to sudden artillery "strafes" on communication trenches with some harassing fire at night. Croix Blanche and V.C. Corner on the Rue de Bois were particularly dangerous spots, as were most of the entrances to the various communication trenches. Nevertheless, the front was a quiet one. Daily papers and illustrated periodicals were received nightly in the trenches, and canteen stores were easy to obtain. The weather was a most glorious springtime. Wild flowers carpeted the ground and ran riot over the neglected fields. The celebrated Flanders poppy was seen at its very best. Almost every day was one of brilliant sunshine, and the spirits of the battalion soared. Meanwhile, no time was lost in improving the firing line—no matter how good defences were, there was always room for this.

A system of granting furlough to the United Kingdom —"Blighty"—was now in full swing. Anzac veterans were the first to enjoy this privilege. Duty, however, was a first consideration, and, where really useful tuition was to be had, the efforts of the Australian soldier to perfect his military knowledge were always serious and earnest. The bombers, scouts, and particularly the Lewis gunners, were all very keen, and when, on the night of May 19-20th, the battalion was relieved by the 9th Battalion, all ranks marched back to new billets across the river from Sailly with the feeling that they had spent an instructive period in the line. During this tour of front-line duty two drafts of reinforcements, totalling 67 other ranks and two officers (Second-Lieuts K. Bayley and F. W. Morton), joined up. The battalion's losses were 5 killed, 6 wounded, and 20 to hospital.

Eight days' leave to England was now granted to the commanding officer, Lieut-Col O. G. Howell-Price, whose rank and command had recently been confirmed. During his sojourn in London he was decorated with the Military Cross—won at Lone Pine—by H.M. the King. Major D. T. Moore took over command of the battalion during his absence.

Combat training was now actively proceeded with, all companies perfecting their organization as well as restricted quarters would permit. All ranks paraded to the divisional baths near Sailly to revel in copious quantities of hot and cold water, a form of enjoyment of which the troops never tired. Small schools of instruction for specialists were held daily, and in every department the men rapidly approached a high standard of efficiency.

On May 25th, a further draft of reinforcements (83 other ranks under Second-Lieut L. C. Watson) arrived from the base. On June 1st, the 1st Infantry Brigade was inspected by the Prime Minister of Australia, Mr W. M. Hughes, for whom the bombing platoon "staged" a demonstration "raid," which was also filmed.

A week later the 14th reinforcements joined the battalion as a company of 150 other ranks, and, before absorption in the companies and platoons, caused interest and comment at battalion headquarters by reason of their specially fine appearance and physique. The infusion of this fine draft brought the battalion's strength up to 29 officers and 1053 men.

On the following day it marched out of billets around Croix du Bac to take over close support billets and trenches from the 7th Battalion in the Fleurbaix sector. At midnight on June 9th the following posts were taken over: Croix Marechal, Ferrets, Cain and Abels, Durhams and Central Keep. The duties of the supporting battalion at Fleurbaix were similar to those at Petillon and Rue de Bois. Heavy engineering fatigues were supplied, and the chances of war were in every way the same.

B Company's billet near Croix Marechal was heavily shelled on June 18th, and totally destroyed. Fortunately there were very few casualties, due in some measure to the distinguished conduct of Sergeant E. H. Jackson. This sudden strafe was but one indication of the increasing liveliness now evident on this front. Raids by the Australians on the enemy trenches were being made frequently, and greater artillery activity, as well as the bombarding of the German lines with 60-lb. "plum pudding" bombs, served to liven the trench warfare very considerably. Open movement of parties of more than ten men by daylight was almost certain to draw hostile fire, and the billets in Fleurbaix received unwelcome attention on more than one occasion. This state of affairs was the source of some satisfaction to the troops, as it indicated that the enemy was resentful of aggressive Australian pressure on his front, and that the initiative had definitely passed into the hands of the Australians.

Very heavy fatigues were continually supplied by the battalion. Often the whole unit, less essential guards and cooks, were employed on Dead Dog, Tin Barn, and Convent Avenues, the main supply trenches in the sector. Excellent defences were thus constructed, and the once neglected lines became heavily fortified. Frequent gas alarms were a feature of the front-line experiences at this time. Nervous sentries were often deceived by the marsh mist which drifted across from the enemy lines. The sounding of one startled sentry's gong—usually a brass shell case suspended on a piece of wire—would be sufficient to rouse the whole countryside. Like a midsummer bushfire, the stampeding of the gongs took some checking.

A convent, or what was left of it, was here by far the most conspicuous feature of the landscape. Its much battered walls provided excellent cover for enterprising snipers and machine-gunners.

Artillery and trench mortar activity was now general on both sides, and casualties from these causes mounted steadily. Air combats and balloon strafing were spectacular incidents of the daytime. When night came, wiring and patrolling parties worked energetically in No-Man's Land, and easily maintained ascendency in that direction.

On the night of the 29th a party, under Captain P. L. Howell-Price from the 1st Battalion, successfully raided the enemy trenches opposite our lines. Some assistance was rendered to the raiders by Second-Lieut R. F. Bulkeley and his patrol who reconnoitred the enemy wire. Heavy retaliation followed. Several gaps were made in our breastworks, in one or two gaps sufficiently large to have allowed a horse and dray being driven through. However, these breaches were repaired before daylight.

A 3rd Battalion raiding party, under Captain A. R. Edwards, was kept in training, but an opportunity for its employment did not arise.

Losses to this date included Second-Lieut E. B. Watson (died of wounds), and Lieuts Tyson and Lamrock (wounded), while Captains Burrett and Stronach and Lieuts C. F. Elliot and Kemmis had been evacuated because of sickness. The enterprising sergeant of scouts, Bob Graham, had been wounded. The total losses were 14 killed and 65 evacuated for wounds and sickness.

The average nightly expenditure of small arms ammunition was 1600 rounds, while Lewis gunners and rifle bombers expended 2200 and 29 rounds respectively.

On the night of July 3rd, the persistent work of the patrols was rewarded by the capture of a German prisoner, a sniper of the 20th Bavarian R.I.R. Incidentally it was the battalion's first prisoner in France. The actual capture was made by Private "Nugget" Byrnes, a big burly sundowner with an infectious smile. In a final struggle, Byrnes reached the height of his ambition by presenting his German opponent with a glorious black eye.

The 3rd was relieved by the 45th Battalion on the night of July 4th-5th. The relief was carried out without incident. The march back to Sailly, where the battalion went into billets, was made in a heavy thunderstorm. Some shell-fire was experienced during the early stages of the march, and a sudden gas alarm made the night a most exciting one. As the following day was practically a holiday, bathing parades and a general clean-up were the order from headquarters. Favourite *estaminets* were revisited and old friendships renewed.

Our time at Sailly was all too short. Rumour had it that the battalion was shortly to take part in the great Somme Battle which was then raging in the south. When officers were issued with maps of the Somme area the destination was settled beyond doubt.

On July 9th, the battalion marched to Oultersteene, about nine miles distant. The march discipline was excellent. The men, now thoroughly acclimatized and hardened by their recent experiences and toiling in the northern sector, tramped along the highways to the accompaniment of mouth organs and ribald songs. The big leavening of reinforcements had been highly trained and, for general efficiency, the troops considered themselves second to none in the Allied armies. This happy feeling was due, in the main, to the splendid influence and enthusiasm of the battalion's youthful commander, Lieut-Col O. G. Howell-Price. A model soldier, he was fearless in action, while on the parade-ground he inspired great respect. The colonel was a teetotaller yet by no means a "wowser." Altogether he set a wonderful example to officers and men. He criticized in his usual searching way the marching troops, and, upon arrival at the bivouac at Oultersteene, subjected the battalion to a vigorous personal inspection. The parade was not dismissed until he had satisfied himself that the fighting equipment was complete in every detail, and the men in good shape.

That night spent in open bivouac was a happy one. Merris was not far distant, and from there supplies of champagne and light wines were obtained. The site chosen for bivouac was near the field where the battalion put up such a wonderful fight in the spring of 1918.

At 11 p.m. on July 10th, the battalion marched out

of Oultersteene for Bailleul, a distance of about five miles. There a troop train was waiting. By 2.35 a.m. entrainment had been completed. The whole operation of loading men (forty to a truck), horses, waggons, etc., was completed in 35 minutes. The rail journey came to an end at dawn on the 11th, when the troops detrained at Candas. Thence they marched about 11 miles to billets in St Ouen.

This town was by far the largest in which the battalion had, till then, been quartered in France, and its inhabitants were in a very liberal frame of mind. Being the centre of a large industrial area, the operatives of the factories and mines were less conservative than the somewhat cold and calculating peasant classes of the north. The men, naturally, thoroughly enjoyed themselves.

One company commander struck trouble at St Ouen. The madame at his billet refused to allow the troops to use soap in the horse trough. Good-naturedly, the company commander—a school teacher by profession—tried to soothe the outraged feelings of the woman in his best French. The result was tragic. Whether the lady thought that the officer was doubting her parentage or not would be hard to say, but the fine battle of words only ended when the officer, suddenly relapsing into English, exclaimed, "Oh, you be eternally damned, woman." Madame beat a hasty retreat.

At 8.45 a.m. on July 12th, the battalion marched out of St Ouen for Vignacourt. On the following day it continued its journey to Allonville, a distance of twelve miles. Here the troops were billeted in an old aeroplane hangar, but the majority of the men preferred to sleep in the open fields. Three days were spent at Allonville, practising formations for wood and village fighting, and on Sunday, July 16th, the unit marched to Warloy-Baillon. The distance, ten miles, was covered in three hours. During the stay at Warloy, battle lectures which stressed every particular of the coming fight were given and careful inspections of fighting equipment were made. Senior officers visited the battle front, and inspected with care the positions marked down for assault. Large patches of pink cloth were issued to the troops, to be sewn on the backs of their tunics. This extra badge of identity had been found necessary in the new form of shell-crater fighting that was being evolved. It allowed of easy identification by aeroplane observers when normal means of communication broke down, as it so often did under terrific artillery-fire. Old hands remembered how, at the battle of Lone Pine, similar colour patches had been used.

Warloy witnessed one of the happiest incidents in the history of the battalion. Word came through that Company Sergeant-Major Morris had been awarded the Military Cross—a distinction rarely given to an N.C.O. It was said to be but the second occasion when this decoration was granted to an Australian N.C.O. C Company officers celebrated by entertaining Morris at the house where they were quartered, much to the astonishment and somewhat to the consternation of some English artillery officers in adjoining billets. They did not understand the familiarity and friendship which always existed between officers and men of the A.I.F.

CHAPTER XXII

THE CAPTURE OF POZIÈRES

DURING the afternoon of July 20th the battalion, in "battle order," marched out of Warloy for Albert on its way to the line, to take part in the 1st Division's first major operation in France. The day was fine and warm, and the route at first ran through pleasant cornfields almost ready for harvest. The spirits of the men were high. The comparatively easy tours in the line in front of Sailly and Fleurbaix had merely whetted appetites for more serious fighting. The temper generally may be judged from the fact that a man in D Company, suffering from a sprained ankle, actually wept when ordered to the rear for purposes of evacuation. Incidentally, that same soldier, when he rejoined the battalion after Pozières, was consoled by one of his mates who grimly remarked, "Well, Bill, you ain't missed much."

As the marching "fours" approached Albert, the cornfields were replaced by all those things significant of a great "push." Endless horse-lines, batteries of artillery, piled-up shells, dumps of every description, and troops representative of all arms of the service. Bustle and activity characterized the whole countryside, which was humming like a bee-hive. The Australians could not help but wonder what the German artillery was doing within easy range of such splendid targets, almost entirely without concealment. Then it was realized that the Germans had been temporarily driven from the air; secondly, that their guns were far too busy with counter-battery work, and other preparations for resisting the

British advance, to have any time to deal tangentially with movements farther back.

The evening before moving out, the battalion had first heard from afar a real barrage—one of those which were put down from time to time, either as a feint or as a preparation for the real attack—and in spite of the distance, had been amazed, appalled almost, by its intensity. It was not to be compared with any artillery-fire the battalion had previously known on Gallipoli or in France.

Along the horizon, to north and south, rode an endless line of British "sausages" (observation balloons), swaying gently far above their moorings, a further proof of British mastery in the air. High over the town of Albert protruded the partially ruined brick tower of the basilica, surmounted by the great gilded statue of the Virgin and Child, leaning perilously over the street like a diving figure—"Annette Kellerman," as the Diggers were quick to name it. The French said at the time that the fall of the historic figure would presage the end of the war. Actually, it was displaced in April, 1918, during the German occupation of the city, more than six months before the Armistice.

As Albert was being shelled frequently, the battalion marched through the town by platoons at distances of fifty paces. They passed right under the leaning statue at which many an apprehensive glance was directed, so imminent did its fall appear.

At the foot of the slope rising just beyond Albert, a halt was called on the left of the main road leading to Bapaume and the evening meal taken while the battalion awaited guides from the 68th British Brigade, who were to lead it to the particular support trenches to be occupied. At dusk the guides arrived and we moved off, by platoons, over open ground pitted with shell-holes and traversed by straggling strands of shattered wire-entanglements, and permeated with the pungent sickly-sweet smell of a recent battle—an odour of T.N.T., cordite, ammonal gas, and blood.

Though the night was comparatively quiet, the Germans were shelling the support area intermittently with "5.9s"; and, on arrival at its destination, the battalion found that the companies it was relieving, although they had taken no part in the actual fighting, were in a bad way because of the continuous shelling. They were very glad to be relieved.

C Company (Capt. E. W. G. Wren) and D Company (Capt. J. R. O. Harris) were located in a support trench running across "Sausage Valley." A (Major A. R. Edwards) and B (Capt. Kemp) were accommodated in a communication trench running back from D Company's trench and in another parallel support trench in rear. On the left flank of the latter trench, Lieut-Col Howell-Price established his headquarters in an old German dug-out. In a shallow cutting to the left of the battalion sector were the remains of a light railway line. At one point this cutting was choked with British and German corpses. Indeed, unburied dead lay thickly all over the ground, and before advancing to the assembly trenches it was thought advisable to send out parties of veteran soldiers to bury the bodies adjoining the route, for the sights were well calculated to unnerve the younger soldiers.

In the midst of these dreadful surroundings the battalion spent two days perfecting details of equipment, receiving instructions as to the advance and the attack, writing letters home, and—in the case of officers and N.C.Os—taking occasional trips to the front line, which, in the sector immediately in front, was held by the 1st Battalion A.I.F. Among the "issues" made to officers were so many scale maps that they filled all pockets, gas-helmet satchels, and haversacks to repletion. One company commander solved the problem by handing all except that indicating Pozières to his batman, a utilitarian who used them subsequently during a shortage of fuel to boil a dixie of tea. The area was fairly heavily shelled by "5.9s" day and night, but the casualties were negligible. Many of the shells were duds, and few caused casualties in the trenches.

From the support area two roads, intersecting both the British and German front lines, ran forward towards the village of Pozières. One ran from "Casualty Corner," a sunken cross-road near the head of Sausage Valley, past the "Chalk Pit" (a quarry used as an artillery dump) and through the left of the village; the other from Contalmaison wood into the centre of the village.

Briefly, the projected operations of the 1st Australian Division, forming part of the third phase of the Franco-British offensive on the Somme, envisaged an attack upon three objectives, to be launched by the 1st and 3rd Brigades on the night of July 22nd-23rd. The 2nd Brigade would be in reserve. The first objective was Pozières Trench, the second objective a supposed line of trenches about half-way between that trench and the main Albert-Bapaume road; these were to be taken, from left to right, by the 2nd, 1st, 11th, and 9th Battalions. The third objective, a supposed line immediately south of and parallel to the main road, would be stormed by the 4th, 3rd, 12th, and 10th Battalions. A line of shell- and bullet-splintered telegraph poles, running across No-Man's Land in the general direction of the village, marked the boundary between the 1st and 3rd Brigades.

Although there was a definitely marked trench on the first objective, hardly anything in the nature of trenches by now existed on the second and third objectives; it is possible they had been obliterated by previous bombardments. In any case, it is difficult to understand why the third objective was fixed along a line so close to such a salient feature as a main road. Its position certainly cost our battalion dear in the subsequent German bombardments.

The lines of the three objectives were not parallel, but converged and met on the south-west side of the village. To the north-east, where they ran into the "O.G." (Old German) lines, which the main road intersected at right angles, they were about 300-400 yards apart. The distance from the Australian front line to the final objective in the 3rd Battalion sector was from 800 to 1000 yards.

Each battalion was to attack on a two-company frontage. The rear battalions taking the third objective would utilize two of their companies for the purpose, holding the other two as local reserves. The operation was one to which the term "leap-frogging" was applied, because, after the leading companies had captured the first objective, the two lines in rear would pass through and over them to the more distant objectives. Each attacking line was to be still further divided into three waves—first, a line of scouts and wire-cutters; second, at a distance of 50 yards, the main attacking force; third, 20 yards farther back still, a party carrying picks and shovels, extra sand-bags, ammunition, bombs, and other stores. As all three waves composing one line of attack had shelter in the same assembly trench, the difficulties of arrangement were considerable.

On the night before the attack, the 1st Brigade battalions in support (the 3rd and 4th) received orders to move forward and prepare, immediately in rear of the fire trench, assembly trenches for the attacking companies, and, along the road leading through the front, similar positions for those in support. The front-line battalions (1st and 2nd) also dug assembly trenches in No-Man's Land in front of the line, so that there were three parallel lines of trenches to shelter the attacking troops. The whole of this work was successfully carried out, except the trenches along the road for the support companies. Here the digging troops quickly struck rock, with the result that the trenches reached only to a depth of two feet, a fact that had serious consequences for the support companies at the time of the attack.

Two circumstances added considerably to the difficulties of the 3rd Battalion in its attack: (*a*) the front line in the middle of the right-company sector bent sharply at a right-angle to the south; (*b*) the line of the third objective was not parallel even to part of the jumping-off trench. In consequence the 3rd's attacking companies received instructions to straighten out, on moving into No-Man's Land, the kink caused by the right-angle bend in the trench, and, secondly, to swing their whole line quarter left till it was parallel to the third objective—two manœuvres difficult enough in daylight under peace conditions, but absolutely impossible, as it proved, in the darkness and confusion of battle. However, it was said that after the battalion crossed the second objective a suitable rallying line would be found in a partially demolished light-railway line (a continuation of the line intersecting the 3rd Battalion trenches in the support position), which was roughly parallel to and about 200 yards from the third objective.

To make the above explanation of the battle dispositions clearer, two sketches are appended. No. 1 shows the village of Pozières, the main Albert-Bapaume road, and the three objectives of the 1st Division. No. 2 shows the dispositions of the 1st and 3rd Battalions immediately before the attack.

Although the construction of the assembly trenches was carried out without serious interference from enemy machine-gun or artillery fire, the area immediately in rear of the front line was subjected to a heavy bombardment of gas-shell. These were distinguishable from ordinary shells by the "wobbly" sound of their flight and

LIEUT. H. MEAGER WITH HIS PERISCOPIC RIFLE
Meager was killed at Lone Pine.
Photo: Aust. War Memorial Museum.

WHILE THE BILLY BOILS. LIEUT. E. C. H. RITCHIE (LEFT),
PTE BAILEY AND PTE TIMOTHY NOLAN
Photo: Aust. War Memorial Museum.

A TYPICAL "POSSIE." 3RD BATTALION TRENCHES. ANZAC
Photo: *Aust. War Memorial Museum.*

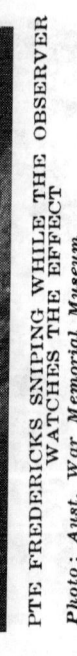

PTE FREDERICKS SNIPING WHILE THE OBSERVER WATCHES THE EFFECT
Photo: *Aust. War Memorial Museum.*

by the faint "plop" of their explosion on impact, the charge being just sufficient to split the case without widely dispersing the gas content and thus weakening the deadly effect.

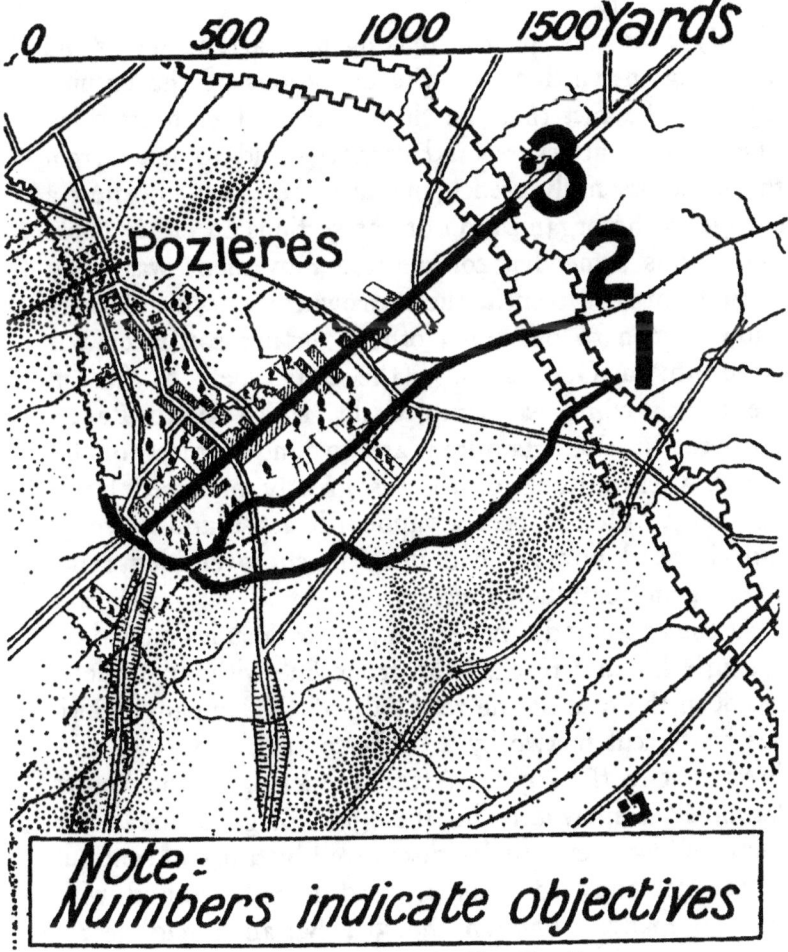

BATTLE OF POZIÈRES (MAP No. 1)
Copyright: Aust. War Memorial Museum.

An officer of the battalion, passing through the gassed area on his way back to the support trenches, had hastily to don his helmet, for the ground was smoking with phosgene. Blinded by the dimness of the eye-pieces, he promptly fell into two deep shell-holes. Deciding that it was better to be partially gassed than to break his neck, he compromised by taking off the mask and covering his nose and mouth with the impregnated material, leaving his eyes clear.

July 22nd was spent in making final arrangements and in giving instructions for the operations of the ensuing night. The fact that the three waves of each attacking line—scouts, attackers, and carriers—had to issue from the same assembly trench, made it necessary to effect a change in the organization of the sections on either flank. While this somewhat complicated movement was being carried out in a trench, the narrowness of which hardly allowed men to pass each other, further confusion was caused by a German 5.9 (the only shell to fall in the trench while we occupied it), which killed Lance-Corporal A. D. Hamilton and wounded most of his section. Hamilton's death was greatly mourned by D Company. He had been a vaudeville artist, and his songs and cheerful humour had done much to enliven route marches and battalion concerts.

At the appointed time, 8 p.m., the companies moved off in single file and reached the front line without incident, except in the case of the rear half of D Company, which was neatly cut in two by a traffic-control man, who misdirected it to the right. After wandering in the "outer darkness" somewhere in the 3rd Brigade area, the "tourists" were eventually discovered by a patrol sent out by the company commander, and were re-united with their company. Though the 3rd Battalion had nearly four hours (from 9 p.m. to 1 a.m.) to wait, almost the whole time was occupied in sorting out and reorganizing the attacking lines. This task was carried out under moderate to heavy machine-gun and artillery fire, which rather rattled the men and made it impossible to carry out the precise details of the plan. As it happened, the right company (D) escaped serious shelling, but the left (C) and supporting companies (A and B) suffered severely, the loss in the two last mentioned being mainly due to the shallowness of their assembly trench.

At 12.28 a.m., two minutes before zero, the full force of the British and Australian barrage fell on the German front line with an intensity not hitherto experienced or contemplated by our men. The flashes of the exploding shells were so close and continuous that they formed an almost unbroken wall of flame crowned by rolling columns of smoke illuminating the inferno below. The noise could only be described as tremendous. Separate explosions were quite indistinguishable, being fused into one continuous roar. No order could be heard unless shouted into the ear.

Punctually at 12.30 the first line went over, the forms of the men silhouetted for a moment against the fiery background. In a few minutes—they seemed like hours—news filtered back that the first objective had been captured without resistance. The second line moved out and disappeared. Then, at 1 a.m., the attacking companies of the 3rd Battalion received the signal to advance, the scouts having already gone forward. But partly owing to the din and confusion, partly to the eagerness of the line of carriers to be "in at the death," the instructions to advance in two lines were disregarded. All attempts to straighten out the line and swing it to the left were found to be wholly impracticable, and the men moved across No-Man's Land in small groups which kept edging to the left in an effort to keep touch. The result was that Captain Harris, who moved out on the extreme right of the battalion in order to keep that flank extended as far as the line of telegraph poles which marked the boundary of the battalion sector, found himself deserted by all except his batman.

However, before the barrage lifted from the third

objective (the main Albert-Bapaume road), the men of the 3rd's attacking companies generally were posted along the light railway, which served as a rallying line for the final assault. In fact, some of D Company's No. 13 Platoon, including its commander, Lieut Paul White, and

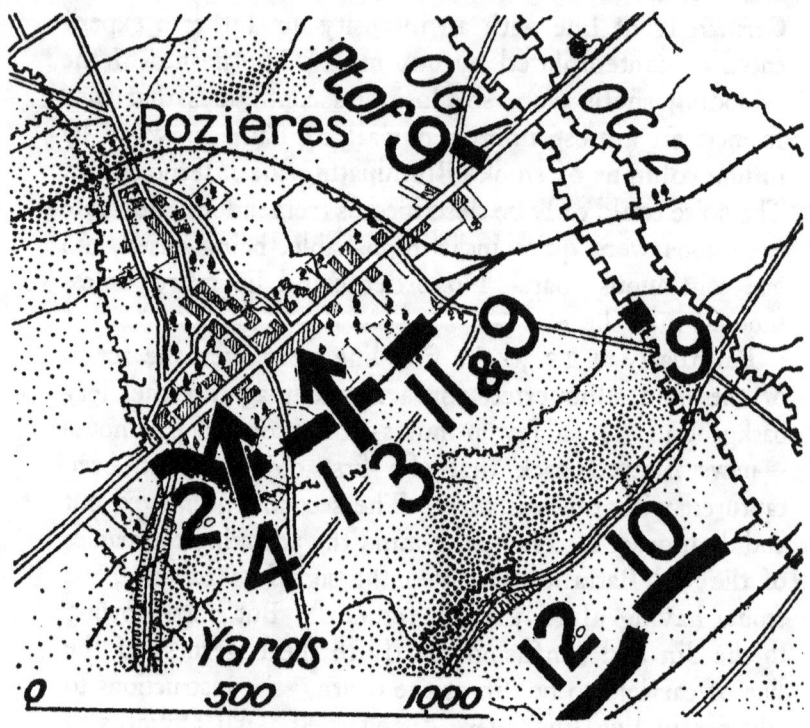

BATTLE OF POZIÉRES (Map No. 2)
Copyright: Aust. War Memorial Museum.

Sergeant "Denny" Campbell, overran the railway line and were caught by their own barrage, sustaining some casualties. The successful organization of the final attack was largely due to White and the intelligence officer, Lieut R. F. Bulkeley.

In this sector there was no semblance of resistance on the part of the Germans. No regular trench-line was discovered, either on the second or third objective, and the few casualties sustained were due to distant machine-gun fire or to men running into our own barrage. So great had been the confusion of the advance that C and D Companies were found practically to have changed places. D was now on the left and C on the right; and the line included men from almost every company of the 1st and 3rd Brigades.

Officers quickly laid out a trench-line among the shell-holes and mounds of rubbish—all that was left of the cottages on the south side of the road—and the men began digging-in feverishly with their entrenching tools. They bitterly regretted the lack of picks, which had been jettisoned in the advance.

Patrols quickly linked up with the 4th Battalion on the left flank. On the right, however, there was, for a time, a perilous gap, caused partly by D Company having edged to the left during the advance, and partly by reason of the fact that the left-flank companies of the 3rd Brigade had either not yet reached, or had considerably overrun, the third objective in their sector. To obviate the danger of a German counter-attack driving a wedge through this gap, a Lewis gun post was established on the 3rd Battalion's extreme right flank, and a patrol was sent out with orders to range wide in the hope of making contact with the 3rd Brigade. In addition, in case of need two platoons were brought up from A Company; before their arrival, however, connection had been established on that flank also, and at daybreak the division was strongly entrenched on the third objective.

In the meantime the heterogeneous mass of men had been organized in temporary platoons and sections, and sufficient supplies of ammunition and bombs had been collected to repel any counter-attack. But, if we had only known what was happening on "the other side of the hill," we would have been spared any anxiety about an immediate counter-attack. For the time being the Germans had had all the fight knocked out of them by the fierceness of the preliminary bombardments, and, except in O.G. 1 and O.G. 2, they were on the run all along the divisional line. Moreover, additional protection was being afforded us by the artillery barrage, which was still falling, if in greatly diminished strength, about 100 yards beyond the main road.

Meanwhile, A and C Companies had lost their commanders. Shortly after leaving the jumping-off trench, Captain Wren was severely wounded, and subsequently lost his right arm. Major Edwards, who went to Wren's assistance, was also badly wounded while endeavouring to ascertain his injuries. That ended the service of these two officers with the battalion. Before the day was out the battalion also lost two of its best N.C.Os in Company Sergeant-Majors G. A. Morris and W. Woods. Just a week before, Morris had been awarded the Military Cross, a rare honour for an N.C.O. Woods was a champion spring jumper, and had appeared in many countries as a vaudeville artist. During a sports' meeting at Tel-el-Kebir, early in 1916, he gave an exhibition of trick jumping—in a standing jump he cleared the colonel's horse. The regimental sergeant-major, Sid Rudkin, was wounded.

Lieutenant H. L. Cooper, a reinforcement officer, was another victim of the first phase of the attack. Both his legs had been injured to such an extent that it was impossible to move him. Captain S. C. Fitzpatrick, the medical officer, went out through heavy shell-fire and made a desperate effort to save his life. But Cooper was too far gone. An eye-witness reported that Fitzpatrick tackled the job as coolly as if doing his ordinary hospital rounds.

Lieut A. O. Duprez took charge of A Company, while Lieut C. H. Howie assumed command of C. Duprez was an officer who had seen service in the Matabele campaign. During the Boer War he achieved fame by winning the Queen's Scarf—a very high honour.

Shortly after daybreak the first contact plane appeared. It was flying low along the new front line at a height of about 200 feet, and green flares, in groups of three, were immediately lighted at intervals to indicate to it the extreme limit of the advance. Soon afterwards Lieut-Col Howell-Price who, when his men were in the line, was seldom happy in any position in rear, came up and personally resumed the direction of affairs. Men belonging to other battalions were sorted out and sent to the rear and flanks, and, as the line was now adequately manned, the reinforcing platoon from A Company was sent back. C and D Companies, though retaining the reverse positions into which the confusion of the advance had thrown them, were as far as possible reorganized in their proper platoons and sections.

While the C.O. was discussing the general position with his officers, standing in the open in rear of the trench, a German sniper opened fire from the ruined cottages beyond the road. The party took cover without suffering any casualties, and patrols were sent out to search the ground across the road right up to and even through the barrage. A few Germans were hunted out and killed, and some prisoners were brought in.

And now followed one of those strange lulls which may be compared to the windless area in the centre of a cyclone. As so often happens when the artillery on either side is uncertain as to the position of its own front line, the barrage had almost completely died down. Our front trench was held by sentry-groups at fairly wide intervals, the remainder of the men, after two sleepless nights, and worn out by the strenuous digging and the reaction from the excitement of the attack, having dropped in their tracks and fallen asleep. The front line took on almost the semblance of the peaceful Fleurbaix-Armentières "nursery," where the battalion had received its first introduction to active service conditions in France.

The whole of July 23rd was, in fact, comparatively uneventful in the front line. About 10 a.m. some fifty Germans, apparently without arms, were seen about 200 yards beyond the main road, running across the front from right to left. Several posts in the 3rd Battalion line opened fire, whereupon some of them dropped into shell-holes. The remainder ran back in a northerly direction until they disappeared below the slope of the hill in the direction of the cemetery.

Towards midday our scouts patrolled the ruins of the village north of the road and brought in 15 or 16 Germans. The leader, an N.C.O. who was wearing the black and white ribbon of the Iron Cross, was interrogated in French by one of the officers. He had been a schoolmaster in civil life, and he volunteered the information that his men had experienced a very bad time, our bombardments having cut off all communication with the rear. For the previous three or four days they had subsisted mostly on soda-water and cigars. Though their uniforms were neat and clean, they certainly looked pale and haggard and showed emphatic traces of the intense mental and physical strain they must have endured.

Though the new front line was as yet almost entirely free from bombardment, the approaches and communication trenches leading to it from the rear were heavily shelled throughout the day, with the result that it was a very difficult matter to get rations and stores forward, or to send messages by runner either way. This interruption was doubtless responsible for the following extraordinary circumstances: At 4 p.m. Captain Harris, who was in command of the 3rd Battalion's front-line companies, was visited by Lieut-Col J. Heane, of the 1st Battalion. Lieut-Col Heane, who said that he was in command of the front line of the 1st Brigade, gave Captain Harris verbal orders to push forward an attack through the village north of the road at 5 p.m. Preparations for this attack had already been indicated by an intensification of the barrage, which had been falling lightly all day just across the road. But Harris refused to carry out the order unless it was confirmed by instructions from 3rd Battalion Headquarters, and when the barrage lifted at 5 p.m., in the absence of more definite orders, no advance was made by the 3rd Battalion. Two Lewis gun posts were, however, established in the ruins of cottages about 100 yards north of the main road.

The difficulty of maintaining communication with the front was still more emphatically indicated by the events of the following night. The commander of the 1st Brigade had received the 8th Battalion (2nd Brigade) as a reinforcement, and decided to utilize it in establishing a series of posts on the north-western edge of Pozières village. But the front-line battalions received no notification of this intended movement. Shortly before midnight the commander of the front-line companies (Capt. Harris) of the 3rd received a message from the C.O. of the 4th (Lieut-Col I. G. Mackay) that a German counter-attack was to be expected during the night. The 3rd immediately stood to arms.

Just after midnight shadowy forms were seen quietly stealing across the front from right to left,* about fifty yards away. The men of the 3rd, who, naturally, were inclined to be "jumpy" as a result of the alarm, had their fingers on the triggers, and a catastrophe was only averted by the peremptory orders of officers and the courage of Lance-Cpl C. Dowling of D Company, who, on instructions from the company commander, moved out from the trench and ascertained the identity of the newcomers. The rest of the night passed quietly without further incident.

* Dr C. E. W. Bean in the *Official History of Australia in the War of 1914-1918* (in the map on p. 538, Vol. III) represents the party as moving from left to right. The company commander, however, says that he has an intimate recollection of the incident, as he sent L/Cpl Dowling out, and is sure that they travelled from right to left.

At 6.30 a.m. next day, July 24th, the German artillery (5.9's mostly) opened on the 3rd Battalion trench, now the support line, as the new front line had been formed by posts from the 8th and 12th Battalions. At this stage the obvious folly of siting a trench along a main road and of packing it with men became apparent. It should be explained, however, that the battalion and company commanders had had no choice in the matter; their orders as to objectives had been quite definite.

An easy target, it was bombarded from front, right, and rear. The shells from the front, while they repeatedly caved the trench in and buried the occupants, were not as deadly as those coming from the right. The latter, dropping almost perpendicularly, were visible during the last moment of flight. As there were no dugouts—indeed no shelter of any kind from the fire of these enfilading batteries—casualties soon mounted up. There was nothing to do but to try and keep the trenches clear and dig out the men who were buried. In spite of most heroic efforts, the stretcher-bearers could not keep pace with the casualties.

D Company was unfortunate in losing C.S.M. H. F. Stead and its four platoon sergeants (S. Garrard and R. Macdonald, killed; R. Y. V. Macdonald and W. H. Spicer, wounded). The company commander had called a meeting of platoon sergeants, who, owing to casualties among officers, were commanding their platoons. Fortunately for Captain Harris he was a few minutes late in returning from the other end of the line, which he had been inspecting. On arrival he found that a large shell (probably of 9-inch calibre) had fallen right on company headquarters with disastrous results for his N.C.Os.

"The extreme difficulty of clearing the wounded," says Dr Bean, in Vol. III of the *Official History*, "was in that part, met by the resource of a middle-aged private named Jenkins." Quoting from an account written by Captain Harris, Dr Bean continues: "During the heaviest of the bombardment this man constituted himself the attendant of those wounded men who could not be removed. Under heavy shell-fire he raised a shelter for them where there was a little more protection than in the trench, and took them over one by one across the open. He looked after them with the utmost tenderness, expended the last drop of water in his bottle to alleviate their thirst, and, when a small quantity of fresh water was brought up, refused a drink himself in order that his patients might have more. He cheered them up by telling them that the stretcher-bearers would soon be along . . . and I firmly believe kept several of them alive by his efforts. Every single one of these wounded men was eventually taken out and recovered; but at the end of the day he himself, while taking along a dixie of tea to the sufferers, was blown to pieces by a shell."

Lieut-Col Howell-Price, invariably to be found in the hottest places, stayed in the front line all this day, doing his best to keep up the spirits of the men, who were almost cowed by the storm of shell which rained upon them almost without intermission for nearly twelve hours. The ration- and water-parties sent up from time to time during the day were almost all destroyed by the heavy shelling, the only food that arrived consisting of two cold dixies of boiled onions. One could hardly have imagined a more nauseous and unpalatable form of sustenance in the circumstances.

Towards 6 p.m. the bombardment slackened, and the parched and exhausted survivors, whose strength had been reduced to half both in the front and support lines, gained a short respite from their troubles. About this time there arrived a little water, most of which was commandeered by Jenkins for his patients. The remainder was sparingly doled out in the proportion of about one-eighth of a pint to a man. Advantage was taken of the lull to evacuate the wounded, but the survivors were too few and too weary to clear out the trench, which had been almost flattened by the ferocious shelling.

Throughout the night of the 24-25th the enemy again heavily shelled the Australian position, and no sleep was possible for the defenders. The battalion was still south of the main road, A and B Companies having relieved C and D in the firing line.

July 25th opened with a tornado of shells from the German "heavies," and losses continued at such a rapid rate that Lieut-Col Howell-Price, after a personal reconnaissance, ordered a forward move close up to the 8th Battalion line, hoping thus to escape the worst of the barrage. It was at this stage that Captain R. O. Middleton and Lieut J. S. F. Bartlett, both acting as company commanders, were killed. They had gone back for the purpose of guiding their companies forward but were caught in the curtain of gun-fire. Howell-Price thereupon led the survivors forward himself. By 10 a.m. this manoeuvre was completed.

Just prior to the advance, Lieut H. S. Chapman, the battalion signalling officer, was examining a map in company with Major D. T. Moore and several signallers, when a high velocity shell hit the back of the trench. Chapman was killed by the concussion and Signaller W. A. Oates was blown to pieces. The same shell killed Signallers Clarrie Page, "Snow" Pickering, and Rupert Clarke. Strange to relate, Oates predicted, while at Gallipoli, the actual date of his death.

"I decided to push forward one company," wrote Howell-Price in his report on this day. "But when I returned to my trenches I found they were quite untenable. A Company had been practically wiped out, and as the enemy shells were going over the first line at the time I decided to move forward closer up to the 8th Battalion line. As soon as this movement commenced the enemy artillery shortened range and we were obliged to pass through a terrific barrage of high explosive. My officers and N.C.Os had been greatly reduced, especially the most experienced being killed and wounded, and a great number of men had been buried. Many brave actions were performed, especially by the most experienced stretcher-bearers who attended the wounded without hesitation, and for whose work I am unable to speak in high enough terms. I was reduced to less than one officer per company and after advancing I collected my battalion about a 'strong point' and commenced to consolidate, which work was done in splendid style. Two companies of the 6th Battalion reported to me and were put on digging in and connecting the brigade line with the 'strong point' above, and from there to the cemetery, with the result that when I was relieved practically the whole of the line was completed with a good firing line and communication to the rear."

And so ended the 3rd Battalion's share of the fighting in the grim struggle for the village of Pozières. At 1 a.m. on July 26th, the 2nd Brigade commenced the relief of the worn-out warriors. By dawn the majority of the survivors were sitting round the company cookers at the bivouac in Bécourt Wood, where the cooks served out a very welcome hot meal. Many of the men were badly shaken by their experiences, and more than a few were observed with bandages on roughly dressed wounds. Some of the lads were so tired that they just dropped off to sleep, fatigue quite overcoming their desire for food. As the day brightened, a miscellany of dusty, clustering figures slept profoundly in the poppy-dappled fields about the bivouac camp.

At the muster parade held near Bécourt Wood on the 27th the losses were shown to be:—*

OFFICERS: 3 killed, 9 wounded, 2 died of wounds.
OTHER RANKS: 101 killed, 366 wounded, 43 missing.

In addition to those already mentioned, the officers who fell included Lieut J. T. Philpot, who succumbed to his wounds on July 25th. Philpot, who had been a chemist at the Small Arms Factory at Lithgow, was one of the many Gallipoli veterans who perished at Pozières, others being Sergeants Dick Rosser (a Coronation cadet), Victor Speller, F. H. Mathieson, L. S. McCallum, and Corporal H. T. Harris—all men with fine records.

---

* The *Official History* (Vol. III, p. 593) shows the loss of the 3rd Battalion as 13 officers and 484 men. The battalion diary on July 14 gives the strength of the unit as 27 officers and 1063 other ranks, and on July 31 as 13 and 562, a difference of 14 and 501.

CHAPTER XXIII

THE SECOND POZIÈRES

THE march back from Pozières is described by Signaller Len Jones: "On July 27th the battalion moved to woods at the rear of Warloy-Baillon, arriving at 10 p.m. Next day the battalion marched out for La Vicogne. Warloy was packed with troops, either waiting their turn to go into the line, or, like the 3rd Battalion, on the way out. The 4th Australian Division was in waiting. Scottish and English units were everywhere.

"The men had now been able to remove, to an extent, some of the dirt and traces of the Pozières trenches. With equipment straightened up the battalion moved along the inevitable sunken road. What a difference our entrance into Warloy now compared with the 16th! Headquarters signallers and pioneers had been reduced to a few men. The companies were minus old commanders and platoons were just skeletons. Barbed-wire had taken its toll of uniforms. Faces were grey and lined and many men were suffering with stomach trouble caused by gases from the devastating enemy barrage. But they marched as the 3rd Battalion could march when it wanted to.

"On the road bank stood a lone Scotchman, dressed in his picturesque kilt with khaki apron. Surveying the passing troops with a critical eye, he called out, 'Where ye froom, chooms?' Someone answered, 'From the other side of Pozières.' Turning round, the Scotty yelled to some pals, 'Hi! Coom and see the Aussies whoo've taken Pozziares.' One man became a crowd. Troops came running from all directions. In a matter of seconds the bank was lined with thousands of troops. Someone called out, 'Give these boys three cheers.' The cheering was taken up right along the line and the battalion marched out to La Vicogne through an avenue of shouting troops. Lieut-Col Howell-Price obviously was pleased and looked back proudly at his men. Faces brightened, shoulders straightened, and arms gave an extra inch to the swing, but nevertheless the men marched silently. Gone for the moment their usual flippancy and buoyancy and desire for humorous repartee with all comers, there were so many still on the other side of Thiepval Ridge. All ranks were, it seemed, relieved when the battalion reached the open country and faced the ten miles' trudge to La Vicogne. Here the battalion slept for the night under apple and pear trees in an orchard."

On July 29th the backward trek was continued by route march to Bonneville, and the following day a four-hour march brought the 3rd to the picturesque Picardy village of Pernois. Here the task of reorganizing the battalion was continued, and the inevitable training operations were soon in full swing. While there were reasonable periods of rest, the men were not allowed to feel that this respite would be of long duration. Indications were many that the battalion would shortly be called upon to do some more "scrapping."

There was a certain amount of grumbling, as always, by a few—the "hard heads"; but the orders of the army commander—"Get the men into fighting trim and make every man physically fit"—were inexorable. There was no alternative. Now but a very small unit in a colossal assembly of troops, the battalion moved almost automatically according to a fixed schedule of days, hours, and minutes, which was plotted weeks in advance. An exacting high command had learned to calculate accurately just how long an infantry division could be expected to stand the strain of the fighting now in progress—so many days

LIEUT.-COL. E. S. BROWN
Killed in action.

LIEUT.-COL. D. M. McCONAGHY, C.M.G., D.S.O.
Killed in action.

LIEUT. J. HAMILTON, V.C.

in the initial attack, so many in reserve, so many in attack again. There was no escape.

The great battle of the Somme had now reached a stage when the conflicting armies might have been compared with giant wrestlers who, locked together in fierce and evenly-matched dispute, pause and fumble breathlessly for the decisive hold that will bring mastery. The tactical situation was such as almost to brand the British offensive as a total failure. The impregnable resistance of the German flanking fortress-positions at Thiepval and Guillemont was casting a shadowy eclipse upon hope of a decisive victory. British blood had been poured out like water, the utmost of sacrifice and heroism had been demanded and made by the flower of Empire troops. Yet, although the enemy appeared to be staggering and ready for the knock-out blow, there was not yet available to British arms any decisive answer to the German massed artillery and bravely served machine-guns.

On August 9th the 1st Australian Infantry Brigade retraced its steps to the line. By La Vicogne-Herissart-Vadencourt Wood the unit moved in stages that led to a bivouac on the brickfields near Albert. Among the new officers who now led platoons were Second-Lieuts C. O. Clark, H. Ferguson, R. B. Allport, C. Blumer, H. M. Bishop, J. V. Pestell, H. D. Robb, B. C. Berry, C. Leslie, and C. Sturt (all ex-sergeants), F. T. Maisey, E. R. Shelley, and C. T. Clifton (ex-privates). All subordinate ranks were again in full complement.

At Albert packs were dumped and "battle order" was donned. On the evening of August 15th began the long approach march, via Tara Hill and shelter trenches in the old British front line, where a brief halt was made, to the new front line in the Pozières Ridge—Mouquet Farm Sector. Rain was falling in torrents, and the chalky, shell-churned soil was soon a slippery quagmire that caused many hard falls and made the relief, begun before 1 a.m.

on the 16th, a movement of singular hardship. Most of the troops were unable to reach the front before daylight, and found it the most grotesque sector of the fighting front it had so far been their fortune to inhabit. Utterly featureless, a dun-coloured wilderness of inter-lipping craters strewn with corpses, this north-north-eastward slope of the Pozières ridge had become the most active section of the Anzac front.

General Gough's* tactics directed that the I Anzac Corps should continue to exploit the valuable ground gained on the Pozières heights by making northward thrusts along the old German third line, in order to seize the ground behind the large isolated Mouquet Farm and so command the rear of the stubborn bastion at Thiepval. To this end the 4th Australian Division had already struggled for more than a week against the redoubtable 16th (Rhineland) Division, which was supported on its flank by the 24th (Saxon). These German troops, supported by favourable ground and the almost fantastic situation of the attackers, had stoutly met every assault and had yielded ground only after the most bitter struggles. Evidence of this was apparent on all sides, and the 3rd Battalion stretcher-bearers were kept busy removing wounded of the 49th and 51st Battalions from isolated holes in No-Man's Land. Privates R. Pattinson and C. Clutterbuck, in particular, were conspicuous at this work in all the daylight hours, braving a very troublesome sniping fire. Pattinson was awarded the Military Medal for his work at Pozières.

The general situation was most dangerously obscure. The position held by the 3rd Battalion was the point of a sharp salient, some 1200 yards deep, that thrust like a horn into the left flank of the Mouquet Farm defences. On the left, fronting the farm—which was visible only as a heap of reddish rubble and tumbled wooden beams on

---

* General Sir Hubert Gough, commanding the Fifth Army.

the distant northward skyline—the 4th Battalion occupied the only really habitable trench in the whole Australian sector. The remainder of our defences, for the most part, were merely remnants of the churned-up German lines, fortified with such T-head saps as could be hastily constructed in the face of practically continuous artillery-fire. The lack of any natural feature from which trustworthy bearings could be taken made the recognition of map reference points extremely difficult, and this grave danger was immediately recognized by Lt-Col Howell-Price and his scout officer, Lieut R. F. Bulkeley, whose excellent survey work in the face of danger had been repeatedly commended. Here again, as in the first tour at Pozières, Lieut Bulkeley, supplied his information with an exactitude that was invaluable to his commanding officer, and was certainly the means of saving some lives, although, alas, not in time to save all.

The first suspicion that something was amiss came on the evening of the 16th, when, in answer to a call for fire on the battalion S.O.S. line on the occasion of a determined enemy counter-attack at 7.30 p.m., many of the shells of our side harassed the front and rear of the battalion's most forward lines. In spite of this and the heavy German barrage, our left company (A) assisted the 4th Battalion to drive off the attackers, but the losses were so heavy that, in order to strengthen the line, A Company was moved up from support on the afternoon of the 17th to take over portion of the 4th Battalion right flank.

This movement was immediately detected by the ever watchful enemy, and the curtain of fire—which, hour by hour, normally harassed the long and difficult lines of communication on this front—was immediately thickened, and progress of any sort towards the front line was almost entirely stopped. Troops could filter through only by short rushes, and this led to much confusion and loss. Less than one-third of A Company's personnel was reassembled in the line. Moreover, this movement doubtless put the enemy on the alert for the attack which was impending at this critical point. Much activity was observed along his shell-hole line, and his snipers, unusually aggressive along this front, added an extra spice of risk to all open movement in daylight. On the other hand our own riflemen accepted the German challenge, and found many fine targets. Our line, from left to right, was now held by A, B, C, and D Companies, under Lieuts Paul White, C. H. Howie, Captain J. G. Tyson and Lieut G. E. Blake respectively.

The northward thrust behind the Mouquet Farm was now planned for the late evening of August 18th, and when, on the 17th, the artillery liaison officer gave notice that preliminary demolition fire would at 6 p.m. that day be opened by "heavies" on a line corresponding to points R.34, a.3.8 and 9.9 on the maps, an urgent warning was immediately despatched by runner to brigade headquarters that the line indicated was actually a part of the 3rd Battalion's front line! Telephone communication was out of the question; so furious was the enemy's fire on every communication trench and track, that the signallers, toil as they might over their severed wires, were unable for nearly three whole days to get a line in working order. However, brave men—although they took two hours—ran the gauntlet with messages in an attempt to stay the artillery's fire. Unfortunately they were too late, and at 6 o'clock the British heavy guns opened fire and a proportion of their shells duly exploded in the 3rd Battalion's position with disastrous effect. Lieut R. F. Bulkeley was killed almost in the act of delivering a confirmation of his previous surveying observations.

While blame for this calamitous occurrence was hardly attachable to anyone, feeling in the battalion at the time was bitter. Only the skilful survey of Lieut Bulkeley, in an area from which every natural feature had been blasted, had detected the error in the accepted plan of the line, and, had telephone communication been possible, the disaster might not have occurred. As it was, the divisional staff only reluctantly accepted the correction after an aerial reconnaissance of the line, in which flares were lighted by the troops. Even so, there can be no doubt that, when the bombardment opened again on the evening of the 18th, there were still some British guns laid on to the line of the battalion's trenches. It might be here noted that, as several British divisions also took part in the attack, the strength of the supporting artillery employed was really enormous. Consequently the rechecking of its detail orders was probably a task of some difficulty.

The preparations for the attack were completed on the afternoon of the 18th, when the 1st Battalion relieved the three right companies of the 3rd and thus allowed them to concentrate further to the left front. This movement, carried out in broad daylight over open ground, was undoubtedly observed by the enemy, for much sniping and low shrapnel-fire gave on indication of his ready alertness and boded ill for the success of the attack.

At 8 p.m. our bombardment opened, and the enemy guns at once countered heavily from the front and either side of the narrow salient. This shelling continued until 10 p.m.—the hour fixed for the "hop-over." The assembly positions being badly wrecked, Lieut-Col Howell-Price ordered the attacking lines to stand fast, and pushed forward strong fighting-patrols to test the activity of the enemy, at the same time supporting the 4th Battalion with a bombing drive on the left flank. His caution proved to be most wise. As soon as contact was made with the German listening-posts, the whole enemy front directed a heavy cross-fire with rifles and machine-guns on taped ranges along the line of the objective.

The point of junction between the 16th and 24th German Divisions was directly opposite the 3rd Battalion's right front, but the enemy commanders acted in close harmony in their plan of defence. They had strict orders to prevent any further penetration in this area towards the "Fabeck Graben"—the line which guarded the Thiepval fortress—and their machine-guns were massed so as to bring intense enfilade fire to bear upon this already critical salient point. The 300 yards of extra ground which was inside the battalion's new objective was, therefore, absolutely untenable for trench-digging troops, although the plan of infiltration into shell-hole posts was possible. This plan was followed with a ready initiative which might well have been copied elsewhere on the front at this time. A couple of old German gun-pits were seized and occupied on the right front of the new line. This gave adequate flank protection on the left to the 4th Battalion's objectives, which were much deeper owing to its need to conform with the 3rd Battalion's already advanced line. But the 4th, meeting opposition similar to that experienced by the 3rd, could only filter forward into a line of shell-hole posts, most of which proved quite untenable in daylight hours. Further to the left, the British attacks were equally abortive.

On August 19th the troops were mostly concerned with an intolerable sleeplessness and fatigue and with the ceaseless scream and crash of German shells from all sides. There was little laughter anywhere. The labour conditions, too, were almost intolerable. Communication avenues were repeatedly blown in, and frequent calls had to be made for more and yet more men to volunteer to keep them open. The front lines were little more than wide shallow ditches strewn with the sad, still bodies of comrades newly slain. But worse than all this was the rankling sense of bitterness engendered by the short shooting of some of our supporting artillery. The men were ready and willing to assault, but, because their faith in the trustworthiness of their own artillery had been shaken, there was in the mind of every one of them a depressing doubt as to the final outcome of the struggle.

Rain, in insidious soaking showers, was a final damper to the spirits of the men. Already the losses of the battalion in this second immersion on the Somme were nine officers and 151 other ranks killed and wounded.

At 6 p.m. on August 19th, with the sun still high in the west, the 10th Battalion began to relieve the 3rd from the trenches opposite Mouquet Farm. At the time the German artillery was laying a shrapnel barrage on all tracks and communication trenches, but the relief was completed by 11 p.m. and the 3rd escaped without a casualty.

A weariness, the inexpressible weariness of body and mind similar to that of an athlete who has run himself to a standstill, was the paramount feeling of every man in the much-battered battalion as it filed out by way of Sausage Valley and other tracks to Albert. At no other time in its history, perhaps, was the 3rd Battalion ever to know such a deep feeling of despondency. Tired and worn, and silent with the memory of comrades who had fallen, there was a decided contrast between the feelings and appearance of these men and the strong companies which had moved forward over the same route four days before.

But this feeling of depression did not linger. Clear at last of the tumbled and chaotic ground of the Pozières crater-fields, and moving at last with light steps down the broad highway of the old Roman road that led to Albert, some of the old gaiety returned and tired feet picked up the rhythm of the march once more. The Ursna Tara Hill was crossed and soon the light of the gun flashes disclosed spasmodic views in silhouette of the battered streets of Albert, where, after crossing the square that was over-hung by the now familiar golden virgin on the tower of the great basilica, the battalion turned right into the Rue de Aveluy to find billets for the rest of the night, and an appetizing meal prepared by the cooks.

The battalion rested all that day in billets while Colonel Howell-Price and Lieuts Blake and Sturt attended an inquiry at Divisional Headquarters into the artillery inaccuracies during the recent fighting. At 8.30 a.m. on the 21st we marched out of Albert, via Bouzincourt and Senlis, over the rolling Picardy uplands to Warloy nestling in its green cup in the hills, and took over billets for the night. Next day the march was continued in very hot and oppressive weather via Contay and Herissart to Val-de-Maison, where the battalion went under canvas about noon.

Here energetic plans for re-organization and recreation were put in hand. The tented field the battalion now occupied had been Anzac rest camp, and the matter of absorbing 27 old hands (just returned from hospital) and 76 reinforcements, who were waiting there, was done at once. The more vital and delicate task of re-organizing the ranks of the battalion engaged the attention of the commander.

The men entered into the programme of sport and recreation with vim and vigour. At the concert held in the camp on that first evening, and at the sports meeting on the following day, the morale of the battalion was never better. To balance the sense of loss for comrades who had "gone west," there was a strong conviction that the unit had upheld the traditions of Anzac, and he men were able to laugh and sing and yet silently to prize their inner knowledge that all that courage and effort and self-sacrifice could do, had been done, and not in vain.

On the afternoon of August 23rd the whole brigade was reviewed at La Vicogne by General Birdwood, who presented ribbons to those who had been awarded medals for distinguishing themselves during the first tour at Pozières. The medical officer, Captain S. C. Fitzpatrick, and the late Lieutenant R. F. Bulkeley were honoured with the Military Cross, and Sergeant Douglas and Stretcher-bearer J. B. Saxby received the Distinguished Conduct Medal. The corps commander acted in sympathy with the general feeling when he cut his usual laudatory peroration short on this occasion. Then the battalion quick-stepped it back to camp to entertain itself with another concert and with the general's personal assurance that a move to Belgium was immediately imminent.

CHAPTER XXIV
TO BELGIUM

AT 9.30 on the following morning the move commenced with a long march to Gezaincourt, near Doullens, with a marching strength of 20 officers and 590 men. Next day final preparations for entraining were completed. To keep to the schedule the battalion mustered at 3 a.m. on Saturday, August 26th, in marching order, and by 5.45 the entrainment was completed at Doullens North Station. In addition to the troops, 71 horses, 2 four-wheeled waggons, 36 two-wheeled and 6 Lewis gun carts were entrained. Lieut Howie (O.C., B Coy) and 103 other ranks were temporarily left behind on entrainment duties.

The route followed was a short one, via St Pol and Hazebrouck, through the rich meadow-lands of the Artois region. After the bare hedgeless roads of Picardy and their stiff and regular lines of trees, the grassy glens beside the line seemed very calm and restful. To the east of the line, glimpses were to be had of the distant mine derricks and slag heaps of northern France. Presently the train rolled into the market-garden region north of Hazebrouck, where every possible inch of the ground is closely tilled, and the countryside is criss-crossed with paved roads and endless ditches and canals; and at last it came to a final halt at the old Flemish village of Poperinghe. Detraining at 1 p.m. the battalion was fifteen minutes later drawn up in readiness to move, and at 1.25 it marched off to the "Toronto" camp area (lately vacated by the Canadians), where a spell was enjoyed for the remainder of that day, and the next. Bathing parades, to Poperinghe, were enjoyed by every man in the unit.

On August 28th preparations were begun for the relief of the 10th British Brigade (4th Division) in the Hill 60 sector. During a preliminary inspection of the trenches Second-Lieut J. V. Pestell was shot through the head by a sniper and killed.

Rain fell continuously during this period, but the evening of the 31st was fine, and at 9.30 p.m. the battalion entrained in the "Ypres Express" at Brandhoek siding, arriving at Ypres Asylum siding twenty minutes later. The desultory long-range shelling of the siding and the line gave an added spice to this unusual method of proceeding to the trenches. The relief of the close support position was completed by midnight, battalion headquarters moving into the "Railway Dugouts," near Zillebeke. Only one casualty occurred, through a man slipping on the rough, muddy track and injuring his hip.

The battalion was now holding the right flank of the brigade front from the Ypres-Menin railway to Fosseway —a position that had seen much bitter fighting.

The following night A and B Companies took over the front-line trenches from the 2nd Battalion, Royal Dublin Fusiliers, C Company going into support and D into reserve.

The trenches and other defences in the sector were in a badly neglected state, and the German snipers had apparently been allowed to gain the upper hand. Heavy requisitions for engineers' material were immediately sent to brigade headquarters, and the work of cleaning and strengthening the defences was actively proceeded with for several days. Owing to the closeness of the opposing trenches—a bare thirty yards in some places—the work was extremely dangerous, for the enemy made the most of his temporary superiority by bombarding us with *minenwerfer* and rifle-grenades. In the first four days on this now comparatively quiet front our casualties were three killed and seven wounded.

What with drainage, rebuilding (especially in the firebays) and duckboarding, the trenches were soon put into a better defensive state. "Sniperscopes" were then introduced and experts in the use of these weapons soon quietened the enemy marksmen, the Australian advantage being manifest from the night of the first inter-company relief. Heavy rain on September 7th put a severe test on the constructional work, and parts of the trenches collapsed; but superiority of rifle- and grenade-fire kept the enemy low until repairs had been effected. On the night of the 6th the 1st Battalion relieved the 3rd, which moved back to supports at the dugouts under the embankment of the Ypres-Menin railway line, where there was ample accommodation for headquarters and A and C Companies. B and D Companies occupied neighbouring strong-posts. Large fatigue parties were supplied for various engineering works until September 12th, when at 11 p.m. the 11th Battalion took over, and the 3rd marched by way of the Lille Gate and "Shrapnel Corner" to Asylum siding, whither it entrained for Brandhoek and so to "Dominion Camp."

An active period of organization and vigorous training was now begun. At the same time a most welcome innovation was the establishment of well-stocked canteens, both wet and dry. Bathing parades were also a pleasing feature of this period. The list of Military Medal awards to men who had distinguished themselves during Pozières operations was promulgated here, and met with general approval.

The countryside around the camp was a source of never-failing interest to all with a bent for history. In particular, the ancient and once beautiful Flemish city of Ypres was the Mecca of eager sightseers, who spent many precious hours in examining its medieval ramparts and the remains of its other points of historic interest. Destruction was by now a commonplace to those accustomed to modern war, but there still remained in Ypres an abiding air of the dignity of age that the German artillery had been unable to efface.

On the evening of September 25th, the battalion returned to the line, taking over from the 7th Battalion support positions at the "Bluff" tunnels. Battalion Headquarters occupied Swan Château, about a mile south of Ypres, and for a fortnight the 3rd enjoyed a quiet time. As fighting was confined to desultory shelling and indirect machine-gun fire, it was possible to approach the forward positions in comparative safety. Gas precautions were, of course, never relaxed; and as the autumn was now well advanced and rain frequent, particular attention was paid to the care of the men's feet. Very large fatigue parties were again actively engaged, and they accomplished a considerable amount of engineering work. During this time some reinforcements, consisting of a few men from the 3rd Division in England, joined the battalion.

On the night of October 7th, we took over the front line from the 1st Battalion—a relief that occupied but forty minutes, from advance parties to final completion, and was easily the smartest in the battalion's record.

The line now held included the Bluff mine-craters on the right bank of the Ypres-Comines canal, and extended to the left close to the Verbrandenmolen road. The battalion fire at all times was superior to that of the enemy and our own patrols were active. On the brigade front during this tour rifle-grenades were lavishly expended, and an aggressive machine-gun fire was maintained by both Vickers and Lewis guns up to a nightly expenditure of 16,000 rounds. Trench mortars were active also.

With a view to identifying the German forces opposed to us, and, incidentally, to inflict losses upon them, a special party from the battalion raided the enemy trenches on the night of October 12th. This party (three officers and 44 other ranks), which had undergone four days' training for the purpose, climbed into No-Man's Land at 8.20 p.m., and crawled to within 35 yards of the enemy's line. When at 8.30 our artillery opened and the party rushed pell mell for the enemy trench, they were met with a heavy fusillade of bombs. Although an entry was made, so strong and stubborn was the resistance that the taking of prisoners was rendered impossible. One man was in fact secured, but, owing to his violent struggles, he had to be killed. Some twelve other Germans—who belonged to the III Battalion of the 416th Infantry Regiment, 204th (Württemberg) Division—were also killed in the mêlée.

The battalion lost one officer and three other ranks wounded, and one other rank (Private Frost) missing, believed killed. Throughout the rest of the night, patrols made a careful but unsuccessful search for him.

On the following night our tour in the Bluff tunnels ended, the 14th Battalion (4th Division) taking over the line. Once again our outward route was by way of the gaunt and melancholy ruin of Ypres and the handy relief train, and at 1.30 a.m. on the 14th the battalion was "all correct" in Dominion Camp. No time was lost here, however, for seven hours later we took the road to Steenvoorde, marching via Ouderdoom, Poperinghe, and Abeele. After a night in billets the march was resumed in perfect autumn weather, and before long the battalion was breasting the lower slopes of the noble, solitary hill of Cassel. This height, the most prominent feature of western Flanders, carried the road in a sudden rise of 500 feet above the plain, and from its crest a clear view was to be had over a wide stretch of France and Belgium. Officers and men were intensely interested in the few remaining traces of the ancient castle gate that had once guarded the entrance to the town, which still managed to retain something of its quaint medieval air, despite the fact that it had then housed the busy headquarters of the Second Army (General Plumer). As the battalion marched through its cobbled streets strict march discipline was maintained.

The battalion was now vastly improved both in fitness and spirit, in every way comparable with the old companies that had used the Cassel road for march exercises six short months before. But the men, having acquired a more certain knowledge of the task they had to do, were graver now and dourly efficient withal.

Six miles beyond Cassel a halt was made at Arneke, and next day the route was continued for thirteen miles, via Watou, with its massive Norman castle, and Bayenghem-lez-Eperlecques to the Château de Questmont, where the battalion was billeted for several days.

Preparations for the return of the I Anzac Corps to the Somme had for some weeks been in hand. Accordingly, at 1 a.m. on October 21st, the battalion marched six miles to St Omer, and immediately entrained. After passing through Calais, Boulogne and Etaples, our journey came to an end at Longpre, where billets were had at L'Etoile. On the 23rd a convoy of French motor buses conveyed the battalion from Mouflers to within four miles of Fricourt camp, and the return to the Somme front was an accomplished fact. The transport section of the battalion had, in the meantime, moved down by road.

CHAPTER XXV

FLERS

AFTER a tiring march over very muddy, sloppy, congested tracks we bivouacked near Fricourt under hastily erected tarpaulin shelters. The early winter rains which are a feature of this region had now set in, and the troops passed an uncomfortable night. But much worse was to follow, for next day, through very heavy rain, the march was continued another four miles to an open bivouac on a mud-hill near Mametz Wood.

The battalion now mustered 24 officers and 820 other ranks, and the procedure of moving in regulation manner over the congested country roads and tracks, which were giving way under the abnormally heavy traffic and the shelling of the last four months, was well-nigh impossible. The prolonged rains had turned them into quagmires in which long unending streams of men, guns, transport and ambulance waggons, caterpillar tractors and other paraphernalia of modern armies crawled and slithered and splashed on their way to and from the front. Little wonder, then, that the infantry could only filter through this mass of chaotic traffic.

The camp on the mud-hill was intended to be but a temporary halting place on our way to the line, to take part in a major operation, but the conditions on this muddy battlefield were such that further large-scale attacks were quite impossible. Very little shelter being available for the men on this now desolate moorland, "bivvies" were hastily built or burrowed in the chalk. To make matters worse, the impassable state of the roads

LIEUT.-COL. O. G. HOWELL-PRICE, D.S.O., M.C.
Killed in action.

3RD BATTALION GOING INTO RESERVE TRENCHES, ZONNEBEKE, NOVEMBER 5, 1917, FOR PASSCHENDAELE

Photo: *Aust. War Memorial Museum.*

caused delays in the delivery of the rations, so that all had often to go light. For several days much work was done by fatigue parties in repairing the roads under the very wheels of the traffic.

On October 28th final preparations were made for the relief of the 29th Division in the line. Full battle equipment was issued, including the familiar colour "attack" patch for sewing on the back of the tunic. At noon next day the companies, acting independently, abandoned the mud-hill and floundered forward through the crawling press of traffic to relieve the 16th Middlesex Regiment in close support at Trones Wood. The rain continued to fall steadily.

Various officers visited the front line daily in front of Flers, from Factory Corner to Gueudecourt, with a view to becoming acquainted with the position and with the routes to and from brigade, battalion, and the different company headquarters. Owing to the mud, conditions in the communication trenches were almost indescribable, while in many of the front-line posts men stood day and night in slush and mud up to their knees.

The road forward through Longueval and by Delville Wood was subjected to desultory shell-fire. It was a common sight to see small parties, and sometimes transport, caught by these sudden bursts. Casualties were often inflicted on troops who had just been relieved and were on their way out. On all sides there was much evidence of the wastage of war—wrecked guns, derelict tanks, overturned G.S. waggons, shell-lashed limbers, dead horses and mules, and a heterogeneous array of useless equipment. One unusual spectacle was the remains off-road of a fine staff car badly riddled by shell-fire.

On the night of October 28th, the enemy artillery, searching for the broad-gauge railway which ran from Meaulte and Fricourt to the rail-head at Bazentin, tossed some heavy shells round about our camp. No material damage, however, was done, although all hands had the "wind up" as clods of mud fell on the bivouacs.

After two days in the Trones Wood position, B and D Companies moved into the line in front of Cheese Road, between Gueudecourt and Grass Lane, relieving the 1st Battalion. A and C Companies went into support at Bull's Road, south-east of Flers. The front-line companies moved out into No-Man's Land and dug a new trench 150 yards in front of the old one, which had become just a wet, muddy ditch, quite uninhabitable. The new line was deep, clean, and wide—till the next rain fell—when it also became a morass and in places impassable.

The communication trench from company headquarters in Cheese Road to the line was so bad that at night all traffic deserted it and went across country. In daylight it was simply a case of trying to flounder through the slush, or of going over the top and risking enemy snipers who, fortunately for us, had their own problems and so were not particularly troublesome.

In the ruins of Gueudecourt, over a small rise to the battalion's right rear, a heavy shell would regularly land every few minutes, the enemy apparently being determined to keep his opponents, if possible, away from the dugouts and other shelter there. These shelters would have been invaluable for rest and protection for a portion of the garrison in this muddy sector, and would have enabled the men to dry their feet at intervals, thus minimizing the risk of trench feet.

Early on November 2nd, Lieut-Col O. G. Howell-Price and Lieut L. W. S. Loveday were standing in a machine-gun sap running forward from the main firing line, discussing details of an attack to be carried out by the 1st Battalion within a day or two. At the time there was coming from the German line a considerable amount of sniping fire, directed at ration parties on their way forward. Howell-Price had just given an order for one of our machine-guns to retaliate when he appeared to stumble, and fell across Loveday's arm. Loveday thought he had fainted, but on lifting him up found his own arm covered with blood. The colonel had been shot in the face, the bullet lodging in the base of the skull.

The sad and depressing news of our gallant leader's wounding spread through the lines like wildfire. Padre B. C. Wilson, who was with the battalion at the time, afterwards wrote: "As eight ambulance men were preparing to carry their colonel out to the nearest ambulance post, one thousand shell-hole-strewn yards away, two men of the battalion, Sergeant-Major Douglas and Corporal McLachlan, stepped up and brushed the bearers aside. Douglas said, 'No one else must carry our colonel out.' And these N.C.Os would not allow one of the bearers to touch the stretcher during the long, dangerous trek to the dressing station."

Lt-Col Howell-Price lingered for two days, only once, and for a very short period, regaining consciousness. Major J. W. B. Bean—our original R.M.O., who happened then to be specially attached to the British casualty clearing station outside Heilly, to which the C.O. had been taken—asked Howell-Price if there was anything he could do for him. "Only one thing, Doc," was the reply; "Will you write a note to the Padre and ask him to give my love to the battalion." Those were Howell-Price's last words. Relapsing into unconsciousness, he died shortly afterwards. But those words summed up the whole of his service in the A.I.F.—love for the battalion. Underlying all his sternness and austerity was a deep and single-minded loyalty to his unit—a unit to which he devoted so unsparingly the last years of his life.

Undoubtedly there were men in the A.I.F. who equalled Howell-Price in courage, resource, and leadership, but there was surely none who held a deeper and more secure place in the hearts and minds of his men and fellow officers—a man *sans peur et sans reproche*.

Pending the return of Major Moore from hospital, where he was recovering from wounds received at Pozières, Captain A. F. Burrett was appointed to the temporary command of the battalion. The senior captain, J. R. O. Harris, had the previous day gone to the 1st Divisional School at Tirancourt as second-in-command.

At 12.30 a.m. on November 5th the 3rd Battalion acting in co-operation with the 1st Battalion, which assembled in the front line to attack "Bayonet Trench," raided "Lard Trench." Several attempts had previously been made by British troops to capture this position, but each had failed.

The leadership of the 3rd Battalion's operation was entrusted to Lieut Loveday, who had spent several nights reconnoitring the German lines. His force was split into three parties, as follow:

No. 1 Party: Lieut L. W. S. Loveday, 8 bombers, 17 infantry, 2 runners, 1 Lewis gun and 3 gunners, 2 stretcher-bearers.

No. 2 Party: Lieut L. F. Kemmis, 8 bombers, 17 infantry, 2 runners, 2 stretcher-bearers.

No. 3 Party: Lieut H. McK. Bishop, 8 bombers, 17 infantry, 2 runners, 2 stretcher-bearers.

As soon as the barrage crept forward in Lard Trench, No. 1 party was to rush the trench and bomb forward to a position on the left of an old roadway and there establish a strong-post. No. 2 party was to co-operate with the 1st Battalion, and No. 3 would push forward when the other two had entered Lard Trench and would consolidate the position.

Before leaving the lines to take up a preliminary position in No-Man's Land, Loveday addressed his men and told them that they now had an excellent opportunity to avenge the death of their colonel.

"It was," wrote one of the party, "a dirty night in more ways than one, dark, wet and terribly muddy." As the artillery-fire lifted, Loveday yelled "Come on," and made for the only gap in the wire—or where the only gap had been the day before. It was too dark to see anything, but they plunged through the mud and the retaliatory barrage, for by now the Germans were wide awake and shelling heavily. Loveday was the only member of the party who knew where the gap was, but the majority of the men were old hands and all knew their job. Privates Weger and Meaker, who were following him, had been selected as the two first bayonet-men, with instructions to slip one each side and "start the dirty work" as soon as they encountered the enemy. Their moment came when Loveday got a bullet through the sleeve of his tunic. By the light of the gun flashes they saw German helmets glistening with wet. Everything went like clockwork. Weger and Meaker—both about six feet and very brave soldiers—carried out their orders to the letter. Then began a particularly fine piece of work with bomb and bayonet. After each bay was bombed, the bayonet-men finished off those who were unlucky enough to survive. Behind came others, who ferreted Germans out of shelters which had been cut into in the straight part of the trench and covered with waterproof sheets and gas blankets.

One of the chaps with less experience than the others found a German in a shelter and reported the fact to a sergeant. The latter told him to "fix" the German, but the private said he couldn't kill a man that way. The sergeant said, "Go on, you haven't killed one yet; I'll give you one more chance and then I'll fix him myself." The other still delayed, so the N.C.O. stuck his bayonet through the blanket and the German.

"When we had fought our way half the length of the trench," says one of the raiders, "we caught a German, smaller than the others, who could speak some English, and, instead of killing him, 'booked' him and passed him round the traverse of the trench. Loveday decided to keep him for identification purposes, 'frisked' him for bombs, knife, and artillery, and told him to come along with us. We couldn't have saved anyone better, because when they got him back to headquarters he gave about four pages of information about the Germans engaged opposite the Australian lines. He even knew the number of men in Luisenhof Farm and the names of the commanders.

"Finally we reached the end of the trench with three other prisoners in tow. There we set to work to dig in on the top of the bank and just this side of another trench occupied by the Germans who had been left for dead in the trench below."

Loveday placed the Lewis gun on the left flank, because he expected to be attacked from that direction as soon as dawn broke. In the event of the 1st Battalion not succeeding, it would mean that the Germans would be in front, behind, and on the left of him. When the gun was tested, it fired a burst or two and then went out of action. Almost immediately German flares went up behind our men, and Loveday knew that the 1st Battalion attack had failed and this, his, position was practically untenable. However, his orders were to hold on. The engineers who had been detailed to follow up the 3rd Battalion and help in the work of consolidation had not arrived, and it was imperative to make the position stronger. He thereupon decided to send back for two more machine-guns and ammunition, as well as bombs and reinforcements. Some of the best men were wounded, and none of the others, good soldiers as they were, fancied the job of taking a message back to battalion headquarters. Not sure of the way, it would have been dangerous enough to go back through the heavy barrage and the mud, but now there was the added danger of running into the enemy whose whereabouts were not precisely known.

Loveday, who considered that Sergeant Yorke had done enough fighting that night to last him a year, explained the position to him and asked if he would try and get back with a message. Yorke replied laconically, "All right, I'll go back through the trench and fix up those —— Huns, their moaning has been getting on my nerves." So Loveday wrote, "Home and dried. Send two machine-guns, bombs and ammunition."

Loveday, who thought a great deal of Yorke, hated to think of anything happening to him, but Yorke got back to headquarters, and after delivering the message was told he could go to the reserve line and rest. He refused point blank, saying that he was "Going back to the boy (Loveday) and the mob."

Yorke then guided back to the strong-post a party under Lieut H. Robb. By 4 a.m. a trench had been dug 200 yards long and about three feet deep, with two machine-gun saps. Everything was ready for the counter-attack, and the raiders were ready to "bump off" a few of the enemy before themselves being "bumped off."

"Then," to quote the previous writer, "at daybreak a message was received that, as the other attack had failed, we were to get out and get out quickly. After all the good hard work, the men were almost disappointed at leaving such a nice home and not being allowed to see what it was like to be attacked on three sides at one time. After a lot of growling we began to crawl homewards. It was foggy, and we had to move as quickly as possible. The small German prisoner stuck to Loveday, occasionally informing all and sundry, 'Der Kaiser ist no blutty goot,' etc. The other prisoners 'went for a stroll.'

"Loveday told us to follow him and, if we ran into the German lines, to throw all we had with us and get over to the left, where we must run into Australian lines somewhere. This happened, and eventually we reached our own trenches.

"Loveday had told us the night before that there was to be no rum issue before the fight, but that if only one man came out of the stunt he would get the full issue, two jars. The survivors got the rum as promised and began to sample it, the German prisoner in their midst moistening his tongue with envy. Loveday said, 'Well, the stunt is over, why don't you give him some.' It hadn't struck us that Germans could drink rum just as well as we could. So we filled a big mug full and he tossed it off like granny tossing off gruel. After a couple more he was led off, reciting like a parrot his piece, 'Der Kaiser no blutty goot ist . . . ,' only this time loud enough for the Kaiser back in Potsdam to hear him."

Lieut Kemmis's party, after killing a few of the enemy, had met with heavy opposition, and was compelled to retire. Bishop's linked up with Loveday's and helped to consolidate his position.

In all, five members of the 101st (Saxon) Regiment were captured, and it was estimated that 35 of the enemy were killed. Our casualties were four men killed and 22 wounded.

For their good work and bravery that night Weger and Meaker each received the Distinguished Conduct Medal, and Loveday and Kemmis the Military Cross. Loveday recommended Sergeant Yorke for a decoration, but was informed that the brigade commander had already noted him for an award. Six months later Yorke was shot through the brain by a German sniper while gallantly attacking at Bullecourt.

Later in the day Lieut Bishop and nine men were killed by the short-shooting of British heavy artillery. Bishop, who had been promoted from C.Q.M.S. in August, had a happy, smiling disposition, and his passing was regretted by all ranks. There was nothing the infantryman hated more than shells from his own artillery falling short. He would stand any amount of shelling from the enemy, but short-shooting by his own guns quickly demoralized him.

On November 6th Lieut "Nobby" Clark returned from a school of instruction and was detailed to proceed to a training battalion in England. It was with mixed feelings that we saw him go. He had earned and needed a spell from active service, but his cheery countenance and happy personality were missed from the battalion for six months.

During the afternoon of the 7th, the 3rd Battalion was relieved by the 11th. Two companies went back to Trones Wood and two to the switch trenches south-east of Flers, headquarters being in Flers itself. The next four days were occupied, as far as the surrounding conditions would permit, in a general clean-up, and the four nights—during which the greater portion of the battalion was employed in digging and on carrying fatigues—in getting dirty again.

The digging parties were located in Chalk Lane, a communication trench running from Bull's Road, east of Flers, to Cheese Road, where close supports and front-line company headquarters existed. Chalk Lane was eight feet deep, and wide enough for two men to move abreast. Those who were not digging were engaged in carrying forward a variety of material. At any time during the night long strings of men, led by an officer and a guide and followed by a sergeant, could be discerned carrying duckboards, A frames, revetting material, sand-bags, corrugated iron, ammunition, bombs (in boxes of 12), two-gallon tins of water (often tasting strongly of petrol), picks, shovels, and the hundred-and-one things required by a battalion in the line.

Just after dusk and before daylight were to be seen, or heard, the ration parties going up to the forward positions, and an everlasting vote of thanks is hereby given to all quartermasters and their staffs for their devotion to the troops, especially when in the line. Each morning hot porridge and tea came up in what were really huge Thermos flasks, and sometimes, in addition, an issue of rum. Of an evening the flasks would contain hot stew and hot tea; bread, butter, jam, etc., were packed in sandbags. These hot meals, which went astray so seldom in normal times, meant a great deal to the men in the line and in a large degree helped to maintain that cheery optimism which always distinguished the Diggers.

On November 10th, thirty-two kite balloons ("sausages") and fifty-two aeroplanes, all British, were visible in the air at the one time. On the 13th the battalion was relieved by the 49th (4th Division), and we moved by easy stages to the rear. The first night was spent at Bernafay Wood, but a low-trajectory naval gun firing over our bivouac put sleep out of the question. The next night, at Fricourt, just behind the old British front line of July 1st, we got into the first clean bivouac for three weeks. Here the battalion was issued with pay, made a creditable toilet, and enjoyed a good night's sleep. In the morning we embussed for Buire and went into billets, and the following day moved to Flesselles for rest and training.

It was at Flesselles that the adjutant, Lieut R. Agnew, reported back from a school of instruction. For the next nine days the battalion practised a variety of training, going through section, company, and battalion drill. Fortunately there was little marching during this period, as a number of the men were sore-footed after three weeks with their feet continually soaked.

On Sunday, November 19th, a commemoration service was held for the late Lt-Col O. G. Howell-Price, representatives from the other units of the 1st Brigade attending.

The opportunity was taken of sending officers to various schools of instruction—Howie to the Fourth Army school;

MacDougall and Ormiston to the 1st Divisional school, at Tirancourt; Jackson to the Lewis gun school, at Le Touquet, where the instruction was good and the hours short, and where the troops had ample opportunity for inspecting golf links, tennis courts, and the V.A.Ds on the sea front. Incidentally, it was noticed that the C.O. always selected single, unattached officers for the L.G. school. Lieut Clifton also was detached from the battalion at this time, for duty at 3rd Brigade headquarters.

After training at Flesselles, the battalion moved back to Buire for corps fatigues. Two companies marched daily to Dernancourt to assist in the repair of and general work on billets under the superintendence of an R.E. company. On their return each evening these companies were met by the band at the big A.S.C. dump mid-way between the villages, and played back to their billets. It was noticed that the members of the band always wore their packs and regularly met the companies close to a large coal dump, and that before long the packs became blacker and blacker. Other parties were daily employed at other A.S.C. dumps, unloading lorries containing all manner of supplies.

The total casualties in the battalion during November were 2 officers and 32 other ranks killed, and 1 officer and 70 other ranks wounded. R.S.M. Sid Rudkin and R.Q.M.S. Doug. Oakley, both of whom had been with the battalion since its formation, were now given commissioned rank. None in his respective branch knew his work better than either of these men. Rudkin remained with us for a further ten months, until he was badly wounded at Broodseinde, and Oakley until the end of hostilities in 1918.

All ranks were pleased to welcome Major D. T. Moore back to the battalion after recovering from wounds he received at Pozières. Shortly afterwards he was promoted to the rank of lieutenant-colonel, and commanded the battalion till the end of the war. Quiet and unassuming, one of the youngest battalion commanders in the A.I.F., Moore was never known to be upset, no matter how serious the situation or what the crisis. He had joined the battalion as a lieutenant on its formation, and received both his captaincy and majority in Gallipoli, where he was severely wounded during the Lone Pine engagement.

Captain F. C. Kemp also returned in December to command A Company. It was a month of much rain, and all working parties had to carry out their duties under very uncomfortable conditions. Orders received on the 14th for four officers to proceed to the front line gave reason for the belief that the unit would soon be on the move forward again. Later came directions to relieve the 8th Battalion on the 22nd in the sector we now knew so well—between Gueudecourt and Factory Corner.

CHAPTER XXVI

WINTER WARFARE

ALL ranks now saw in orders "Joe" Burrett's promotion to major.

Before the battalion moved up to the front 140 partly trained reinforcements joined. With them came an order to the effect that they were not at present to be used as garrison troops in the front line, but only as carrying parties in the forward area. The move forward started on the 20th, the first night being spent at "Melbourne" camp (Mametz), the following one at Bernafay B camp, and the relief of the 8th Battalion in the line taking place during the next afternoon and evening.

"When the battalion marched out from Melbourne camp on December 21st, 1916," wrote Private W. H. Nicholson, "a sharp snow-storm had whitened all the route via Montauban to Bernafay, where we camped in little shelters for the night. Those who were 'hardheads,' forewarned by their knowledge of previous hardships in this part of the line, immediately turned to advantage the last few hours of daylight and foraged far and near for whatever extra canteen stores their luck allowed them to find. Canteens were few and far between thereabouts, and even a hard walk of two or three miles was not considered fruitless if it produced an extra tin of coffee and milk or a couple of spare 'Tommy Cookers.'"

Next evening, after making ready, the battalion moved up by way of Delville Wood and the now well-duck-boarded "Cavalry Track" to the support positions in the

Gueudecourt sector. That elegant wooden footway was a world removed from the old slippery, muddy slough through which the battalion previously struggled to the line, and so were the tunnels newly excavated in the chalk and occupied behind the support lines. That someone had laboured mightily was very clear. Members of the unit all felt very kindly towards the brawny Australian pioneers. Whole companies could now shelter securely in those burrow-like chambers, and, what was vastly more important, they would be out of the wet.

"What did it matter," wrote Private Nicholson, "if there was only room to sit up and sleep? What did it matter if you had every part of your anatomy tramped upon by the muddy boots of the inevitable traffic that moved up and down in the rich purple fog of the tunnel? For a few hours at least you were safe from that freezing, soaking sleet that sifted persistently down from the dark and lowering winter sky. For a few hours at least you could relax into a restful slumber and, furthermore (oh, blessed relief!), you could slip off your sodden boots and tenderly massage the agony of cramp from your long-suffering feet."

That tour of duty called for 36 hours of front-line work, alternately by each half-battalion of the brigade. The support companies had to supply the hot-ration fatigues for the men in the outpost-line. Punctually at midnight, the men detailed for the work would emerge from their subterranean burrows and move off in Indian file into the pitch-black, rainy dark to where the village of Flers showed its ragged outline of shell-blasted trees in the bottom of the valley. And no time was ever lost. By some happy trick of efficiency the smoky "babbling brooks" were always ready. A short approach-march up the deserted main street to where the cook-house was sheltered by a partially shattered wall; a short pause to gulp down a pannikin of strong, hot tea.... And then away on the two-mile trek up to the line.

Two trips were made each night, about eight miles in all. But such miles! Wading all the way through half-frozen slush, strafed unmercifully when the enemy detected the approach, only the grateful thanks of the hungry men in the freezing outposts made the march at all tolerable.

The communication trenches were ignored at all times by the hot-food parties, partly because they were for the most part well nigh impassable, partly because the trick of carrying the heavy, steel thermos containers seemed to call for unlimited elbow room. Bad falls in plenty were the lot of the carriers; and, on returning at dawn to the entrance to the tunnels, it was their usual practice to wade thigh-deep in the nearest shell-hole, so that the thickest of the outer layers of yellow slime might be washed away from saturated boots and puttees, before descending underground to sleep in steaming, rain-sodden clothes.

Christmas eve was the auspicious night selected for the first inter-company relief. The relieving companies for the right half-sector, close to Gueudecourt village, had barely struggled up to the line and taken over, when a chance 77mm. shell found its billet in one of the outposts. The resultant casualties proving to be too much for the already over-worked company stretcher-bearers, volunteers were called for.

The men who volunteered that night for that extra bit of service will never be likely to forget it in this life. Sponsored by the energetic and somewhat excitable "Darky" Scott, a company bearer, the volunteers found their burdens already chilled to helplessness by the biting cold. Swinging them up shoulder high, the bearers began their march, six men to each stretcher. They were hardly clear of the sunken road at Fritz's Folly before the colossal nature of their task confronted them. The rain, which for three days had poured with relentless persistency, had by now joined every shell-hole into a brimming, waist-deep marsh where the depth of the darkness was rendered even more confusing by the occasional ghostly gleam of a soaring enemy flare. To walk upright under such conditions was utterly impossible. Every man fell time and again into freezing, waist-deep water. A bare six hundred yards, someone guessed it was, from that sunken road to the regimental aid-post, but that trip took nearly three hours!

Christmas Day 1916 was mostly distinguished, at least in the 3rd Battalion, for a remarkable shortage of things to eat. Instead of the hearty Yuletide cheer (not to mention beer!) of numberless Australian Christmases which had gone before, dry bread liberally plastered with yellow mud was the common lot, and everyone was wet and cold and comfortless to boot. The rain kept on until nearly midday, and in almost everybody's "bivvy" and dugout the water problem was acute. But that night the hot-ration parties struggled up with hot stew, and there was even a suggestion of Christmas duff—one small plum pudding to forty men!

On Christmas Day the unit lost Padre B. C. Wilson, who was transferred to the 3rd Division. What a great chap he was, and how the men loved him! What a cheery soul in the mess! His place was taken by Stacy Waddy, a former headmaster of The King's School at Parramatta. Many King's School boys in the brigade gave him a warm welcome.

A splendid, fine, clear day followed that inclement Yuletide, and visibility was so good that for those who wanted it there was excellent shooting to be had at the incautious Boche who went wandering in rear of his lines, thus providing that little touch of sport which always goes with the antipodean Boxing Day.

The inter-company relief again took place on the night

HARBONNIERES. 3RD BATTALION FOLLOWING UP AFTER ATTACK BY A.I.F.,
8TH AUGUST, 1918

Photo: *Aust. War Memorial Museum.*

3RD BATTALION N.C.O's, TAKEN AT METEREN, 1918

of the 27-28th, and the relieved company, on reaching the support tunnels, had immediately to make a forced march back to the outposts, with containers of hot food for the garrison there.

Every man now was beginning to feel the exhausting effect of the bitterly antagonistic climatic conditions. When a soldier stumbled and fell with his load, it was almost impossible for him to rise unassisted. The rain had now resumed its pitiless downpour, and the indirect fire of enemy machine-guns and whizz-bangs had the communication trails so nicely "taped" that the casualties among the carrying parties were becoming increasingly heavy. The unfailing regularity of the methodical Boche did, however, supply a remedy for the worst of those periodical shell storms. By taking note of their exact time and location, a certain amount of trouble could be avoided.

On the 28th the line was shelled rather severely, and the battalion lost one of its best-liked and most valuable officers in Lieut C. S. Shappere (of Blayney, N.S.W.). An old Fort-street High School boy, keen and capable, the life and soul of any party out of the line, he died as he would have wished when his turn came—doing his job in the front line.

The winter weather had now set in with redoubled severity, and down underground in the support tunnels the discomfort was almost as bad as it was in the line. Packed tight with hundreds of rain-soaked, steaming bodies, the badly ventilated caves were most unhealthy, and it was only a sleepless and weary company of men that moved out again on the evening of the 30th to take up the outpost-line anew. Rain fell in torrents. The posts were knee-deep in water, which the efforts of the half-dozen men could do little to check.

Withdrawing at dawn from the most advanced outposts, the weary garrison of Fritz's Folly found there were yet other excitements in store for them. About 11 a.m., the first shell from a long 11-inch naval gun heralded its approach with a high-toned menacing scream, and for the next two hours those great four-feet needle-pointed shells continued to arrive with unfailing regularity and with disconcerting accuracy. Their target was the three old German dugouts which sheltered the full garrison of the Fritz's Folly Post, and the plan to destroy them had evidently been well prepared. The loading and firing of an 11-inch gun is no simple matter, and the fact that artillery of such heavy calibre was being used on them served, strange as it may seem, to heighten rather than dampen the spirits of the beleagured troops. In the first hour some thirty shells fell in dangerous proximity. The fuses being timed for demolition purposes, each huge projectile had to penetrate some fifteen feet of earth before the explosion. In consequence, a distinct pause followed the impact of each shell.

Down in the congested dugouts the discomfort occasioned by these violent concussions was very marked. Lights would not burn, and the air was expelled from the underground rooms so violently that everyone was frequently left gasping for breath. Jokes and jeers greeted each successive miss on the part of the enemy artillerymen, but, as the morning drew on, this hilarity gave way to a feeling of exasperation; and then, about noon, there arrived the only shell, of some sixty fired, that was fated to score a hit.

Bursting directly on the centre dugout that was D Company's headquarters, the shell simply crushed it in. Fortunately, most of the company staff had already prepared to evacuate their threatened position, but one officer, Lieut A. O. Duprez, was entombed beneath the wreckage. Volunteer relays were organized immediately to set him free. Willing hands were soon at work, under Sergeant Murn and others, but because of repeated falls of earth due to the continuous bombardment, and the difficulty of forcing a passage through the crushed and splintered dug-out timbers, little progress was made until axes and saws were obtained. Messengers were sent, and the necessary tools fortunately were found quite handy in the possession of one of the ubiquitous engineers. Efforts to free the imprisoned officer were then redoubled. But although every man had to risk his life repeatedly in that hazardous labour, and although there was no lack of ready volunteers for the feat that undoubtedly earned more decorations than were afterwards awarded, Lieut Duprez, when freed, was injured to such an extent that he never rejoined the battalion.

It was with this knowledge of loss that the men faced their last night of outpost duty in the Gueudecourt sector of the line. The cold was now intense, and every man suffered severely from cramps. Tortured by the biting frost, there was at least one case of fatal collapse due to exposure. At the end of that last long night everyone felt that the limit of his endurance had been passed. Yet it was not until 11 p.m. next evening that the 4th Battalion men came in and took over the outpost-line.

Mateship was never more evident in the ranks of the 3rd Battalion than on that weary march out of Gueudecourt. In the inky dark, weakened to the point of collapse by the cruel conditions, many of the sick men would have found the route impossible had it not been for the ready assistance of their hardier mates. For every sick man there was always a willing arm and shoulder, and no mate was abandoned until he was either in the good care of an R.A.P., or sound asleep in some handy shelter in the muddy ditch that was the reserve line.

Then, warmed to his heart's core by a very meagre issue of army rum (hallowed memory!), every soldier laid himself down to sleep in the sloppy Somme mud, comforted with the certain knowledge that he had laboured and endured to the last in the worthy company of determined men.

Captain A. L. Hewish, newly promoted, now returned to battalion from the 1st M.G. Company, with which he had served for nine months. Those of the troops who had served under him in the machine-guns were especially glad to see him. Alas, in another short nine months he made the supreme sacrifice on the muddy slopes of Broodsiende Ridge.

About this time Lieut Eric Shelley had what he considered to be his narrowest escape from death. Stepping down into a trench at Bull's Road to speak to his platoon sergeant, he took a pace forward to avoid a large puddle of water, when a nose-cap from an "archie" landed in the puddle, covering both him and the sergeant with mud and water.

Our casualties for December were—1 officer and 4 other ranks killed; 1 officer and 18 others wounded. Since arriving in France the battalion had experienced a momentous nine months. Many good friends had been lost and many new ones made. What did 1917 have in store? Would the war be over by the end of the year. The prospect did not appear at all inviting.

New Year's Day 1917 found the battalion in Gap and Switch trenches, south-east of Flers, busy digging and carrying, and improving accommodation "possies," as far as the weather and general conditions would allow. The enemy artillery was paying much attention to the duckboard track from brigade headquarters in Longueval Valley to Bull's Road, along which there was a constant stream of traffic, day and night.

Relieved by the 46th Battalion on January 6th, the 3rd moved back to Bendigo camp for the night. Next day it proceeded to Quarry Siding, entrained for Méaulte, and marched thence to Ribemont, where it enjoyed the much-needed three days' rest ordered by the divisional commander. Rugby football matches, both inter-company and inter-battalion, were played; when the game between the 3rd and 4th Battalions took place, the field was deep in mud. At the start, the costumes were of various styles and shapes and colours, but before many minutes were out they were at least all one colour. This was the first of many enjoyable matches played against the 4th Battalion.

On January 13th the 3rd Battalion left Ribemont for Baizieux, staying there under canvas until the 23rd. Here all manner of training was indulged in, interspersed with lots of football and snow-fights, and concert parties at night. Heavy snow and a hard freeze made conditions clean and a welcome change from the mud which had persisted for so long. At Baizieux we met the 1st Battalion in a football match. Before long the field was beaten down into hard frozen snow on which the players found difficulty in keeping their feet, and they quickly learned that it was very hard to fall upon. Nevertheless it was all very enjoyable. Our worthy adjutant, Rupert Agnew, scored the only try of the match.

All ranks were now gratified to hear that their late C.O., Lieut-Col O. G. Howell-Price, had been awarded the D.S.O. The only regret was that he was not still with the unit to receive in person the honour which he had so richly earned.

On the morning of January 23rd the battalion marched out of Baizieux for the village of Bécourt, where the military encampment consisted of Nissen bow-huts. Few members of the A.I.F.—or of other units, for that matter—who spent a winter's night in a Nissen hut can truthfully say they did not pull out some of the lining boards for use as firewood in the Canadian slow-combustion stoves with which these were equipped. During our three days' sojourn at Bécourt, a large proportion of the battalion was engaged in working for the engineers. It was while here that the pleasing news arrived of the award of the D.C.M. to Sergeant "Bill" Hatton, M.M., for further conspicuous work in action. From a musketry school Lieut Hugh Robb, full of information, returned with his usual smile.

Then an officer and some N.C.Os went forward to take over Bazentin camp, to which the battalion was due to move on the morrow. Next day (27th) we relieved the 4th Yorks and the 4th East Yorks in No. 1 camp there. This was one of the rare occasions on which the battalion took over from an English regiment.

The Eaucourt-l'Abbaye sector to which the 1st Brigade was now allotted was some 2000 yards north-west of the old Gueudecourt-Factory Corner region of awful memory. Much of the material for the line was now pushed up on trolleys running on light railway tracks. This welcome innovation lightened enormously the work of the carrying parties, which had been such a burden during the previous periods in the line.

The battalion was here split into halves, B and D Companies being stationed at Yarra reserve, near battalion headquarters, and A and C Companies (under the command of Captain F. C. Kemp) in Flers reserve, some 1000 yards south-east of battalion headquarters. On the afternoon of January 28th, a hurricane bombardment was opened on A and C Companies, four men being killed and two wounded.

In the forward area, conditions were now very different. Gone was the foul and treacherous mud, into which the troops had been liable to sink knee- or thigh-deep, and even, if help was not at hand, to smother; and gone with it was that utter exhaustion and leg-weariness which had attended any effort to cross the old Somme battlefield. But with the passing of the mud went its single redeeming feature—the muzzling of the high-explosive shell-bursts. The mud had often-times allowed a shell to bury itself three to five feet in the ground before bursting, thus minimizing the force and devastation of the explosion. Now on the frozen ground there would be a crash, stinging the ear drums, and shell-fragments would fly horizontally far and wide. As the fumes from each blast discoloured the snow, it was an easy matter to plot the enemy barrage-lines after a shoot. Nevertheless, in spite of the more disastrous shell-bursts, the going was clean and hard, and was appreciated by everyone. Digging on the surface was of course out of the question, but much work went on underground, where shelters and accommodation at company headquarters were constructed.

January 30th was a day of promotions in the battalion. R.S.M. C. L. Smith, Sgts A. S. McMaster, and H. L. Dill were elevated to commissioned rank. McMaster, who came from Adamstown, was one of the most promising junior officers. The battalion, unfortunately, did not have him for long, for he gave his life gallantly leading his platoon at Hermies on April 9th. Dill, who belonged to Brewarrina, had been hit at Pozières, and, six days after McMaster's death, he was severely wounded at Hermies, and never fully recovered. He died in Sydney in 1923. Smith (of Newtown, N.S.W.) was killed at Merris on June 24th, 1918.

On the last day of January, the 3rd took over from the 1st Battalion in the front line, the right of the brigade sector. Muffled to the eyes in woollens, wearing leather or sheepskin jerkins beneath their greatcoats, with sandbags carefully wrapped round their boots, and carrying a varied assortment of military stores and gear, the companies straggling forward in single file over the crest of High Wood ridge might well have been mistaken for a party of gold-seekers rushing to the Klondyke over the High Divide.

The position occupied—Yarra Bank—faced a German stronghold known as The Maze, which had resisted several frontal attacks by both British and Australian troops. B and D Companies held the front line for the first spell of four days, being then relieved by A and C.

The cold that now gripped the devastated area of the Somme battlefield had frozen the crust of the earth to a depth of about four feet, and new problems arose. Probably the most difficult was how to approach the forward outposts over sloping snow-covered ground, entirely exposed to the view of a hostile enemy. For the most dangerous patrols and listening posts, white overalls of a nightgown pattern were provided, and these proved to be an excellent method of disguise. For the normal outposts, and the positions within seventy yards of the enemy, the men had to find their way forward by whatever means they could. Very little ingenuity, however, was necessary, for it soon became apparent that the enemy also was being harassed by the weather and for the moment was more concerned with his own problems.

"Yarra Bank was a place where the trenches had all been about six feet deep with five feet of water in them," wrote Lieut Geoff. Leslie. "When the frost came the water froze and the trenches were only a foot or so deep. The troops on both sides had to wriggle along them on their tummies or get shot. We fraternized in this sector, for the first and only time that I can remember. No one fired at the enemy for about three days. Anyone could walk openly along the trench parapet to within 40 yards of the German line, and their rifles would remain silent. We signalled and shouted to each other across No-Man's Land. A party of six or seven Germans sat on their parapet and invited us to share a jar of something that looked very much like 'S.R.D.' We were reluctantly compelled to decline.

"The unofficial armistice ended in a peculiar way. My batman, McMillan, one afternoon asked me if I would like to practice with the revolver. I said yes, so Mac casually picked up a rum jar, climbed up the parados of the trench, and walked out about 30 yards behind it. Just as he was stooping to place the jar on a little rise, a single rifle report came from the enemy lines and Mac ran back to our trench with a slight wound in the shoulder. After this it was real war again, and a very uncomfortable time we had in those ice-stuffed trenches.

"Our period of rest in supports was not much better. We had to go back about 150 yards to a deep dugout and spend the whole day inside it. There were plenty of men to fill it, and they used to boil their dixies by tying sand-bag strips around a candle and lighting the candle. This made quite a warm fire, but the smell of the burning, tallow-soaked bagging was dreadful. I felt rather annoyed with the Huns for shooting my pet batman, but managed to square accounts a little later when I observed a party of them one night digging a trench near the front line. I took careful note of the position, rang the artillery, and had the satisfaction of seeing five or six shrapnel bursts right on them, effectively stopping their work."

Hot tea and stew were brought to the front line after dusk and a hot breakfast at dawn, while in the coldest of the early morning hours there was a strong rum issue.

Enemy action was confined chiefly to desultory shelling, with 5.9's and 77s, on the supply dumps and communication tracks at Turk Lane and Cough Drop Siding. Occasionally heavy bombardments would be directed against the right company's position at Yarra Bank, and also against the left flank where the substantial ruins of the old abbey were doubtless suspected of giving shelter to Australian heavy trench-mortars. The "flying pig" experts were relentless in their attention to the German position about The Maze, and the enemy replied to their fire with showers of "pineapple" bombs. As a result, the approach to the front line had to be made with the utmost caution. Carrying parties had a very strenuous time, owing to the slippery nature of the ground and the difficulty of handling ice-encrusted burdens. A feature of this tour was the effect of artillery-fire. A shell striking the frozen ground had the effect of scattering blocks of ice in the air like chaff.

On February 5th the inter-company relief took place, and the companies fresh from the line took over the duties of transporting supplies from Clarke's and High Wood East dumps. After spending four more days in these trenches, the battalion moved out to Site 5 at Bazentin camp, leaving several parties behind on divisional fatigue duty at Clarke's Dump. During this tour in the line the general health of the troops had been exceptionally good, and casualties from all sources very light.

The heavy demand by divisional headquarters for fatigue parties now took away so many men that training operations had more or less to be suspended. The competitive spirit of the battalion, however, was kept at a healthy pitch by the introduction of barrack-room competitions. On February 12th some 90 reinforcements joined, bringing the battalion strength up to 28 officers and 913 other ranks.

Next day the first signs of an early spring were present, in lowering clouds and sleety rain. This change was the signal for an increased alertness on the part of all troops. On the 14th an order was received for the battalion to move back to Dernancourt for training, but this was countermanded when it became known that the enemy had begun to retire to positions before Bapaume. Preparations for a hurried pursuit were made, and, after many false alarms, orders were at last received to relieve the 11th

Battalion, which was following the Germans in the direction of Le Barque.

We moved again on February 27th. As reports indicated that the 11th Battalion had already pushed its patrols through Le Barque and Ligny-Thilloy, the battalion headquarters went to Yarra Bank. The outpost-line was taken over by one company, with the other three in support. The approach to the abandoned German lines was made difficult by reason of mud and the sloppy nature of the ground, but beyond them and around the shell-stricken ruins of the two captured villages were firm stubble fields and green grass. Clumps of tangled woods and isolated farm-houses offered a strange contrast to the desolate moorland on which we had spent the winter months.

Sniping fire was actively directed on enemy movement on the high ridge in front, which sheltered from view the town of Bapaume. Retaliation from the enemy's artillery was immediate. One shell obliterated the regimental aid-post, but fortunately there were no casualties. Curiously enough, its arrival coincided with the departure for England of the medical officer, Captain S. C. Fitzpatrick, who was relieved by Major F. T. Beamish.

The combative spirit of the battalion was kept at a high pitch by patrolling, and there occurred several sharp brushes with the enemy. At 6 a.m. on March 2nd, under cover of a thick fog and assisted by a half-hour's preparatory bombardment of a somewhat violent nature, strong detachments of the 4th German Guard Division raided the posts of the 1st Australian Division. In the 1st Brigade's sector one such party, making its way through the 4th Battalion posts by the Bapaume road, succeeded in capturing a dozen Australians and a Lewis gun. The fog lifting at this stage, Lieut A. H. Boileau, in charge of B Company of the 3rd, brought rifle and machine-gun fire to bear on the Germans. Supports of the 4th Battalion and survivors from a dugout that had been bombed* also attacked them, and an all-in fight took place. Most of the Australian prisoners escaped, although unfortunately four lost their lives. As to the Germans, some were killed and others surrendered. The Lewis gun was recaptured and sent back to the 4th Battalion.

Other parties, belonging to the 5th Foot Guard Regiment, were to attack Thilloy and Ligny-Thilloy. One of these surprised an isolated post of B Company in "Trip Trench," taking prisoner its entire garrison of twelve. These men, in accordance with instructions, after observing all night had with the appearance of daylight just dismantled their Lewis gun and were preparing to conceal themselves when they were overwhelmed.†

The loss of these good men, and of others who were killed or wounded in the affray, was a grievous blow to the battalion. As far as the enemy's losses were concerned, our outposts took toll of his storm-troops to the extent of 16 killed and 11 prisoners, six of whom were wounded. A number who were less seriously wounded managed to escape in the fog.

On March 6th, the weather turning bright and clear, airmen on both sides were particularly active. Observers

---

* Lieut G. H. Leslie, who was in the dugout at the time, says that it contained about 30 men of the 4th Battalion and 10 of the 3rd, including himself, all of whom had been sent there to sleep. Bombs thrown down the stairway caused many casualties and filled the dugout with suffocating fumes. Donning their respirators, the survivors made several unsuccessful attempts to rush up the steps. In these rushes many were killed or wounded. A captain of the 4th Battalion had his leg blown off and died a little later, while Lieut Boileau of the same unit was wounded. Eventually, ten or fifteen minutes later, the imprisoned troops were able to get out of the dugout and take part in the fighting.

† The captured men included Corporal Howarth and Privates Spriggs, Kinsella, Edwell, Hanna, Lindfield, and O. L. Smith. As prisoners of war, the first part of their internment was spent at the Cambrai Citadel, which at the time was used as a reprisal camp. "We rose at 4 a.m.," writes Private Spriggs, "when we were issued with a small quantity of bread and a tin containing black coffee. We would then fall in and march away to work. We worked all day without anything to eat, returning just before sundown. We were kept at this for seven months, toiling on the canals, roads, and barges near the St Quentin Canal."

on the ground witnessed a stirring aerial duel, as a result of which a British pilot made a sensational landing within our lines.

This day we were relieved by the 18th Battalion (2nd Division), and marched to Site 4 at Bazentin camp for the night, continuing next day to Mametz Wood. The casualties for the week's tour are recorded as—officers, 1 wounded, 1 evacuated; other ranks, 7 killed, 3 died of wounds, 19 wounded, 17 missing.

Very little military training was undergone at Mametz Wood camp, but football and other games were played daily, to keep the men in good trim. The padre was particularly active in organizing boxing tournaments and concerts. On March 16th the battalion moved to billets in the village of Dernancourt on the River Ancre. During the five days spent here we were exercised in open fighting and the capture and construction of strong-points. The specialists indulged in their own particular training. Bathing facilities were available at Vivier Mill, near Albert.

On the 22nd the Battalion went further down the river to Ribemont, a nondescript hamlet, both cold and cheerless, which crowned a slight eminence opposite a natural ford on the Ancre. It is true that the nearby villages of Heilly* and Méricourt provided some diversion of a more cheerful sort, but no regrets were expressed when, on April 3rd, after a further ten days of intensive training in open warfare and outpost work, the battalion left Ribemont's dilapidated barns and dwellings and marched, via Dernancourt, to Montauban, on yet another stage towards the new firing line.

---

* At Heilly, many men took the opportunity to visit the grave of their former commander, Lieut-Col Howell-Price.

CHAPTER XXVII

GERMAN WITHDRAWAL—THE BATTLE OF HERMIES

THE Germans were still doing their utmost to delay the British advance, and to impede attempts to reconnoitre the Hindenburg line on which work was even now being feverishly carried out. But on April 2nd the I Anzac and other corps of the Fifth Army had wrested from them all the villages in front of that line, except three—Boursies, Demicourt, and Hermies—on the southern flank of the Australian sector. None of these were included in the objectives set for that day, the task of capturing them being left to the incoming 1st Division, which was finally ordered to carry out the operation on April 9th.

When, on the morning of April 4th, the 3rd Battalion marched out from the hutted camp at Montauban, it passed many places which had become familiar during the past six months. The dry and comparatively clean conditions of the latter half of January and all February, during which the countryside was frozen hard, had again given way to mud and slush, but a great part of the route was now over duckboarded tracks. Reaching our old front line, the battalion continued on across the No-Man's Land over which many of us had looked, patrolled, and sometimes fought, in recent months, and, crossing the old German trenches, went by way of Riencourt-les-Bapaume and Beaucourt to Frémicourt, where it rested for the night. At first sight of these villages, hopes ran high at the prospect of getting into better billets, but closer inspection disclosed the fact that many of the buildings had been so badly damaged by the enemy prior to his withdrawal that they offered very little in the way of shelter. Then again, the villages were already overcrowded with other troops. However, all ranks were pleased at the thought of leaving the mud and slush of the old battlefield and moving into cleaner country. Apparently with the idea of impeding the advance of our artillery and transport, a number of the trees bordering the roads had been felled by the Germans and lay sprawling in the way. In some cases even isolated fruit and ornamental trees in the village gardens had been cut down and destroyed in a wanton, useless manner.

The night of April 5th was spent in Lebucquière, and on the afternoon of the 6th the battalion moved into Vélu Wood. While A and B Companies proceeded to the line facing Hermies, C Company settled down in outbuildings of the damaged château, and D went into bivouac. Much of the surrounding country was under hostile observation, so much so that only small parties of two or three were allowed to move about during the daytime, but the wood gave excellent cover to the companies standing by for the impending attack on Hermies.

Vélu Château—surrounded by beautiful park-like grounds, once the pride of some landscape gardener, but now neglected and overgrown with weeds—had been considerably damaged by the retiring enemy. Apparently it had been used as a hospital, and further evidence of German "kultur" was available in the form of a cemetery established in the grounds some two or three hundred yards distant and in full view of the main outlook from the ancient building.

During the two nights prior to the attack on Hermies, officers and N.C.Os carried out what reconnaissance they could in order to become familiar with the best routes to assembly points from which the attack was to be launched, and also with a view to gaining as much information as possible regarding the German positions. But the patrols found it a difficult task to make contact with the enemy, No-Man's Land being explored to a depth of several hundred yards without any sign of a field-grey uniform.

Such great freedom of movement, after having been more or less caged for a twelvemonth within confined limits, was a distinct novelty. Moreover, the ground was now firm and clean. Consequently the activity of the patrols was considerably increased.

Private Bill Clarke was one of the most energetic of the scouts at this time. Unhappily his enthusiasm in this direction was eventually responsible for his death.

One reconnoitring party, under the leadership of Major A. F. Burrett, came upon the bodies of two members of the 13th Australian Light Horse Regiment about 800 yards in advance of the front-line posts. At the time it was a problem of much interest and speculation how members of the light horse, in full marching order, had reached this forward position, it not being known that the mounted troops had performed much scouting work for the 2nd and 5th Divisions' columns advancing from Bapaume.

Many "booby" traps and "delayed action" mines had been left behind by the enemy, and any object at all suspicious or out of the ordinary was left severely alone. Captain C. F. ("Dad") Elliot and Lieut Eric Shelley, returning one night from a reconnaissance—during which they crossed the Canal du Nord and established contact with the 20th British Division—noticed a small wooden sleeper, left behind for some reason when the enemy had removed a light railway line. Elliot offered Shelley 100 francs if he would pull it up. But Shelley had seen others "stung," and the offer was declined with thanks.

On the 8th of April, 1917, the enemy occupied the line Boursies-Demicourt-Hermies-Havrincourt Wood, with advanced posts thrown out in front. Next morning the 3rd Brigade was to attack Boursies, and the 1st Brigade

3RD BATTALION OFFICERS AT METEREN, 1918

STRONG POINT. 20TH SEPTEMBER, 1917

VERBRAND-ENMOLEN ROAD

VIEW FROM OBSERVATION POST, RAVINE WOOD

YPRES-BRUSSELS RAILWAY CUTTING, NEAR HILL 60

Demicourt and Hermies, while the 60th British Brigade would assist by directing fire on to Havrincourt Wood. The attack on Hermies was entrusted to the 2nd and 3rd Battalions, the latter's task being to advance from the south-west and clear the area from the Canal du Nord to the Hermies-Vélu railway. Subsequently it was to make junction with the 2nd Battalion, which would attack the village from the north-west. As the attack was to be a surprise, there would be no covering bombardment.

The German strongholds were admirably sited on high ground from which a commanding view of the whole countryside was to be had. In addition, in the railway embankment the enemy had a first-rate defensive position. The Australian positions, approximately a mile distant and in much lower country, were thus completely dominated by the enemy.

C Company, consisting of six officers and 193 other ranks, and D Company, five and 194, were chosen for the attack. They were to be assisted by a carrying party 20 strong, and by another, made up of scouts, signallers, and other specialists, totalling 10. Each company would advance in two waves, each wave consisting of two lines of men.

At 3.30 a.m. the companies deployed for the attack, each sending out a protecting screen of patrols and scouts. Fifteen minutes later the order was given for the leading line to advance, and the troops went forward at a walking pace along the southern side of the railway line to engage the south-western defences of the village.

When the first wave debouched from the assembly point in the sunken road, the enemy opened with machine-gun fire. Two platoons of the left company (C) met strong and determined opposition at the railway station, where the enemy had established a heavily wired strong-point. A machine-gun there held up the advance for half an hour, and was responsible for most of the casualties in this company. Lieut A. S. McMaster got to within 20 yards of the gun before he was killed.* Another platoon leader, Lieut G. R. MacDougal, was wounded. Sergeant G. N. Goode and Private J. W. Quinn also were killed at the same place.

At this stage Captain J. G. Tyson pushed out the right half of C Company through the enemy wire and gained the railway line. Meanwhile D Company, further to the right, captured a number of the enemy and a machine-gun. The 2nd Battalion, entering Hermies from the north, enabled the left half of C Company to continue its advance, and at 5.20 it linked up with the 2nd.

D Company in its advance ran into considerable machine-gun fire and was repeatedly held up, one enemy post after another having to be dealt with. At 5.30 a.m., this company entered the cemetery, where a post was established.

At 3.30 a.m., just as D Company moved out, No. 13 Platoon on the extreme right had the misfortune to lose a very fine N.C.O., Sergeant Claude Dowling, who was killed by fire from a machine-gun immediately in front. Soon afterwards the gun was bombed and silenced. After advancing some 300 yards, the leading line of D Company surprised a number of the enemy in a bivouac. The prisoners, a number of whom had been wounded, provided our men with some very fine hot coffee and cognac from their water-bottles. The issue had only just been made to the Germans, and was much appreciated by their captors on this cold morning.

At the damaged bridge, where the road running south from Hermies crossed the canal, No. 13 Platoon was lashed by machine-guns from the opposite side. Corporal W. C. Tilbrook (of Kempsey, N.S.W.) was killed while

---

* McMaster should have left the previous evening on furlough, but at the eleventh hour his leave was postponed to enable him to take part in the attack. According to Private Atkins and several others, he had a premonition of personal disaster.

gallantly returning this fire. The gun was then engaged and silenced by Lance-Corporal Lee and Private P. F. Day, with the aid of rifle grenades. The position of this gun bore out a suspicion of the previous day that the flank would be open. However, at the time of the attack it was too dark to see across the canal, which was about 60 feet in width and had bricked sides stretching 15 feet sheer to the water, and a tow-path on either side. During the morning of the 9th the 20th British Division moved up and secured the open flank.

The attack was a complete success. Thirty-one Germans (two of them wounded) and three machine-guns were captured by us. The battalion's casualties amounted to 72, including 2 officers. The Germans were now at last driven into their Hindenburg line all along the front.

Immediately the objectives were gained, steps were taken to consolidate our position. "After making our position a fighting one, and ourselves comfortable possies," wrote Sergeant A. Bray in his diary, "we decided to look over the captured ground and the Hun dugouts. This tour of inspection proved to be a profitable one. In all the dugouts we found parcels. It was apparent that the defenders had just received a big batch of mail and had not had time to open the parcels before our attack was launched. These parcels contained eggs, bacon, tobacco, and lots of those gifts which it is usual for soldiers to receive in occasional and welcome parcels. All these things we put to good use. We also found plentiful supplies of bottled beer, wine, brandy and whisky. None was wasted."

During the Hermies "stunt," one of C Company's runners, Fred Kennaugh, was given a bunch of about thirty Fritz prisoners to take in to headquarters. He arrived there sitting up on a stretcher carried by two of his prisoners while the others marched ahead, and with his hands in his pockets. The officer to whom he handed over his prisoners wanted to know what he meant by coming in like that, and was told that that was the easiest way he could think of on the spur of the moment, and that it kept some of his prisoners busy and gave him a good view of the others. When told of the risk he ran by having his hands in his pockets, and no weapon, he removed his hands and showed a Mills bomb in either hand. "What'll I do with these," he asked, "now I've finished with them?" "Throw them down," said the officer. Kennaugh prepared to do so and asked, "Can you run?" "Yes," replied the officer. "Why?" "Then run like b——," said Ken, as he threw them, "because the pins are out." It is said that the officer broke "evens" in the rush to safety, and that Ken, although a professional runner, was a very bad second.—Private W. Atkins.

The dawn ushering in wet and cold conditions, the various groups established in small open posts had an uncomfortable time, especially those of D Company, which had gone into the attack without greatcoats or blankets. That night a party went back for greatcoats, but by the time they returned the troops were wet as a result of falling snow.

Rain and snow continued to fall throughout the following day, and in consequence the work of improving the new line was held up. C Company was withdrawn from the front line, two of its platoons remaining in close support on the right and two falling back on battalion headquarters. A and B Companies relieved part of the 2nd Battalion on our left flank, and linked up with D Company on the right. During the night a line of picquets was thrown round the eastern side of the village, and by 11.20 p.m. had joined hands with the 1st Battalion.

On the night of the 10th, when the rations were issued, each man was given a pair of hand-knitted socks, a most welcome gift from the 3rd Battalion Comforts Fund.

The weather on the 11th and 12th was unchanged, so

that there was little activity beyond digging at night and the making of shelters with material salvaged from Hermies. Of this there was an abundance—doors, sheet iron, and the like. On the 12th the brigadier, General W. B. Lesslie, paid a visit to the front line.*

With the twofold object of securing better observation and improving our field of fire, the corps line was to be pushed forward to within less than a mile of the Hindenburg line. On the 3rd Battalion's sector this meant an advance of about 1000 yards, which was undertaken by B, A, and D Companies (from left to right) at 10 p.m. on April 13th. The night was exceptionally dark, and platoon officers were faced with a difficult task—to march on a compass bearing, establish posts on a map location, and keep in touch with the units on either flank.

No. 5 Platoon, of B Company, moved out with scouts in front and came without opposition to a point some 200 yards from the Hindenburg line and opposite a natural butte of land, heavily fortified. In this advance a sergeant, attempting to join the scouts, lost his way, and walked unsuspectingly into the German lines, where he was made a prisoner. Before No. 5 Platoon could dig in, the enemy sent up flares and opened fire with rifles and machine-guns. Fortunately the platoon could be seen only by the Germans directly opposite, and, to prevent them from having it all their own way, a Lewis gun was sent out to the flank where it kept up a continuous fire, harassing the enemy in the trenches while our men dug in. The post was established with the loss of one man killed.

---

* On April 11th the 4th Australian Division was thrown against the Hindenburg line east of Bullecourt, without the assistance of artillery. The tanks which accompanied them—and on which far too much reliance had been placed by General Gough of the Fifth Army and other high leaders—broke down, in most cases in No-Man's Land, and the infantry were left to get through the broad, rusty wire-entanglements by their own efforts. The 4th Division, however, nothing daunted, went on and gained a lodgment in the German lines, but was eventually driven out, after particularly gallant fighting, with heavy loss.

A and D Companies did not advance as far as was hoped, with the result that the right flank of B was 150 yards ahead and about the same distance to the left of A. The digging of the new trenches in a solid chalk formation was a long and tedious job, and somewhat difficult to accomplish before daylight. The protecting screen of scouts thrown out in front reduced the number of men available for the work.

The 14th was a bright sunny day, and as far as possible, all ranks were allowed to rest. The only work carried out was in the direction of straightening out a few posts and consolidating the new line. On the German side hurried preparations were being made for a spectacular counter-attack by four divisions against almost the whole of the 1st Australian Division's front and part of the 2nd's.

At 1 a.m. on the 15th the enemy artillery began to shell Hermies and its immediate surroundings intermittently, but at 4 o'clock it laid down a heavy barrage on the east and south of the village. The Australian battery-positions west of Hermies were also heavily shelled by 5.9's.

At that hour a sentry of No. 5 Platoon (B Company), the most advanced and isolated of the battalion, observed the enemy massing in front of their own barbed-wire, and gave the alarm. Lieut Geoff. Leslie, the platoon commander, with characteristic coolness, lost no time in arranging for the bringing of all the defensive forces of the battalion into play. Five minutes later No. 5 Platoon was attacked fiercely. Its successful defence was due in great measure to the splendid work of the Lewis gun section under Corporal W. Marshall. Marshall kept his gun in action continuously for about two hours, rushing it from one end of the trench to the other, wherever the attack was strongest. On several occasions the gun was mounted on the parados and fire was brought to bear on enemy parties which had pierced the Australian line further north. Rifle-grenades also were used with great effect, four nicely placed along a line of Germans, sending 20 or more of the enemy helter-skelter back to their own trenches. The telephone line to Leslie's post was cut at 4.15, and half an hour elapsed before communication was re-established with him.

Meanwhile at 4.7 a.m. the remainder of B Company's posts were attacked, and three minutes later the 4th Battalion line, immediately to the left, was also heavily engaged. The enemy advanced in two waves at about 5 to 10 yards' interval, with approximately one yard separating individual infantrymen, and got to within twenty yards of B Company, which brought the attack to a standstill by the concentrated fire of rifles and Lewis guns and the judicious use of bombs and rifle-grenades. At 4.15 our artillery opened on their S.O.S. lines in response to the call for assistance. No S.O.S. flare, however, was sent up from the posts engaged.

At 4.10 a.m. a thrust was also made against the 3rd Battalion's centre company (A), but meeting a heavy fire, the enemy retired.

At daybreak the Germans finally retired in disorder, many of their wounded crawling away. The dead and wounded lying out in front of the 3rd Battalion posts were estimated at 200. Two prisoners from the 4th Ersatz Division were taken—one a member of the 4th Company, 360th I.R., the other of the 10th Company, 361st I.R.

After daybreak the Germans began to collect their wounded, the stretcher-bearers coming out with Red Cross flags. Our own wounded were sent back at the same time. Before long, however, the Germans who had retired were seen to be digging in behind their stretcher-bearers, about a hundred yards or so away. Fire was immediately directed on them, with the result that two German machine-guns opened on Lieut Dill's post, wounding Dill and three of his N.C.Os. At 5.30 a.m. Lieut C. L. Smith was sent up to take charge of Dill's post, and had to crawl for the last 200 yards. During the remainder of the day the Germans kept all B Company's posts under machine-gun fire, while the battalion generally was subjected to heavy shelling. Our losses amounted to 7 men killed, and 1 officer and 26 other ranks wounded.

During the attack the enemy bombarded the quarry captured on the 9th. Under some pine trees near the quarry, a number of packs had been neatly stacked, including those belonging to the band. Most of the packs were scattered over the countryside by the shell-fire, about six or eight being flung up into the trees, up which, later on, the men had to climb to retrieve what was left.

One of the fatigue parties taking forward the early morning coffee, bacon, and bread had an exciting experience. Surprised by the enemy attacking troops, its members dropped the rations and quite wisely beat a hasty retreat. The Germans thereupon helped themselves to the meal intended for this company, which perforce had to do the next 24 hours on iron rations. Sergeant L. Furneaux Cook, one of the party, afterwards wrote:

"A few others—including Pte. G. Williams (an original), J. Smith, E. Younger, S. Thomas, E. Bennett—and myself were detailed as a ration party and escort for a number of reinforcements. After proceeding a fair distance, it became evident that our guide had mistaken the direction and that we were 'bushed.' We found ourselves in an excellent, but very precarious, position which enabled us to view the enemy preparatory barrage with its accompanying display of flares. This barrage commenced on our extreme left and provided a most spectacular sight, especially for the reinforcements who were making their way to the front line for the first time. We others, however, knew only too well what was in store.

"With amazing rapidity and deadly precision the barrage was on top of us, and our troubles commenced. The new chaps bunched together and disregarded our shouts to them to spread out and lie down. Consequently, we were obliged to drag them down and take advantage of the slight cover, afforded mostly by small tree stumps. ... Flares of every description and star shells were going up, transforming the night into day, while the heavens seemed to be belching shells which ploughed up the ground. Adding to the general din were the machine-guns and the unholy whine of their vicious bullets as they passed us. In front and all around the bullets were kicking up the dust, and, as shells exploded, we would be smothered in earth, which gave us a most uncomfortable feeling in the pit of the stomach. However, we kept our eyes glued to our front, waiting for the barrage to lift.

"Then, at a distance possibly of 100 yards, clearly visible in the glare of the bursting shells and the flares, came the Germans ... in, it seemed, an unending stream. They advanced towards us in wave formation, and I was astonished to notice that they appeared to be kicking in front of them balls of fire. Our position now became desperate, for we were lying in an elevated position without a depression to crawl into, and by this time the machine-gun fire had become intensified. Looking round me for a better position, I could discern on my left what appeared to be a sunken road, so I shouted to my companions to make a dash for it and get under the lee where we would have a fighting chance. One shouted back that the distance was too far, and that, as we had not been hit so far, it would be better to stay as we were. The words were scarcely uttered when a shell exploded to our rear, and I heard someone sing out. Wondering who had been hit, my speculations were cut short when I received what felt like a kick in the middle of my back. One of my two companions cried out that he had been hit, and, putting my hand behind me, I discovered that I also had received a knock. By some means or other I scrambled to my feet and turned to dash for the sunken road. Before I could do so, I heard my companion scream out not to leave him as he was wounded. There was no time to use a field dressing, so I bent down to grab him and saw that he had been badly hit in the right thigh. I also noticed that the other chap had vanished. I think he, too, was hit, for although I could not see him, I could hear someone crying out, 'Oh, my eye.'

"I managed to get the first chap on my shoulder . . . and half-running, half-stumbling, made a dash for the road. I was probably more than half-way, when a shell exploded directly in front of us, blowing my unfortunate burden clean out of my grasp and suspending portion of his body in a tree. I received the balance of the shell in both legs, and the shock had the effect of making me run all the faster, but, unfortunately, in the wrong direction. When I ultimately collapsed I found I had been running towards the advancing Fritzies. . . . They passed very close to me, and one half-turned me over with his foot, but, seeing that I was in such a frightful mess, probably thought I was done. . . . Some of them were wearing the field-grey round caps instead of tin hats. I have thought since that they may have been German A.M.C.

"Gradually realizing my helpless position, being without a rifle, bombs, or even a tin hat, a new and terrifying thought entered my head, that I might be taken prisoner. With sweat pouring out of me, probably with fright, for it was a cold night, I commenced to drag myself back towards the sunken road. As it was slow and painful work I tried to get on my feet, but found my legs were useless, and so was forced to continue the journey on my stomach. Dawn now began to break, and, just as my senses appeared to be leaving me, there came yet another terror—the counter-barrage by the artillery. . . . I thought that every moment I would be blown to smithereens. This terror gave me added energy, and I continued to drag myself along the ground, but had not proceeded very far when I got another knock in the back that seemed to take all the breath out of me. Astounding as it may seem, I now struggled on to my feet and ran like mad, reaching the road, into which I collapsed head first.

"Lying there, the first thing I remembered was hearing someone running towards me. Thinking they were Germans, my terrors returned, and I lay on my stomach and did not dare look up. I think now they must have been some members of C Company going up to strengthen the posts on the right. I heard someone shouting for Captain Tyson, and knew that at last I was back among my own chaps. Then I discovered that my position was very insecure owing to my being almost in the direct range of a machine-gun which constantly fired straight down the road. Again dragging myself along, I tried to improve my position. Failing to find any cover for my head, I extracted a tin of bully-beef out of my haversack and set it up in position.

"It was now daylight. I seemed to have been lying there for hours. It was bitterly cold, and seeing someone pass me I cried out and he came over. It was Sergeant-Major Hewland. I asked him if my legs were off. He laughed and gave me a good nip of rum out of his water-bottle, and the next thing I remember was Pte J. Smith fixing up my legs. I asked him also if my legs were off, as I could feel nothing from the waist down.

"I was put on a stretcher, and we commenced a nightmare journey. Instead of taking me down the road, they took me over the top, evidently a short cut. My bearers were only small chaps and, not being supplied with straps, soon found themselves in difficulties. To add to the discomfort, Fritz started to snipe at us with whiz-bangs, which forced my bearers to drop me and seek cover. They then went to get straps, saying that they would only be gone a few minutes. But they did not return. The German artillery continued to shell, and I certainly had the "wind up," being so near and yet so far from comparative safety. Repeatedly I waved my arm in the hope of someone seeing me. At last two stretcher-bearers arrived, one being, I think, Clutterbuck and the other Private Pickering."

So ended the German counter-attack that was planned with the intention of administering a crushing defeat on their opponents while the latter were incompletely dug in. It is true that in the Lagnicourt sector the enemy succeeded in penetrating to the advanced battery-positions and damaging five guns, and that the I Anzac Corps suffered 1010 casualties, including the loss of some 300 men captured. But the total loss of the Germans in this action, according to their own figures, was 2313, of whom 362 were taken prisoner.

The relief of our three companies from Hermies at 2.30 a.m. on April 17th was perhaps one of their most trying experiences up to this time. Rain fell in sweeping torrents and, with the impenetrable blackness of the night, made the long march back by vague and broken tracks to Beaumetz a hardship to be remembered. Shell-fire, too, added strain to nerves already frayed by the severe fighting of the previous ten days; and, when it was found that the ruins of Beaumetz provided no shelter whatever, the position appeared to be hopeless. But the older soldiers, summoning strength from some source that never seemed to fail, were soon at work making what cover they could. On the other hand, some of the latest reinforcements, utterly exhausted, flung themselves prone in the mud and slept while the rain lashed their unconscious bodies.

The strain put on all officers by these adverse conditions was most marked. Happy was the company commander who, by his skill, or even by a stroke of luck, could provide some additional comfort for his men.

Captains H. E. Butler and F. C. Kemp were now evacuated through sickness. This loss, added to the casualties already suffered (3 officers and 120 other ranks), made the Hermies victory a costly one. Nevertheless, it was agreed on all sides that the record of the battalion had been worthily maintained.

CHAPTER XXVIII

THE SECOND BULLECOURT

THE battalion occupied the outposts round Doignies and Demicourt from April 20th to 24th, when the 6th Battalion, York and Lancaster Regiment, took over that part of the line. By way of Vélu Wood and Haplincourt, the 3rd marched to a camp at Riencourt-les-Bapaume, from which it moved on the 26th to the Vaulx-Vraucourt-Morchies support lines, relieving the 18th Battalion.

This manœuvre was but one of the opening moves in a plan which had as its object a repetition of the attempt by the Fifth Army to pierce the Hindenburg line about Bullecourt on the day when the Third Army resumed its offensive, known as the Battle of Arras, which had begun on April 9th. In this combined operation, which was set down for the morning of May 3rd, fourteen divisions would be attacking on a front of sixteen miles, from Vimy to near Quéant. The division chosen for the right flank of the attack was the 2nd Australian, the one next to it on the left being the 62nd British, whose task was to advance through and beyond the village of Bullecourt.

In the Australian sector the attack would be launched by the 5th and 6th Brigades, which had been relieved from the line by the 7th Brigade on April 20th, and withdrawn to the region of Bapaume for rest and further training. The 1st Brigade was lent to the 2nd Division in case further support was needed during the attack; in the meantime, it garrisoned the support-line on the occasions when the 5th and 6th rehearsed their parts at Favreuil.

Throughout the night of May 2nd the attacking units of the 2nd Division were moving up to the front. Some hours before this the 3rd Battalion's dispositions had been arranged. D Company moved to Noreuil to occupy posts defending that village, while two platoons of C were detailed as a special escort to a forward group of field-artillery in the same area. Battalion headquarters, together with A and B Companies and the other two platoons of C, remained at Vaulx. A special nucleus of officers, N.C.Os, and specialists had meanwhile been sent back to a details camp at Vaulx.

Promptly at 3.45 a.m. on May 3rd the British barrage opened along the huge front from Lagnicourt to Vimy. On the extreme right flank in the re-entrant between Bullecourt and Quéant, the Australian brigades—6th on the left, 5th on the right—began their advance towards the Hindenburg line.* Within an hour the 5th Brigade's effort had been crushed at the wire-entanglements by the machine-gun and rifle-fire of the Württembergers. The 6th Brigade, however, broke through the German defences and quickly gained the first objective—the two Hindenburg trenches, known as O.G.1 and O.G.2; and, despite the heavy bomb-fighting, reached the second objective two hours after the start of the attack, but with troops barely sufficient to hold it. To the left of the 6th Brigade the 185th Brigade (62nd Division), whose extremely difficult task was to capture the ruined village of Bullecourt, also failed through machine-gun fire. The flanks of the 6th Brigade, which had penetrated nearly half-a-mile into the German position on a front of only 500 yards, were thus in the air, and after the defeat of the first general counter-attack, the second objective was abandoned. By the afternoon the whole

---

* During the last quarter of an hour there had been a little confusion and some consternation when a sharp German bombardment fell on the assembling rear waves.

of the 7th Brigade was drawn into the desperate fighting, the 28th Battalion, together with some remnants of the 5th Brigade, capturing part of the O.G. trenches on the right of the 6th; but at 9 p.m. the Germans regained that portion of the line. So the 6th Brigade held on by itself all night in the Hindenburg line, facing the enemy in front and on both flanks.

But to return to the 3rd Battalion. At 3 a.m. on May 3rd the companies "stood-to" in their support positions about Noreuil and Vaulx, and about dawn A moved forward to close support behind the 28th Battalion. As the day advanced several urgent, yet contradictory, orders were received. These gradually drew the battalion closer to the scene of the fighting. At 8 p.m. the G.O.C. of the 6th Brigade (Brigadier-General Gellibrand) gave orders for the 3rd Battalion to relieve his four shattered battalions in the captured position. The battalion was then in the vicinity of a new communication trench that led across the old No-Man's Land to the captured German lines—a work of excavation a thousand yards long that will stand to the everlasting credit of the 2nd Australian Pioneer Battalion. Our fighting strength that morning had been 17 officers and 543 other ranks,* and the fact that it was sufficient to occupy the brigade frontage was a striking testimony to the severity of the fighting through which the 6th Brigade had passed.

Mere words could not express the admiration of the 3rd Battalion for the magnificent effort of the tired but indomitable Victorians, so we performed the most soldierly service in our power by relieving them as promptly as possible and not asking unnecessary or detailed questions regarding the line taken over.

---

* Throughout the whole of May 3rd the German shelling of the old Australian front and support positions was severe. Captain J. G. Tyson, commanding C Company, was killed and Lieut R. R. Morgan wounded, while 60 other ranks also became casualties.

DRAINING IRON ALLEY

IRON ALLEY, ZILLEBEKE, HILL 60

COMMUNICATION TRENCH, BULGAR WOOD

HEAD OF COMMUNICATION TRENCH, HILL 60

THE LACE SCHOOL, YPRES

EXTERIOR, ST PIERRE CHURCH, YPRES

THE CLOTH HALL, YPRES

INTERIOR, ST PIERRE CHURCH, YPRES

THE SECOND BULLECOURT

And what questions might have been asked! It was quite obvious that the battle which had raged in these captured lines had been of unparalleled severity. With a loss of 68 officers and 1524 men in twenty-four hours, the 6th Brigade had been reduced to the strength of a single battalion. Evidence of the terrific struggle could be seen in the many dead and wounded who lay around. The wounded men presented a colossal task to the valiant stretcher-bearers, whose work at this time can never be adequately praised.

The relief was complete by 4 a.m. on the 4th, the distribution of the battalion in O.G. 2 being (from right to left)—A Company (Captain S. F. P. White); C Company, less two platoons still on escort duty at Noreuil (Lieut Ben Berry); Battalion Headquarters (Lieut-Colonel D. T. Moore); B Company (Captain G. E. McDonald); D Company (Captain C. F. Elliot). At 4.30 the enemy, advancing up the old communication trenches, launched a general counter-attack against the right and left flanks of the battalion in an attempt to hem us in. A furious bomb-fight raged for half-an-hour, with Mills and stick bombs crossing in the air. But finally the Germans were driven off with heavy loss. Particularly prominent in this defence was the N.C.O. in charge of the extreme right post, Lance-Cpl A. Hudson, of the bombers who, in face of the determined pressure of this heavy onset, had been forced to give ground temporarily. But, quickly reorganizing the remaining men of his section, he led them back and drove the enemy from this all-important post, killing and capturing 20 Germans there. During the action he was severely wounded, and eventually lost a leg.

The left-flank post, behind a barricade in a sunken road which here ran through O.G. 2, was in charge of Sergeant P. Kinchington, who had mounted a Lewis gun and a captured German machine-gun on the road-bank immediately in rear of it. All at once 150 Germans, without rifles, were observed coming down the road. Kinchington got alongside the machine-guns, telling his men not to fire until he gave the order. When the Germans were

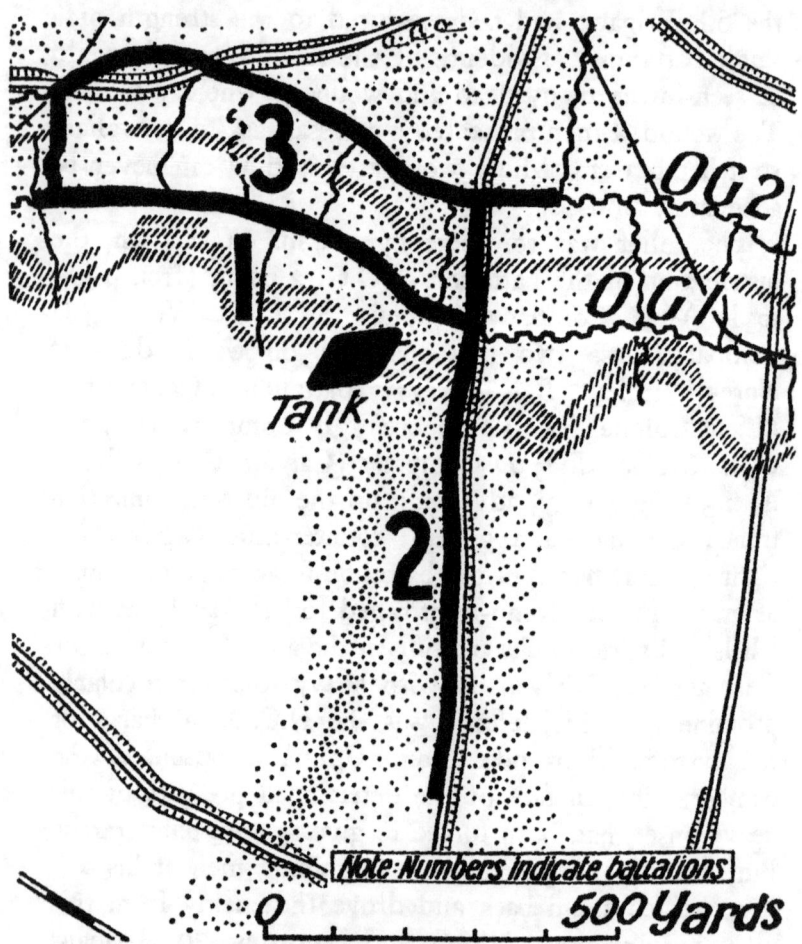

THE SECOND BATTLE OF BULLECOURT
Copyright: Aust. War Memorial Museum.

about forty yards distant, one of them shot a jet of flame into the bank, and the Australians realized that this was from a *flammenwerfer*, the first they had seen. Kinchington shot the carrier, his bullet going through the German's body and setting fire to the *flammenwerfer* can at the back; and the machine-guns immediately opened on the others. The carrier toppled into a hole in the road with about a dozen men on top of him, all of them appearing to catch fire. Bombs fell thick and heavy, D Company using German egg-bombs (a supply of which had been found in the trench) as well as Mills. The nearest German reached five yards from Kinchington's post.

At 1 p.m. D Company launched a bombing attack along O.G. 2, the 1st Battalion behind them, doing likewise up O.G. 1. D Company's attack was to some extent supported by a trench-mortar of the 6th Brigade, but the bombers under Captain Eliott found stubborn resistance from machine-guns and stick grenades at every post. When the attack passed over the low crest of land on the left, it penetrated into a depression that was commanded by several enemy posts, and the battalion's bombing sergeant, John Yorke, M.M., and several other N.C.Os who were assisting the bombing drive, were killed or wounded here. Private C. Clutterbuck was another who was particularly active in all this close fighting, on many occasions rushing out alone to hurl bombs at the enemy. He was afterwards awarded the D.C.M.

After an hour's heavy fighting, D Company joined hands with the 1st Battalion in a short length of communication trench which ran between the lines. The attack here caused great anxiety to the 123rd German Grenadier Regiment, remnants of four of whose companies were holding that flank. By the time the fight ended one of these companies, the 4th, had lost 98 out of a "trench strength" of 110 The regiment had now used up all its supports, and orderlies and batmen were hurriedly summoned to the headquarters in the Bullecourt-Hendecourt in case the Australian attack reached that critical point.

All day long the men worked hard to consolidate the position. At 10 p.m. the enemy launched another heavy attack along the battalion front. On the right and centre A and B Companies repulsed the Germans with ease, but on the extreme left flank the post of D Company was forced to withdraw when it ran out of bombs. At 11 o'clock the enemy again heavily bombarded our lines, severing all telephone communication with the rear. Much short shooting by our own supporting artillery was also experienced, as a result of which we suffered some casualties.

On May 5th the battalion was strengthened by the arrival of the detached platoons of C Company, which now moved to the left flank and relieved D. The latter was put in to hold the right centre, between A and B Companies.

At 10.15 p.m., fresh troops assailed A Company with bombs, but the S.O.S. barrage quickly dispersed them. From 1 a.m. until the hour of dawn on the 6th, the German artillery poured a heavy barrage into the entire captured position. Its infantry then made a determined frontal attack on A Company and on the 11th and 12th Battalions to our right, as well as an attack on those two battalions along O.G.1 and O.G.2. The frontal attack was completely defeated by the concentrated fire of rifles and Lewis and Vickers guns, as well as of the artillery. On the flank of the 3rd Brigade the Germans, with the assistance of flame-throwers, met with some temporary success, but they were soon routed, and the Australian hold was slightly extended. During the morning six platoons of the 4th Battalion arrived to reinforce the 3rd, but, as its left flank had not been attacked, they moved into O.G. 2 to strengthen the 11th and 12th Battalions. Shortly afterwards they were ordered to return to the railway embankment, the 10th Battalion taking their place.

As the 3rd Battalion was by now sadly reduced in numbers—in some platoons only a handful of men remained—the 2nd Battalion was sent in to relieve it, and at 10 p.m. on the 6th the tired survivors moved back, as did those of the 1st Battalion, which was relieved by the 4th. But for the time being rest was out of the question, the relieved units being called on to provide parties to carry supplies to the front line. Next day the 9th Battalion took over these duties from the 3rd, which was accordingly withdrawn to the Vaulx defences. On May 9th the battalion was relieved here by the 29th, and moved back to Riencourt-les-Bapaume, from which, on the 13th, it went to Bazentin-le-Petit.

With the exception of one post abandoned by D Company, not an inch of the consolidated line had been lost to the enemy. Nor had he once obtained a firm footing in the battalion's trenches—indeed, more ground was gained by the battalion.

Throughout the operations the battalion had despatched many carrying parties to the rear to bring up large supplies of ammunition, bombs, and rifle-grenades. Sometimes less than 50 per cent of these parties succeeded in returning through the German fire, that of the light and heavy trench-mortars and the machine-guns being particularly troublesome.

The casualties—56 killed, 8 missing, and 245 wounded—had sadly thinned the ranks of the battalion. The losses among officers, however, had not been considerable, and reorganization was therefore quickly affected at Bazentin, where we were joined by a party of 56 reinforcements under Second-Lieuts A. N. Buckley and A. E. Smith. On May 21st, after an easy rest, the greater part of the battalion marched to Buire-sur-Ancre, where we picked up another batch of reinforcements, numbering 70. For the time being C Company was left at Bazentin to load material into trucks at Bernafay Wood.

Major W. B. Carter was now temporarily in command of the battalion, Lieut-Colonel Moore having gone on leave to England.

CASUALTIES: Captain J. G. Tyson, killed; Lieut R. R. Morgan, died of wounds; Lieut A. G. Cormack, wounded; Second-Lieut M. McL. Keshan, wounded. Other ranks, 56 killed, 245 wounded, 8 missing. (The battalion went into Bullecourt with a strength of 17 officers and 543 other ranks.)

The list of decorations awarded for distinguished conduct at Bullecourt contained the following names:—

MILITARY CROSS.—Captain C. F. Elliot.

D.C.M.—No. 2607, Lance-Corporal A. Hudson; 1666, Private C. Clutterbuck.

MILITARY MEDAL.—No. 2167, Sergeant H. W. Maston; 1396, T/Cpl S. McGee; 561, T/Cpl R. R. Bonney; 3290, Lance-Cpl J. L. Roberts; 1147, Lance-Cpl N. Murray, 2848, Private W. L. Wallace.

CHAPTER XXIX

THE THIRD BATTLE OF YPRES

JUNE began in a burst of glorious weather. In the invigorating warmth of a teaming spring-time, the units of the I Anzac Corps in back areas, far from the line, were settling down to a period of rest and hard training that was to last until well into September.

The 3rd Battalion had suffered to such an extent in the Bullecourt fighting that in two companies immediately afterwards only a bare 30 men had answered the roll call. The loss of trained N.C.Os was proportionately high. These gaps were to some extent made good by the return of "old hands" from schools and from the base depôt, but even so, the four companies were at this time only about half-strength.

All ranks were cheered considerably by the news that the Americans had at last joined in the struggle. It meant, save for some great accident, that victory was ultimately assured.

The inauguration of divisional competitions were an incentive to thorough training. These began in the battalions during the first week in June, when D Company won the inter-company contest in the 3rd. In the 1st Brigade competition which followed, D Company was again successful. This win gave it the right to compete against the winners in the other brigades—C Company of the 8th Battalion, and D Company of the 10th. The brigade results were made known at the divisional sports meeting held near Hénencourt on June 12th; and the following day D Company marched from Buire to billets in Hénencourt, where the final test took place a week or so later. Ably led by Captain A. L. Hewish, D Company of the 3rd emerged victorious and thus gained the coveted divisional cup. The battalion band, under Sergeant Bert Williams, played the winners back to Buire with appropriate airs, and seven days' leave to Amiens was promptly granted to the men by Lieut-Colonel Moore.

On one of our rests at Buire-sur-Ancre, the local miller was also known as the brewer, not that he brewed, but he wholesaled *biere Suisse* to the local *estaminet* proprietors. On one trip from the railway goods yard over a mile away he had just pulled up his team of big white Percherons at the mill-yard gate, when some of the lads asked him how many barrels he had brought. "Six," he replied; whereupon he was told that there were only five on the waggon and that he must have dropped one on the way. He let out a great roar, jumped down from his cart, and, without waiting to check his load, rushed back along the road to locate and secure the missing barrel before the troops got hold of it. By the time he had gone to the railway and back, the whole of the beer had been unloaded by the troops and rolled to the bank of the river, where a great camp-fire was soon organized and the evening devoted to singing and consuming the good brown stuff so freely provided. Some went into the officer's mess, some went into the sergeant's mess, and the rest was successfully surrounded by the lads in the good old-fashioned way. The brewer, after an all-night search, discovered at break of day his missing barrels busted in and very empty bobbing about alongside the weir. Of course no one was able to afford any information regarding the occurrence.—Private W. Atkins.

But nothing succeeds like success. The battalion was now called upon to provide a guard of honour to no less a personage than the Duke of Connaught, who was visiting the Third Army Headquarters. This guard, furnished by 100 men from D Company, under Captain Hewish and Lieuts Shelley and Taylor, carried out its duties in an admirable manner at Albert on June 18th.

The same day, the remainder of the battalion moved from Buire to bivouacs round Englebelmer and Mailly-Maillet, and for a week took part in field manoeuvres over the old battlefield of Beaumont-Hamel. One night was spent in practising a full dress night attack.*

Back to Buire, the battalion on July 6th supplied a guard of honour on the occasion of the unveiling by General Birdwood of the monument at Pozières to the men of the 1st Division who fell in the operations there in July and August, 1916. On the following day the accidental explosion of a bomb during instruction wounded Second-Lieut A. Croll and eleven other ranks.

On July 12th the units of the 1st Brigade lined the Albert-Amiens road while King George went by. Next day a move was made by route march to the Bray area, and for ten days further exercises and training were carried out in the old French lines there. On the 27th we entrained at Buire for Flanders, our destination being Nieppe, close to the village of Ebblinghem where the battalion had occupied its first billets some eighteen months before.

"Old Pop," assisted by his second wife, very much his junior, and three daughters too old to be much attraction, conducted an *estaminet* opposite our billets at Buire. Still he enjoyed fair patronage owing to good *biere* and accessibility at all hours, legitimate or otherwise, as the well in

---

* It was during these manoeuvres that an incident occurred which set the battalion chuckling for several days. Private Jack Dean, the wit of the unit, over six feet in height and thin as a whippet, a man who stuttered badly, was the central figure. At the rear of the battalion he and a few others were carrying sand-bags filled with grass, to represent ammunition. A staff officer, appearing on the scene, selected Dean as a likely man to question.

"What part of the outfit do you represent, my man, and what have you in the bag?" he asked.

"B——y m-m-m-edals for the S-S-Staff," came the ready reply.

his yard contained good water and furnished a reasonable excuse for being found on the premises out of hours. One evening Madame announced that the *estaminet* would be closed the next day, as she and the daughters would be spending the day in Amiens. Apparently "Pop" could not be trusted to hand over all the takings. After tea we heard knocking, and found that "Pop" had been locked up in the cellar for safe-keeping. Readily he agreed that if he were liberated he would open up as usual, and as the doors, etc., were only secured in the usual careless French fashion with wooden pins thrust into doorposts, no difficulty was experienced by the liberators. In token of his appreciation all drinks were on the house, and a good time was had by all until about 9 p.m., when we were rudely disturbed by the arrival of Madame and the three ugly daughters. Poor "Pop" was soundly belaboured by four infuriated women when they found no beer and no money was the result of the evening's trading. A tarpaulin-muster next pay day compensated "Pop" for his sufferings on the condition that not one sou of it was to go to Madame; he assured us he had a secure plant for such few coins as eluded Madame's eagle eye.—Private W. Atkins.

The return to well-known and happily remembered scenes was in accord with the humour of the troops generally. Although it was a leaner, graver, and older regiment, with much hard campaigning behind it, the men were still as appreciative of the spontaneous, open-hearted welcome of the cheerful Flemish folk. There was a richness, too, about the landscape that was a welcome change from the barren uplands of the Somme. Fresh vegetables became welcome additions to the common menu. Even if they did appear suddenly on the official platters, mysteriously and unexplained—no questions were asked.

On July 29th there was a heavy thunder-storm, the

prelude to a deluge of rain such as had not for many a year been experienced during the summer in Flanders. For a whole week the downpour was continuous, and everyone was depressed at the thought that the great British offensive east of Ypres, which had begun on the 31st, and in which the I Anzac Corps was destined to take part, was thereby probably doomed to failure.

The move eastwards of the battalion began on August 9th, when it marched some 12 miles to Grand Sec Bois. Curiously enough, this march through the Hazebrouck area coincided with a heavy bombardment of that railway junction by German long-range guns, and many civilians seeking a temporary refuge in the fields passed the marching troops.

That night and the following day, further rains drenched the battlefield which was now little short of a vast bog. Nevertheless the offensive was resumed on the 16th, under frightful conditions, and the French and British troops were almost everywhere driven back with heavy loss, the same fate befalling a number of local attacks against "Inverness Copse," "Glencorse Wood," and Nonne Bosschen on the following days. So it happened that on August 26th Sir Douglas Haig decided to make the southern heights of the Passchendaele-Staden ridge the centre of his ensuing attacks, the planning and carrying out of which he now entrusted to General Plumer's Second Army. The date of the attack was fixed for September 20th, the I Anzac Corps being chosen to capture the key position on the ridge.

Meanwhile the battalion continued its training around Sec Bois. All ranks thoroughly enjoyed the respite in this lush and smiling region, which had yet to feel the defacing hand of war. Then in September inspections by the divisional commander, the corps commander, and the army commander followed in quick succession; and several of the battalion officers, including Major J. R. O.

Harris and Captain R. I. Moore, returned from "other duty."

On September 13th the battalion numbered 40 officers and 916 other ranks, but 10 officers and 96 men were left behind as a nucleus when the battalion that day moved on to Meteren. The final "Instruction in the Preparation of a Division for Offensive Action" was a feature of the new and extraordinarily improved battle organization. Next day the troops marched to "Ottawa" camp, near Ouderdom, for the special purpose of becoming acquainted with the nature of the ground over which they were to fight. This was done by means of a large relief map, constructed with great care on a closed area of ground by specialist engineers. On this model every significant feature of the Menin Road battlefield was shown, and lecturers briefly explained the objectives of the forthcoming operation. For purposes of reconnaissance, officers and N.C.Os were given special facilities for studying this map.

The objectives were easy to understand. The natural strength of the enemy position on the wide semicircle of heights to the east and north-east of Ypres was shown to be truly remarkable. Instead of garrisoning the front line continuously in strength, the Germans, since the advent of Ludendorff to the Western Front, now held the forward area by means of scattered posts, with machine-gun nests (many of them in concrete blockhouses, known as pillboxes) distributed over a wide area behind them. Behind these again were the supports and strong reserves and more machine-guns, in great depth. The enemy's tactics were to keep these reserves out of reach of the first attack, so as to use them in a swift counter-stroke before their opponents had time to settle down and consolidate the positions gained.

Never before on the Western Front were the Australian divisions more confident than now. For the first time two of them were to advance side by side, the 1st Division, on the right, attacking the main ridge, the 2nd Division "Anzac Spur." The operation would be made in three stages of 800, 400-500, and 200-300 yards respectively, and each division's front of attack was 1000 yards. Opposite the 1st Division, which was using the 2nd and 3rd Brigades, the remains of Glencorse Wood and Nonne Bosschen bog provided obstacles that seemed likely to break up any attack. "Zero" hour was fixed for 5.40 a.m. on September 20th. The 1st Brigade was to be in close reserve.*

On the 16th, the 3rd Battalion moved to Dickebusch and forthwith began battle preparations, detailing D Company for work in the forward area and several other parties for carrying work. At 5 p.m. on the 19th it moved forward another stage, to Château Segard area, passing through an almost incredible array of the material of war. For three miles before the front was reached, the cannon stood almost row on row. In the I Anzac Corps alone, more than 500 guns, field and heavy, had been allotted to support the attack.

Success was instantaneous. At every point where the blockhouses showed fight, the attackers with a ready initiative outflanked and quickly suppressed them. All objectives were attained. With the easy dexterity that months of training had perfected, a "crater-line" was swiftly formed and organized in depth to withstand the barrage fire.

At 1 a.m., four hours before the attack, the 3rd Battalion had moved to support trenches near "Half-way House," beyond Zillebeke, whence at 7.40 (two hours

---

* The front of attack was eight miles in extent, from the Ypres-Comines canal, in the Second Army sector, to the Ypres-Staden railway, in that of the Fifth Army. In all, 11 divisions were to be employed—9 British and 2 Australian. Five would attack on the left of the 2nd Australian, four on the right of the 1st.

after zero) it moved in artillery formation to occupy the old front line from which the 2nd Brigade had advanced.

Very heavy shell-fire was the outstanding feature of this battle, the enemy's answer to the avalanche of British shells, that roared overhead like the passing of a hundred express trains, being a continuous rain of "daisy-cutters" (5.9's fitted with instantaneous fuses), which took heavy toll. Work was consequently hampered. In the old front line, the battalion suffered some 70 casualties, including Second-Lieut E. C. H. Ritchie (of Bega, N.S.W.) killed. But the spirit of the men was invincible. Everywhere buoyant morale was apparent. The stretcher-bearers, signallers, and runners, whose duty took them continually over the exposed tracks and pathways of this awful crater-field, were particularly selfless.

On the night of September 21st, the 3rd moved forward and took over the newly captured "Green Line" from the 7th and 8th Battalions, the relief being completed by 1 a.m. on the 22nd. The front occupied was on the southern slope of the Polygon Wood ridge, astride the faint trace of a road leading to an old pre-war artillery training ground known as the Polygone de Zonnebeke, which remained the one recognizable landmark upon the desolate crater-field. The wisdom of avoiding here the construction of a continuous front-line trench which enemy aircraft could easily discover, was now most apparent. Very few shells fell upon the front positions; instead the support lines were heavily battered, battalion headquarters being harassed to a marked degree. Snipers and machine-guns also caused endless trouble. Second-Lieut P. I. H. Owen, son of our beloved old colonel, was this day killed by a burst from one of these guns. A native of Wollongong (N.S.W.), he had come to Sydney in 1916 from his rubber plantation in the Federated Malay States to enlist in the A.I.F., and had left in command of the 7th reinforcements for the 58th Battalion, later transferring to the 3rd.

Twenty-four hours completed the 3rd Battalion's front-line service on this occasion. No counter-attack developed, and at 11 p.m. on the 22nd the line was handed over to fresh troops. The 56th Australian Battalion took over on the left of the Polygon road, the 8th York and Lancaster and 9th Yorkshire of the 98th Brigade (33rd Division) moving in on the right.

The manner in which the 3rd Battalion conducted itself in these difficult days was most meritorious. The enemy's harassing fire, particularly at night, reached a crescendo of fury difficult to describe, while the inflammatory shells, sent over for the purpose of range-finding and the destruction of ammunition dumps, cast a weird and confusing light over the whole chaotic scene. The British guns, belching sheets of orange flame everywhere in the darkness, added to the frightful din, making the successful completion of the intricate troop movements over the battlefield a matter of great difficulty.

Captain C. F. Elliot and Lieut G. H. Leslie were wounded during this tour. In addition, 22 other ranks were killed and 91 wounded.

Moving back by way of Half-way House, the battalion rested at Dickebusch camp on the 23rd, marched next day to Ottawa camp, near Ouderdom, and on the 25th, having picked up the "nucleus," went by 'bus to the Steenvoorde area. The billets here were poor and scattered, and conditions were not improved by a transport break-down, which for two days delayed the delivery of kits and surplus gear. Consequently, all ranks had to remain in the garments worn during the tour in the line and to wear "tin hats" instead of the typical felts which the Diggers so dearly loved to don after a period in the forward area.

Until September 29th the days were spent in all

manner of training and recreation, inter-company football matches being a feature each afternoon. Lieuts L. W. S. Loveday (M.C.), E. R. Shelley (M.C.), and C. O. Clark (M.M.) were paraded before General Birdwood, who presented them with the ribbons of the decorations they had won. Sergeants H. W. Maston and C. H. Rae and Corporal J. L. Roberts received their Military Medals also.

The move forward again commenced on the 30th, after a church parade in the morning. Sunday movements were of frequent occurrence during the life of the battalion in France. At a bivouac camp at Café Belge in the Château Segard area, we relieved the 10th Battalion, which in its turn moved a stage nearer the front. Next day, while the battalion rested, and enjoyed the receipt of a huge mail from Australia, several officers visited the front area to become acquainted with the route to the line and the sector in supports which had to be taken over from the 10th Battalion on the night of October 2nd.

All ranks now heard with regret of the death of Second-Lieut F. T. G. Smith, caused by hostile aeroplane bombs while on duty at the divisional baths at Reninghelst. Smith had joined the battalion in the previous April, and taken part in the Bullecourt operations in the following month. During the summer it came to the C.O's notice that Smith's heart was affected, the cause doubtless being due to the strain of the Bullecourt bombardments, so he was detailed for light duty at the baths. And now he was dead. It was indeed a cruel stroke of fate that his end should come in such circumstances.

On the evening of October 2nd, the battalion left the bivouac camp and moved to Anzac Ridge, on its way to take part in the great battle set down for the 4th. Already on September 26th, in the Battle of Polygon Wood, the 4th and 5th Australian Divisions—after the latter had succeeded in defeating a most powerful counter-

LA BREARDE WINDMILL

BILLETS, STEENVORDE

BILLETS, SEC BOIS

RAILWAY CROSSING, STRAZEELE

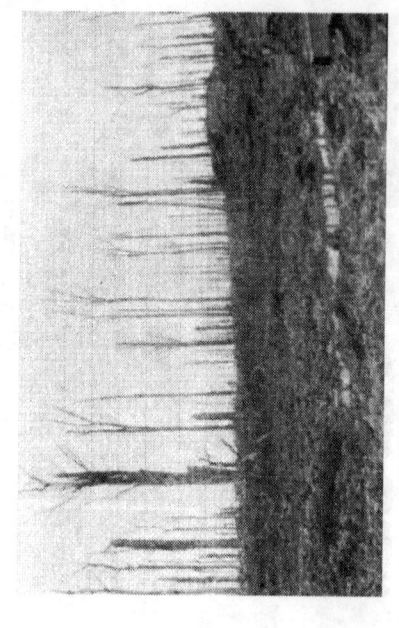

GERMAN OBSERVATION POST, RAVINE WOOD

RAVINE WOOD, HOLLEBEKE

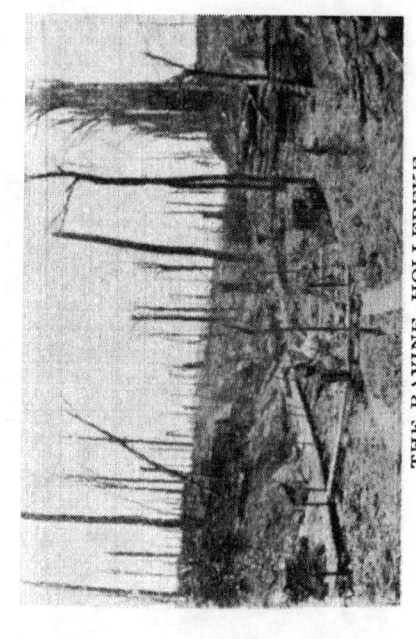

THE RAVINE, HOLLEBEKE

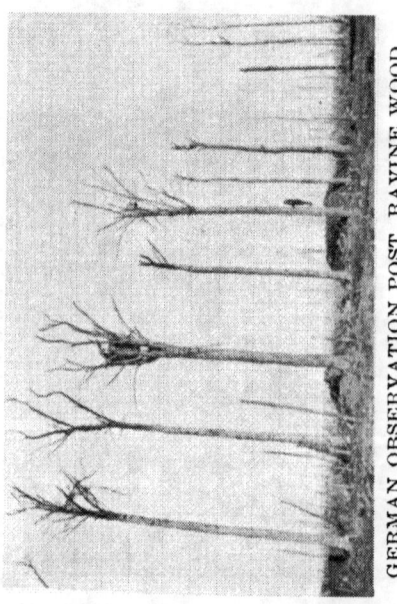

A FINAL RESTING PLACE NEAR WYTCHAETE

stroke on the previous day—had carried the advance another 1000-1200 yards, five British divisions co-operating with them.

Enemy aircraft, very active throughout this offensive, now bombed the column, inflicting numerous casualties on the 1st Light Trench Mortar Battery, which happened to be marching in rear of the battalion. As usual after dusk, the route was very much alive and congested, G.S. waggons, pack trains, ration parties, and all the other normal traffic of the forward area also being on the move. The latter part of the road was corduroy, this being the only method by which the main routes in this shell-stricken area could be maintained for the passage of guns and wheeled transport.

The manner in which the numerous working parties—of engineers, pioneers, tunnellers, and infantry—carried out the difficult task, often under heavy shell-fire, rightly earned the praise of the higher commanders, and contributed in no small measure to the success of the battles of the Menin Road, Polygon Wood, and Broodseinde.

The trenches taken over from the 10th Battalion on Anzac Ridge lacked sufficient space for the companies, and in consequence an uncomfortable 20 hours were spent here until the time came to move to the assembly positions in the early hours of the 4th. During the 3rd, Lieut Eric Shelley, who was to act as liaison officer with the left-flank brigade (the 2nd), proceeded to the Butte at Polygon Wood to observe a trial barrage on the enemy's lines. The shooting was good. So was the German artillery's retaliation. As for the enemy snipers, they were most active along the front.

The transport officer, Lieut Ted Clark, was now reported as having died of the wounds he received while hurrying forward the battalion rations on pack-horses the previous day. Lieut Clark, who was formerly a police detective in Sydney, will ever be remembered for the efficient way he maintained the battalion transport. It was barely a month since, at a march-past, his section had been the subject of favourable comment by the brigade commander.

The battle now about to be fought was the most important operation in the whole Third Ypres offensive. The objective was the Broodseinde ridge, which had been

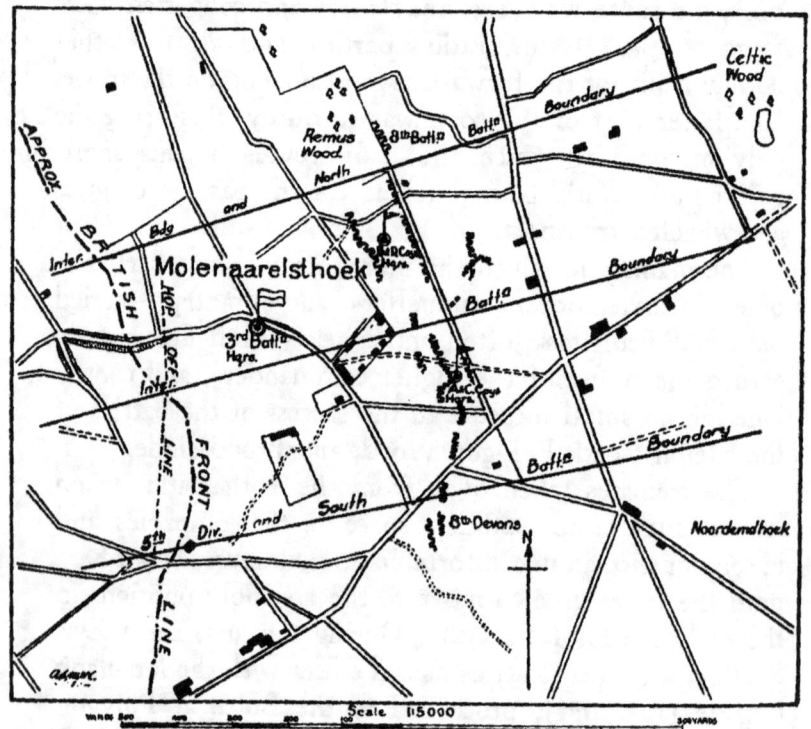

THE ATTACK ON BROODSEINDE RIDGE

captured by the Germans in 1915. "Crowded with headquarters and observation posts," says Dr Bean, in the *Official History*, "it looked out on the famous British salient as on a spread-out map." For the main attack on the ridge the 1st and 2nd Australian Divisions had again been selected. Alongside them on the north would be the 3rd Australian Division, and next to it the New

Zealand. In all, 12 divisions and parts of two others were to advance on a 14,000 yards' front, from "Bitter Wood" (south of Tower Hamlets) to the Ypres-Staden railway.

At 2 a.m. on the 4th the move began to the assembly position for the attack. The brigade intelligence officer, Lieut Hughie Robb, had laid white tapes (they did not remain white for very long) along "Jabber Track" to guide the companies to the line. Otherwise it would have been well nigh impossible to distinguish the route, because of the deplorable conditions of mud and slush. In many places it was quite a simple matter to slip from the track into the morass. Those who had the misfortune so to do had to be helped out, the usual gear taken into an attack hanging all round them. Occasional enemy shells and some indirect machine-gun fire came close to the marching column, and in places the bullets of our own supporting machine-guns seemed to pass close overhead. The snappy reports from the guns rattled and tortured the ear-drums all the time.

The battalion was in readiness on the "jumping-off" tape at 4 a.m., having two hours to wait until "zero." Some of the men were in the front trenches occupied by the 2nd Battalion, while others lay out on the tape, or were in "possies" in front of the line. The position here was on rising ground, fairly well drained. Consequently the mud was not nearly so troublesome as on the route from Anzac Ridge. The 8th Battalion was on our left, and here the liaison officer found a small gap. Both battalions maintained that they had each taken up their allotted frontage, but the gap was automatically filled as soon as the advance commenced.

At 5.30 a.m. hostile artillery-fire opened rather sharply on the front line. Numerous *minenwerfer* shells also came over, growling as they staggered aloft and swooped to earth, their fuses burning against the dark sky. Most of these fell just behind the front line, unfortunately among the waiting men of the 1st Battalion. Among the killed was Major P. L. Howell-Price, D.S.O., M.C., brother to our late C.O., and one of the most gallant officers in the 1st Brigade. It was subsequently learned that this hostile fire was preparatory to a general counter-attack which the enemy had planned to launch against the British line at 6.10 a.m.

However, the British barrage opening at 6 a.m. put an end to all the German plans. The troops were only too ready to advance and so escape from the German fire that had been harrying them for half-an-hour. The British attack, opening 10 minutes before the enemy's projected assault, added to his confusion. In many cases the Australians came upon German sections with machine-guns and *flammenwerfer* equipment packed up ready to advance. Rather strong opposition was met at a row of pill-boxes in the centre of the line, the enemy sending over showers of stick-bombs, but after a short, sharp fight our Mills bombers succeeded in ousting them. Soon the Germans broke ground and retreated through the barrage, pursued in many cases by Australians with the bayonet. This over-eagerness to get to holts with the enemy was the cause of not a few casualties, from our own shrapnel and, in one case at least, from Lewis gun fire.

Referring to our shell-fire, Lieut Shelley wrote: "At this point I turned for a few moments and faced the west, being rather far forward, waiting for our men to come up. I was rewarded by one of the finest sights of the war. In the slowly breaking dawn I could see, not tens, not hundreds, but literally thousands and thousands of slabs of orange flame belching from the mouths of our guns to north, south, and west. It looked for all the world like some gigantic field packed full of twinkling lights—a wonderful spectacle."

The enemy barrage now fell rather more sharply than

before, the 2nd Battalion in the old front line getting much of the backwash and suffering many casualties. The routes and tracks to the rear also were severely shelled during the day, and many of the wounded were again hit while being taken back.

In the dim light of the breaking dawn the enemy were often mistaken for our own men. Lieut Loveday, commanding B Company, anxiously guiding the direction of the troops, mistook a party of Germans for Australians. Calling out "Keep to the left"—"Keep to the left," he suddenly found himself in a life and death struggle with a German under-officer. He was getting by no means the best of the encounter when one of his men managed to work his bayonet between the struggling figures and dispatched the German.

Another deadly duel took place between Private W. H. Nicholson and a powerfully built German bayonet-man, the latter protected by heavy armour. Nicholson thought the German was about to surrender when the Hun suddenly lunged at him with his bayonet.

Nicholson automatically parried the thrust and was being overpowered when two shots from Sergeant Sully's revolver ended the German's life.

A remarkable incident occurred while the battalion was lying out on the tape waiting for the signal to advance. One of the men fell asleep. When the artillery barrage opened he woke with a start, grabbed his rifle, and charged the Germans all on his own.

It so happened the enemy were massed for attack, so the solitary Australian soldier was received with open arms. Two men escorted him to a neighbouring pill-box. From their actions one of them wanted to cut his throat, but the other was equally emphatic about saving his life. Before the issue had been decided the Australian attack was launched, the pill-box and its occupants were captured. Then, by signs and gesticulations, the one German made it clear that it was up to the Australian to now save his life. And so he did.

There is no record of the fate of the other man.

The 3rd Battalion, with the 8th on its left and the 8th Devons on the right, reached the first objective on time, and consolidation began at 7 a.m. Battalion headquarters was established in one of the row of pill-boxes where the bomb-fight had occurred. But the enemy batteries had these well registered, and they came in for a good deal of shelling throughout the day. During the night an entire ration party and some prisoners were all either killed or wounded just outside Colonel Moore's headquarters.

After the companies had reached the objective, Lieut Shelley was making his way to the 8th Battalion headquarters, when he came upon a badly wounded German sergeant. This man asked him in good English: "Did the whole b———y Australian army attack this morning?" Poor chap, he was just about done for, his right leg having been almost severed by shell-fire.

Among those killed in the advance was Lieut Humphrey Watson. An Englishman, irrigation engineer and surveyor in private life, always keen on his job, capable, highly respected, and a good fellow in and out of the line, he was the type of officer the battalion could least afford to lose. Lieut Bret Allport, who was seriously wounded, was another bright and cheery soul whose influence was afterwards missed in the battalion. With a fractured leg and jaw, a hole in one shoulder, and the loss of an eye, he reached the C.C.S. safely and thence proceeded to England and finally to Australia.

At 8 a.m. the 1st and 4th Battalions moved through the 3rd, and attacked the second objective. This operation also was carried out according to plan, the consolidation taking place under hostile shell and machine-gun fire, which continued to fall on the ridge and positions in rear

YPRES

throughout the day and far into the night, but slackened off before dawn on the 5th. Small parties, stretcher-bearers and others, could be seen moving over the captured ground on the nearer side of the ridge, identifying the fallen and taking stock of the surroundings.

4.10.17.

The fighting strength of the battalion at zero hour was 27 officers, 462 other ranks.

CASUALTIES: Killed in action, Lieut H. J. F. Watson, Captain A. L. Hewish, Captain R. I. Moore (M.C., D.C.M.); died of wounds, Lieut E. Clark, Second-Lieut F. T. C. Smith; wounded, Lieuts G. R. MacDougall, R. D. Allport, A. G. Cormack, Second-Lieuts A. N. Buckley, W. F. Elliott, A. E. Smith, F. G. Fitzpatrick, T. S. Rudkin, C. B. Christoe, Captain L. F. Kemmis (M.C.). Other ranks, killed 51, died of wounds 8, wounded 170, missing 10.

October 5th was a fairly quiet day, but towards dusk the German artillery renewed its fire, and the 10th Battalion had an unpleasant time moving up to take the place of the 3rd. But, after a slight delay, the relief was completed by 10.30 p.m., our companies then moving back to the positions on Anzac Ridge that we had occupied on October 3rd. Just after the relief, we had the misfortune to lose the O.C. of D Company, Captain Les. Hewish (of Albury, N.S.W.). Without doubt, he was one of the most promising officers in the brigade, and all ranks were genuinely sad because of his death.

On the 6th and 7th the battalion was employed on salvage work over the battlefield and in improving the existing trenches. On the 7th the battalion suffered further serious loss among its leaders, when a stray shell landed on B Company headquarters, killing Captain R. I. Moore, M.C., D.C.M., and seriously wounding Captain L. F. Kemmis, M.C., who lost both legs but survived. Both were natives of Armidale (N.S.W.). Moore had won the D.C.M. at the landing at Gallipoli and the M.C.

at Lone Pine. These were very serious losses to the battalion—gallant, well tried and most capable officers.

During the latter days at Anzac Ridge there was some talk of the battalion returning immediately to the front line for a further tour, but it was apparently groundless. We moved back to the Dickebusch huts on the 8th, after spending the day burying cables.

Who, among those who were fortunate enough to witness it, will ever forget the sight of Lieut "Nobby" Clark leading out his platoon. All were plastered with mud, red-eyed from loss of sleep, and unshaven, and there were few among them who had not been blackened with the soot of bomb and shell explosions. And at the head of them all, dirtier than any, strode "Nobby" with his beaming smile, his teeth being the only white thing about the whole grimy outfit.

That night the battalion moved back a further stage by bus to the Wippenhoek area. The huts and tents were poor, and, as the weather was wet during our week's stay here, very little outdoor training could be undertaken. On the 16th buses took us forward again, this time to the Belgian Château area, where dry and comfortable quarters were found in Nissen huts beside the main road to Ypres. Close by battalion headquarters occupied a two-storied house, the top floor of which had been blown off some time before.

It was common knowledge, however, that the troops had not returned to the forward area for the mere purpose of enjoying comfortable billets. Over 120 details of all ranks had rejoined, and Sergeants A. D. Arnold, D. Ross, D. R. Desbois, and E. Hawkshaw had been promoted to commissioned rank. Fatigue parties were told off and the whole battalion worked hard and continuously for the next fortnight, constructing and repairing roads and railways, delving drains, and laying cable lines.

The British front had now advanced to a point where preparations for the inevitable winter quarters in the new salient were to a certain extent possible. The clearing of the Passchendaele ridge was almost complete, and to contribute to the final effort while the weather held dry was the task set the 3rd Battalion and every other unit that could be spared. It was now dangerously late in the year. The weather could not be expected to hold much longer, and the tremendous quantities of ammunition and supplies yet required had somehow to be got forward. So we were kept busy constructing light and heavy railways across the crater-field towards Broodseinde.

This work was as difficult as it was dangerous. The roads and railways were continually under the observation of German aircraft, and it was only by destroying them and preventing their reconstruction that the enemy could obtain any relief from the British shell-fire which harassed him day and night. All paths and tracks were therefore heavily shelled, and the fatigue parties of the battalion which daily worked with the 9th Canadian Railway Company and other engineering detachments had a trying time.

From the moment of leaving camp by the light railway that conveyed them to "Hell Fire Corner" siding, whence all parties moved forward independently to their work, all came under a galling fire such as was not frequently experienced, even in the front line. The main railway crossing of the Menin-Ypres road, which had been melodramatically dubbed "Hell Fire Corner," was a particularly dangerous spot, as were the valleys in the immediate vicinity of Hooge and Westhoek. German bombing planes assisted in this persistent harassing of the working parties, and several powerful squadrons attempted daylight raids, dropping bombs, fortunately in most cases without considerable results. At night, large Gotha bombers made repeated raids over the back area about

Ypres, and on October 27th they succeeded in inflicting heavy casualties on the 2nd Battalion in an adjoining camp at Château Belge.*

Casualties occurred repeatedly among the working parties, but astonishing escapes were much more frequent. By the last day of the month the light railway had been pushed forward nearly two miles, to Anzac Ridge. Much damage was continually done to this line, but persistence triumphed in the end, and the troops had the satisfaction of helping forward on its rails the big howitzers that were destined to hammer the German artillery which for two years had dominated the British positions on the Ypres flats.

Camp life near Château Belge was not entirely colourless. A divisional concert party had been organized, and its efforts were much appreciated, as were the more solid creature comforts obtainable from an excellent wet-and-dry canteen.

The war, however, was paramount, and on November 5th, in broad daylight, we marched to the line, and at 11 a.m. relieved the 11th Battalion in the support positions before Zonnebeke. This bold move proved conclusively with what completeness the Germans had been deprived of their strategetic advantage. The new position was immediately on the left of the Ypres-Roulers railway, and no particular activity on the part of the enemy was noticeable. On the 6th, however, the Canadian Corps, on the left, launched an attack on the ruins of Passchendaele and this finally brought some barrage fire upon the main support positions. B Company in particular was ill-treated by this fire, but fortunately no serious loss resulted.

On November 8th the battalion took over the left sector of the brigade front from the 2nd Battalion, a relief

---

* A number of the 2nd's men were paraded for an issue of clothing when a bomb landed among them. Officers and stretcher-bearers of the 3rd Battalion rendered what assistance they could to the wounded.

that was only remarkable because of the extraordinary circumstances accompanying it. The night was extremely dark, and the condition of the crater-field, which had now become waterlogged by the early winter rains, absolutely defies adequate description. "It was," writes Sergeant A. E. Bray, of A Company, "a quagmire within a quagmire. It was a wonder to us that human beings had ever been able to walk across such ground, let alone fight across it successfully!"

The relief was completed in good time, despite the fact that some of the companies became intermingled with Canadian units which were relieving on our immediate left in preparation for a further assault on the 10th. This circumstance had no ill-effects, but the Australians had the opportunity of hearing some picturesque Canadian oaths. The Canadian assaults duly came off as arranged, and were assisted by Australian divisional artillery. Again the enemy's retaliatory barrage severely punished the 3rd Battalion positions.

The trenches in occupation were in a very bad state, having been dug in ground that was now rapidly turning to slime. Ration parties and all supply details were considerably hampered by these conditions, and the rations had to be boldly "packed" forward by daylight. The battalion quartermaster and his always dependable assistants gave yeoman service on the shell-blasted trails and tracks, but it was very difficult to get hot meals to the front line, and in consequence the discomfort of all hands was greatly increased.

Heavy rains set in again on the 10th, the day on which the Canadians made a further attack at Passchendaele. To add to the miseries of the already bone-tired men, all the trenches showed signs of collapsing. A Company was seriously affected in this way, for the enemy opened on their position with a heavy strafe which utterly wrecked all dugouts and shelters and brought the total casualties of the battalion on this tour to 13 killed and 45 wounded.

When spirits generally were at their lowest ebb, the welcome order came which prepared all hands for relief that night by the 2/7th Lancashire Fusiliers, and guides from the companies met the incoming troops near Birr Cross-Road. The company which had been in support was on its way out at 7 p.m., but the others had to wait until midnight for the relief to reach them.

The conditions of the march back to Ypres that night were unforgettably vile. Shells had obliterated most of the tracks, and in the bewildering darkness many parties were lost upon what was indubitably the most dreadful area of desolation that it had ever been the misfortune of man to behold. Many men were drenched through and through, and in their heavy equipment at times almost drowned when they fell into brimming shell-holes, some of which were more than ten feet deep. One party of A Company found itself wading into the centre of Zonnebeke "Lake," a considerable expanse of water that could in no way be distinguished from the rest of that trackless quagmire.

No wonder the nerves of the men frayed under these impossible conditions! Fortunately the possibility of a difficult or disastrous relief had been anticipated, and all the slightly wounded and weaker men had been sent ahead to make their way back to Ypres as best they could by daylight. Only the strongest were called upon to face the hardships of the night, and even some of these were forced to abandon every particle of their equipment before they could reach the firm footing of the corduroy track. Tales of fortitude to a degree almost incredible were told of this night march through the ghastly morass of the Zonnebeke valley, and it is certain that never before were the spirits of the men drained to so low an ebb. The Australian Comforts Fund hot drink dépôts in the back areas were little heavens on this night.

As the men arrived in small, weary groups at the rendezvous at the canal dugouts at Ypres, many were quite unable to eat the hot food the cooks had ready. Falling prone upon the earth, careless of everything since they had got through to this goal, they slept like dead men until they were aroused for a late breakfast.

Everyone had again been tried to the limit of human endurance. Exhausted men who had been out in the muddy hell all night continued to straggle in right up to the time the main body of the battalion moved off at 10 a.m. for Halifax camp, near Ouderdom. All were plastered with mud from head to foot, and more than half the men were suffering acutely with sore and swollen feet. The short march of three miles was made in what the terse, but adequate, military phraseology describes as "independently," or the irate sergeant-major "column of lumps." However, the trek was completed before noon, and the unit set about the inevitable task of reorganizing. A general inspection of uniforms and equipment disclosed a very heavy list of shortages. These were promptly made up, and, with the return of the invigorating self-respect that a washed and shaven well-being always brings to tired troops, the "Chocolate and Greens" began very noticeably to recover the old snap and verve that had lately been in eclipse.

From Ouderdom, the battalion moved by route march to the Berthen area. No packs were carried and, as a multiplicity of foot trouble had developed, motor lorries had to be provided for men so afflicted. On the following day a further march was made to the Ebblinghem-Wallon Capel area. This time 300 of the men had to be carried by train.

CHAPTER XXX

THE WINTER OF 1917-1918

ALL were now aware that they were moving to a back area. This was very pleasing news, and, when the nucleus under Lieut C. H. D. Champion rejoined the battalion, the move back was made immediately, by way of Henringham, Assinghem, Senlecques, to Halinghen, where on November 19th preparations were made for an extended stay.

An easy syllabus of training was embarked upon, recreational work being practised in a manner calculated to give the troops the utmost benefit from their rest period. The alacrity with which the men forgot their arms and turned to sport demonstrated how small an immediate effect the disasters of war had upon their courage. Sport, with its levelling and recuperative effect on all ranks, was one of the brightest phases of the military life of the A.I.F., and it did much to keep the competitive spirit at a high pitch and develop the unit *esprit-de-corps*. Inter-company contests were accordingly inaugurated, and D Company again emerged as the champions, with an aggregate of 692 points.

The extensive city and seaport of Boulogne was only about ten miles distant, so as much leave as possible to visit it was granted to all ranks. Bathing parades to Étaples by motor-bus were also popular.

Early in December, however, it became evident that the exigencies of war would compel an early return of the resting units to the fighting line; and on the 14th, in heavy marching order, the battalion, 868 strong, moved to Enquin, proceeding thence to Ledinghem and Assinghem on succeeding days.

The old stone mill at Assinghem which had been the battalion's billet on the previous visit, was utilized again, but, the weather having become very severe, the place was, if anything, colder than before. And fishing (with bombs) in the old mill-pond was not so good on this occasion.

The forward journey was continued on the 17th, when reveille at 3 a.m. called the men out into weather that threatened a blizzard. Throughout the whole of the march to the railway centre at Wizernes, a fierce storm raged. Seven inches of snow fell, while a head wind blew with cutting force into the faces of officers and men and made the burden of their soaked and freezing gear a torture. After some delay in the station yard at Wizernes, a train was provided at 6 a.m. to convey the battalion to d'Kennebak siding in Mont Kemmel area. Here, about noon, quarters were found in Ramilles camp.

In this very comfortable camp the unit fortified itself against the severe weather that now set in. Snow-storms were incessant, as were black frosts. Training was carried out only by companies.

A happy Christmas season was spent in Ramilles camp with *beaucoup bière* and other comforts, supplied mostly from the battalion canteen. Immediately afterwards arrangements were made to relieve the 6th Battalion at Oosttaverne in the Messines-Wytschaete sector, south of Ypres, and on the 30th, advance parties moved up to take over stores and allot positions. The relief was duly completed at 8 p.m. on December 31st. Between 9.30 and midnight D Company, in reserve in "Ouse Trench," lost an N.C.O. killed and 3 men wounded from shell-fire.

The front line in this area consisted of a series of unconnected posts in low-lying, muddy and marshy ground, and could only be reached with the greatest difficulty. The positions held by the 3rd and 4th Battalions were separated by a small stream, the Wambeke, which here ran through a valley. For about 200 yards on either side of it the country was a quagmire, "pitted" by shell-holes full of water. It was impossible to establish posts here, but at intervals throughout the night patrols from each battalion visited its neighbour's flank posts.

Duties in this area were those of ordinary trench-warfare—the improving of the support trenches and avenues of communication, and the sending out of frequent patrols. The patrol work was of course hampered to a great extent by the boggy nature of the ground. On the night of January 4th the flank patrol (one N.C.O. and four men) acting in liaison with the 4th Battalion was attacked by an enemy party about eight strong.

After a hand-to-hand scuffle, in which two of our men were wounded, the Germans were driven off. The same night a fighting patrol of one officer and 26 men discovered an enemy working-party and dispersed it with Lewis gun fire.

On January 6th Lieut-Col Moore left us for a month's furlough, Major A. F. Burrett taking charge of the battalion until the 24th, when Major W. B. Carter returned from hospital and assumed command. At this time the quartermaster, Lieut D. G. Oakley, received official notification that he had been awarded the Military Cross. Such a well-merited honour was fully approved by the whole battalion.

"It was rather a peaceful war for us just then," wrote Major Burrett afterwards, "and the Diggers were really having a 'front line rest.' However, 'the heads' suddenly discovered that they wanted identification of the German troops opposite, and we were ordered to get this urgently. Nevertheless, we were forbidden to do the usual trench-raiding stunt.

FLETRE

RUINS OF CAESTRE

RUINS OF CAESTRE

RUINS OF FLETRE

R.C. CHURCH, PRADELLES

SUPPORTS, SHREWSBURY FOREST

DESERTED STRAZEELE

D COY HEADQUARTERS, STRAZEELE

"For a few nights fighting patrols went out, but not a sign of a wandering Fritz was seen, and 'nil' reports were rendered. This brought a 'strafe' from the 'brig.' In desperation I offered 100 francs each for the first six Huns brought in dead or alive. The only stipulation was that corpses must be 'warm' and not 1914 models. This offer appealed to the troops, and for the next few nights the front line was deserted—the whole 3rd Battalion was out on patrol. But the Germans very wisely stayed 'at home,' and finally we were relieved from the line without getting the desired identification.

"Before we left the line 'Dad' Jarvis composed a verse or two, which were sung to the tune of 'In the Evening by the Moonlight.' One stanza I remember went somewhat as follows:

> Down the Wambeke, see them go,
> Keen to catch the Major's dough:
> Creeping through the German wire,
> Meeting Hun machine-gun fire.
> First they whisper, then they yell,
> As they run like "Nancy Bell."
> In the evening, down the Wambeke,
> With the wind up,
> Running with the wind up, wind up, wind up,
> Running with the wind up, all night long.

This tour of duty came to an end at 8.30 p.m. on January 15th, when the 6th Battalion returned to the line. The 3rd moved back to a rest camp near Wytschaete, and during the next week the opportunity was taken to fumigate blankets, visit the divisional baths, and wash our clothes. Only very small working-parties were supplied to assist the engineers.

At 7.30 p.m. on the 22nd, we relieved the 1st Battalion at Oosttaverne. The same night that battalion, which had gone into supports, sent a party into No-Man's Land to search for Lieut Bull and several men who had gone out on patrol on the 19th and had not returned. The search was unsuccessful. In the meantime, however, Lieut Bull, who had spent the three days behind and in front of a German post, came back through our lines. The majority of his patrol had been captured by the enemy.

Our next relief took place at 10 p.m. on January 30th, the 56th Battalion (5th Division) taking over the line. Shortly after noon on the 31st we arrived at Ramilles camp, at Kemmel, and an hour or so later left by bus for Meteren. By now the battalion numbered 32 officers and 656 other ranks. On arrival at Meteren, the companies moved off to billets, principally in farms spread over a considerable area. The most distant company was closer to Merris than Meteren, and battalion headquarters was in Meteren itself. Generally speaking, the billets were good, being commodious, well protected from the weather, and supplied with plenty of fresh straw. The health of the unit was excellent.

The time spent at Meteren was devoted to a rigorous course of training, which included a number of long route marches. The mornings were usually occupied in military exercises, the afternoons in football and other games. At night picture shows and concert parties in Meteren helped towards making the stay here a pleasant one. The divisional competition, carried out in a spirit of friendly rivalry, was won by the 1st Battalion.

During the few weeks spent here members of the battalion became well acquainted with the surrounding country-side, and the knowledge then gained stood us in good stead when in April we had to help drive the enemy out of Meteren and other villages in the neighbourhood.

Our occupation of this area came to an end on February 27th, when we marched to Murrumbidgee camp, near La Clytte. Next day we relieved the 50th Battalion (4th Division) at Ridge Wood camp, north of Vierstraat.

Ridge Wood was a hessian-hutted camp, the buildings of which were built up outside with sand-bags as protection against aeroplane bombs. In addition to officers' and sergeants' messes, it contained a large recreation hut for the men. To make the huts more comfortable and cleaner, they were tarred.

While at this camp the demand for fatigue parties was very heavy. Almost the whole battalion was utilized daily in the forward areas and at De Seule and d'Kennebak dumps. The only men not detailed for this work were the Lewis gunners, scouts and signallers, who carried on with their specialist training, and a party that was being organized for raiding purposes.

About this time, raids by the enemy were frequent along the divisional front, and it was expected that he might at any time make an attempt to break through. At 10 p.m. on March 1st the whole battalion was ordered to stand by during the progress of one of these raids, but there were no serious developments. The same night, selected officers and N.C.Os were sent from each company to acquaint themselves with the topography of the forward area.

On March 6th C Company moved up to the "Spoil Bank," south-west of Verbrandenmolen. Here it came under orders of the brigade-major, who employed it in renovating and constructing dugouts. In the following week Captain G. F. Plunkett and Lieut E. H. Jackson, D.C.M., rejoined the battalion after a period of duty with the 1st Training Battalion in England. On the 21st, thirty-two men were gassed while working in the forward area. Fortunately, most of them escaped permanent injury.

On the night of March 22nd, the 3rd Battalion relieved the 2nd in the front line at Verbrandenmolen. During the ensuing tour of duty patrols and scouting parties were kept busy, while the Lewis gunners occasionally found good targets at "Pool," "Pack" and "Long" farms. Enemy aircraft was active, especially on the 24th. At

12.45 p.m. that day our Lewis gunners engaged a hostile plane and it turned back, apparently damaged.

At last, on the night of the 25th, the 8th and 9th Battalions of the Lincoln Regiment, belonging to the 63rd Brigade, took over the task of holding the front, and early next morning we returned to the comparative comfort of Ridge Wood camp. For the next week the battalion was called upon to supply heavy fatigue parties. Those of March 27th may be taken as a typical example of a day's work. On this day 4 officers and 100 men were provided for wood cutting in Bois Carré, 1 officer and 23 men for hut building at "Dead Dog" farm, 23 men to work under the direction of the camp commandant at Larch Wood, and 37 at the 1st Divisional Train's coal dump. Meanwhile, three companies spent happy hours in the baths at "Confusion Corner."

CHAPTER XXXI

THE DEFENCE OF HAZEBROUCK

By the end of 1917 Germany had succeeded in pushing Russia, Serbia, and Rumania out of the war, and quite recently had delivered Italy a staggering blow at Caporetto. She was thus free to shift numerous divisions from these fronts to the west, and to concentrate her attention on a great offensive against the Franco-British Armies.

The blow fell on March 21st, against the Third and Fifth British Armies. The actual front of attack was from Croisilles, on the Sensée River, to Vendeuil, on the Oise, a distance of over fifty miles. The British troops, hopelessly outnumbered, fought with great valour, but they were pressed back so quickly that within a week the Germans were in possession of the old Somme battlefield of 1916 and were threatening Amiens and even Paris.

At the outset the Australian Corps was holding a sector miles away to the north of the threatened split, and the 3rd Battalion was on the point of re-entering the line at Verbrandenmolen. But by March 30th the appalling seriousness of the situation had impressed itself upon every man in the B.E.F. Sir Douglas Haig issued a special message to the troops. Already the 3rd and 4th Australian Divisions had been rushed south to help stem the German flood, and the 2nd and 5th were following in their wake. In the 1st Division, which was ordered to stand ready to move, officers reduced their kits to a minimum, and all spare gear and equipment was collected and forwarded to various dumps. The departure of the

Australians from this region, where they were held in such high regard by the civilian population, caused consternation among these people, many of whom freely remarked, "When you go, the Germans will attack here."

At last on April 2nd came the call to the 1st Division to proceed south. The battalion travelled by light railway from Ridge Wood to a camp at "Fuzeville," near Reninghelst. Here three reinforcement officers, Second-Lieuts C. L. Wainwright, M.M., H. F. Baily, and A. T. Anderson, reported for duty.

On the 5th the journey was continued by route march to Godewaersvelde, where C Company boarded a waiting train which at 4 p.m. departed for Amiens. Arriving at that city at 3.30 the next morning, it immediately began the task of unloading the 1st Brigade's transport. A, B, and D Companies, together with battalion headquarters and the transport section, left at 10.5 p.m. and reached Amiens twelve hours later. Here the battalion (less C Company) received orders to march to the village of Cardonnette, where it went into billets for a few days.

On April 9th, when the battalion moved to Frechencourt, the congestion on the roads was very bad. Marching troops had to use tracks or second-class roads, leaving the main routes for guns, motor transport, and other heavy vehicles. Rain having fallen, these side tracks were reduced to liquid mud, and the troops found the going most fatiguing. It was in such conditions that long Jack Deans made one of his characteristic retorts. Because of bad feet, Jack was usually carried in some form of transport when the battalion was on the move, but on this occasion he had to march with the others. The inevitable happened. Jack was straggling about one hundred yards behind the rest of the battalion, wallowing miserably in the mud. Brigadier-General Lesslie must of course ride up at this juncture. "Hullo, Jack," he said, "falling out?" "Ye-e-s, B-r-r-rig," stammered Deans, "M-m-me b——y old p-p-p-paddles have g-g-gone on me!"

The following day the march was continued to Baizieux, which was reached at 3.30 p.m. Officers from units of the brigade immediately reconnoitred the forward area, but the fates decreed that the 1st Division was not to participate in the fight for Amiens.

Up north, the Germans had now broken through on the Lys and were making a desperate effort to reach the Channel ports. From Hollebeke to Festubert, along a fifty-mile front, the Allied line was in full retreat.* The position was not only serious. It was critical. Suddenly the British High Command decided to withdraw the 1st Australian Division from the Somme and send it hustling back to the north to assist the hard-pressed troops there. Five British divisions were also ordered thither.

The first stage of our return to the north began at 10.30 p.m. on the 10th, when the battalion set out from Baizieux along the very road it had come but eight hours before. B and C Companies, under Major A. F. Burrett, went into billets at Frechencourt, A Company at Beaucourt, and D Company and battalion headquarters at Château Montigny.

General Birdwood visited the battalion on the 11th, shortly before it left for Amiens, which was reached after a three hours' march. D Company went direct to St Roche station to entrain, the remainder of the battalion going into billets at the Hospital St Victor. At 8 p.m. an enemy airman dropped a number of bombs round the hospital. One bomb wounded four men, two fatally. Five horses were killed and four injured.

This was the day on which the British Commander-in-Chief, Sir Douglas Haig, issued his simple but moving

---

* The first to give way was the 2nd Portuguese Division. Many of the British divisions engaged had already been worn out in the fighting on the Somme the previous month.

appeal to his troops to endure to the last. After briefly surveying the events of the past three weeks and expressing the admiration he felt for "the splendid resistance" offered by all ranks of the B.E.F., he finished by saying: "There is no other course open to us but to fight it out. Every position must be held to the last man; there must be no retirement. With our backs to the wall, and believing in the justice of our cause, each one of us must fight on to the end. The safety of our homes and the freedom of mankind alike depend upon the conduct of each one of us at this critical moment."

At 6.30 a.m. on the 12th the remainder of the battalion left St Roche station on the long and weary journey northwards. That night, at 8.30, the train pulled into Hondeghem, and three-quarters of an hour later men, horses, and equipment were clear of the station.

Captain A. McDermid marched the companies for some little distance outside the village and there embussed them for Strazeele, which was reached shortly after midnight. In the meantime the transport section moved by road to Pradelles.

Major A. F. Burrett, the second-in-command of the battalion, had accompanied Captain G. E. Blake with D Company, which had arrived at Hondeghem at 10 o'clock that morning. "When we got out at the little railway siding," says Major Burrett, "the sights we saw were most pathetic. The civilian population was fleeing in droves. Old women wheeling their all in perambulators, old men and children struggling to safety as best they could. I remember those who passed close, rushing up and asking whether the 'Australiens' were coming back. When I told them 'Yes' they stopped—many of them as if by magic. One old Frenchman said to me—'Thank God, we're all right now.' It was a confidence which inspired us Australians, and was a very wonderful thing to witness."

Lieut Hughie Robb, now brigade intelligence officer, also travelled in the advance train. On arrival he immediately rode out some miles beyond Strazeele in an endeavour to gain an idea of the general situation. The Tommies he met retiring were dejected, disorganized, and apparently beaten. None knew where the enemy were. The only information vouchsafed was—"They're coming." So it was almost instantly decided to defend Strazeele, a vital spot on the main road to Hazebrouck, which, being an important railway junction, was one of the immediate objectives of the enemy.

Strazeele was deserted. The advance of the Germans had been so rapid that the majority of the inhabitants just packed a few clothes and fled in panic. Half-finished meals and food left cooking over kitchen fires provided evidence of their hurried departure. An old curé, who suddenly put in an appearance, advised the Australians to go into the houses and help themselves to whatever they fancied. "If you do not," he said, "the Boche will—*c'est la guerre!*"

One Digger, at least, followed this advice. Entering a rather prosperous looking home, he came out dressed in corsets, a canary-coloured waistcoat, and a frock coat. Long-pointed French boots had replaced his Aussie pair, and his tin helmet was superseded by a top hat. From somewhere or other, too, he had commandeered a perambulator which was loaded to capacity with bottled Bock. So garbed, with his rifle slung across his shoulder, and pushing the pram, he headed for the firing line. But he did not proceed far. The C.O. suddenly appeared on the scene to say some vitriolic things, and a sadly chastened and sobered Digger surrendered the mobile *estaminet* and went sheepishly back to recover his own apparel and equipment.

The local farmers had simply walked off their farms, leaving everything behind them. Kine in the second best bedrooms and swine in their cosy kitchen homes. That was the position as the 3rd Battalion discovered it. Stray cows were accordingly rounded up, and kept the troops supplied with milk. Fresh eggs and poultry were plentiful, and pork was no longer a luxury. Wine was on every menu. Indeed, so fastidious did some of the Digger combatants become, that they would not imbibe until the cobwebs had been brushed off the bottles souvenired from ancient cellars, so as to ascertain whether the date of the particular vintage was to their liking.

For once the troops lived and fought like the proverbial fighting cocks. This high living, however, exacted its toll, for several weeks later there was an outbreak of boils in the battalion such as it had never before experienced.

When it left Amiens as advance guard of the battalion, D Company had been detailed for the duty of unloading trains at Hondeghem, but so serious did the position now become that every available man was sent in to consolidate the line in front of Strazeele.

During the night of the 12th and the early hours of the 13th, the four companies of the 3rd strove to consolidate their new position. The line, from left to right, was held by B, D, and A Companies, with C Company in support. B had its headquarters in the front trench, D in the mill at Strazeele station, and A in the *estaminet* near the railway. On the left the 4th Battalion's line conformed to that of the 3rd. The 7th Battalion (2nd Brigade) was on our right flank.

Before dawn on the 14th patrols made touch with the British troops on the Australian flanks. These proved to be remnants of the 29th and 31st Divisions and of the Grenadier Guards. They were ordered to move through the Australian lines to the rear for the purpose of reor-

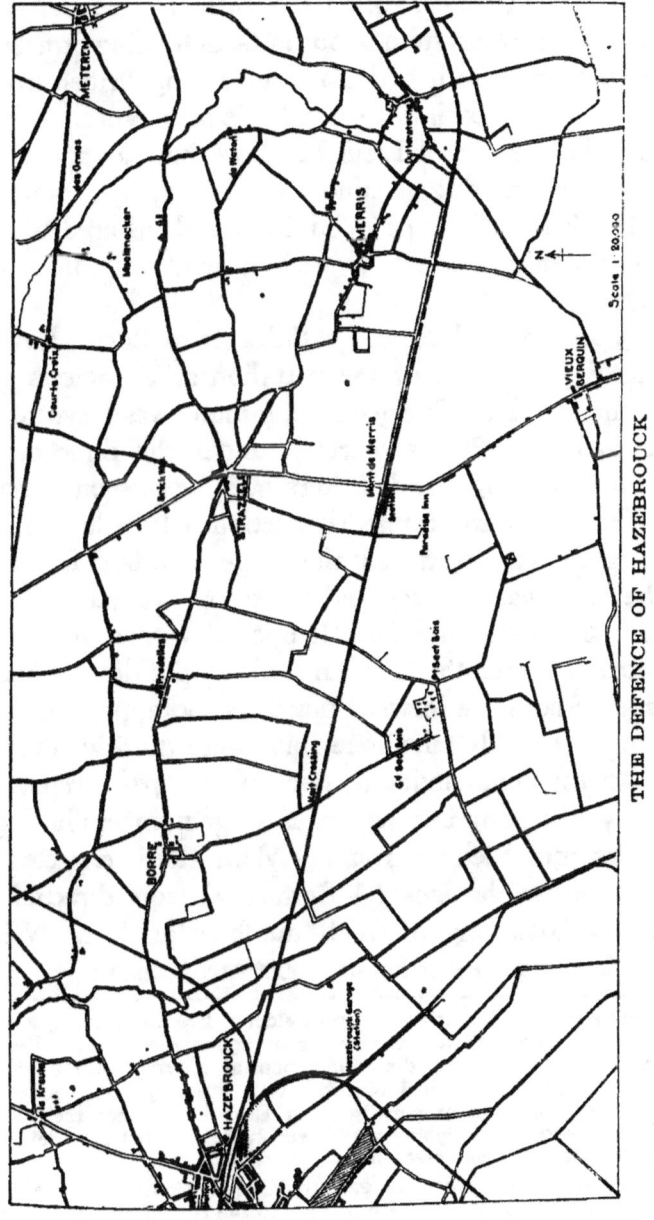

THE DEFENCE OF HAZEBROUCK

ganization.* At daybreak on the 14th the 3rd Battalion held the front by a system of outposts, defending Strazeele.

Instructions were issued that the retiring British troops should be organized into a second line of defence. Under the capable direction of Lieut E. Hawkshaw, an additional defence-line was dug, behind the village, by Tommies, who, fortified with some good food and inspired with a new confidence, bucked in with a will and did good work.†

At 5 a.m. a nucleus was withdrawn to Borre, leaving the fighting strength of the battalion at 29 officers and 596 other ranks. Every spare minute was devoted to consolidation. Stokes mortars, under the direction of Captain F. E. Page, and Vickers guns were soon in position, and ready for immediate action. In addition, 27 Lewis guns were scattered along the battalion frontage.

The stage was now set, and the troops waited patiently for the play to commence. It opened with a vengeance at 6.40 a.m., when the German artillery put down a heavy barrage on both the forward positions and approaches and on Strazeele. All telephone lines were quickly severed. At 7.30 the commander of our left company reported: "Enemy advancing into Merris in large numbers in single file; also into Vieux Berquin. Main attack expected to come against right flank (A Company) from direction of Merris. Advancing in small numbers on left. Wires cut. Enemy on right about 1000 yards distant."

---

* Among the retiring troops was an elderly English colonel, accompanied by two privates carrying a box of ammunition. Lieut Desbois ordered these men to drop the ammunition, as it was required for the firing line. The old colonel objected very strongly. He threatened Desbois with all sorts of penalties, but Desbois was not the type to stand on ceremony. Whipping out his revolver, he stated very definitely, "That ammunition stops right here." And so it did.

† A few days later, when the gate to Hazebrouck had been definitely shut, all such British troops were ordered to the rear to rejoin their own formations. But one delightful little chap, only a boy, who had been virtually "adopted" by the headquarters details of the 3rd, refused to go, and the Diggers fully intended souveniring him permanently. There was great sorrow when he was killed shortly afterwards.

The German attack was made in three waves, but the rush was met by a particularly cool firing line. So confident were some of the company commanders, that they withheld fire of their men until the enemy were within 20 yards of the position.

Prior to the attack on Mont De Merris, Lewis guns had been pushed well forward, and these fired until the enemy came within 75-150 yards of them. The guns were then withdrawn to the outpost lines, the gunners behaving with great gallantry. It is interesting to note that during this action one of the Lewis gunners fired no less than 94 panniers of ammunition without a stoppage. This achievement was believed to be a record.

Corporal P. Turvey, D.C.M., M.M., recounting in *Reveille* his experiences during these exciting days, says: "Reaching a position about 300 yards in rear of 'Gutzer' farm, I was required to take out my company Lewis guns and act as a covering party, while new trenches were dug. The night was slipping away fast, and we knew Fritz would attack at dawn So every man had to 'step on it.'

"While scouting for gun positions in the semi-darkness, I discovered the bodies of a young woman about 25 and a girl of 8. Evidently they had been caught by enemy gun-fire during the day. At the sight of those poor souls, I saw 'red' and swore to take toll of Fritz if an opportunity came.

"Digging operations being completed just before daybreak, my guns were withdrawn to the front line. But the position at Gutzer farm appealed to me as an observation post, and I received permission from Lieut 'Dad' Jarvis to take a Lewis gun out there. Four men readily volunteered to come with me and carry ammunition.

"We had scarcely got into position and were gazing towards the village of Merris, over the undulating country, when we saw miles of infantry, slowly, but surely, goose-stepping towards us. Officers on grey horses were riding up and down the column. It really was a wonderful sight. I sent one of my men back to headquarters with a message, and in a few minutes the most awful slaughter was going on. However, in spite of terrible losses, Fritz kept coming on, and was soon within point-blank range of my gun. So I decided to present him with 1150 rounds of S.A.A.

"It was like firing into a haystack—one could not miss. The Germans were about six deep in places. They became very much unsettled in front, but kept creeping up on both flanks. I sent the other three men back to the line while I emptied the remaining magazines. As I finished there were 'Hocks' uncomfortably close, so I grabbed the gun and bolted across No-Man's Land, followed by a hail of bullets. I reached the trench without a scratch, though one bullet tore a hole through the back of my tunic. Can any of the old B Company remember shouting, 'Come on, Turvey'?"

At 10.30 a.m., taking advantage of a lull in the fighting, Lieut C. H. D. Champion, commanding B Company, ordered Lieut C. G. Prescott and his platoon of 20 men to attack Gutzer farm, about 100 yards out in front. A sniper posted in this farmhouse picked off Sergeant Jack Mott, Frank Guest, and Ernie Corby, but subsequently was himself killed by one of our snipers.

After a short bombardment by Stokes mortars, Prescott's party advanced under covering fire from other posts. Entering the farmyard, it came upon fifty Germans, and at once fired into them at a range of fifteen yards. Becoming demoralized, the enemy rushed towards a small gate forty yards away, offering a splendid target as they bunched together at the entrance. Only ten escaped. The remainder were killed. Meanwhile, unknown to the raiding party, about 30 of the enemy escaped under a hedge thirty yards from one of our platoon posts, which shot down every one of them.

As no good purpose could be served by occupying it, Prescott now withdrew his platoon from the farm. Five of his men had been killed. After the retirement Private W. H. Reid (of Hornsby, N.S.W.) gallantly went out sixty yards towards the farm, through murderous fire, and brought in a wounded man. He also volunteered to go back and search for any others who might have been wounded. To our great regret he was killed shortly afterwards.

Handfuls of men acting boldly, as this platoon did, very soon materially altered the situation. At the sight of eager Australians on the move, large numbers of the enemy on the flanks ran back, offering very favourable targets for machine-gunners and snipers. These sorties appeared to demoralize the whole German line in the neighbourhood, and their success naturally had a heartening effect on our troops. Prescott subsequently received the Military Cross for his excellent leadership.

Shortly after midday the position was moderately quiet, but at 1.55 an enemy force, about 1200 strong, was observed assembling in four waves opposite the right and left companies. The artillery was at once informed; and at 2.15 an S O S flare went up on the left company's front.

As the Germans swept across the open on this flank, Lieut F. J. Jarvis (known as "Old Dad") produced a tin whistle and, mounting the parapet, played in shrill strains "Australia Will Be There." "The machine-gunners nearby," says F. M. Cutlack,* "laughed at the sight of him— he awoke memories of many a comic turn at concert parties —and they cheered like mad as the tune died away in the noise of their emptying gun-belts. Having finished that tune, he told them he would play something to line the Huns up thicker and make a better target, so he began to whistle 'Die Wacht am Rhein,' whereupon, it is said, the

---

* In *The Australians: Their Final Campaign, 1918*, p. 151.

annoyed Huns concentrated their machine-gun fire in his direction and he was forced to abandon his efforts, for they were only a hundred yards away."

At this stage Corporal Turvey observed what he considers to be the finest example of bravery in his whole experience. A German officer, on foot, leading his men, "yelled out something like 'Forverts, forverts!' but a volley from our lines sent him and many others to grass. He struggled to his feet, however, and again called to his men to advance. Another volley sent him in a heap, and it seemed that he was done. But, to our utter amazement, he gallantly struggled to his feet and, lurching unsteadily from one side to the other to get his balance, called again, 'Forverts, forverts!' This time he took the full count. And perhaps some of us were sorry. A brave enemy!

"I also recall the bravery of Private A. O. Compton, of Goulburn," says Turvey. "He had lost a brother at Anzac in 1915 and had sworn to avenge him at the first opportunity. This was the first real chance he had had of point-blank shooting. With reckless courage he stood right up on the parapet and did some great execution. It was not long before he was hit—mortally."

Under the devastating effect of concentrated rifle and Lewis gun fire, the Germans broke and retired to their own trenches. The attack on the other flank was suppressed by fire from the centre and right companies, and did not develop to any extent.

At 3 p.m. a platoon of C Company from supports was sent forward to reinforce the left company (B), which had lost about 40 men. About the same time two enemy field-guns came into position on the Vieux Berquin-Strazeele road, and two companies of infantry were observed near by. The Lewis gunners opened fire and scattered the Germans in all directions.

TRENCH AT MERRIS ROUND A DUD MINNEN-WERFER

STRONG POINTS, 20TH SEPTEMBER, 1917

DUG-OUTS, SPOILBANK

SWAN CHATEAU, DICKEBUSCH

LIEUT.-COL. D. T. MOORE, C.M.G., D.S.O., V.D.
Order of Couronne (Belgium), Croix de Guerre (Belgium)

The last effort of the enemy to pierce our line was made at 7 p.m. A party, estimated at 150, attacked B Company on the left, but was annihilated by a withering fire from rifles and Lewis guns. The company commander, Lieut C. H. D. Champion—son of the Rev. A. H. Champion, formerly headmaster of The King's School, Parramatta—was fatally wounded during the action. Throughout the day he had fought bravely and well, and the quick and effective repelling of the enemy attacks was due in very great measure to his inspiring leadership, coolness and initiative.

No finer tribute has been paid to the 1st Division for its defence of Hazebrouck than that by Sir Arthur Conan Doyle, who, in *The British Campaign of 1918,* says: "The German attack was once again a complete failure, and it was clear that the Australians had the historical honour in Flanders as well as on the Somme of saying 'Thus far and no farther,' upon the sector which they manned." *

Individual acts of gallantry and initiative had inspired the men greatly during this engagement, which was crammed so full of incident. Sergeant Bridle, of B Company, who was wounded, was recommended for the Victoria Cross by an English company commander, who was chagrined when he discovered that Bridle had received only the Military Medal. Private G. A. E. Gilbert, a mere boy but already holder of the Military Medal and bar, put up an outstanding performance. Time and again he went out into the thick of the fighting to

---

* Sir Arthur also states that "the Germans, advancing behind a deadly barrage, came forward through Merris and Vieux Berquin. They soon found, however, that they had before them fresh and steady troops who were not to be driven. The immediate German objective was the high ground from Mont de Merris to Strazeele. The 2nd Australian Brigade was on the right and the 1st (Lesslie) on the left. Both were equally attacked and both met their assailants with a shattering fire that piled the plain with their bodies. Three lines swept forward, but none reached the shallow trenches of the Digger infantry. The 3rd and 4th Battalions held the line to the north where the pressure was greatest."

repair telephone wires after they had been cut; he came through the day's great dangers without a scratch.

According to Major Burrett, at the end of the fight "our defence was merely one line of Diggers, with practically nothing between them and Hazebrouck and victory for the Huns. A French cavalry division was, I believe, the only reserve near by, and I remember a French cavalry staff officer coming to me. *'Bon jour, monsieur,'* he said, as he pulled out his map. *'Boche la—Boche la?'* he queried. I nodded or denied. *'Bon jour, monsieur, merci,'* and he was gone. He certainly was the most business-like person I met on the Western Front. About the 16th a senior staff officer from Second Army headquarters called on me. 'You do not realize, my boy, what your battalion has helped to do during these couple of days, and I want you to tell them from the army commander that they have saved the Channel ports. Had the Germans broken through to Hazebrouck the ports must have been lost.'"

April 15th and 16th passed off quietly in the 1st Division's sector, the enemy devoting his attention to attacks on the British line farther north. During the 15th we spent our time improving the outposts and throwing out barbed-wire entanglements, as well as straightening several sections of the line. Enemy shelling was intermittent throughout the day; and shortly after 6 p.m. our 18-pounder batteries registered satisfactorily on the battalion SOS line, though not before the company headquarters had been hit.

For three and a half hours from 9.15 on the morning of the 17th the German artillery laid down a barrage on our sector; fortunately it fell just in rear of the front line. As his infantry were seen to be massing, messages were passed on to our artillery, whose excellent shooting prevented them from essaying any attack.

That night at 11.30 p.m. the 2nd Battalion took charge

of the front area and we moved back into supports at Sec Bois. The duty of the unit occupying this position was to counter-attack in the event of the front line being breached. Four nights later the 18th Battalion, Durham Light Infantry, relieved us of this responsibility, and we marched to a billeting area around Borre and Pradelles.

The casualties for the period April 11th-22nd were 1 officer (Lieut C. H. D. Champion) and 43 men killed, and 4 officers and 85 men wounded. The officers wounded were Captains A. G. Cormack and G. F. Plunkett, and Lieuts C. L. Sturt and C. J. McDonald.

For the next few days training was carried out by companies. Working-parties were supplied to the forward areas, and experiments were made with a new rifle-grenade discharger. The civilian inhabitants who had not deserted the area were now being evacuated by the French authorities.

"I wandered into the prosperous looking farm-house occupied by battalion headquarters," says a member of the 3rd, "and opened a door leading into one of the rooms. Sitting at a roll-top desk was a very fine type of old Frenchman going through his papers. A few he set aside. Others he tore up and put into a big basket. Although he must have known I was there, he took not the slightest notice of me. Mechanically his work went on. Every now and then just a murmur: '*Ruine!*' '*Ruine!*' '*Ruine!*' I left him to pull down the past.

"The same day, and to the same farm, came a young woman about 20, almost in a state of collapse as the result of hunger, fatigue, and mental strain. A few weeks previously she had been with her father and small brother on their farm—the mother was in hospital in Baillieul—when the Germans were reported to be within a short distance of the place. The father told the girl to go back a little way and wait at the cross-roads until he came along with the son in their farm cart. She ran back and waited, but her kinfolk did not come. Only when she saw the German advance-guard a few hundred yards off did she move. Apparently the father had delayed too long and his retreat had been cut off. Baillieul, in the meantime, had been very heavily shelled and bombed and eventually captured, and the girl did not know whether her mother was alive or what had been her fate. A few of us gave her a little money, and old Tom Avery took her back in the officers' mess cart to the refugees' camp. I have since often wondered what became of her—if eventually she found her family safe and sound."

On April 26th Lieut E. R. Shelley, Second-Lieut S. L. Robertson, and 48 "old hands" rejoined the battalion. Reinforcements to the number of 109, under Second-Lieut G. P. Darlow, also reported for duty. Two days later the 3rd was back in the firing line,* this time opposite Meteren—but a very different Meteren from that which the troops had known in April 1916. Then it was full of civilians and practically untouched by the war; now it was in the hands of the enemy and in ruins.

On our side posts had been established across the main road running into the village from the west, and others were in the hop-fields. Each night patrols and working-parties were kept busy at their respective tasks, and they also displayed much activity. Gas was projected against the enemy position on the night of the 29th. The only immediate response was that the Germans shelled their own front line, in the belief that the Australians had broken into some part of it. However, a shower of distress signals from the garrison quickly brought about a lengthening of the range.

On the night April 30th Sergeant G. H. Buckley, accompanied by two men, raided an enemy post and

---

* On this occasion Lieut Shelley took charge of A Company, its commander, Captain Higinbotham, who was due for a spell, staying out with the nucleus.

brought back a prisoner, thus enabling the intelligence staff to identify the German regiment and division opposed to us.

Four nights later we were relieved from front-line duties by the 4th Battalion. Our new position, back in reserve, did not lie immediately behind the part of the line that it would be our duty to reinforce in case of need, but was somewhat to the north of it. A Company headquarters, near a road junction, was shelled on one occasion. A limber and two horses were knocked out and rations for one of the platoons blown up. Second-Lieut Robertson had a miraculous escape from injury.

On the night May 9th a battalion of the East Yorkshire Regiment took over this position, and the 3rd marched back to a camp at Wallon-Capel, for rest, training, sport and a fresh issue of clothing. Air raids were now nightly affairs. On one such visit a hostile plane dropped near the transport section's lines a bomb which blew a crater 17 feet in diameter.

Brigade sports were held on the 16th, the battalion securing the transport prize and winning a number of the athletic events. The 1st Battalion put a wonderfully good football team into the field. The same day Captain F. C. Kemp rejoined the 3rd after having visited Australia on sick leave.

On May 19th the battalion went back to Strazeele, and took over a section of the front line some distance to the south of the position it held during the previous tour. The front posts crossed the railway line at Strazeele station, the left flank resting on the summit of Mont de Merris. The crops in the surrounding fields were now about three feet high, and gave excellent cover to the patrols and scouts of both sides. It was about this time that daylight raids became a feature of the Australian operations.

At 6 a.m. on May 22nd, Sergeant J. Bruggy (of

Harden, N.S.W.) left the battalion lines by himself and, crawling through the crops for some 500 yards, ran into an enemy post. He killed two of the garrison and badly wounded four more. Collecting their identity disks, he returned to company headquarters and made his report. Captain McDermid found it somewhat difficult to credit his amazing story, whereupon C.S.M. Pat Kinchington volunteered to accompany Bruggy on a second trip. This was undertaken at 7 a.m. Arriving at the post, the N.C.Os found the two dead and two of the wounded Germans, and also trails of blood leading to a hedge through which the others had obviously escaped. Additional clues, in the shape of shoulder straps, etc., were secured and brought back, for the dual purpose of substantiating Bruggy's claim and assisting the higher staffs in their never-ending task of unravelling the German dispositions. An aeroplane was afterwards sent up to photograph the area in question, and it was not until the prints arrived that Bruggy's brilliant feat was fully appreciated. As a reward he received a commission and the Military Medal. Some few months later Kinchington, too, was appointed to commissioned rank. The aerial photograph was circulated to all units of the 1st Division.

On the night of May 27th, Lieut J. H. Nixon led a party against a post in front of D Company, killed three of the garrison and brought back two prisoners. Shortly afterwards the 12th Battalion moved into our section of the line, and we marched back to La Kreule, between Hondeghem and Hazebrouck, for rest and further training. All ranks were kept busy, large parties being detailed for work every night.

While at La Kreule members of the battalion became only too well acquainted with a 15-inch gun, which was mounted on a special railway truck. Regularly in the early hours of the morning the crash of its discharge and the shriek of its shells disturbed the peace of the sleeping troops. The gun was frequently sought by enemy planes, and during the process many bombs were dropped in the vicinity of our camp.

On June 3rd the battalion moved farther back, to Sercus. The camp was situated in a square of timber, with a clean, grassed parade ground in the centre. Sport, musketry exercises and other training filled the days; at night many visits were exchanged between members of the various units in the brigade, some of them extending to the early hours of the morning.

A change in the command of the 1st Infantry Brigade now occurred, Brigadier-General W. B. Lesslie leaving us to return to the British Army. There was not an officer or man in the brigade who was not sorry at Lesslie's going, for he had invariably given us a strong lead and a fair deal. He had been with the brigade for upwards of eighteen months; but many of the old hands treasured earlier and vivid recollections of him, a compelling figure on Anzac Beach and Watson's Pier, always in his shirt sleeves, frequently hoarse with shouting orders all through the busy hours of the night, and more often than not in the daytime one of the first to dash to the aid of a stricken man when the cry of "stretcher-bearers" or "wounded" went up on that dangerous strip of foreshore.

In General Lesslie's place came Lieut-Col I. G. Mackay, who was destined to command the brigade for the remainder of its victorious career up to the Armistice. Ever since the days of the Landing and Lone Pine he had displayed qualities of the first order, and in the next six months was to enhance the reputation he had already made as one of the foremost fighting leaders of the A.I.F.

The battalion remained in the delightful surroundings at Sercus until June 7th, when it returned to the support line at La Kreule. The strength of the unit at this date was 32 officers and 721 other ranks.

On June 17th the battalion's turn to garrison the front

line came round again; and at 8.40 a.m. on the 20th A Company (Captain L. H. R. Higinbotham) carried out a daylight attack against a German post, the capture of which gave us better observation of the territory held by the enemy.

Nos. 1 and 2 Platoons, under the command of Lieuts F. W. Taylor and C. J. McDonald, respectively, carried out the assault. Covering fire was provided by four three-inch mortars. The platoons, advancing at the double, negotiated the barbed-wire without difficulty and entered the enemy trench. The Germans withdrew in great haste, and the raiders hurriedly built a bomb-stop. Just as the objective was reached, Lieut Taylor was dangerously wounded. He lingered until the 22nd, and then died.

Between 9.30 a.m. and 2 p.m., three separate counter-attacks were made by the Germans, but each was repulsed. Later, a further attempt was made by about 25 of the enemy in the vicinity of the bomb-stop. Conspicuous in this assault was a German officer in a cloth cap, who displayed great spirit and courage in urging on his men, and himself advanced boldly, using a rifle with deadly effect. Time and again he exposed himself to our fire, and appeared to bear a charmed life. He was killed about 4 o'clock, and the attack petered out. Still persisting, however, the Germans made a fresh attack at 4.40, but it shared the fate of its predecessors.

Six hours later about 150 Germans, advancing under an artillery barrage, made a last bid for the position, but a withering fire from Lewis guns and rifles drove them off. It was about this time that Captain Higinbotham, while leading reinforcements forward, was badly hit. Like his colleague Taylor, he succumbed to his wounds the following day. Higinbotham shared the fate of many company commanders of the 3rd Battalion. In practically every engagement in which the unit took part—from the landing at Anzac onwards—the casualties among company commanders were unusually heavy.

Our casualties in this action were: Officers, 2 died of wounds; other ranks, 9 killed, 2 died of wounds, 23 wounded, and 2 missing.

At 8.30 p.m. on the night of June 22nd, an enemy force, estimated at 200 strong, made a determined attack on one of the battalion's posts. Although the invaders were driven off with heavy loss, we suffered a number of casualties through shell-fire. Second-Lieut J. Bruggy was wounded, and three other ranks were killed and nine wounded.

Half-an-hour after midnight of June 23rd-24th, two platoons of B Company under Lieuts L. W. S. Loveday and E. Hawkshaw, respectively, attacked under cover of an artillery barrage some enemy positions 300-500 yards in advance of one of our outposts. A similar raid was carried out at the same hour by the 2nd Battalion on our left.

Hawkshaw's platoon reached its objective with only one casualty, but Loveday's men were quickly involved in serious trouble. The entanglement protecting the German position not having been destroyed by the covering artillery-fire, the raiders, including two Lewis gunners, were compelled to throw their rifles and guns over the wire and then dive after them. Gun flashes and Very lights disclosed that the enemy post was strongly held. As one of the survivors remarked, "The b——s were so thick, you couldn't poke a stick between them." After some fierce fighting at close quarters, every man in Loveday's party, with the sole exception of the platoon sergeant, was hit. Nevertheless the position was taken. The sergeant dashed back for assistance and Lieut C. L. Smith rushed his platoon forward, but every member of it quickly became a casualty. Smith himself was killed by shell-fire.* Lieut A. O. Arnold's platoon eventually occupied the post.

While in the captured post, Lieut Loveday received severe abdominal wounds. The first two medicoes through whose hands he passed would not touch him, so hopeless did his case appear, but a sister at the casualty clearing station persuaded the doctor there to give him a fighting chance. And so Loveday came through.

The desperate nature of this engagement is made clear by the casualties the battalion suffered: 1 officer and 6 other ranks killed, 2 officers and 26 other ranks wounded.†

The battalion remained in the forward zone until the night of June 27th, when, relieved by the 8th Battalion, it marched back into reserve at La Kreule. After a general clean-up at the divisional baths, the days that followed were devoted to the reorganizing and re-equipping of the unit and to intensive training.

On June 30 officers drawn from each unit of the 1st Division visited divisional headquarters to bid farewell

---

* This officer was one of the select few in the A.I.F. to receive a Military Cross while serving as a warrant officer.

† Before the "stunt," while the platoons were applying the last touches to their equipment and waiting for "zero" hour to arrive, an American officer and two sergeants strolled into the line looking very much the worse for wear. It appeared that they had crawled most of the way from the back area on their stomachs. After greeting Loveday in the usual breezy Doughboy style and shedding their equipment, the officer asked the Australian to have a drink. Meanwhile, Loveday, out of the corner of his eye, had watched the American's equipment disappear round the bay of the trench—and reappear. The invitation was readily accepted by Loveday—but, to the astonishment of its owner, the water-bottle was found to be empty!

The officer explained that he and his sergeants had come along to "see how one of these gol-darned raids wur-r-ked." Invited to join in, he cheerfully replied, "Say, boy, I have the finest bunch God ever put breath into. I'm not going to have them killed in no raid before they go into battle together."

It was now time to move off. Our covering barrage had opened and enemy shells were also screaming through the air. A succession of heavy detonations shook the trench, columns of smoke and dirt hurtling skywards. One or two sand-bags thudded off the parapet into the trench. "What about it; are you coming?" queried Loveday. "Say, sonnie, if this is only a raid I want to be in no darned battle," replied the Yank, as he settled down good-naturedly into the trench.

to Major-General Sir H. B. Walker, who was on the point of returning to the British Army.

"Hooky" Walker was another British officer to whom the A.I.F. owed an enormous debt of gratitude. Coming to us in December 1914 as chief of General Birdwood's staff, he took the first opportunity of exchanging this appointment for a front line command. This was not long in coming, for on the day of the Landing he was given command of the New Zealand Infantry Brigade, whose own commander had fallen ill. Several days later, on the death of Colonel MacLaurin, Walker came to our brigade, and on May 20th, after General Bridges had fallen to a sniper's bullet, he assumed command of the 1st Division, which since then he had led almost continuously. An English gentleman of the first water, it was natural that he should possess a high sense of honour, and it was no surprise afterwards to learn that he had invariably sunk his own interests for the good of the A.I.F.

Our new commander, Major-General T. W. Glasgow, was probably the strongest leader in the A.I.F. Forceful but just, and straight as a die, he was typical of the finest product of the Australian countryside. Joining the 2nd Light Horse Regiment in 1914, he commanded the 1st Regiment in the August offensive at Anzac, but since early 1916 had been G.O.C. of the 13th Infantry Brigade (4th Division).

On July 5th the battalion proceeded by route march to a position between Strazeele station and the villages of Borre-Pradelles, where it relieved the 9th Battalion, then in reserve. Large parties were supplied nightly for work in the forward areas, the remainder of the battalion indulging in various military exercises.

A week later we took over the 1st Battalion's front in the deserted farm lands about Strazeele. The wide spaces of No-Man's Land provided happy hunting grounds for the Australian infantry, who roamed through the crops both day and night.

After dark patrols were sent out in force. In the early hours of the 14th, Sergeant W. Delaney and twelve men encountered a large force of the enemy, estimated at 70 strong. Delaney withheld the fire of his party until the Germans were but ten yards distant. He then gave the signal to fire. Many of the enemy fell, and the survivors scattered through the crops, their squealing and shouting being heard distinctly in our front line.

Sergeant Delaney accompanied Lieut C. L. L. Burrett on another patrol some hours later and helped to locate several enemy posts. Parties left the lines again at 11.30 a.m. and 12 noon, the second one under Sergeant Campbell, who was wounded by an enemy sniper.

The last patrol of the day went out at 5 p.m. under the guidance of Lieut H. D. Robb, for the purpose of ascertaining whether or not certain positions were in the hands of the enemy. The information was obtained, but not before some sharp fighting took place, during which Robb and his sergeant, McDonald, were wounded. That was the last the battalion saw of the broad smile and beaming countenance of Hughie Robb, an excellent officer whose training and experience as a surveyor had been invaluable on more than one occasion when correct locations were essential for the safety of the battalion, as it waited on the tapes for the covering barrage to lift.

At 10 o'clock that night, A and B Companies of the 1st Border Regiment—part of the famous 29th Division—moved into the sector and took over the front line from our A and B Companies, which caught up with the remainder of the battalion near La Kreule. For a week the customary training exercises were resumed, with occasional sporting events and plenty of bathing parades.

On July 22nd the 3rd was detailed for duty as reserve battalion, and came under the tactical direction of the 3rd Infantry Brigade. During the course of the next week training continued in the daytime, and large fatigue parties were engaged at night in the arduous work of burying cables in the forward areas. On the 29th the battalion moved to Racquinghem.

CHAPTER XXXII

THE ADVANCE TO VICTORY

THE successes achieved in the Strazeele fighting, and the news that we were to rejoin the Australian Corps on the Somme had a wonderful effect on the morale of the troops. For almost four months the 1st Division had been attached to the XV Corps under the command of Lieut-General Sir Beauvoir de Lisle. How well our job was done is indicated in his farewell message of August 4th, 1918, to Major-General T. W. Glasgow, our G.O.C.:

> Before your magnificent division leaves my corps, I wish to thank you and all ranks under your command for the exceptional services rendered during the past four months.
> Joining this corps on April 12th, during the Battle of the Lys, the division selected and prepared a position to defend the Hazebrouck front, and a few days later repulsed two heavy attacks with severe losses to the enemy. This action brought the enemy's advance to a standstill.
> Since then, the division has held the most important sector of this front continuously, and by skilful raiding and minor operations has advanced the line over a mile on a front of 5000 yards, capturing just short of 1000 prisoners, and causing such damage to the troops of the enemy that nine divisions have been replaced.
> The complete success of all minor operations, the skill displayed by the patrols by day as well as by night, the gallantry and determination of the troops, and their high state of training and discipline have excited the admiration and emulation of all, and I desire that you will convey to all ranks my high appreciation of their fine work and my regret that the division is leaving my command.

General Sir Herbert Plumer, commander of the Second Army, also sent the 1st Division a message of appreciation, and requested that the men should be told how sorry all ranks of his army were to lose them. On a number of occasions we had served under General Plumer, and learned to respect and admire his fine qualities of leadership. His snow white hair and moustache, his heavy cheeks, the eye-glass that kept jumping out, only to be peremptorily put back again, and his picturesque appearance generally, is a lovable memory to us all. As events turned out this was our last farewell to the Second Army.

Since we were last with the Australian Corps, General Birdwood had left it to take charge of the newly constituted Fifth Army, his place in the corps command being filled by General Monash from the 3rd Division. General Birdwood, however, was still the administrative head of the entire A.I.F. overseas, and he continued in that rôle until long after the Armistice. "Birdie" had brought us safely through many trying experiences, and there was very genuine sorrow at his departure from the corps. The memory of him will always remain dear to Australians, particularly those who saw so much of him on Anzac. Of a friendly disposition and personally brave, he was never happier than when visiting the line or mixing among the troops.

Up to August 5th the battalion was billeted in the Racquinghem area, about three miles south of Ebblinghem, the village in which we had received our first taste of life in billets on arrival in France more than two years previously.

Little routine training was carried out during these days, most of the time being devoted to sport and military competitions. In these the 3rd more than held their own; at football we defeated the 4th Battalion (8-nil); at cricket with the 4th our side managed to win by a margin of 11 runs; in the brigade band competition, the 2nd and 3rd tied for first place; in the brigade sports we were runners-up to the 1st Battalion in the aggregate number of points awarded.

On August 4th Lieut A. ("Wonga") Littlejohn, and 25 other ranks, represented the battalion at a Second Army church parade and review in commemoration of Britain's entry into the war.

This short rest proved most enjoyable, and the men were in great heart. It was always a wonderful and extraordinary thing to witness the battalion's rapid recovery after coming out of the line. No matter how gruelling the tour, twenty-four hours after relief the men were all spruced up and happy, and the more adventurous among them would be looking out for some way to get into mischief.

At 6.30 p.m. on August 5th the battalion moved hurriedly by route march to Wizernes, three miles south-west of St Omer, and shortly after 3 o'clock next morning left by train for Pont Remy, south-east of Abbeville. Detraining here at 2 p.m., we marched about a mile to the château at Liercourt, rested there till 8, and again took the road, this time in buses. After travelling for six and a half hours down the main road on the south bank of the Somme, through Amiens, we alighted near Daours, and at 3.30 a.m. on the 7th bivouacked in a sheltered field north of that village. The transport section of the battalion travelled overland from Racqinghem and joined us at noon on the 7th.

The ambitious offensive now about to be undertaken was entrusted to the Fourth Army, under the command of General Sir Henry Rawlinson, who decided to launch three army corps against the Germans: Canadian on the south, Australian in the centre, and III British on the north. There seems to be no doubt that our own corps commander, Sir John Monash, played a leading part in the elaboration, if not in the actual formation, of the plan, but history has yet to apportion his share and that of other responsible leaders.

MAJOR A. F. BURRETT, D.S.O.
Photo: *Dickenson-Monteath.*

LEFT TO RIGHT: LIEUT. A. H. BOILEAU, M.C., LIEUT. E. JACKSON, D.C.M., LIEUT. G. H. LESLIE, M.C.

LEFT TO RIGHT: CAPTAIN S. F. P. WHITE, LIEUT. L. W. S. LOVEDAY M.C., LIEUT. E. HAWKSHAW, M.C.

THE ADVANCE TO VICTORY

Briefly, the battle plan for the initial attack by the Australian Corps was for two of its divisions, each on a two-mile frontage, to penetrate to a depth of approximately five miles. The boundaries of this section of the attack were from the Somme on the north to the Péronne railway line on the south. "Zero" hour was eventually fixed for 4.20 a.m. on August 8th.

The 1st Brigade now came under the orders of the 4th Division (Major-General E. G. Sinclair-MacLagan), and went into divisional reserve in place of 13th Infantry Brigade, which had been detailed to hold the front through which the Canadians were to attack. This decision had been arrived at rather late, and our arrival on the Somme was accordingly hastened by urgent orders from the corps commander.

Early on the morning of the 7th, orders for the battle arrived from brigade headquarters. Our rôle was simply to follow the 4th Division, and to be available as a striking force, if required. By 3.20 a.m. on the 8th the 1st Brigade was to be in its first assembly position, the 2nd, 3rd, 4th, and 1st Battalions (in that order, from right to left) on a general line about 1500 yards south-east of Corbie and some 2500 yards in rear of Hamel. At 6.20 the 4th and 12th Brigades which would previously have assembled in front of the 1st Brigade's position, were due to advance. When their rear companies got clear, we were to advance 4500 yards to another position, 2000 yards south-east of Hamel. At 8.20, when this movement was completed, the 3rd Battalion (left) and 4th (right) would be slightly in advance of the 2nd and 1st. The method of advance was to be a process of filtering through rather than a forward march of the whole brigade. Battalion commanders were to use their discretion regarding advance formations, the movement of which would be governed by the state of the ground and the hostile fire.

v

Troops to keep clear of roads. Finally, the orders expressly stated that no battalion of the brigade was to become involved in the fight without direct orders from the brigadier. It was anticipated that the attacking troops would reach the final objective by 11 a.m.

August 7th was a busy day for all. Packs, blankets, greatcoats, valises, and surplus gear were handed over to the quartermaster (Captain Douglas Oakley), and extra rations, bombs, ammunition and other fighting stores were drawn from the dumps. Pack-horses would carry the battalion's reserve of S.A.A., and a maltese cart and a limber the signalling gear.

As many officers and N.C.Os as possible visited the area in which we had to assemble before the attack, but it was not possible to reconnoitre the country to be traversed later. The battalion intelligence officer (Lieut C. O. Clark) and his section, together with the company scouts, did valuable exploratory work that day, and it is in no small measure due to their efficiency that the battalion marched in the darkness without a hitch to the assembly point.

During the afternoon Major Burrett mustered the battalion together, and explained the operation. Since their morning's orders, a message received from brigade headquarters stated that in the event of the British troops being held up on the north bank of the Somme, the 3rd Battalion might be required to get across the river somehow or other and render assistance to them. A hearty cheer greeted the announcement of this unhealthy possibility.

Sir John Monash's famous message "To the soldiers of the Australian Army Corps" was then read to the assembled troops. As it created a profound impression, the full text is given hereunder.

For the first time in the history of this Corps, all five Australian divisions will to-morrow engage in the largest and most important battle operation ever undertaken by the Corps.

They will be supported by an exceptionally powerful artillery, and by tanks and aeroplanes on a scale never previously attempted. The full resources of our sister Dominion, the Canadian Corps, will also operate on our right, while two British divisions will guard our left flank.

The many successful offensives which the brigades and battalions of this Corps have so brilliantly executed during the past four months have been but the prelude to, and the preparation for, this greatest and culminating effort.

Because of the completeness of our plans and dispositions, of the magnitude of the operations, of the number of troops employed, and of the depth to which we intend to overrun the enemy's positions, this battle will be one of the most memorable of the whole war; and there can be no doubt that, by capturing our objectives, we shall inflict blows upon the enemy which will make him stagger, and will bring the end appreciably nearer.

I entertain no sort of doubt that every Australian soldier will worthily rise to so great an occasion, and that every man, imbued with the spirit of victory, will, in spite of every difficulty that may confront him, be animated by no other resolve than grim determination to see through to a clean finish, whatever his task may be.

The work to be done to-morrow will perhaps make heavy demands upon the endurance and staying powers of many of you; but I am confident that, in spite of excitement, fatigue, and physical strain, every man will carry on to the utmost of his powers until his goal is won; for the sake of AUSTRALIA, the Empire and our cause.

I earnestly wish every soldier of the Corps the best of good fortune, and a glorious and decisive victory, the story of which will re-echo throughout the world, and will live forever in the history of our home land.

This day, every wood and valley around Daours which offered cover from enemy observation, concealed troops, horses, tanks, artillery, and dépôts of all description. It seemed impossible that this huge massing of troops and material would not be discovered, but subsequent events proved that the attack came as a complete surprise. All this speaks volumes for the efficacy of the staff work of the various formations.

At 11 p.m. the battalion moved off in column of platoons at fifty yards' distance, and marched via Aubigny and Fouilloy to its assembly position. "All correct" was reported at 2.40 a.m. Here a hot breakfast was served from the battalion "cookers," which came forward from Daours. There was now nothing further to be done but rest and wait for that word to which war had given a new and dreadful meaning—"zero."

Dawn, 4.20 a.m., was heralded with a mighty crash from more than a thousand guns.* The heavens lit up with a sheet of flame, terrifying in its dynamic splendour, and the earth seemed to burst open with volcanic fury. The crunching noise of the tanks, the rumble of batteries of artillery moving forward, the whirl of planes—all showed that the fight was on.

A heavy fog, together with the smoke from bursting shells, made it impossible to discern anything except at a very short distance. At 6.30 we began to move in artillery formation towards the second assembly-position, A Company followed by D, on the right, B Company followed by C, on the left. Headquarters, with a screen of scouts thrown out in front, led the battalion. The platoons of each company moved in "diamond" formation, with fifty yards' interval and distance.

This march was a severe test of training and discipline—deployment in the fog and smoke, marching forward in unknown and difficult country, across old trenches and wire-entanglements, skirting guns in action. But the battalion was again admirably guided by Lieut Nobby Clark and his trusted scouts. About 7 o'clock the sun suddenly broke through and showed the battalion in per-

---

* On the morning of August 8th 1083 guns were under the command of Brig.-General Coxen, the G.O.C., R.A., Aust. Corps. This is said to be the largest number of guns under the direct control of one man in a battle in the British Army's history.

fect formation, marching steadily onward—a magnificent sight. Nothing better was ever done by it in any training operation.*

It was soon realized that the attacking troops must have penetrated the enemy's defences to a depth sufficient either to capture his artillery or force its retreat, for hardly a shell burst in our vicinity. Valleys and folds in the ground provided excellent cover, so the battalion gradually adopted an irregular column of route formation, with the platoons and companies at a safe distance.

At 8.20 a.m. the battalion was in position at the new assembly area—the old German support position. The country ahead was immediately reconnoitred. Prisoners —in most cases in formed parties without escort—were now streaming back everywhere, apparently only too anxious to get as far back as they could.

The 1st Brigade was eventually released from reserve, in order to take over, from portion of the 4th Brigade, special outpost duties along the south bank of the Somme. This became necessary through the British troops north of the Somme not gaining Chipilly, and it was feared the

---

* Commenting on this march at a later date, Lieut-Col (then Major) A. F. Burrett, who was in command of the battalion at the time, wrote: "It was simply a case of trusting that everything was all right, as there was nothing I could do. This went on for half-an-hour or more, and I was extremely anxious to know whether the battalion was in formation and keeping direction in the rather difficult and unknown country. Of course immediate connecting links kept reporting 'O K' to me—but what of the others? The sun suddenly broke through, and there was the whole battalion in perfect formation—scouts out, connecting files, platoons and companies as if on parade ground. In fact, I can remember thinking that it was the best bit of parade-ground work I'd ever seen the battalion do. I can assure you, I felt relieved and proud.

"It may be argued that with the visibility so bad, a closer formation should have been adopted, but it must be borne in mind that it was not then known how the fight was proceeding. There was the possibility that, despite the cover given by the fog, the battalion might at any moment come under a barrage, or that when the fog lifted, as it showed signs of doing, we might offer, in close formation, a perfect target for the German artillery. In any case, it would have been difficult and dangerous, even if desirable, to change at the last moment the orders issued at Daours the previous night for the advance formation."

enemy might cross the river and attack the Australian Corps on its left flank.

At 2 p.m. the 3rd Battalion moved due north for 1000 yards, and formed a defensive flank facing north-east along the Somme, the left of the battalion being thrown back. Our position was consolidated at 6.15, A Company on the right and B on the left, with C and D Companies in reserve. At 9 o'clock C Company moved to a new position, with its left flank resting on the main bridge at Bouzencourt. A Company extended its frontage to Gailly. On our right the 1st Battalion guarded the important crossings leading from Cerisy to Chipilly, while the 2nd, farther still to the right, occupied the country to Morcourt and beyond. The 4th Battalion was in reserve on a plateau 1500 yards in rear of the centre of the Brigade outpost-line.

The 3rd Battalion was now responsible for about 2500 yards of river frontage, but as no attempt was made by the Germans to cross the stream, all hands spent a peaceful night.

Such was the battalion's part in the glorious battle of the 8th of August, 1918. It is true that it was not a very spectacular part; but our turn was soon to come. The strength of the unit in the line was 26 officers and 567 other ranks. At Daours were 5 officers and 155 others, made up of the nucleus, the transport section, and the quartermaster's staff, all under the command of Captain S. F. P. White.

We spent a quiet day on the 9th in the outpost-line of the previous night. During the afternoon we had a clear view of the spectacular advance of the British and American troops along the opposite bank of the river, on to the Chipilly spur, and ending in the occupation of Chipilly itself. Mention must be made of the extraordinarily fine work done by a patrol of six N.C.Os and men of the 1st Battalion under C.Q.M.S. Hayes, which crossed the river and virtually guided the attacking troops into the village.

The 2nd and 3rd Brigades, after making a forced march from a detraining point near Amiens, came into action during the afternoon in front of Lihons, on the extreme right of the Australian Corps, linked up with the Canadians, and conformed to their advance on the south of the main Péronne railway.

The 1st Brigade now received orders to rejoin the 1st Division. After dark we were relieved by the 13th Brigade, the 49th Battalion taking over from the 3rd about 8.30. The 1st Brigade's instructions were to proceed by route march to an assembly position skirting west and south of Harbonnières, over which the Australian flag had been hoisted at noon the day before by the 5th Division.

The first-line transport and the quartermaster's details moved early in the night to a position west of Bayonvillers. The remainder of the battalion, together with its battle transport, set out by route march, 100 yards separating companies and 50 yards the platoons. It was a beautifully clear night—ideal for flying and bombing. Consequently, before the battalion moved off, orders were given that if hostile planes were heard the men were to sit down and remain as still as possible.

It is doubtful whether any of the dreadful practices of war had a more demoralizing effect than bombs dropped from the air at night, particularly on troops in the open. To hear the machines above without being able to see them, to know that at any moment there would be a series of terrific explosions and destruction, to be helpless other than by remaining still, and waiting, though having an almost irresistible urge to move somewhere for cover, even to the smallest shrub—is suspense enough to break the nerve of the strongest——

About 11.30 p.m. when the head of the column was approximately 1000 yards north-east of Bayonvillers the drone of enemy planes was suddenly heard. The battalion halted at once. But we had been seen, and after circling above us for a few minutes they commenced their attack. The first bomb, a dud, fell within five yards of the leading portion of battalion headquarters. The next one exploded in the middle of the second portion, almost every man of which was a highly trained specialist, and practically wiped it out. Among the killed was the Lewis gun officer, Lieut H. H. Fergusson.* "Fergie," who came from North Sydney, was an original member of the battalion who was given his commission after Pozières. He had amassed a wealth of knowledge concerning the employment and care of Lewis and Vickers guns and infantry weapons generally, but, apart from the loss to the battalion of his technical skill, his cheerful disposition had made him a popular figure.

Fortunately this was the only direct hit registered on the column, but some additional casualties were caused by splinters. Altogether sixteen bombs were dropped, and the total loss was 33. Captain C. F. Elliot, M.C., then in command of A Company, was badly wounded.†

The battalion completed the disastrous march at 3.20 a.m. on the 10th, bivouacking in a field west of Harbonnières. Early next day we moved forward along the Péronne railway line to Rosières, and at 2 p.m. took up a strong defensive position in an old trench-system north-

---

* Just before the battalion moved off that night, Fergusson jokingly remarked, "I'll cut the cards for a full issue (death) or a blighty (a slight wound)." A black was to denote "full issue," a red "blighty." The cards were shuffled and cut, and out came a black. "Make it three cuts," said Fergusson. The following cuts were also black. (His brother, E. J. Fergusson, was killed at Anzac in May 1915, while serving with the 1st Battalion.)

† The casualty list for this day gives the following as being killed: 3717, Cpl L. J. Campbell, D.C.M., M.M. (of Tempe); Pte W. H. Burgess (of Newcastle); 3033b, Pte J. Clydesdale (of Lidcombe); 2630b, Pte W. E. Eldred (of Enfield); 6503, Pte W. Flaherty (of Warren); 6883, Pte Dougal McDougall (of Paddington); 1398a, Pte S. McGee, M.M.; 5188, Pte J. F. Stapleton (of Cobargo); 1639a, Pte L. A. Webb (a Londoner); 3942, Pte W. L. Whiting; and 3943, Pte H. Whiting (cousins, both of Adelong).

THE ADVANCE TO VICTORY

east of the village. Lihons and the Lihons ridge, the latter some 3000 yards to our front, had been captured during that morning by the 2nd and 3rd Brigades after a very stubborn resistance by the Germans. The 1st Brigade was now in reserve to the 1st Division.

It was very interesting to see the huge enemy dumps at Rosières, the engineering material alone being sufficient to supply the needs of the Australian Corps to the end of the war. One large dump consisted solely of articles of brass, such as door knobs, ornaments, and other fittings, which were obviously intended to be used in the manufacture of shell-cases. The most interesting capture at Rosières, however, was the giant 11.2-inch "railway" gun, mounted on two great bogies and complete with trucks and carriages for the gun-crews, workshops, and ammunition. This monster's daily task had been the shelling of Amiens.

At 3 a.m. on August 11th A and C Companies on the left flank moved forward 500 and 650 yards respectively into an old system of trenches. This enabled the battalion to form a better defensive position in depth, as well as being closer to the front for counter-attack purposes if necessary. During this move Lieut T. J. Vallis was killed by a shell. He had been with us only a short time, but had acquitted himself very well indeed.

This night at 9 o'clock the battalion moved up to the front line, taking over from elements of the 5th, 7th and 8th Battalions that had become mixed up in the capture of Lihons. The relief was completed at 2.20 a.m. on the 12th. The 3rd was now responsible for a frontage of approximately 2000 yards on a general line 500 yards in front of Lihons, running to the southern boundary of the corps. All four companies (from left to right B, C, A, D) were in the forward area, each having three platoons in the front and one in close support. A Company of the 1st Battalion, under Major

G. A. Street, was detailed to act in general support of the position.

On our left was the 2nd Battalion, supported by the remainder of the 1st on a general line 500 yards in rear of Lihons. The 4th Battalion constituted the brigade reserve 1500 yards farther back. Two guns of the 1st Light Trench Mortar Battery were at 3rd Battalion headquarters; the 1st Machine Gun Company placed its Vickers guns in strong positions over the brigade area.

The country in front of Lihons was a labyrinth of old trenches, dug during the early years of the war, and now almost overgrown with weeds. Barbed-wire entanglements spread in all directions. The trenches naturally afforded our posts excellent cover, but the enemy enjoyed a similar advantage. On account of the wide front and the difficulty, through the broken nature of the country, of watching all approaches, nothing smaller than platoon posts were established in selected localities, with a system of strong patrols maintaining communication between them.*

On the night August 16th-17th the battalion was organized on a two-company frontage. B and D Companies, each with four platoon-posts, held the front line, with A and C, also disposed in platoon-posts as far as possible covering gaps in the front line, in close support. Major Street's company then rejoined the 1st Battalion. During the six days the 3rd Battalion held this frontage, two enemy patrols attacked the line—one was easily driven off, but the other caused three casualties before retiring. Our patrols and snipers, on the other hand, were constantly active in the old saps leading into our front.

One of C Company's patrols (Lieut J. R. Baird and

---

* An interesting event took place at corps headquarters at Bertangles on August 12th, when, in the presence of 100 men from each of the five Australian divisions, and other distinguished visitors, His Majesty the King conferred the honour of knighthood on General Monash.

three men) were working along an old sap near the Lihons-Chaulnes road when it came upon a party of some twenty Germans talking at the entrance of a dugout. One of the enemy was shot and bombs were thrown right among the remainder. But heavy machine-gun fire, opened from close range, forced the patrol to retire before completing the job. The target, however, was such a good one, and the bombs were thrown so accurately that a number of casualties must have been inflicted on the Germans. Lieut E. Hawkshaw also did good work in this area, leading strong fighting-patrols.

The German artillery was aggressive during this period, but most of the shells fell harmlessly in unoccupied areas. There was also considerable activity in the air, but our planes held the supremacy.

At 3.40 a.m. on the 17th we were relieved by the 45th and 46th Battalions, and moved to a bivouac about three miles in rear. After a short rest and breakfast we marched to Vaux-sur-Somme, a delightful spot twelve miles from Lihons, and went into billets. Lieut-Col D. T. Moore rejoined us from the nucleus and took over command of the battalion. Since August 8th we had suffered 45 casualties.

CHAPTER XXXIII

THE BATTLE OF PROYART*

THREE clear days were spent at Vaux-sur-Somme before the battalion was once again on the move. Apart from watching and participating in a demonstration near Hamel of infantry attacking in co-operation with tanks, most of the time was spent in resting and cleaning up.

The Australian Corps line now stretched from in front of Lihons on the south through Proyart and Mericourt to just behind Bray on the north. So far the northern boundary of the corps was roughly the River Somme which immediately south of Peronne turns west, and after a series of irregular bends to north and south, flows past Amiens to the sea. These bends presented a most difficult problem, particularly if the enemy was allowed to consolidate his position to any large degree. So as to prevent this consolidation and force the Germans practically to retire across the Somme, the battle of Proyart was launched on August 23rd.

At 9.30 p.m. on the 21st the battalion moved from Vaux to a position immediately south of Mericourt, bivouacking in old trenches and sunken roads. Next day battle stores were issued, the men were rested, and officers and senior N.C.Os reconnoitred the forward areas and assembly positions. The company cookers, located about 600 yards behind the battalion, were shelled at midday and a number of casualties inflicted. The actual

---

* The official designation of this second main British attack in the offensive is "The Battle of Albert, 1918." It began on August 21st, to the north of the Australian Corps. Next day the 3rd Australian Division and certain British divisions attacked near Bray, north of the Somme.

THE ADVANCE TO VICTORY 317

battalion attacking strength was 25 officers, 539 other ranks.

The divisional plan was to clear the enemy from the Chuignes valley and from the bend of the Somme at Cappy. In the first phase of the operation the 3rd Battalion (less C Company) would follow in support of the other battalions of the 1st Brigade. C Company (Captain A. McDermid), was to be attached to the 1st Battalion, which would have three of its own companies in the front line attack, the fourth being in support. C Company of the 3rd would be in reserve during the first phase, but after the first objective had been gained, it was to push through on the right of the 1st and help in the capture of the second objective, namely, the high ground overlooking and commanding Chuignes. From this position the second phase of the brigade's attack would take the form of "exploitation" by the 3rd Battalion, C Company in the meantime having rejoined as support company.

C Company moved off at 1.30 a.m. on the 23rd, and two hours later reported to the 1st Battalion that it was in position about 100 yards due east of Proyart, formed up immediately in rear of D Company of that battalion. Here a section of the 1st Machine-gun Battalion, in charge of Lieut Hall, came under orders of Captain McDermid. Shortly afterwards, at 3.45, the remainder of the 3rd Battalion—B Company (Captain A. G. Cormack) on the left; A Company (Lieut F. T. Maisey) in the centre; D Company (Lieut E. H. Jackson) on the right—were in position close behind the northern portion of Proyart, with instructions to move forward at zero hour (4.45 a.m.), and be in position 2000 yards forward of that village, astride the Chuignes road, by 6.15.

The battle opened with an intense artillery barrage. Tanks moved in front of the infantry and deployed. After a short time Captain McDermid, believing that

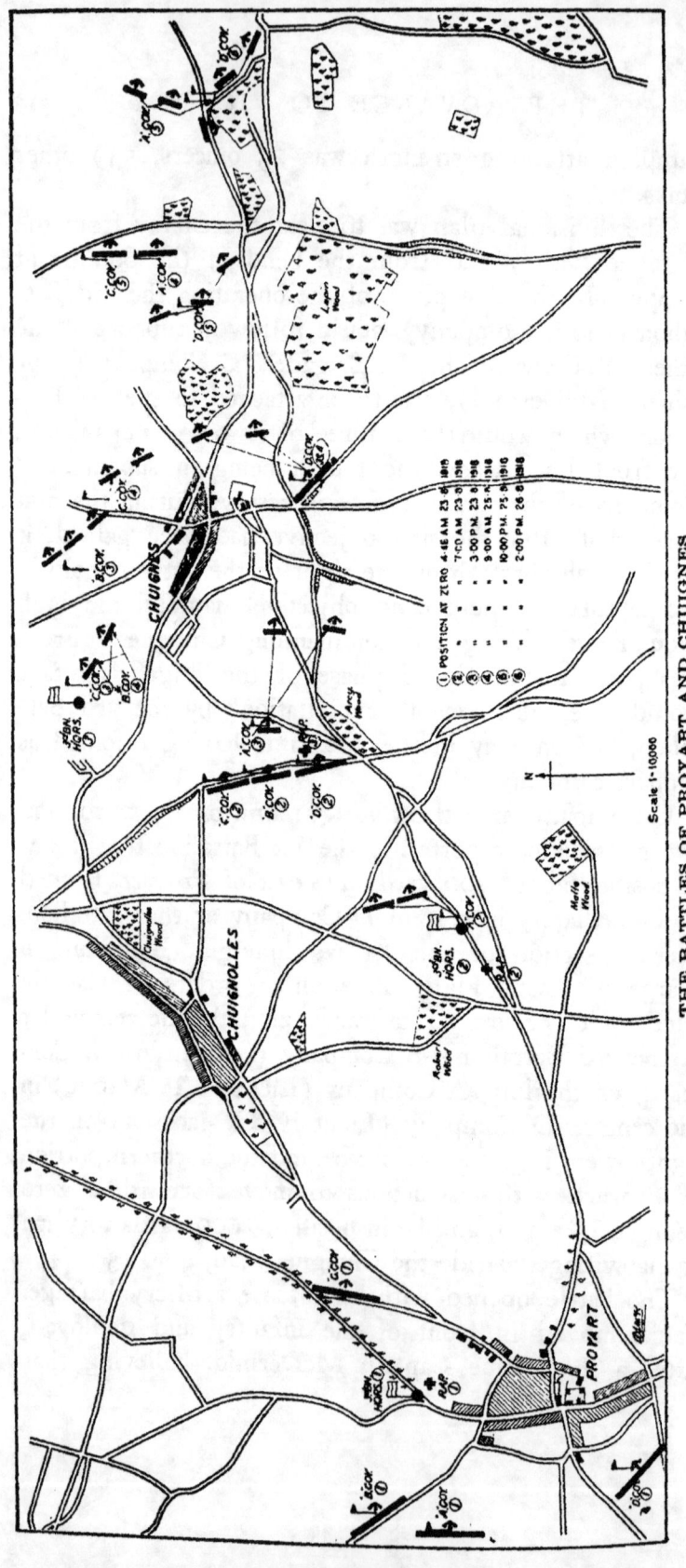

THE BATTLES OF PROYART AND CHUIGNES

THE ADVANCE TO VICTORY

D Company of the 1st Battalion was losing the barrage by advancing too slowly, and thereby allowing the enemy to enfilade both the flanking companies of that battalion, endeavoured to speed things up and finally sent messages to 1st Battalion headquarters and to the flank companies that he was passing through the centre B Company and would attack its objective. McDermid accordingly linked up with the flank companies and with them captured the first objective.

While the barrage halted for fifteen minutes, C Company was reorganized. When it lifted McDermid launched his attack on the second objective. During this advance No. 11 Platoon, working through "Arcy Wood," came unsuspectingly upon a 14-inch naval gun, which the Germans had already put out of action by means of a demolition charge. Since June it had wrought havoc almost daily in Amiens. So far as can be ascertained No. 5208 Pte J. N. Doughty was the first Australian to reach it.*

After passing Arcy Wood splendid co-operation by the tanks, overhead machine-gun fire, and the artillery barrage enabled C Company at 7.10 a.m. to take the objective practically on the south-western outskirts of Chuignes.

C Company has the distinction of being the only company of the 3rd Battalion ever detached for duty with another unit in a battle. At Chuignes it fought with bull-dog tenacity, the individual bravery of the Diggers being quite outstanding, while McDermid displayed superb leadership and initiative in the handling of his command. The company's casualties in the entire action

---

* Sir John Monash, referring to the gun in *The Australian Victories in France in 1918* (p. 163), says: "This is the largest single trophy of war won by any commander during the war, and it was a matter of great regret to me that the cost of its transportation to Australia was prohibitive. . . . So long as any Australian soldiers remained in France this spot was a mecca to which thousands of pilgrims wandered. . . . There, in the shade of Arcy Wood, the great ruin rests, a memorial alike to the sufferings of Amiens and of the great Australian victory of Chuignes."

numbered 4 officers and 60 other ranks out of a "jumping-off" strength of 5 and 100. Ten of its members were afterwards decorated for their conduct in the battle.

To return to the 3rd Battalion itself. At zero B and D Companies moved forward past the north and south of Proyart respectively, A Company following B after an interval of two minutes. A sudden German barrage caught No. 2 Platoon, A Company, only four of its members escaping wounds or death. Among the killed was the platoon commander, Lieut M. McL. Keshan (of Sydney). As A Company was passing "Robert Wood" it was fired on by enemy snipers, but a party at once entered the wood and "mopped up" twenty Germans. Punctually at 6.15 B and D Companies were in position behind Arcy Wood, where they came in contact with C Company. When C took its final objective and B and D passed through it to gain the exploitation line, the 1st Battalion relinquished its control of McDermid's company, which again came under the orders of the 3rd, to support its sister companies. B Company moved forward without any very serious opposition, but D (with C in close support) came under heavy machine-gun and anti-tank gun fire from the ridge north-west of Chuignes. It was here that the sole surviving officer of D Company (Lieut E. H. Jackson, D.C.M.) was wounded, but he remained on duty until the remnants of his command were temporarily incorporated with those of C Company under Captain McDermid. McDermid, seeing that it was a useless waste of life to persist in the work of exploitation without adequate artillery support, consolidated a position on the western entrance to Chuignes.

Arrangements were now made for an artillery barrage to be put down, and at 12.30 p.m. the battalion was warned to keep in readiness to move at any time. At 2 p.m. a very effective artillery bombardment commenced, and B and D Companies advanced. D was now

LIEUT. C. J. McDONALD, M.C., LIEUT. C. O. CLARK, M.C., M.M., CAPTAIN D. G. OAKLEY, M.C

OFFICERS OF WINNING COMPANY, DIVISIONAL COMPETITION, JUNE 1917

BATTLE OF MENIN ROAD. 3RD BATTALION GARRISONING THE LINE AT CLAPHAM JUNCTION

Photo: *Aust. War Memorial Museum.*

commanded by Lieut C. L. L. Burrett, who had been sent from battalion headquarters for the purpose.

This advance, although strong opposition was encountered, gave us the village of Chuignes and the final objective of the 1st Brigade. Contact was established with the 4th Battalion on the right and the 12th on the left. B and D Companies were retained in the front line and C was withdrawn to a supporting position on a cliff north-west of Chuignes, while A Company, in reserve, guarded the south-western portion of the village. The battalion's advance during the day was approximately 5000 yards.

On August 24th, 25th, and 26th, by constantly relieving the front-line companies, the battalion pushed further forward by means of fighting patrols. By the time we were relieved by the 24th Battalion, at midnight on the 26th-27th, our line had been advanced 2500 yards east of Chuignes, and Fontaine-les-Cappy was in our hands. In all, four German officers and 155 other ranks, as well as 6 guns, 15 machine-guns, and 6 trench-mortars, were captured by the 3rd Battalion during the course of the operations since the 23rd.

Our casualties in the operation were: officers, 2 killed and 9 wounded; other ranks, 39 killed or died of wounds, and 181 wounded. The officers killed were Captain A. G. Cormack and Lieut M. McL. Keshan; those wounded were Lieuts O. C. Kellner, E. Hawkshaw, A. D. Arnold, W. L. Lamrock, A. J. S. Croll, E. H. Jackson, D.C.M., C. L. Wainwright, M.M., G. P. Darlow, and F. J. Jarvis. Jarvis, however, was not evacuated. Cormack, a Scotsman, was an unassuming officer who could always be relied on to do his job; Keshan was a fine type of clean-living young man whose splendid physique and physical fitness were an inspiration to his men.

Two N.C.Os, with fine records, C.S.M. Pat Kinchington, M.M., and Sergeant W. H. D. ("Bill") Sully, D.C.M., M.M., were now gazetted second-lieuts.

CHAPTER XXXIV

THE BATTLE OF HARGICOURT

From August 27th till September 6th the battalion was in bivouac in the Morcourt area, almost on the banks of the Somme Canal. Training, cleaning up, and recreation filled in these few days' respite. How wearisome it had all become—front line—training—cleaning up—recreational sports—front line ... until lying on the tape or kicking a football meant just about the same. The battalion was tired and done up. It had been fighting heavily since April, and was weary, both mentally and physically.

At midday on September 6th the battalion left Morcourt in buses and bivouacked that night near Hem, on the north bank of the Somme, moving again on the 8th to an old hutted camp in the Tincourt-Boucly area, about three miles east of Péronne, which had fallen during the past few days after the magnificent Australian victory at Mont St Quentin. The Somme was behind us and no longer an obstacle and the enemy was well on the run back to the Hindenburg outpost line, which was, in reality, the old British front line of March 21st.

On the 10th September we took over from the 38th Battalion in its support position 1000 yards east of Roisel, remaining here until relieved by the 5th Battalion on the night of the 14th-15th. We then moved back to the huts near Tincourt.

Some battalions of the A.I.F. had fallen so low in effectives that they had been disbanded, their remnants being absorbed by the other battalions in their respective brigades, so as to bring those units, also reduced in numbers, nearer to establishment. To anyone who did not fight in one of the sixty glorious infantry battalions of the A.I.F., the indescribable sadness attaching to the disbandment of one of them, the heartbreaking wrench of giving up the colour-patches, cannot be even remotely understood. Every Digger loved his battalion, and for it to die out was a personal and inexpressible sorrow. However, be it to the everlasting credit of those battalions that were unfortunately disbanded, their members carried on just as loyally and gallantly with their new units.

On September 15th the 3rd Battalion was forced through depleted numbers to reorganize anew on a three company basis, the new designations of the companies and their commanders being X (Lieut C. J. Clifton), Y (Lieut E. R. Shelley), and Z (Captain G. E. McDonald). So far as the 3rd was concerned A, B, C, and D Companies going "west" was bad enough; but everyone in the entire 1st Brigade hoped and prayed that neither the 1st, 2nd, 3rd, nor 4th Battalions would have to lower its flag on account of the disastrous wastage of war and lack of reinforcements. However, at this stage there was talk of it, and it was no doubt a distinct possibility.

The strength of the 3rd Battalion was now round about 400 all ranks, and it was tragic, almost cruel, to think of the thousands of gallant men who had fought in its ranks, and to see this remnant struggling on to keep alive the tradition set by those gallant fellows. As an illustration of the terrible wastage of war, at a parade on the 1918 anniversary of the Landing at Anzac there were present with the battalion only one of its original officers, two of its original sergeants, and fourteen others —out of approximately 1100 who landed on the Peninsula on the 25th April, 1915.

At midnight on September 17th the battalion moved to its assembly position in the old trenches just forward and north of Hesbécourt, and was in position at 4.15 a.m. Rain fell during the march, and the going was very heavy. The 1st Brigade was to attack on the left flank of the Australian Corps, which was employing two divisions—the 1st and 4th—in the battle.

In the coming battle,* set down for September 18th the 1st Brigade was to penetrate about 6000 yards on a 2000 yards' frontage, taking in its stride the village of Hargicourt. The 2nd Battalion on the right and the 4th Battalion on the left would carry out the first phase of the attack, the 1st and 3rd Battalions subsequently passing through them to capture the final objective.

A very effective barrage was put down at 5.20 a.m., but a heavy fog, thickened by smoke shells, made visibility very poor, and the start of the battalion was delayed for fifteen minutes. During portions of the advance behind the 4th Battalion some of our platoons lost touch, but with good leadership they continued on in the general direction, and at 7.40 we were able to report all correct at the second assembly position at Hargicourt. So far the battalion had suffered no casualty.

While the protective barrage for the second phase fell east of Hargicourt the companies got their men together. At 8.30 a.m., when the fire lifted, the 3rd Battalion (little more than 300 strong) moved through the 4th, attacking in open warfare formation on a 1000-yard frontage. In support was a mobile battery of artillery, a trench mortar section, and two sections of the 1st Machine-gun Battalion. All these were under the immediate command of the acting C.O., Major A. F. Burrett. Z Company (Captain G. E. McDonald) followed in reserve.

---

* Known by the British officially as the "Battle of Epehy," being a phase of the "Battles of the Hindenburg Line."

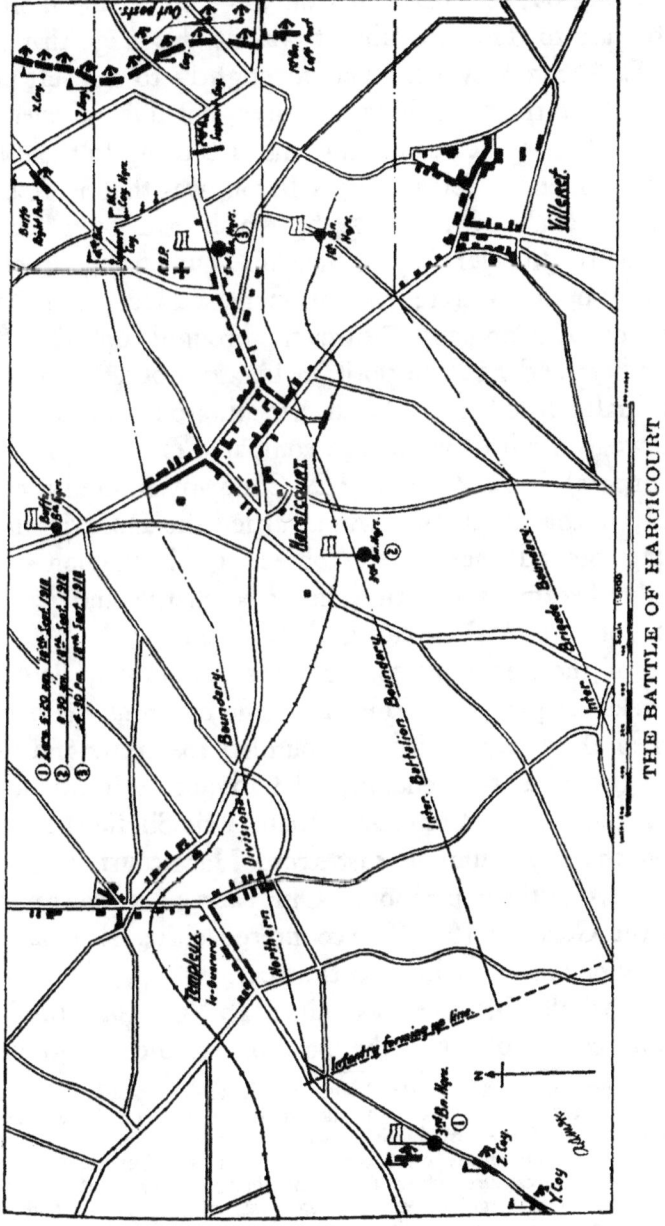

THE BATTLE OF HARGICOURT

Moving out of Hargicourt our direction changed from north-east to due east, and it was at this stage that the left flank company (X) veered slightly to the left and so fought in the 74th Division's area, but this was eventually righted. The reason for this, according to the company commander, Lieut C. J. Clifton, was that he desired to keep touch with the 74th, which had been forced further to the left by a machine-gun firing from a strongly-built concrete emplacement. Lieut E. Hawkshaw of X Company, however, brought up his riflegrenadiers and had the position knocked out.* The gap was finally filled in by Lieut Kinchington's platoon who followed on with the reserve company Z.

Corporal J. L. Roberts of X Company figured prominently in this attack, and was awarded the D.C.M. when, during the advance to the objective his platoon commander became a casualty, he took charge and led his men forward with great gallantry and skill. At one stage of the attack his platoon was temporarily held up by machine-gun fire from two enemy guns. Roberts worked ahead and killed or wounded the crews and captured the guns, thus enabling the advance to continue.

On the right Y Company (Lieut Eric Shelley) moved along the spur running east from Hargicourt, and met with very little opposition. Our barrage was excellent, and the Germans that Y encountered either surrendered readily or rushed wildly to the rear.

The whole objective was gained at 10.15, and the line companies consolidated the position in the old trench-

---

* Commenting on this battle, Lieut Pat Kinchington (Z Company), wrote:—"After passing through the southern end of Templeux-le-Guerard, some of the 74th Division were held up. I had to lie on the ground to see the enemy on account of the mist. Getting in behind the Germans we captured 28 of them, and then relieved Lieut Truscott's party of the 15th Battalion, Suffolk Regiment, which was in a bad way. On reaching 'Minnow Trench' I personally captured a German who was guarding a dugout. This dugout was found to contain a battalion commander, 4 other officers, and 55 men. All of them were made prisoner."

system known here as "Minnow" and "Triangle" trenches. Touch was established with the battalions on our flanks. Patrols were sent forward to exploit the success, but enemy reinforcements, bringing heavy machine-gun fire to bear on them, prevented any appreciable advance.

The advanced posts of the 10th Buffs on our left withdrew, leaving our flank rather "in the air." During the afternoon enfilade machine-gun fire was severe, but the night passed quietly. Every dugout was carefully examined for "booby-traps" before being occupied.

It was now decided to capture the high ground overlooking Bellicourt and so pave the way for a further advance by the Corps, against the Hindenburg Line itself. This preliminary attack, which would take place at dawn on September 21st, was entrusted to the 1st and 3rd Battalions and the 10th Buffs (74th Division) on their left. On the night of the 20th the 1st Battalion accordingly took over a section of our front, on the right; both X and Y Companies of the 3rd were now in support to Z Company (Captain G. E. McDonald), which would carry out our part of the attack.

At 5.40 a.m. under cover of artillery and machine-gun barrages the line advanced to the attack. Posts were established by Captain McDonald 500 yards ahead. The enemy established posts in the left rear of Z Company about midday, as the British troops on our left had retired. Z Company was then subjected to severe machine-gun and rifle-fire, and, as this could not be returned, the posts were withdrawn to Minnow trench.

The 10th Buffs relieved us along portion of the line during the night, and twenty-four hours later our 5th Battalion took over the remainder. Our strength that day in the front zone was 12 officers and 245 other ranks.

Taking into consideration the ground won, our casualties—13 killed and 82 wounded—in the last few days' fighting were comparatively light. Lieut C. J. McDonald, M.C. (of Bowral, N.S.W.) died of wounds. He was an exceptionally brilliant young officer, courageous and popular, and to him falls the tragic honour of being the last officer of the 3rd to give his life for Australia. Lieuts E. R. Shelley, C. J. Clifton and E. Hawkshaw and Second-Lieuts S. J. Holman and P. Kinchington were among the wounded.

CHAPTER XXXV

THE ARMISTICE AND AFTERWARDS

AT 3.15 a.m. on September 23rd the battalion arrived in the Roisel area, and the day was spent in resting and passing through the baths at Marquaix. Next day a route march by way of Péronne and Halle brought us to Biaches, where we went into bivouac. The nucleus joined us here, and on the 26th, about 2 p.m., the whole battalion—21 officers and 390 other ranks—entrained at La Chapellette for Longpré, from which at 6 o'clock it marched to Bellancourt, taking over billets there five hours later.

The battalion rested and trained at Bellancourt till October 6th, when it marched to Villers-sous-Ailly. Four days later it moved on to Epagne, where training exercises were continued, on November 8th marched to Pont Remy to entrain for Tincourt-Boucly, which was reached the following day. On the 10th the Battalion was again on the move, buses conveying it to Bazuel, near Le Cateau. The billets in this place were poor and comfortless. Many of the houses had been used as cages for prisoners of war, and on the walls of many of them were scrawled the regimental numbers and names of prisoners, including those of Australians. It was in these cheerless surroundings that we received the news of the Armistice.

There was now much speculation as to the future movements of the battalion. Popular opinion favoured the occupation of Berlin. On the 13th we marched to Busigny, on the 21st to Mazinghiem, next day to Prisches, and on the 25th to Solre-le-Chateau, where the educational scheme was first put into operation with a view to preparing the men for post-war work. On December 15th we at last crossed the Belgian border and went into billets at Barbencon. The following day Pry was reached. Then on the 17th we entered Gerpinnes, six miles south-east of the city of Charleroi. In this town comfortable quarters were secured, and many weeks were spent here. To keep all ranks occupied, football matches and winter sports were arranged. A favourite pastime was tobogganing on improvised sledges in the snow.

In the meantime the repatriation of the A.I.F. went on steadily. On the 27th of February, 1919, it was decided to amalgamate the 1st and 4th Battalions at Acoz, and the 2nd and 3rd at Bouffioulx, small villages on the outskirts of Chatelet, a suburb of Charleroi. The band of the 3rd Battalion rose to fame during these days, being one of the first British bands to play in Brussels after the war. It proved to be so popular that it was stationed in the capital for some weeks.

At last, on May 6th, the battalion, together with the rest of the 1st Brigade, entrained at Charleroi on its way to the coast, *en route* to England, Lieut-Col D. T. Moore being in command and Major G. E. McDonald second-in-command. Both officers had enlisted with the original battalion.

And so the 3rd Battalion closed its account with the Germans and their Allies. It had been a long road from Randwick Racecourse to Hargicourt, full of hardships, suffering and sacrifice, but throughout it all that marvellous bond of comradeship, *esprit de corps,* and love of Australia moulded the 3rd Battalion officers and men into a glorious unit from which sprang epic deeds of heroism and bravery, both individual and collective. We share the glory of the A.I.F., the greatest thing Australia has yet produced—a force that gave Australia nationhood and **Anzac.**

If one man's spirit lived throughout those years as an inspiration to the 3rd Battalion, it was that of our first commanding officer—Lieut Col R. H. Owen, C.M.G., dear old "Dad." His high principles, courage, absolute fairness, and understanding of human nature, early gave the battalion an ideal, which was carried on by Bennett, McConaghy, Howell-Price and Moore.

We survivors of the 3rd are proud to have taken some part, no matter how small, in building up its glorious history—Anzac—Lone Pine—The Evacuation—Pozières—Flers—Hermies—Bullecourt—Broodseinde—Passchendaele—Hazebrouck—Chuignes—Hargicourt . . . . a veritable trumpet-sound of names.

To the present generation and to generations unborn, we hand on unsullied the chocolate and green of the 3rd Battalion as a proud heritage, and to the everlasting glory of those who made the supreme sacrifice.

BATTLE HONOURS

SOMME, 1916, 1918
POZIERES
BULLECOURT
YPRES, 1917
MENIN ROAD
POLYGON WOOD
BROODSEINDE
POELCAPPELLE
PASSCHENDAELE
LYS
HAZEBROUCK
AMIENS
ALBERT, 1918 (CHUIGNES)
HINDENBERG LINE
EPEHY
FRANCE AND FLANDERS,
    1916-18
ANZAC
LANDING AT ANZAC
DEFENCE OF ANZAC
SUVLA
SARI BAIR—LONE PINE
GALLIPOLI, 1915
EGYPT, 1915-16

HONOURS AND AWARDS LIST—3RD BATTALION A.I.F.

Victoria Cross
No. 943—Private J. Hamilton.

Companion of the Order of St Michael and St George
Lieut-Col R. H. Owen
Lieut-Col D. T. Moore (D.S.O.)
Major D. M. McConaghy

Distinguished Service Order
Lieut-Col D. T. Moore (C.M.G.)
Lieut-Col O. G. Howell-Price (M.C.)
Major A. F. Burrett
Major G. F. Wootten

Military Cross

Lieut Agnew, R. R.
Lieut Baird, J. R.
2/Lt Boileau, A. H.
Lieut Bulkeley, R. L.
Lieut Clark, C. O. (M.M.)
Lieut Clifton, C. J.
2/Lt Desbois, L. D.
2/Lt Dill, H. B.
Capt Elliot, F. C.
Capt Fitzpatrick, S. C.
Lieut Hawkshaw, E.
Capt Howie, C.
Lieut Kemiss, L. F.
Lieut Leslie, G. H.
2/Lt Littlejohn, A.
2/Lt Loveday, L. W. S.
2/Lt McDonald, C. G.
2/Lt Moore, R. I. (D.C.M.)
C.S.M. Morris, G. A.
Capt Oakley, D. G.
Capt Page, F. E.
Lieut Prescott, C. G.
Capt Price, O. G. Howell-
Lieut Robb, H. D.
Lieut Shelley, E. R.
C.S.M. Smith, C. L.
Lieut Sturt, C. L.
Capt Tyson, J. G.
Chaplain Wilson, B. C.

Distinguished Conduct Medal

2327 Pte Abraham, G.
32 Sgt Berry, G. G.
3717 Cpl Campbell, L. J. (M.M.)
2666 Pte Clutterbuck, C. (M.M.)
1320 Sgt Douglas, B. A.
4459 Cpl Druery, R. W.
1088 Sgt Edwards, A. G.
2451 Cpl Ewart, L. A.

325 Pte Farmer, A.
1355 Sgt Fawcett, F.
1354 Pte Freeman, W.
2648 Pte Gaukrodger, A. G.
2149 L/Cpl Graham, N.
  20 Cpl Graham, R. L.
 932 Sgt Hatton, W. B. (M.M.)
2607 L/Cpl Hudson, A.
1293 Pte Humbertson, R.
 140 Sgt Jackson, E.
 164 L/Cpl Marshall, W. A.
5136 L/Cpl Matthews, G. S. A.
2750 Pte Meaker, H.

3152 Cpl Meers, C. J.
2097 Sgt McMillan, T.
1151 Cpl Moore, R. I.
 165 R.S.M. Newland, W. J.
3290 Cpl Roberts, J. L. (M.M.)
5534 Pte Saxby, E. J.
1579 Sgt Seccombe, A. H.
2669 Sgt Sully, W. H. D. (M.M.)
 748 Sgt Thompson, J. H.
2693 Cpl Turvey, P. (M.M.)
1843 Pte Ward, P. H. (M.M.)
2101 L/Cpl Weger, J. C.
1156 Cpl Williams, R.

Military Medal

2877 Pte Alexander, F. J.
 763 Pte Bailey, E. W. H.
6718 Pte Bain, W. H.
3019 Pte Baldwin, C. C. H.
1445 Pte Beeves, W. E.
1488 Sgt Blumer, C.
 561 Pte Bonney, R. R.
1081 Pte Bradford, G.
2567 Pte Breen, F. L.
4965 Pte Breitman, G.
  98 Sgt Bridle, H.
 308 Sgt Bruggy, J.
4588 Pte Burt, R. V.
1511 L/Sgt Byrne, J.
 790 Pte Cameron, J.
3717 Pte Campbell, L. J.
       (D.C.M.)
6489 Pte Campbell, P. W.
5661 Pte Carr, J. T.
2590 Pte Carter, G.
6404 Pte Charters, F.
2113 Sgt Clark, C. O.
2666 Pte Clutterbuck, C.
       (D.C.M.)
5667 Pte Croydon, A.
       (D.C.M.)
3054 Pte Daniel, R.
3740 L/Cpl Dare, H. S.
2584 Pte Day, P. F.
 486 Cpl Dick, G. C.
5208 Pte Doughty, J. W.

1348 Sgt Dowling, C.
3745 Cpl Driscoll, V.
6159 Pte Duncan, J. E.
4167 Sgt Dykes, P. J.
1738 Cpl Edwards, E. H.
5073 Pte Elgood, A. W.
1359 Cpl Fletcher, A. N.
1547 L/Cpl Flynn, J. T.
2823 Pte Freeborn, W.
3831 Pte Gilbert, G. A. E.
 332 Sgt Gordon, G.
 334 Pte Gordon, W. H.
 239 Pte Green, W. A.
4127 Pte Griffiths, J. G.
6289 Pte Hall, A. F.
 936 Sgt Hanlon, H.
 932 Sgt Hatton, W. B. (D.C.M.)
5104 L/Cpl Haynes, G.
 734 L/Cpl Heathcote, A. W.
6026 Pte Holt, R. A.
2668 Pte Hopson, F. R.
 135 Pte Howarth, J. E.
4498 Pte Kearns, J. T.
5122 Pte Kevin, W. T.
2695 Pte Kew, W.
2623 Cpl Kinchington, P.
6309 Pte Lang, E. G.
2629 Pte Lee, N.
6800 Pte McDonald, D.
1398 L/Cpl McGee, S.
1366 Cpl MacLachlan, L.

PTE C. M. GEDDES

SGT. KEITH MARTYN

SGT. L. F. COOK

PTE W. H. NICHOLSON

CAPTAIN C. E. LEER
Killed in action.

CAPTAIN W. B. DOUGLAS
Killed in action.

MAJOR G. E. McDONALD, V.D.,

LIEUT. S. RUDKIN

LIEUT. E. N. LITCHFIELD

DECORATIONS

1191 L/Sgt Millard, J. W.
2648 L/Cpl Milner, G.
2167 L/Sgt Maston, H. W.
37 Sgt Murn, F. J.
1998 L/Cpl Murray, J. A.
1147 L/Cpl Murray, N.
1159 Pte Murray, S.
2662 L/Cpl Nurse, C.
6802 Pte O'Donnell, F. B.
4258 Pte O'Sullivan, W. D.
166 L/Cpl Page, C. G.
2140 Pte Parry, R. A.
1606 Pte Pattinson, R.
5726 L/Cpl Putre, J.
16 Sgt Ravell, D.
1375 L/Cpl Ray, C. H. E.
176 Sgt Ritchie, F. E. L.
1793 Cpl Ritchie, L. G.

3290 L/Cpl Roberts, J. L. (D.C.M.)
3269 Pte Scott, C. J.
3224 Pte Stuart, L. A.
6816 Pte Sullivan, J. R.
2269 Sgt Sully, W. H. D. (D.C.M.)
2881 L/Cpl Thomas, J. H.
4570 Pte Thomas, L.
976 Cpl Traynor, J. G.
2693 Cpl Turvey, P.
4571 Pte Usher, L. J. N.
2206 — Wainwright, C. L.
2848 Pte Wallace, W. J.
1843 Pte Ward, P. H. (D.C.M.)
3268 Cpl Watkins, J. W.
19 T/Sgt Wood, A. W.

Bar to Military Medal

3831 Pte Gilbert, G. A. E.
1147 L/Cpl Murray, N.

Meritorious Service Medal

1507 C.S.M. Bubb, J.
301 Pte Fishlock, G.
3076 Pte George, B. W.
2365 Sgt Mann, P. A.

956 Cpl Morrison, J. A.
362 L/Cpl Powell, J. H.
2218 C.S.M. Regan, C. C. A.
1657 Cpl Thomas, P.

Order de la Couronne (Belgian)

Lieut-Col D. T. Moore (C.M.G., D.S.O.)

Croix de Guerre (Belgian)

Lieut-Col D. T. Moore (C.M.G., D.S.O.)
1137 Sgt Wells, M. E.
294 Sgt McKenzie, A. S.
5686 L/Cpl Irvin, J.

Croix de Guerre (French)

Captain E. W. G. Wren

NOMINAL ROLL—3RD BATTALION, A.I.F.

* Killed or died of wounds.   † Denotes original officer.

LIEUTENANT-COLONELS

†*Brown, E. S.
†*Howell-Price, O. G. (D.S.O., M.C.).
†Moore, D. T. (C.M.G., D.S.O.).
†*McConaghy, D. M. (C.M.G., D.S.O.).
†Owen, R. H. (C.M.G.).

MAJORS

†*Austin, C.
†Bennett, A. J. (D.S.O.)
Brand, C., D.S.O.
Burrett, A. F. (D.S.O.)
†Carter, W. B.
Edwards, A. R.
Harris, J. R. O.
†Lamb, M. St J.
†McDonald, G. E.
Wootten, G. F. (D.S.O.)

CAPTAINS

Agnew, R. R. (M.C.)
†*Beeken, W. C.
Blake, G. E.
†Butler, H. E.
†*Burns, R.
†Chester, J. L.
*Cormack, A. G.
†Coulter, C. W. H.
†Cowey, R. O.
*Dawson, E.
†*Douglas, W. B.
Elliot, F. C. (M.C.)
Goldenstedt, P. L.
*Hewish, A. G.
*Higinbotham, L. H. R.
Holland, A. C. S.
Howie, C. (M.C.)
Kemmis, L. F. (M.C.)
Kemp, F. C.
†*Leer, C. E.
†*MacFarlane, E. M.
McDermid, A.
*Middleton, R. O.
*Moore, R. I. (M.C., D.C.M.)
Oakley, D. G. (M.C.)
Page, F. E. (M.C.)
Plunkett, G. F.
Phipps, W. B.
†*Smith, T. O.
Stronach, A.
Tarleton, A.
*Tyson, J. G. (M.C.)
†Wall, G.
White, S. F. P.
*Wilson, G.
†*Wilson, J. C.
Wren, E. W. G.

Lieutenants

Allen, H.*
Allport, R. B.
Anderson, A. T.
Arnold, A. D.
Backhouse, A. N.
Bailey, H. F.
Baird, J. R. (M.C.)
Barber, G. F.
†*Barlow, J. E.
*Bartlett, J. S. F.
Bayley, K.
Bayley, R. B.
Beary, C. G.
Berry, B. C.
*Bishop, H. M.
*Blaydes, A. M. D.
Blumer, C. (M.M.)
Boileau, A. H. (M.C.)
†*Brodziak, C. E. M.
Browne, E. E.
Bruggy, J. (M.M.)
Buckley, A. N.
*Bulkeley, R. F. (M.C.)
*Burley, L. J.
Burrett, C. L. L.
Butcher, W. E.
Butler, A. W.
†*Cadell, T. L.
*Champion, C. H. D.
Chapman, E. W.
*Chapman, H. S.
Chapman, W.
Christoe, G. B.
Clark, C. O. (M.C., M.M.)
*Clarke, E.
Clayton, C. E.
Clifton, C. J. (M.C.)
Cochrane, A. B.
*Cooper, H. L.
*Cotterill, F. J.
Croll, A. J. S.
Daniel, A. H.

Dare, H. S. (M.M.).
Darlow, G. P.
Dayas, A. J.
Denoon, W.
Desbois, D. R. (M.C.).
Dill, H. L. (M.C.).
Duprez, A. O.
*Elliott, L. S.
Elliott, W. F.
*Evans, T. H.
*Ferguson, H.
Fitzpatrick, F. G.
*Garnham, S. M.
*Gibbins, N.
Giblett, W. N.
†Goldring, E. G.
†Goldring, H. W.
Greyson, G. W.
Griffith, J. B.
Hadfield, R. D.
Hamilton, J. (V.C.)
*Harrison, J. H.
Hawkshaw, E. (M.C.)
†*Hinde, K. J.
Hine, A.
Holman, S. J.
Howard, A. K.
Hutchison, J.
Jackson, E. (D.C.M.)
Jarvis, F. J.
Kellner, O. C.
*Keshan, M.
Kidd, A. C.
Kinchington, P. (M.M.)
Lacey, J. L.
Lamrock, W. L.
Layton, K. C.
Leggett, N. C.
Leggett, R. O.
Lemon, G. D.
Lenehan, P.
Leslie, G. H. (M.C.)
Litchfield, E. N.

NOMINAL ROLL

Littlejohn, A. (M.C.)
Lord, J. N.
Loveday, L. W. S. (M.C.)
MacDougal, G. R.
*McDonald, C. J. (M.C.)
McCarthy, E.
McCarthy, J. S. E.
McLachlan, L. (M.M.)
*McMaster, A. S.
*Maisey, F. T.
*Marshall, J. J.
*Mason, A. C. S.
Matthews, J. H.
Montague, J.
*Morgan, R. R.
Morton, F. W.
*Mulholland, D. V.
Murn, F. J. (M.M.)
Nixon, J. S.
Norman, E. R.
Ormiston, I. W. L.
*Owen, P. I. H.
*Palmer, H. L.
*Pestell, J. V.
*Philpot, J. T.
Pinkstone, N.
Pinkstone, S. A.
Prescott, C. G. (M.C.)
Ray, C. H. E. (M.M.)
*Ritchie, E. C. H.
Robb, H. D. (M.C.)
Robertson, D. H.
Robertson, S. L.
Rogerson, A. G.
Ross, D.
Rudkin, T. S.
Sedgwick, W.
*Shappere, C. S.
Shelley, E. R. (M.C.)
Sheppard, L. S.
Sillar, J. W.
Smith, A. E.
Smith, C. L. (M.C.)
Smith, Forbes
*Smith, F. T. C.
Smythe, V. E.
Stanger, J. H.
†Stevenson, L. S. K.
†*Street, L. W.
Sturt, C. L. (M.C.)
Stutchbury, E. W.
Sully, W. H. D. (D.C.M., M.M.)
Symonds, A. B.
*Taylor, F. W.
Thompson, C.
*Vallis, T. J.
Wainwright, C. L. (M.M.)
*Watson, H. J. F.
*Watson, L. C.
*White, C. H. O.
†White, C. J. A.
Whitworth, A. R.
Wilson, H. L.
Woods, P. W.

MEDICAL OFFICERS

†Bean, J. W. B., Captain
Beamish, F. T., Major
Blomfield, B. B., Captain
Dunlop, L., Captain
Fitzpatrick, S. C. (M.C.), Captain
North, H. M., Captain
Pattinson
Phillips

CHAPLAINS

†The Very Rev. Dean Talbot
The Rev B. C. Wilson, M.C.
The Rev Stacey Waddy
The Rev J. W. Dains

OTHER RANKS

2327	Pte	Abraham, G. (D.C.M.)	6457	„ Allen, W. F.
6456	„	Ackland, A.	2958	„ Allt, P.
*306	„	Ackling, C.	2423	„ Allthorpe, F. W.
*6157	„	Ackroyd, G. C.	691	„ Almond, G.
6999	„	Acland, A. J.	2555	Cpl Alt, J. F.
*1703	„	Adams, C. H.	550	R.Q.M.S. Ambrose, J. J.
1505	Cpl	Adams, C. J.	1203	Pte Ambrose, C. G.
84	Sgt	Adams, C. S.	5027	„ Amiet, V.
3001	Pte	Adams, P. C.	2554	„ Amourin, A. G.
2105	„	Adams, R.	*2779	„ Amodeo, A. S.
2326	„	Adams, S. C.	2249	„ Amourin, L.
1506	C.Q.M.S.	Adams, S. J.	94	„ Amourous, L.
1298	Sgt	Adams, W. H.	*701	„ Anderson, A.
*7191	Pte	Adams, W. H.	5028	„ Anderson, A. A.
*564	„	Adamson, H.	1511	„ Anderson, A. T.
3229	„	Adcock, F. W.	5646	„ Anderson, C.
6	C.S.M.	Agassiz, C. T.	702	„ Anderson, E.
3686	Pte	Agnew, R. F.	2983	„ Anderson, E. L.
*2633	„	Ahearn, F.	2780	„ Anderson, E. S.
3002	„	Aikens, W.	2556	„ Anderson, F.
3685	„	Ainslie, T.	3003	„ Anderson, J. A.
1101	Cpl	Ainsworth, A.	6946	„ Anderson, N. J.
5966	Pte	Airey, T. A.	582	„ Anderson, R. C.
*1869	„	Aitkins, F. K.	4129	„ Anderson, V.
2990	„	Akhurst, C. W.	5969	„ Andrews, A. S.
5026	„	Alcock, T. H.	7193	„ Andrews, C. P.
6702	„	Alewood, G. R.	7441	„ Andrews, W. H.
6788	„	Alexander, F. J. (M.M.)	5968	„ Andrews, F. T. J.
			6412	„ Andrews, G. H.
*7437	„	Alexander, W. H. H.	4091	„ Andrews, H.
			*2424	„ Andrews, L.
*2776	„	Alexander, J.	2554	L/Cpl Andrews, R. W. J.
*2555	„	Alford, E. S.		
3676	„	Allan, E. S.	6274	Pte Andrews, T. R.
996	„	Allan, J. J.	*5029	„ Anelzark, L. R.
4587	„	Allbrand, E.	3682	„ Angus, F. J. G.
2106	Cpl	Alldritt, N. B.	4622	„ Annan, K. H.
4002	Pte	Allen, A. H.	*1296	„ Annesley, R. R.
1510	„	Allen, A. W.	2124	„ Anness, F. A.
3222	„	Allen, E. L.	2123	„ Anness, H.
59461	„	Allen, J.	690	„ Annetts, J. A. H.
3005	„	Allen, J. W.	*244	Cpl Anschau, G. G.
65704	„	Allen, L.	1701	Pte Anson, H.
1901	„	Allen, R.	2859	„ Appleton, J. R.

2070	„	Apthorp, W. E.
*1297	„	Archer, B. C.
*1093	„	Archer, F. W.
4030	„	Archer, J.
6947	„	Archer, L. P.
*6212	„	Ariansen, V.E.H.
1663	„	Arlidge, W.
7436	„	Armes, S. G.
*1309	„	Armfield, L.
*1650	„	Armitage, W.
2939	„	Armitage, W. J. E.
7582	„	Armour, A. G.
*6414	„	Armstrong, D.
6275	„	Armstrong, E. E.
2101	„	Armstrong, J. H.
6433	„	Armstrong, R.
2102	„	Armstrong, S. D.
4100	Cpl	Arnold, H. W.
3992	Pte	Arnott, J.
65707	„	Arthur, K.
2509	„	Ash, J. McM.
7438	„	Ashburner, H. P. W.
7439	„	Ashcroft, J.
126	„	Ashdown, S. A.
2475	„	Ashton, A. E.
2552	„	Askby, J. E. E.
*1094	„	Aspinall, B. F.
6604	„	Aspinall, R.
*5649	„	Asquith, J.
2777	„	Asquith, J. M.
3677	„	Atherton, W.
693	„	Atkins, G.
6211	„	Atkins, H. G.
2103	„	Atkinson, F. S.
*1503	„	Atkinson, J.
3676	Cpl	Atlee, L. W.
754	Pte	Attwood, S. J.
5201	„	Audet, A. P.
1191	„	Auld, J.
59462	„	Austin, J. E.
1055	„	Austin, L.
2328	Sgt	Avant, R.
3004	Pte	Avery, T.
3716	„	Avery, T. J.
3002	„	Ayers, C. T.
2864	„	Aylett, W. P.
30	„	Ayre, G. H.
*3687	Pte	Badger, A.
1630	„	Baggett, E. W. G.
3688	„	Baigent, W. H.
*597	A/Cpl	Bailey, A.
9	Cpl	Bailey, A. G.
7457	Pte	Bailey, E. H.
763	„	Bailey, E. W. H. (M.M.)
291	Bglr	Bailey, J.
1286	Sgt	Bailey, J.
6952	Pte	Bailey, L.
6458	„	Bailey, T. H.
2147	„	Bailey, W. J.
894	„	Bailey, W. J.
7448	„	Bain, G. C.
6718	„	Bain, W. H. (M.M.)
6229	„	Baird, J. B.
*2253	„	Baird, W. G.
*1704	„	Baird, W. H.
2567	„	Baker, A.
895	„	Baker, A. W.
*106	„	Baker, C. W.
*1104	„	Baker, E. H.
*6704	„	Baker, J. P.
2111	„	Baker, W. H.
7599	„	Baldacchino, G.
59486	„	Baldock, L.
*1493	„	Baldwin, H.
6949	„	Baldwin, R. A.
*3019	Cpl	Baldwin, C. C. H. (M.M.)
*2559	Pte	Bale, A. E.
2107	A/Sgt	Ball, S.
1101	Pte	Ballantyne, J.
395	„	Balkwill, A. C.
2108	„	Ballinger, A. P.
3010	„	Bancroft, H. W.
1563	L/Cpl	Banks, C. H.
311	Pte	Banks, F. A.
1313	„	Banning, R. H.
1912	„	Bannister, W. J.
5977	„	Barber, P. C.
3007	„	Barber, R.

6219	„	Barclay, A. C.	5356	„	Bastian, H.
*1518	„	Bare, D.	5335	„	Bastian, H. E.
1305	„	Barkell, V. J.	1317	„	Batchelor, F. A.
4589	„	Barker, E.	3004	„	Bates, A.
3013	„	Barker, H. F.	39	„	Bates, A.
6610	„	Barker, L.	65869	„	Bates, A. A.
1914	„	Barker, H.	1521	„	Bates, C. F.
6705	„	Barker, T.	65723	„	Bates, D.
*6415	„	Barlow, A. E.	1102	„	Bates, P. C.
309	„	Barlow, F.	933	„	Bates, S.
6708	„	Barnes, D.	4437	L/Cpl	Batey, R.
*2104	„	Barnes, L. J.	*1909	Pte	Batts, R. M.
2425	„	Barnes, T. R.	6220	„	Batty, A. J.
3009	„	Barnes, H. A.	7443	„	Batty, S.
2561	„	Barnes, N. M.	4006	„	Batty, T. C.
2472	Cpl	Barnes, T. R.	*7505	„	Baulch, E. R. L.
7455	Pte	Barnes, W. H.	2329	„	Baxter, E. J.
*3691	„	Barnett, A.	*5650	„	Bayley, A.
3016	„	Barnett, R.	6221	„	Bayliss, G. T.
2193	„	Barnie, G.	*6234	„	Baylis, J. E.
*2558	„	Barnsley, C. C.	4431	„	Bazzina, M.
*2566	Sgt	Baron, H. J.	*898	„	Beal, W.
3281	Dvr	Barr, J.	*6459	„	Bean, J. G.
3019	Pte	Barrett, C.	2789	„	Beard, G. C.
95	„	Barrett, L.	3020	„	Beattie, F.
4255	„	Barriere, R.	2109	„	Beaumont, G. W.
3007	„	Barrow, A. V.	4429	„	Beaven, J. W.
*517	Sgt	Barrow, J. W.	*6716	„	Bear, J. W.
*1007	Pte	Barrow, E. V.	*6961	„	Beasley, L.
2382	„	Barry, J.	*6719	„	Beaton, D. J.
2135	„	Barry, P.	65726	„	Beattie, R. A.
34	„	Barry, H. A.	1513	„	Beauchamp, A. F.
2577	„	Barry, P. J.	*3694	„	Beckhaus, J. R.
*2562	„	Bartels, J.	3692	„	Bedford, W.
1705	„	Bartlett, J. C.	*1110	„	Beeby, R.
*3235	„	Bartlett, W. G.	2561	„	Beechey, L. J.
6708	„	Barter, D.	4578	„	Beechey, J. C.
*1102	„	Barter, F.	*507	„	Beeken, F. W.
3008	„	Bartley, J.	1107	„	Beern, J.
2130	„	Barton, H. P.	1913	„	Beesley, W. G.
*2110	„	Bartrop, H.	1445	„	Beeves, W. E.
6956	„	Barwick, H.			(M.M.)
*1314	„	Bass, C. E.	*1311	„	Behenna, H.
2329	„	Bass, S. F.	*1707	„	Behen, B.
*2463	„	Bassett, O.	3006	„	Bell, C. C.
99	„	Bassage, W. A.	6460	„	Bell, E. J.
*2572	„	Bassford, J.			

NOMINAL ROLL 345

1304	,,	Bell, E. W.
788	,,	Bell, F.
*5034	,,	Bell, G. F.
1303	,,	Bell, J.
*6461	,,	Bell, J. C.
6232	,,	Bell, H. R.
599	,,	Bell, L.
2766	L/Cpl	Bell, L.
*1509	Pte	Bell, W.
*2562	,,	Bell, W. J.
*5652	,,	Bellchambers, W.
1512	,,	Belling, A. B.
6116	,,	Bellinger, W. T.
7691	,,	Bellis, T.
7686	,,	Bender, R. H.
4436	,,	Benger, H. J.
2795	,,	Benjamin, D. H.
4433	,,	Benn, F.
1708	,,	Bennett, A. J.
7444	,,	Bennett, J.
2781	,,	Bennett, J. C. A.
3007	,,	Bennett, K. W.
3006	,,	Bennett, L. W.
6959	,,	Bennett, R.
2964	,,	Bensen, J. E.
2947	,,	Bensen, J. E.
*2051	,,	Benson, F. R.
3347	,,	Benson, R.
3021	,,	Bentley, P. P.
8	L/Cpl	Benyon, F. J.
1118	Pte	Benzing, C. W.
*1080	,,	Beresford, B. F.
698	,,	Beresford, T.
6477	,,	Berg, R. A.
*908	,,	Bernays, R. M.
*4010	Sgt	Berry, J. J.
1107	Pte	Berryman, M. H.
*97	,,	Berryman, W. E.
*1027	,,	Besson, W.
4434	,,	Bethel, W.
892	,,	Bettridge, G.
2576	,,	Beveridge, D.
696	,,	Beveridge, R. W.
7449	,,	Beveridge, T. W.
2568	,,	Bevan, E. A.
4013	Cpl	Bewley, G. L.
*6462	Pte	Biden, W. W.

7210	,,	Biggs, T. J.
6835	,,	Bill, J.
2766	,,	Bill, L.
2863	,,	Bingley, E. G.
*7206	,,	Binn, H. H.
*3011	,,	Birch, C. A.
1103	,,	Birch, F.
*1522	,,	Bird, F. G.
7451	,,	Bird, T.
6463	,,	Birkett, S. W. P.
3025	,,	Birse, J.
107	,,	Bishop, H. A.
*3012	,,	Bishop, E. R.
4009	,,	Bishop, L.
2577	,,	Bishop, W. J.
*2492	,,	Bishope, W. R.
1319	,,	Bitmead, C.
65	,,	Black, R.
65720	,,	Black, S. H.
*896	Cpl	Blackburn, T.
*6222	Pte	Blackman, J. H.
5037	,,	Blackmore, T.
1307	,,	Blacklock, E. J.
2950	,,	Blackney, J. E.
6857	,,	Blackwood, R. E.
2383	,,	Blackwood, J. S.
489	,,	Blake, E. F.
1868	,,	Blakeney, C. R.
6154	,,	Blakeney, E. J.
*2384	,,	Blanch, J. D.
6464	,,	Blanchard, E.
*2113	,,	Blanchfield, W.
1328	Sgt	Blaskett, H. A.
2900	Pte	Blaskett, H. A.
700	,,	Bleasby, A.
2782	,,	Bleasdale, J.
*1459	,,	Blend, B.
6418	,,	Blewett, B. S.
*4744	,,	Blomfield, F. G.
7452	,,	Bluett, E. C.
*1508	Cpl	Blumer, G. S.
*2406	Pte	Board, T. W.
1106	,,	Bodley, G. E.
2940	,,	Bodimeade, G. G.
2941	,,	Bodimeade, R. C.
3022	,,	Bodinnar, A. N.
1100	,,	Boland, F. C.

2346	„	Bolt, W. L.	7372	„ Bowson, A.
6539	„	Bolton, T. C.	2194	„ Boxall, C. W.
1709	„	Bolton, L. H.	307	„ Boxall, O.
6466	„	Boncher, J. W.	*6467	„ Boyer, A.
704	„	Bone, A.	6717	„ Boyd, C.
2221	„	Bonnette, C. A.	4	P/Sgt Boyd, G. G.
4007	„	Boni, B.	2330	Pte Boyd, J. C.
3696	L/Cpl	Boniface, G. L.	59469	„ Boyd, R. G.
561	Sgt	Bonney, R. R. (M.M.)	312	„ Boyland, J.
			1403	„ Boyle, T.
3695	Pte	Boot, L. V.	6416	„ Boyton, R. G.
6465	„	Booth, J. A.	*7458	„ Brace, H.
*6960	„	Booth, L. J.	*5041	„ Bradbery, B. A.
1318	„	Booth, W.	4011	„ Brackpool, E. W.
4628	„	Borger, M. C.	2856	„ Braddon, E.
1298	„	Boston, C.	2786	„ Bradford, A.
3020	„	Boswell, R. W.	1081	Cpl Bradford, G. (M.M.)
5038	„	Boswood, A.		
*1306	Cpl	Bosworth, A.	3018	Pte Bradford, W.
1308	Pte	Botfield, W. H.	2547	„ Bradley, H.
3015	„	Bottemley, H.	7450	„ Bradley, W. A.
*5040	„	Bottom, H. J.	1516	„ Bradshaw, H. L.
1097	Cpl	Bottomley, J.	*2252	„ Bradshaw, W. G. M.
*103	L/Sgt	Bouquet, A. H.		
1517	Pte	Bourke, E. A.	7203	„ Brady, E.
*699	L/Cpl	Bourke, C.	*514	„ Brady, W. H.
1517	Pte	Bourke, E. A.	483	Cpl Braga, J.
*4597	„	Bourke, H.	*5656	Pte Bragg, W. G.
*1513	„	Bourke, J.	*2580	„ Brain, P. S. R.
6950	„	Bourke, J.	*2114	„ Bramley, F. A.
*697	„	Bourke, J. J.	1531	„ Brander, W.
1086	„	Bourke, W.	4135	„ Brandric, W. J.
*694	Cpl	Bourke W. A.	2566	L/Cpl Brassil, T.
5798	Pte	Bourn, W.	3014	Sgt Bray, A. E.
*5	Sgt/Cook	Bourne, F.	2088	Pte Brayshaw, C.
1316	Pte	Bouveret, F. V.	3701	„ Brazier, A. E.
65725	„	Bowden, F. W. J.	2567	„ Breen, F. L. (M.M.)
2797	„	Bowen, F.		
5773	„	Bowen, J. A.	4965	„ Breitman, G. (M.M.)
5039	„	Bowen, R. C.		
4013	Cpl	Bowley, G. L.	7461	„ Bremer, C. J.
3348	Pte	Bowling, R.	*1310	„ Brennan, F.
5651	„	Bowman, B. B.	1104	„ Brennan, H. C. T.
1715	„	Bowman, D. McQ.	*589	„ Brennan, J.
			2560	„ Brennan, J. C.
3699	„	Bowness, W.	*104	„ Brennan, P. J.
*3698	„	Bowser, F.	*1099	„ Brennan, W. G.

NOMINAL ROLL

1570	,,	Brent, R.
27	,,	Brent, R.
524	,,	Brett, W.
93	,,	Brettle, W.
1740	,,	Brettle, S.
2729	,,	Brew, F. H.
4432	,,	Brew, W. E.
98	Sgt	Bridle, H. (m.m.)
*310	Pte	Bridges, J. C.
6429	,,	Brien, C. H.
*4627	,,	Briggs, D. G.
*2858	,,	Briggs, F. W.
*63	Sgt	Briggs, H. F.
2960	Pte	Briggs, T. B.
2796	,,	Brightfield, H. J.
7456	,,	Brindle, E. E.
93	L/Cpl	Brindle, H.
502	Pte	Brine, J.
*5042	,,	Brinkman, F. J.
897	,,	Brinkman, J.
7201	,,	Britten, J. H.
6962	,,	Britten, L. G.
17	Dvr	Britton, T. P.
6713	Pte	Broad, S. F. P.
*5655	,,	Broadbent, S. F.
7694	,,	Broadhead, E.
2331	,,	Brocklesby, T. V. M.
*582	Dvr	Broderick, H. J.
3018	Pte	Brodie, R. J.
5973	,,	Bromley, E. A.
1302	,,	Bromwick, C. F. C.
*6158	,,	Brook, F.
2871	,,	Brooker, G. R.
7199	,,	Brookes, E. J.
4591	,,	Brooks. A.
2787	,,	Brooks, E. J.
*4586	,,	Brooks, G. V.
*2857	,,	Brooks, L. V.
*487	,,	Brooks, W. E.
3026	,,	Broome, A. E.
4014	,,	Brown, A.
2115	,,	Brown, A. C.
3476	Cpl	Brown, A. E. (d.c.m.)
2448	,,	Brown, A. E.
1711	Pte	Brown, C.
3705	,,	Brown, C. C.
2789	,,	Brown, C. J.
4449	,,	Brown, C. L.
*1106	,,	Brown, F.
3016	,,	Brown, E. H.
*713	,,	Brown, F.
7204	,,	Brown, G. A.
4760	Cpl	Brown, H. A.
*6226	Pte	Brown, H. F.
*1523	,,	Brown, J.
2470	,,	Brown, J.
*6953	,,	Brown, J. R.
6459	,,	Brown, K. E.
3017	,,	Brown, L.
6395	,,	Brown, M. G.
4427	Cpl	Brown, P. E.
5658	Pte	Brown, R.
2584	,,	Brown, S. I.
65721	,,	Brown, T. H.
4670	,,	Brown, T.
*2789	Sgt	Brown, W. A.
1315	Pte	Brown, W. T.
*7442	,,	Brownlee, W. B.
3022	Cpl	Broxam, J. E.
*6472	Pte	Bruce, C. J.
*4625	,,	Brunshill, H.
2791	,,	Brunyee, G. W.
*519	,,	Bruton, B. J.
*5654	,,	Bryans, E.
3012	,,	Bryant, C. J.
*1301	,,	Bryant, J. H.
1712	,,	Bryant, R. W.
497	,,	Bryant, H.
703	,,	Bryant, W. H.
394	,,	Bryce, C. E.
*2357	Cpl	Bryson, W. G.
101	Pte	Bubb, F. W.
1507	C.S.M.	Bubb, J. (m.s.m.)
*4097	Pte	Buchanan, J. W.
*522	,,	Buckeridge, C. S.
*5975	,,	Buckland, E.
1756	,,	Buckland, O.
6707	,,	Buckland, S.
2570	Sgt	Buckley, A. H.
706	,,	Buckley, G. H.
*2116	Pte	Buckley, L. J.

1098	„	Buckley, W.	*2754	„ Burrows, S. F.
3017	„	Budgett, H.	6471	„ Busch, G. J.
*6233	„	Budge, J.	6138	„ Bush, J. M.
701	„	Budd, B. A.	2875	„ Bush, H. E.
*3711	„	Budd, W. A. J.	*6236	„ Bushby, A. H.
*1103	„	Buffett, A. F.	1300	„ Bushnell, G.
3023	„	Buffier, A.	1502	„ Bushell, S.
2725	„	Bulmer, H. H. J.	2563	„ Butcher, L. J.
96	Sgt	Bull, C. A.	*787	„ Butler, A.
893	L/Cpl	Bull, J.	1649	„ Butler, A. J.
695	Cpl	Bull, R. W.	7202	„ Butler, C. J.
6135	Pte	Bull, R. W. S.	2559	„ Butler, D. A.
4624	„	Bullard, H. A.	6228	„ Butler, F.
166	Sgt	Bulner, R. A.	*6712	„ Butler, J. W.
1911	Pte	Bunner, E.	65714	„ Butler, P. E.
7459	„	Bunt, J. E.	6478	„ Butler, R. W. J.
7454	„	Bunt, W. J.	1063	„ Butler, S.
7447	„	Burford, C. G.	*7460	„ Butt, E.
1312	„	Burgess, D. T.	*2659	„ Buttel, W. R.
2332	„	Burgess, H. C.	*2558	L/Cpl Butters, R. B.
3078	„	Burgess, V. J.	3010	Pte Butterworth, J.
4435	„	Burgess, P.	*1510	Sgt Butterworth, R.
*4438	„	Burgess, W. H.	1506	C.S.M. Button, J. J.
1713	„	Burke, D.	889	Cpl Buxton, J. O.
*64	„	Burke, H.	6715	Pte Byers, W. J. L.
1309	„	Burke, J.	3467	Q.M.S. Byrne, A. J.
*1514	„	Burke, J. J.	102	Pte Byrne, H. S.
565	„	Burke, T.	*1511	Sgt Byrne, J. (M.M.)
1311	„	Burling, C. E.	6706	Pte Byrne, J. J.
7444	„	Burnett, J.	3013	„ Byrne, S. R.
6475	„	Burnheim, V. A.	*7453	„ Byrne, T. J.
6039	„	Burns, F. M.	3011	„ Byrne, W. D.
6963	„	Burns, J. R.	6954	„ Byrnes, G.
3015	„	Burns, J. W.	*6834	„ Byrnes, J.
1299	„	Burns, S.	6476	„ Byrnes, H. O. W.
65709	„	Burrell, C. H.	6711	„ Byrnes, T. P.
*7446	„	Burrell, J. T.		
65710	„	Burrell, W. P.	3257	Pte Cabel, G.
2854	„	Bursill, O.	7709	„ Cadden, E. R.
4588	„	Burt, R. V. (M.M.)	1328	„ Cadoux, C. B.
1065	L/Cpl	Burton, A. A.	6246	„ Cahill, E.
1755	Pte	Burton, A. L.	2387	„ Caiger, V. W.
70	„	Burton, C. R.	5048	„ Cain, E.
*4013	„	Burton, F. R.	*6968	„ Caine, H.
*6479	„	Burton, V. R.	*4449	„ Caine, L. A.
1105	„	Burton, W. H.	*3714	„ Caird, J.
*802	„	Burrows, A.	5922	„ Cairncross, W. D.
6235	„	Burrows, A. E.		

NOMINAL ROLL 349

4162	„	Calder, A. G.
6244	„	Calder, C.
1525	„	Caldwell, A.
5344	„	Caldwell, J. D.
*1716	Sgt	Callaghan, A.
1518	„	Callaghan, W.
904	Pte	Calloway, A. R.
1926	„	Calthorpe, B. W.
*2776	„	Cambage, M. C.
2592	Sgt	Cameron, A.
7467	Pte	Cameron, A. S.
*110	„	Cameron, D.
2801	„	Cameron, E.
5204	„	Cameron, G.H.G.
2942	„	Cameron, H.A.H.
2577	„	Cameron, J.
790	L/Cpl	Cameron, J. (M.M.)
*4964	Pte	Campbell, A. D.
*3716	Sgt	Campbell, A. F.
906	Pte	Campbell, D.
4339	„	Campbell, D. T.
11	„	Campbell, G. F.
3030	„	Campbell, G. McI.
*2388	Sgt	Campbell, H.
*3715	Cpl	Campbell, H. K.
*2117	Pte	Campbell, J.
2334	„	Campbell, J.
3596	„	Campbell, J. A. S.
*3717	Cpl	Campbell, L. J. (D.C.M., M.M.)
1924	Pte	Campbell, M.
7707	„	Campbell, M. H.
3568	„	Campbell, P. C.
520	„	Campbell, P. D.
6489	„	Campbell, P. W. (M.M.)
59483	„	Campbell, R.A.A.
4163	„	Campbell, D.
4159	„	Campbell, W.
1287	Sgt	Campbell, W. E.
*3038	Pte	Campbell, R. H.
707	„	Campbell, V.D.H.
3253	„	Campbell, R. N.
2802	„	Campbell, W.
541	L/Cpl	Campion, C. J.
5995	A/Sgt	Cannon, H.
4769	Pte	Cannon, F. J.
249	„	Cannon, J. H.
1494	A/Sgt	Cannon, W. J.
2799	Pte	Cant, C. H.
1337	Cpl	Cantwell, H. J.
2974	Pte	Cantwell, M. H.
3039	„	Carbury, M. R.
1332	„	Carey, R.
3042	„	Carlaw, J. R.
905	„	Carle, E.
5478	„	Carle, J.
7223	„	Carlyle, R.
6247	„	Carlyle, T.
1917	„	Carmichael, A. J. E.
3720	„	Carmody, B. J.
*3719	„	Carmody, W.
*492	„	Carnell, A. J.
1110	„	Carney, W. J.
*2120	„	Carney, W. L.
5988	„	Carolan, C. V.
*2586	„	Carpenter, F. J.
3035	„	Carpenter, K. J.
5662	Cpl	Carpenter, L. H.
1110	Pte	Carpenter, W. H.
3252	„	Carr, H.
4157	„	Carr, J.
5661	Sgt	Carr, J.T. (M.M.)
*314	Pte	Carr, M. F.
6480	„	Carr, W.
6152	„	Carr, W. A.
6966	„	Carraill, W.
4101	„	Carrig, J.
4092	„	Carriline, A.
1321	„	Carrington, G. H.
*6888	„	Carrington, J. M.
2389	R.Q.M.S.	Carroll, G.
*6241	Pte	Carroll, J.
7215	„	Carroll, J.
4274	Cpl	Carroll, L.
335	Pte	Carroll, P. J.
2471	„	Carroll, R. G.
789	„	Carroll, W. B.
355	Cpl	Carruthers, H. A.
2938	Pte	Carruthers, R. W.
3310	„	Carson, G. J. H.
*1329	„	Carter, F.

2590 L/Cpl Carter, G. (M.M.)
*799 Pte Carter, T.
*710 ,, Carter, W.
4771 ,, Cartwright, E. H.
1108 ,, Cartwright, H.
5049 Cpl Cartwright, J. H.
1717 Pte Casey, J. P.
*1310 ,, Casey, M.
*1916 ,, Casey, T. B.
*109 L/Cpl Casey, W.
5050 Pte Cash, J. W.
*5051 ,, Cash, R. R.
5660 ,, Cassidy, L.
3045 ,, Cassidy, S.
6969 ,, Castle, E. G.
6725 ,, Castle, W. J.
3259 ,, Cathcart, N. H.
725 Sgt Caton, P.
4016 Pte Catts, S. P.
4017 ,, Caughey, J.
*2591 ,, Cavanagh, J.
358 ,, Cavanagh, J. M.
6978 ,, Cavenagh, A.
*1483 Sgt Cavill, W. W.
1324 Pte Cawley, A. N.
5052 ,, Cerise, D.
*313 ,, Chadwick, H.
*1516 ,, Chalk, W.
6481 ,, Chalker, A. A.
6482 ,, Chalmers, A. B.
6605 ,, Chalmers, G. E.
4446 ,, Chalmers, J.
6864 ,, Chalmers, J. W.
6483 ,, Chalmers, S. L.
6483 Cpl Chalmers, S. L.
6484 Pte Chalmers, W. A.
2952 ,, Chambers, H. W.
1114 ,, Chambers, W. L.
1111 ,, Champion, A. J.
5346 ,, Champley, R.
1321 ,, Chandler, R.
1315 ,, Chaundler, W.
6836 ,, Chant, J. C.
2578 C.Q.M.S. Chantrill
1718 Pte Chapell, A. B.
713 ,, Chaplin, L.
1719 Cpl Chapman, A. A.
3260 Pte Chapman, C. W.
1090 ,, Chapman, T. A.
3725 ,, Chapman, W.
1865 ,, Chappell, C. L.
2450 ,, Charet, B. F.
*2576 ,, Charlton, J. J.
*1109 ,, Charlton, M. M.
*6404 ,, Charters, F. (M.M.)
3264 ,, Charters, J.
*712 ,, Cheal, E. H.
*2732 ,, Cheadle, G.
4167 ,, Chenhall, E.
2726 ,, Cherry, H.
2336 ,, Cherry, O. J.
4632 ,, Cherry, R.
1720 ,, Cherry, S. H.
3493 ,, Chilcott, C.
6400 ,, Chilcott, R. W.
6485 ,, Childs, A. W.
5057 ,, Chisholm, R.
5053 ,, Chisholm, R.
*2593 L/Cpl Chisholm, S. H.
5987 Pte Chorlton, F.
4021 ,, Christafferson, S.
*4439 L/Cpl Christensen, F.
*4447 Pte Christian, C. C.
554 Cpl Christie, J.
6722 Pte Christie, N. M.
3495 ,, Chroston, J.
1204 Sgt Church, R. H.
4772 Pte Church, W. C.
1515 ,, Churchill, H. H.
3033 ,, Churchill, J. E.
*900 Sgt Chute, E. C.
69476 Pte Clancy, C. J.
1918 ,, Clark, C. S.
*2297 ,, Clark, D. J.
5054 ,, Clark, G.
1116 R.Q.M.S. Clark, E.
7699 A/Sgt Clark, G. C.
3539 Pte Clark, F. R.
*7463 ,, Clark, J. R.
6728 ,, Clark, J. R.
7000 ,, Clark, V. F.
*2574 ,, Clark, W.

NOMINAL ROLL

*3568	,,	Clark, W.	2571	,,	Clucas, W. C.
5356	,,	Clark, W.	3496	,,	Cluff, A. G.
5664	,,	Clark, W. J.	2781	,,	Clulow
1721	,,	Clarke, A. J.	4767	,,	Clulow, R. E.
*3960	,,	Clarke, A. J. W.	2124	,,	Clune, J. R.
6403	,,	Clarke, E.	1666	Sgt	Clutterbuck, C. (D.C.M., M.M.)
*5993	,,	Clarke, E. C.			
2635	,,	Clarke, E.	*3033	Pte	Clydesdale, J. R.
*1451	,,	Clarke, H.	3034	,,	Clydesdale, A. M.
4158	,,	Clarke, H.	*6981	,,	Clydesdale, W. C. S.
4768	,,	Clarke, H. J. M.			
1530	,,	Clarke, J.	3267	,,	Coady, R.
*4098	,,	Clarke, J.	4148	L/Cpl	Coake, R.
1340	,,	Clarke, J.	3043	Pte	Coates, J. B.
5055	,,	Clarke, L. T. H.	1320	,,	Coates, W. P.
*2195	,,	Clarke, N. W.	*1528	,,	Coburn, H.
7710	,,	Clarke, P. A.	*6967	,,	Cochran, A. J. E.
*3048	,,	Clarke, R.	1398	,,	Cochrane, S.
2579	,,	Clarke, V. J.	2800	,,	Cochrane, W.
4150	,,	Clarke, W. J.	1722	,,	Codyre, J. M.
*6242	,,	Clarke, W. P.	7225	,,	Coffey, L. R. K.
65734	,,	Claxton, R. C.	*6239	,,	Coffey, W. J.
4149	,,	Claxton, W. J.	5424	Sgt	Cohen, N. K. P.
5984	,,	Cleary, A. P.	*113	Pte	Coleman, C. J.
7852	,,	Cleary, F. P.	4766	,,	Coleman, E. P.
*1327	,,	Cleary, P.	*5663	,,	Coleman, E. W.
6486	,,	Cleary, P.	1724	,,	Coleman, H.
2982	,,	Cleary, T.	4774	,,	Coleman, H. G.
1930	,,	Clegg, H. J.	2606	,,	Coleman, J.
*1931	,,	Clegg, T. A.	5985	,,	Coleman, R.
1115	,,	Cleland, R. G.	7468	,,	Cole, A. H.
3028	,,	Clements, R. F. C.	*6837	,,	Cole, E. L.
2146	,,	Clench, O. J.	2570	,,	Cole, N.
4450	,,	Clews, L. G. W.	4630	,,	Cole, R. A.
2596	,,	Cliff, J.	1919	,,	Cole, R. N.
1312	,,	Cliff, S. A.	6975	,,	Coles, H. J.
7352	,,	Clifford, F. M.	*4444	,,	Coles, P. C.
6972	,,	Clifford, J.	3027	,,	Collens, G. P.
6724	,,	Clifford, P.	*1179	,,	Colless, J. W.
26	Dvr	Clifford, T.	2808	,,	Colless, S.
*5000	Pte	Clifford, T.	1339	,,	Colless, C.
59482	,,	Clifton, E. L.	2124	L/Cpl	Collings, L. S.
4775	,,	Clifton, E. W.	*1094	Pte	Colling, A. G.
4773	,,	Clifton, K. J.	6887	,,	Collins, E. J.
3352	,,	Clifton, T. H.	1922	,,	Collins, F. S.
7213	,,	Clooney, J.	5666	,,	Collins, G. M.
3266	,,	Clowes, J. E. H.	3040	,,	Collins, H.

*1341 „ Collins, J.
5058 „ Collins, J. A.
2119 Sgt Collins, J. H.
*3029 Pte Collins, J. W.
*6976 „ Collins, K. P.
*62 Sgt Collins, L.
1520 Pte Collins, P. G.
*2118 „ Collins, R. F.
2599 „ Collins, R. G.
1112 „ Collins, R. J.
4018 „ Collins, S.
1339 „ Collins, C.
4779 „ Collins, J. C.
5057 „ Collison, R. H.
5992 „ Colluson, R. H.
3139 „ Colquhon, G.
3026 „ Colvin, W. C.
15 Cpl Colyer, R. D. W.
*901 Pte Combe, C.
*6977 „ Combo, B.
1514 „ Commins, A. B.
*5998 „ Compon, H. W.
*1333 „ Compton, O. A.
4629 „ Conder, E.
986 Cpl Conmee, J. T.
6390 Pte Condran, E. T.
88 Cpl Conley, S. J.
6140 Pte Conlin, J. W.
3732 „ Conn, F. L.
7222 „ Connellan, N. B. F.
*2337 „ Connolly, E. R.
*1111 „ Connelly, F.
4776 „ Connelly, L.
1723 „ Connelly, R. H.
4448 „ Connoley, W. J.
2587 „ Connor, J. J.
1165 „ Conroy, T. F.
3961 „ Conway, A. E.
7226 „ Conway, G. K.
6727 „ Conyngham, R. A.
2812 „ Cook, C.
4019 „ Cook, E.
*6970 „ Cook, E. T.
3323 „ Cook, J.
5347 „ Cook, J.
4780 „ Cook, J. W.

3733 „ Cook, K.
7700 „ Cook, L.
5059 „ Cook, L. F. P.
7465 „ Cook, T. R.
3634 „ Cook, W.
4781 „ Cook, W. E.
1109 Cpl Cooke, A.
*1338 Pte Cooke, D.
*13 Sgr Cooke, H.
4148 L/Cpl Cooke, R.
3728 Pte Cookson, S. N.
3261 „ Cooling, S. F.
*1920 „ Coombes, A. R.
6730 „ Coombes, E. J.
1656 „ Coombe, F. B.
4785 „ Cooney, J. T.
5060 „ Cooney, T. A.
233 Cpl Cooper, G.
4164 Pte Cooper, C. J.
3353 „ Cooper, E. C.
7702 „ Cooper, E. W.
3544 „ Cooper, J.
1334 „ Cooper, J. E.
*1519 L/Cpl Cooper, H.
2706 Pte Cooper, H.
1725 „ Cooper, J. T.
*315 Cpl Cooper, G. W. L.
6971 Pte Cooper, L.
6139 „ Cooper, W. J. F.
2601 „ Coote, J. C.
5061 „ Cootes, W. S.
*1529 „ Corblett, L. A.
*5665 Cpl Corby, E.
6243 Pte Corbey, M.
3735 „ Corcoran, W.
2607 Sgt Corden, S.
6402 Pte Corfe, H. C.
4020 „ Corkery, W. J.
6973 „ Cornelius, L.
1313 „ Cornelson, R. T.
6389 „ Corner, J.
2499 „ Cornick, R.
7214 „ Corrigan, B.
*6248 „ Corrigan, J. H.
*903 Sgt Cosgrove, N. T.
588 Pte Costello, A. L.
1517 „ Costello, H. J.

LIEUT H. L. DILL, M.C.   LIEUT. H. D. ROBB, M.C.   CHAPLAIN B. C. WILSON, M.C.

MAJOR S. C. FITZPATRICK, M.C.   CAPTAIN F. E. PAGE, M.C.

LIEUT. W. H. D. SULLY, D.C.M., M.M.   LIEUT. L. MacLACHLAN, M.M.   LIEUT. C. J. CLIFTON, M.C.

SGT. R. L. GRAHAM, D.C.M.

LIEUT. COLIN SMITH, M.C.
Killed in action.

SGT. G. GORDON, M.M.

CPL. J. C. WEGER,
D.C.M.

R.S.M. B. A. DOUGLAS,
D.C.M.

CPL. A. HUDSON, D.C.M.

NOMINAL ROLL 353

6419	,,	Cottam, C. E.
*2588	,,	Cottam, J. W.
59477	,,	Couchman, J.
2714	C.S.M.	Coughlan, H. W.
3254	Pte	Coulter, W. H.
4145	,,	Coulton, E. H.
4376	,,	Coulton, M. J.
6729	,,	Covel, C. S.
*1322	,,	Covey, E. H.
65731	,,	Cowan, A. H.
5206	,,	Cowan, C. W.
4592	,,	Cowle, A. C.
1302	Sgt	Cowle, W. C.
*1326	Pte	Cox, E. M.
4778	,,	Cox, H.
5765	,,	Cox, J. A.
2581	,,	Coyle, J. H. W.
5348	,,	Cox, J. T.
*1113	,,	Cox, R.
1923	,,	Cox, S.
3736	,,	Cox, W. G.
1727	,,	Cragg, C. J.
5778	,,	Crago, G.
*1929	,,	Craig, J.
*2031	,,	Craig, R.
1489	Cpl	Crane, J. H.
*2121	Pte	Crane, J. T.
2339	,,	Crane, H. P.
2811	,,	Crassingham, A. O.
2123	,,	Craw, H.
3262	,,	Crawford, C. R.
1726	,,	Crawford, J.
108	,,	Crawford, K.
1331	,,	Crawford, S.
65727	,,	Crawford, T. D.
4443	,,	Crawford, W.
6723	,,	Creagh, J.
4445	,,	Crebert, P.
2338	L/Cpl	Creech, J. J.
7446	Pte	Creed, A. V.
3586	,,	Creed, S. A.
65735	,,	Creek, J.
*2809	,,	Creighton, G.
*7216	,,	Creswick, H. D.
137	,,	Cretan, G.

*1112	,,	Cribb, K. N.
*6488	,,	Crilly, J.
1086	,,	Cripps, O. J.
4999	Cpl	Cripps, T.
	C.S.M.	Crisp, H. W.
4759	L/Cpl	Crisp, W. J. A.
317	Pte	Critchley, R. L. L.
65728	,,	Crittenden, J. W.
2089	,,	Croasdell, R. H.
*4151	,,	Croft, E. C.
*711	L/Cpl	Crocombe, W. C.
*1343	Pte	Croft, H.
7706	,,	Crokery, U.
5766	,,	Cromack, E. H.
1314	,,	Crook, W. E.
6245	,,	Crooks, R. W.
3034	,,	Cross, J.
*2977	,,	Cross, V. S.
6058	,,	Crossley, J. C.
3497	,,	Crossley, H.
1524	,,	Crotty, G. H. J.
7708	,,	Crouch, D.
7097	,,	Crowe, C. L. G.
1927	,,	Crowe, W. D.
5667	Cpl	Croydon, A (M.M.)
3265	Pte	Crozier, W. W.
2248	,,	Cruden, E. J.
*2589	,,	Cruikshank, A.
709	,,	Cruikshank, G.
3357	,,	Crummy, W. H.
4442	Cpl	Crump, G.
6145	Pte	Crumpler, W.
6979	,,	Crutch, W. J.
2815	,,	Cruyve, F. M. T.
6238	,,	Cue, H.
65730	,,	Cuthbert, J. E.
2810	Sgt	Cullen, A. S.
*6838	Pte	Cullen, H. W. P.
112	,,	Cullen, J. P.
*6878	,,	Cullen, L. L.
5349	,,	Cullen, T. H.
6074	,,	Cullen, W. G.
2144	Sgt	Cullivan, E.
318	Pte	Cully, G. B.
*2052	,,	Cummings, E. J.
7705	,,	Cummins, J.

Y

*67 L/Cpl Cunliffe, T.
3032 Pte Cunningham, A. A.
6980 ,, Cunningham, A. A.
3263 ,, Cunningham, E.
688 Sgt Cunningham, E.G.
4340 Pte Cunningham, E.G.
4593 ,, Cunningham, G.
*7219 ,, Cunningham, L.
7701 ,, Cunningham, S.
2976 ,, Cunningham, V. J.
505 ,, Cunningham, W. T.
3037 ,, Curlitza, J.
*1500 ,, Curphey, A. A.
*1457 ,, Curran, J.
6571 ,, Curran, J. J.
1325 ,, Curran, M. J.
5063 ,, Curran, W. H.
*2575 ,, Currans, D. L.
2604 ,, Currie, J.
4015 ,, Currie, J.
4099 ,, Currey, J. H.
66 ,, Currey, J. P.
4783 ,, Currie, R.
3042 ,, Curtan, J. R.
4786 ,, Curtis, H. J.
*1122 ,, Curtis, W. R.
2500 ,, Curwen, E. J.
1336 ,, Curyier, D.
4359 ,, Cutbush, G. A.
7227 ,, Cutler, W.
1526 ,, Cutmore, G. A.

3272 ,, Daggett, H. M.
2978 Sgt Dahl, E. P.
1322 Pte Dahlstrom, G.
1346 ,, Dale, J.
59489 ,, Daley, H. R.
1324 ,, Daley, T.
6737 ,, Dalgleish, A. E.
748 ,, Dalton, A.
6490 ,, Dalton, A. S.
6984 ,, Dalton, J.
*2501 ,, Daly, A.
*1729 ,, Daly, W.
3057 ,, Dan, A.
6491 ,, Danaher, M.

3040 ,, Daniel, C. P.
3054 ,, Daniel, R. (M.M.)
3047 ,, Daniels, R.
2090 ,, Daniher, J.
3058 ,, Darby, B. A.
3740 L/Cpl Dare, H. S. (M.M.)
*281 C.Q.M.S. Dargin, S. N.
*1316 L/Cpl Darling, J. W.
7471 Pte Darnell, A. T.
*6983 ,, Darr, J. F.
1857 ,, Davey, E. T.
714 ,, Davey, F. M.
6132 ,, Davidson, C. T.
2582 ,, Davidson, D. A.
*1936 ,, Davies, F. J.
*2614 ,, Davidson, G. R.
*1539 ,, Davidson, J.
*4360 ,, Davies, A. L.
1540 ,, Davies, E.
1532 ,, Davies, H. C. R.
1344 ,, Davies, H. G.
5477 ,, Davies, J. F.
2340 ,, Davies, W.
1117 ,, Davies, W. T.
1347 ,, Davies, A. G.
4093 ,, Davis, C. H.
65739 ,, Davis, C. V.
*1301 Sgt Davis, D. J. B.
5811 Pte Davis, E. J. H.
65887 ,, Davis, G. A.
3741 ,, Davis, J.
5999 ,, Davis, J. R.
2341 ,, Davis, R.
321 ,, Davis, T.
6989 Cpl Davis, T. S.
2352 Pte Davison, F. E.
1349 ,, Davison, J.
2127 ,, Davison, N. F.
6257 Sgt Davy, H. T.
2612 ,, Dawes, A. R.
1938 Pte Daws, H.
*899 ,, Daws, H. N.
*1091 Bglr Dawson, A. R.
7230 Pte Dawson, F. W.
7470 ,, Dawson, J. C.
1095 ,, Dawson, W. H.

NOMINAL ROLL 355

1323	,,	Day, M. W.
*2125	,,	Day, P. A.
*2584	Cpl	Day, P. F. (M.M.)
595	Pte	Day, W.
503	,,	Day, W.
2872	,,	Deacon, G. H.
*1114	,,	Dean, A. V.
4458	,,	Dean, C. C.
5065	,,	Dean, G. H.
7231	,,	Dean, R. H.
319	L/Cpl	Deane, R. P.
3051	Pte	Deane, U. C.
4461	,,	Deans, J.
5763	Sgt	De Belin, W. C.
4694	Pte	Debons, F.
532	,,	DeCarteret, G.
3742	,,	Deering, E. C.
*1533	,,	Deery, C. P.
7229	,,	De La Garde, S.
4633	,,	Delaney, J.
1317	Sgt	Delaney, W.
716	Pte	De Launey, H. A.
1117	,,	Dempsey, J.
4453	,,	Denham, W. A.
*1730	,,	Dennehey, W. J.
6986	,,	Dennis, J.
68	,,	Denovan, W. G. P.
2498	,,	Dent, W. T.
1939	,,	Denton, J. C.
6000	,,	Denzel, W.
913	,,	Dernee, V. A.
320	,,	De Saxe, L. F.
*173	,,	Dessel, A.
5488	,,	Detmers, O. W. F.
3050	,,	Deunce, J.
2620	,,	De Vere, L. C.
2196	,,	Devidet, L. G.
4594	,,	Devine, T.
5066	,,	Dew, L. B.
4451	,,	Dew, M. L.
4100	L/Cpl	Dewhurst, H. H.
1731	Pte	Diack, W. C. G.
*486	Cpl	Dick, G. C. (M.M.)
6740	Pte	Dickenson, H.
6006	,,	Dickings, F.
2365	,,	Dickson, R. A.
4456	,,	Difford, E. J.
1318	,,	Diggins, J. R.
117	,,	Dignam, D. W.
2743	,,	Dingle, S. W.
6148	,,	Ditchfield, S. F.
5798	,,	Divall, W. J.
*2147	,,	Divorty, G. O.
1869	,,	Dixon, A. D.
2129	,,	Dixon, J. E.
*886	Sgt	Dixon, R. T.
*6259	Pte	Dobbin, F. A.
*1535	,,	Dobson, W. A.
2087	,,	Dobson, W. W.
*916	,,	Docker, N.
6254	,,	Dodd, C.
2589	,,	Dodd, H. G.
1458	,,	Dodd, R. J.
*4094	,,	Dodd, S. J.
36	,,	Dodds, J. W.
2091	,,	Doherty, B.
6985	,,	Doherty, J.
3055	,,	Doherty, M. P.
3203	,,	Doherty, O.
*7469	,,	Doherty, P.
6492	,,	Dominey, R.
2962	,,	Dominic, F. T. V.
*1734	,,	Donaldson, A. J.
118	Cpl	Donalson, C.
*1302	Pte	Donalson, D.
1538	,,	Donnelly, G.
*7233	,,	Donnelly, G.
*115	,,	Donnelly, R. R.
5068	,,	Donnelly, T. F.
*1319	,,	Donnelly, W.
*1523	,,	Donnelly, W. J.
6736	,,	Donnelly, W. J.
6987	,,	Donohoe, J. J.
1534	,,	Donohue, T.
4025	,,	Donovan, J.
2342	,,	Donovan, K. J.
*2093	,,	Donovan, P.
*4023	,,	Donovan, R. J.
910	,,	Doodson, W. V.
21	Dvr	Doolan, J. J. M. H.
3353	Pte	Dooley, H.
*2617	,,	Dooley, J. T.
*4026	,,	Dorman, G. E.

5489 ,, Dormer, H.
2379 ,, Dorrington, F. R.
1521 Cpl Dorrington, W. B.
*1522 Pte Dougherty, R.
1858 ,, Doughty, A.
5208 Sgt Doughty, J. W.
(M.M. AND BAR)
1320 R.S.M. Douglas, B. A.
(D.C.M.)
2092 Pte Douglas, C.
3027 ,, Douglas, F. J.
3041 ,, Douglas, F. J. E.
*6009 ,, Douglas, G.
6493 ,, Douglas, G. H.
909 ,, Douglas, G. P.
*537 ,, Douglas, P.
3036 ,, Doust, E.
2301 ,, Dovey, R.
578 ,, Dowell, S. W.
*1348 Sgt Dowling, C.
(M.M.)
6839 Pte Dowling, E.
*2583 ,, Dowling, J. A.
915 ,, Downer, W. C.
*2587 ,, Doyle, G. H.
*2741 ,, Doyle, N. J.
1105 ,, Doyle, P. H.
1106 ,, Doyle, T.
1735 ,, Doyle, T. R.
6735 ,, Doyle, T. R.
59497 ,, Doyle, V. J.
*1107 ,, Doyle, W. J.
*2343 ,, Drain, E.
3744 ,, Drake, S. J.
229 ,, Draper, F.
*114 ,, Dreves, A. W.
2344 ,, Drennan, W.
2147 ,, Drew, F. P.
3039 ,, Drew, S. W.
2480 L/Cpl Drewe, F. C.
*4452 Pte Drinan, G.
*4024 ,, Driscoll, J. P.
3049 ,, Driscoll, R.
*4455 ,, Driscoll, R. J.
3745 Sgt Driscoll, V.
(M.M.)
*2126 Pte Driver, C. C.

4459 Cpl Druery, R. W.
(D.C.M.)
3038 ,, Drummond, W.
2611 Pte Duck, F. E.
*6141 ,, Duckering, B.
2148 ,, Duckett, A. E.
4789 ,, Duckett, W. C.
523 ,, Ducksbury, J. S.
3042 L/Cpl Duckworth, C.
3043 Cpl Duckworth, H. V.
6252 Pte Dudley, T. J.
116 ,, Duffy, T.
*2619 ,, Duffin, R. E. J.
*119 Sgt Dugay, W. R.
6005 Pte Duggan, A.
*3354 ,, Duggan, J. B.
*2345 ,, Duggan, J. R.
1576 ,, Duggan, T.
6982 ,, Duke, D. R.
297 ,, Duke, J. S.
 ,, Dummett, C.
2967 ,, Dunbar, G.
6494 ,, Duncan, F.
6159 ,, Duncan, J. E.
(M.M.)
*1325 ,, Duncan, J. F.
914 ,, Duncan, L. J.
6255 ,, Duncan, T. R.
1345 ,, Duncan, W.
356 ,, Duncomb, L.
715 Sgt Dunford, L. E.
5209 Pte Dunkley, A.
5210 L/Cpl Dunkley, H. E.
*1542 Pte Dunleary, J. B.
6738 ,, Dunlop, G. C.
1118 ,, Dunlope, W. H.
2588 ,, Dunmill, W.
*3747 ,, Dunn, A.
2082 ,, Dunn, A. W.
1321 ,, Dunn, C. E.
3749 ,, Dunn, H. J.
6611 ,, Dunn, N.
5471 ,, Dunn, R.
*6496 ,, Dunn, R. A.
3281 ,, Dunn, S. H.
6256 ,, Dunn, S. J.
5071 ,, Dunn, W.

NOMINAL ROLL 357

6495	,,	Dunn, W. F. J.
2816	,,	Dunne, J. H.
4595	,,	Dunne, J. K.
322	,,	Dunphy, C.
*2585	,,	Dunphy, C. A.
2346	,,	Durprat, J. F.
3083	,,	Dutton, S.
3026	,,	Dwarte, J.
6002	,,	Dwyer, J. F.
4460	,,	Dyball, G.
1524	,,	Dyball, J.
120	,,	Dybing, A. E.
1525	,,	Dye, F. C.
6988	,,	Dyer, E.
4167	Sgt	Dykes, P. J. (M.M.)
1326	Pte	Eade, J. F.
1526	,,	Eaglesham, T.
6497	,,	Earl, O. G. C.
4634	,,	Earle, W. C.
1121	,,	Earnshaw, T. W.
*3752	,,	Earp, F. C.
7473	,,	Eason, W. T.
2992	,,	East, J. H.
1492	,,	East, R.
*3061	,,	Eastham, A.
*1544	,,	Eather, C. G.
*323	,,	Eather, J.
*1350	,,	Eckland, A.
5212	,,	Eddie, A.
6498	,,	Eddington, D.
6260	,,	Edelsten, R.
*1737	,,	Edgeley, A. B.
5799	,,	Edman, G.
545	,,	Edmonds, F. C.
7237	,,	Edmondston, A. E.
6011	,,	Edmondstone, R.
1352	,,	Edmunds, A.
3060	Cpl	Edward, J. D.
1088	Sgt	Edwards, A. G. (D.C.M.)
7238	Pte	Edwards, A. H.
65748	,,	Edwards, A. R.
*7718	,,	Edwards, C. T.
1738	Cpl	Edwards, E. H. (M.M.)
121	,,	Edwards, F.
*1543	Pte	Edwards, H. E.
3504	,,	Edwards, J.
6744	,,	Edwards, J. W.
6420	L/Cpl	Edwards, L. V.
1545	Pte	Edwards, S.
3308	,,	Edwards, W. H.
5072	,,	Edwards, W. H.
3059	,,	Edwell, E. H.
*1546	,,	Egan, P.
918	,,	Eichler, J. A.
1351	,,	Elam, P.
1135	,,	Elbel, H. E.
917	,,	Elder, M. B.
*2630	Cpl	Eldred, W. C.
*1527	Pte	Eldridge, J. C.
2590	,,	Eldridge, G. D.
*5073	,,	Elgood, A. W. (M.M.)
64	,,	Elliot, C. R. J.
5762	,,	Elliott, E. L.
*717	Sgt	Elliott, H. J. H.
316	Pte	Elliott, J. J.
*816	Cpl	Elliott, J. J.
1120	,,	Elliott, J. R.
7236	Pte	Ellis, B. L.
6990	Sgt	Ellis, F.
1942	Pte	Ellis, G. J.
6500	L/Cpl	Ellis, H.
*7476	Pte	Ellis, H. S.
1353	Cpl	Ellis, L. A.
6301	,,	Ellis, T.
65746	Pte	Ellison, W. R.
59501	,,	Elstub, T.
543	,,	Elton, W. H.
*4464	L/Cpl	Elvin, H. L.
3500	Sgt	Englefield, W. H.
*5792	Pte	Englestad, O.
3044	,,	English, F. M.
6010	,,	Enright, M. J.
*1120	,,	Erekson, H. H.
3046	,,	Erickson, A. V.
2532	,,	Erickson, G. P.
6741	,,	Ericson, B. J.
*7474	,,	Eskildsen, A.
*718	,,	Etchell, W. H.
*4463	Cpl	Etches, D. E.

6261 Pte Evans, A.
6013 „ Evans, A. E.
2631 L/Cpl Evans, A. W.
2993 „ Evans, C. A. K.
6499 Pte Evans, D.
719 „ Evans, E. O.
122 „ Evans, F.
*592 „ Evans, J.
*1119 „ Evans, T. H.
2484 „ Evans, W.
2419 „ Evans, W. B.
6262 „ Evenden, F.
7475 „ Evitt, E. J.
2946 „ Evitt, T.
2451 Cpl Ewart, L. A.
(D.C.M.)
2390 L/Cpl Ewins, H. E.

*324 Pte Fabian, W. A.
5075 Dvr Fage, W. J.
*923 Pte Fahey, H.
*3067 „ Fahey, S. T.
2197 „ Fahey, T. P.
59936 „ Fair, F. G.
6014 „ Fairbairn, C. H.
2368 „ Fairclough, H.
2755 „ Fairmington, H. L.
1291 „ Fairweather, A. C. B.
3052 „ Fallon, J. B.
6842 „ Fallon, J. P.
*325 „ Farmer, A.
(D.C.M.)
4466 „ Farmer, W. J.
3756 „ Farmilo, S.
*1327 „ Farquharson, W. J.
1739 „ Farran, F. S.
1531 „ Farrands, L. R.
5076 „ Farrell, C. M.
586 „ Farrell, D.
*4468 „ Farrell, J.
6844 „ Farrell, J.
*6993 „ Farrell, J. W. H.
1550 „ Farrel, W.
6994 „ Farrell, W. H. G.

3065 „ Fathers, G.
*600 „ Fathers, O.
1365 Sgt Fawcett, F.
(D.C.M.)
*1528 Pte Fawley, W. H.
7487 „ Featherstone, W.
*3765 L/Cpl Featon, H.
*538 Pte Fecitt, G. H.
*1501 Sgt Fegan, D.
*6502 Pte Feilder, A. L.
2922 „ Fenton, C.
5078 L/Cpl Fenton, F. S.
5077 Pte Fenton, H.
5079 „ Ferguson, E. R.
1305 Sgt Ferguson, H. H.
3053 Pte Ferguson, N. R.
*6991 „ Ferguson, R.
563 Sgt Ferguson, R. D.
2347 Pte Ferguson, W. A.
2064 „ Ferrier, F. M.
7480 „ Fetterplace, K. K.
5789 „ Fewell, R. F.
2820 „ Field, B. C.
5668 „ Field, G.
6018 L/Cpl Field, W. J.
7478 Pte Fifield, A. G.
6421 „ Fifield, G. W.
7242 „ Fifield, H. V.
6995 „ Finch, R.
7477 „ Finley, H.
7353 „ Finneran, F. M.
*7241 „ Finucane, F.
2821 Sgt Fischer, J. H.
*922 Pte Fisher, C. W.
4027 „ Fisher, G. F.
301 „ Fishlock, G.
(M.S.M.)
125 „ Fishlock, L.
528 Cpl Fisk, E. L.
(M.S.M.)
2623 „ Fitzgerald, F. J.
7239 Pte Fitzgerald, J.
3763 „ Fitzgerald, J. A.
2251 Cpl Fitzgerald, J. E.
5082 Pte Fitzgerald, P.
*1551 „ Fitzgibbon, M.
4191 „ Fitzpatrick, F. G.

3050	„	Fitzpatrick, J. A. P.	2917	„ Foran, C. J.
*6016	„	Fitzpatrick, J. B.	4467	„ Forbes, A. E.
7481	„	Fitzpatrick, G. E.	6507	„ Forbes, J. A.
1092	Bglr	Fitzsimmons, C. J.	5756	„ Forbes, R.
59503	Pte	Fizelle, E. G.	439	L/Cpl Forbes, V. E.
6965	„	Fizzell, E. R.	*3064	Pte Ford, C. A.
59504	„	Flack, A. S.	530	„ Ford, E.
*1330	L/Cpl	Flaherty, T. P.	1662	„ Ford, G. W.
*6503	Pte	Flaherty, W.	*2863	Cpl Ford, H. J.
6430	„	Flahvin, J.	721	Pte Ford, J. H.
7240	„	Flannagan, N. F.	2595	„ Ford, M. S.
5669	Dvr	Flannery, D. J.	1652	L/Cpl Ford, P. W.
4600	Pte	Flannery, G. L.	4469	Pte Ford, S.
919	„	Flannery, W. D.	*994	Bglr Ford, W.
5083	„	Flannery, W. T.	3055	Pte Foreman, W.
6267	„	Flatman, R. D.	59507	„ Forrest, C. R.
*720	„	Fleming, G. R.	*921	„ Forrest, R.
*7596	„	Fleming, J.	*912	„ Forrester, P.
3764	„	Fleming, W. C.	1121	„ Forsyth, A.
1577	„	Fletcher, A. E.	*3356	„ Forsyth, C. G. S.
1359	Cpl	Fletcher, A. N. (M.M.)	*6746	„ Forsyth, W. G. M.
			6501	„ Forwood, J. T.
			196	Bglr Foster, C. E.
1358	Pte	Fletcher, H.	6266	Pte Foster, F. W.
7655	„	Fletcher, J. N.	*1357	„ Foster, J.
*6504	„	Fletcher, J. H.	3049	„ Foster, S. G.
6992	„	Fletcher, P.	1945	„ Foster, V. C.
2594	„	Fletcher, P. J.	124	Sgt Fourro, F.
1946	Cpl	Flynn, H.	123	Cpl Fourro, W. M.
724	Pte	Flynn, J.	6017	Pte Fowler, C. B.
*6161	„	Flynn, J.	3759	„ Fowler, E. F.
1547	L/Cpl	Flynn, J. T. (M.M.)	5213	„ Fowler, E. V.
			3728	„ Fowler, F.
326	Sgt	Foley, A. A.	*2634	„ Fowler, H. E.
573	„	Foley, E.	*920	„ Fowles, W. E.
6156	Pte	Foley, G. O.	4598	L/Cpl Fox, L. J.
2132	„	Foley, J.	1549	Pte Fox, S. T.
363	Gnr	Foley, J. A.	6602	„ Fraizer, J. J.
488	Dvr	Foley, J. J.	4465	„ Francis, C.
931	Cpl	Foley, P. J.	2133	„ Francis, T.
5084	Pte	Folkard, A. E.	*2348	„ Frank, C. E.
327	„	Follers, A. H.	5670	„ Frankish, G.
*2624	„	Follington, J.	6026	„ Franklin, G. E.
2502	„	Folly, P. J.	2596	„ Franklin, R.
*1529	„	Foote, J. T.	722	„ Franks, S.
*1944	Cpl	Foote, R. V.	*2134	„ Fraser, D.
3054	Pte	Foote, W.	145	„ Frazer, D.

1115 „ Frazer, H. C.
1949 Cpl Fraser, H. C.
1551 Pte Fraser, J.
2825 „ Fraser, J. S.
2591 „ Fraser, L. W. T.
1948 Sgt Frazer, N. H.
1356 Pte Frederick, C.
2823 „ Freeborn, W. (M.M.)
*723 „ Freeman, A. H.
1741 „ Freeman, G. H.
3051 „ Freeman, N. L.
5818 „ Freeman, R. J.
1354 Cpl Freeman, W. (D.C.M.)
2898 Pte Freudenstein, W. J. (M.M.)
*6747 „ Fripp, C. C.
*1667 „ Frith, H.
2592 „ Frith, H.
6750 „ Frith, H. G.
*1943 „ Frost, A. P.
2350 „ Frost, F.
2620 „ Frost, J.
*2626 „ Frost, J. H.
4992 „ Fry, D. B.
*4492 „ Fry, D B.
*3062 Sgt Fry, F. W.
6505 Pte Fry, G.
6506 Cpl Fuller, E. C.
*1947 Pte Fuller, H.
3045 „ Fulton, D. H.
2633 L/Cpl Furnell, W. E.
1648 Pte Fusco, C.
5671 „ Fyfe, B.
3063 „ Fyffe, J. P.

5672 „ Gagen, E. C.
1851 „ Gaisman, I.
6508 „ Gall, S. D.
*726 L/Cpl Gallacher, J.
2135 Pte Gallagher, M. J.
3057 „ Gallagher, L.
2598 „ Gallagher, W. E.
6846 „ Gallagher, V. S.
7355 „ Gallen, A.
*512 „ Galvin, A. St C.

5673 „ Gamble, G. H.
*389 „ Gambling, A. A.
6754 „ Gane, E.
7483 „ Gardiner, C. K.
555 „ Gardiner, F.
5086 „ Gardiner, H. T.
*4028 „ Gardiner, J. W.
27 Dvr Gardiner, W.
2452 Cpl Gardiner, W. S.
926 Pte Garden, J. W.
*2139 „ Gardener, J. A.
*2198 „ Garland, H. F. E.
3380 „ Garland, W.
1857 „ Garner, G. A.
6019 „ Garner, A. E.
1958 „ Garnett, G. W.
2958 „ Garnett, G. W.
*929 C.Q.M.S. Garrard, S. S.
59511 Pte Garthon, C. J.
65750 „ Gastinia, F. J.
7590 „ Gauci, J.
2648 Cpl Gaukrodger, A. E. (D.C.M.)
1552 Pte Gauvin, A.
4602 „ Gavan, J.
3058 „ Gay, B. L.
6998 „ Gay, W. E.
4601 „ Geary, T. F.
927 Cpl Geddes, C. M.
4472 Pte Geddes, H. V.
*6276 „ Gee, H. H.
4007 Cpl Gee, R. C.
40 A/Sgt Gemell, O. E.
7244 Pte Gent, W. F. H.
1331 „ George, A. T.
3076 „ George, B. W. (M.S.M.)
2599 „ Geppert, F. T.
3056 „ Geraghty, W. J.
5087 „ Gess, R. C.
5374 „ Gett, G.
2830 „ Gibbons, F. C.
5088 „ Gibbins, H. O.
*6275 „ Gibbs, W. T.
*515 „ Gibson, B. P.
1742 „ Gibson, C. W.

2592	„	Gibson, F. A.	3074	L/Cpl	Goodman, J. V.
2772	„	Gibson, H.	748	Pte	Goodsall, S. H.
792	„	Gibson, R.	*2654	„	Goodson, J. H.
1332	„	Gibson, W. F.	*1955	„	Goodwin, A. W.
*1333	„	Giddins, O. T.	*1745	L/Cpl	Goodwin, G. V.
2601	„	Gilbert, A.	6020	Pte	Goodworth, A. S.
*2831	Cpl	Gilbert, G. A. E. (M.M. AND BAR)	2138	„	Gordon, A. J.
			2653	Sgt	Gordon, C.
5089	Pte	Gilbert, L. K.	*1090	„	Gordon, J.
*3769	„	Giles, S. T.	*3077	Pte	Gordon, J.
925	„	Giles, T. K.	1698	„	Gordon, J. C.
6273	L/Cpl	Gill, G.	332	Sgt	Gordon, G. (M.M.)
3059	Pte	Gill, H. S.	1363	Pte	Gordon, T. F.
*1122	„	Gill, T. E.	334	Cpl	Gordon, W. H. (M.M.)
2137	„	Gill, W. H.			
330	L/Cpl	Gillespie, J. S.	6392	Pte	Gordon-Smith, R.
*5090	Pte	Gillies, D. W.	*6753	„	Gorick, W. S.
28	Sgt	Gilsenan, J.	*6997	„	Gorman, J. W.
7245	Pte	Gimbert, J. T.	2260	„	Gorrell, R. R.
1123	Cpl	Gimbert, R. W. H.	6756	„	Gottwald, L. J.
			*1123	„	Gough, J.
*5091	Pte	Ginty, M.	1950	„	Gough, J. A.
*7250	„	Gjesing, A.	*930	„	Gould, P. A.
5758	„	Gladstone, R. J.	574	„	Gould, W. A.
1743	„	Glang, H.	4602	„	Govan, J.
6751	„	Glanville, W. A.	2261	Cpl	Gow, C. B.
*6509	„	Glascock, P.	7251	Pte	Grace, G. F.
*391	„	Glasgow, R.	*1124	„	Graff, C. F.
1748	„	Glasson, C. D.	4031	„	Graham, A.
1744	„	Gleeson, E. W.	71	„	Graham, A. B.
*729	Cpl	Godart, T. B.	*5093	Cpl	Graham, D. C.
5092	„	Godbold, P. H.	328	Pte	Graham, J.
331	Pte	Goddard, E. C.	728	„	Graham, J. G.
5674	„	Goddard, G. H.	2149	L/Cpl	Graham, N. (D.C.M.)
2602	„	Goddard, H. J.			
128	„	Godfrey, A.	20	Sgt	Graham, R. L. (D.C.M.)
4474	„	Godfrey, J. G.			
1554	„	Goldsmith, M.	7249	Pte	Graham, R. R. W.
*1537	„	Goldsmith, R. L.	2806	„	Graham, T. L.
*2635	Cpl	Goldspink, J. A.	*2148	„	Graham, W. G.
1957	Pte	Gomer, G.	1362	„	Grange, R.
*329	Sgt	Goode, G. N.	2359	„	Granger, H.
6277	Pte	Goodall, A.	1532	„	Granger, W.
6510	„	Goodger, G.	601	„	Grant, D.
6511	„	Goodhead, F. A.	1624	„	Grant, A. C.
1875	„	Goodman, C. E.	*2649	„	Grant, G. A.
333	„	Goodman, J.	*3075	„	Grant, J. H.

3078 ,, Grant, R. C.
4940 ,, Grant, R. E.
5678 ,, Grant, W. B.
4184 ,, Grant, W. G.
6023 ,, Grass, S.
7246 ,, Graves, J.
1960 Sgt Gray, A.
2136 Cpl Gray, E.
793 Pte Gray, F. R.
*1959 ,, Gray, J.
6274 ,, Gray, H.
4471 ,, Gray, M. D.
4672 ,, Gray, R. T.
4473 ,, Grayston, T. S.
5676 ,, Green, A. E.
7482 ,, Green, A. G.
6752 ,, Green, C.
6278 ,, Green, F. D.
2638 ,, Green, F. S.
59 C.S.M. Green, G. A.
*1360 Sgt Green, G. C.
2832 Pte Green, G. E.
*1361 ,, Green, H. G.
1533 ,, Green, J.
5776 ,, Green, J.
*3766 ,, Green, M.
65754 ,, Green, S. A.
2303 ,, Green, T. F.
6758 ,, Green, V.
239 Cpl Green, W. A. (M.M.).
65751 Pte Greenaway, F. C.
5677 ,, Greenfield, A. C.
*2428 ,, Greenhalgh, E.
2400 ,, Greenshields, E. G.
4022 ,, Gregan, J. W.
3228 ,, Gregg, J.
2086 ,, Gregory, A. J.
3060 ,, Gregory, H. R.
2140 ,, Gregory, W. C.
*1952 ,, Gregory, W. T.
129 ,, Gregson, C. L.
2597 ,, Greig, A.
6022 ,, Greig, W. G.
928 ,, Grey, C. H.
1290 Sgt Grey, G.

380 Pte Grey, H.
2728 ,, Gribbon, G.
4185 ,, Gribben, J. S.
2600 L/Cpl Griffin, V. C.
4127 Pte Griffiths, A. G (M.M.)
3141 ,, Griffiths, C. J.
5675 ,, Griffith, G. A.
*7243 ,, Griffiths, J. H.
5096 ,, Griffith, J. M.
3080 ,, Griffiths, S.
4635 ,, Griffiths, S.
2834 ,, Griffiths, W.
585 ,, Grimes, B.
2604 ,, Grosvenor, K. M.
7248 ,, Groves, G.
1502 Sgt Groves, H. W.
*1535 Pte Groves, J.
7246 ,, Groves, J.
2503 ,, Grundie, C. N.
*6757 ,, Grundy, H.
1747 ,, Gubb, A. M.
4185 ,, Gubbin, J. S.
6996 ,, Guerin, J.
*3406 Cpl Guest, F. T.
3160 Pte Guider, C. J.
3164 ,, Guider, H. A.
3072 Cpl Guillow, B.
1454 Pte Gunn, O.
2647 ,, Gunn, T. J.
7247 ,, Gunther, G.
*1536 ,, Gurney, F. B.
*2250 ,, Guthrie, G. B.
727 ,, Guy, A.
*3768 ,, Guyot, C. W. E.

500 ,, Hackett, L. H.
6290 Cpl Hackett, S. G.
1367 Pte Hackett, W.
2504 ,, Hadlow, J. H. G.
1343 ,, Hagan, J. S.
25 Dvr Hagarty, D.
*1340 Pte Hague, H.
1642 ,, Haigh, B.
*2150 ,, Hains, M.
59517 ,, Hales, L. G.

4669 L/Cpl	Halpin, D. L.	
*4670 Pte	Halpin, T. F.	
1135 „	Hall, A.	
4479 „	Hall, A.	
5097 „	Hall, A.	
6289 „	Hall, A. F. (M.M.)	
1873 „	Hall, C.	
287 „	Hall, C.	
*1485 L/Sgt	Hall, D.	
1564 Pte	Hall, G. R.	
6288 „	Hall, H.	
6291 Cpl	Hall, N.	
*1860 Pte	Hall, R.	
1558 „	Hall, R. B.	
4490 „	Hall, W. E.	
4637 „	Hall, W. E.	
2711 „	Hall, W.	
*935 L/Cpl	Hallam, A.	
6025 Pte	Hallet, A. E.	
1337 „	Hallett, F. G.	
6033 „	Hallet, J.	
3102 „	Halliday, J. M.	
6851 „	Hallinan, C. J.	
6102 „	Hallidah, J. McG.	
*7005 „	Hallman, J. W. H.	
3657 „	Hampton, T. G.	
65764 „	Hamblin, R. P.	
3084 „	Hames, C. A.	
1749 Cpl	Hamilton, A.	
*558 Pte	Hamilton, A. D.	
286 Cpl	Hamilton, A. J. B.	
6408 Pte	Hamilton, C. W.	
1491 Cpl	Hamilton, I.	
*1750 Pte	Hamilton, J.	
*3070 „	Hamilton, J.	
6042 „	Hamilton, J.	
6520 „	Hamilton, J.	
1157 Cpl	Hamilton, J. A.	
1284 Sgt	Hamilton, L.	
*337 Pte	Hamilton, L. W.	
65766 „	Hamilton, T. W.	
*1967 „	Hammond, G. L.	
*733 „	Hammond, L. C.	
942 „	Hamonet, E. C.	
6764 „	Hamshire, H.	
6848 „	Handley, J. W.	
2481 „	Hanbury, N. E. L.	
1126 Sgt	Hancott, A. G.	
3073 Pte	Handley, W. J.	
936 C.S.M.	Hanlon, H (M.M.)	
2491 Pte	Hannah, J. L. L.	
3389 „	Hannett, T.	
5781 „	Hannon, J.	
3089 „	Hanrahan, J.	
342 „	Hansen, A. W.	
1334 Cpl	Hansen, H. G.	
2142 Pte	Hanson, A.	
3104 „	Harbourne, H.	
*1115 „	Harbridge, W.	
5098 „	Harden, W. G.	
5680 „	Hardcastle, W. R.	
*731 „	Hardie, W.	
5788 „	Hardin, A. H.	
*1124 „	Harding, A.	
*1452 „	Harding, B.	
*7356 „	Harding, G.	
2683 „	Harding, H.	
*2675 „	Harding, H. C.	
*1365 „	Harding, P.	
584 „	Harding, W. J.	
*1560 „	Hardwicke, A.	
2835 „	Hardy, J. H.	
7254 „	Hargrave, H. T.	
2844 „	Hargreave, W. J.	
3064 „	Harland, E.	
*1130 „	Harley, J. J.	
5797 „	Harley, M. O.	
2610 „	Harmer, H. J.	
3389 „	Harnett, T.	
7493 „	Harnett, W. C.	
6024 „	Harney, G. W.	
7260 „	Harper, C. O.	
5099 „	Harper, H. M.	
2963 „	Harpley, R. W.	
*3107 „	Harrington, E. R.	
3779 „	Harris, A.	
*2074 „	Harris, A. C.	
*3088 „	Harris, A. H.	

6765 „ Harris, E. C.
3781 L/Cpl Harris, E. F.
2678 Pte Harris, E. T.
*3085 „ Harris, G.
*736 Cpl Harris, H. T.
4485 Pte Harris, J.
*4038 „ Harris, N. P.
*3780 „ Harris, O.
*3090 L/Cpl Harris, S. H.
4483 Sgt Harris, S. J.
*1484 Sgt Harris, W. R.
6036 Pte Harrison, E.
944 „ Harrison, F.
7486 „ Harrison, G.
65760 „ Harrison, H.
6767 „ Harrison, S. A.
1751 „ Harrow, G. W.
2495 „ Hart, F. H.
65763 „ Hart, R. B.
3100 „ Hart, S. C.
*1335 Cpl Hartley, D.
2505 Pte Hartman, R. A.
3091 „ Hartman, W. J.
7492 „ Hartman, W. L.
6607 „ Hartmire, J. J.
801 „ Hartup, H. C.
*7012 „ Hartwig, W. C.
934 „ Harty, P. F.
4821 „ Harvey, C. S.
6513 „ Harvey, G.
6024 „ Harvey, G. W.
2845 „ Harvey, H.
1158 „ Harvey, H. L.
598 „ Harvey, J. D.
396 „ Harvey, L. T.
1557 „ Harvey, R. D.
7738 „ Harvey, L. R.
*2360 „ Harwood, R. O.
*131 „ Harworth, B.
2810 „ Hatch, G. W.
1111 „ Hatton, O.
*7489 „ Hatton, P. J.
*932 Sgt Hatton, W. B.
 (D.C.M., M.M.)
2506 Pte Haugh, J.
2658 „ Haughton, F. T.
2517 „ Hawdon, R. A.

59527 „ Hawke, S.
1962 „ Hawkey, T. S.
4487 „ Hawkins, G.
5101 „ Hawkins, M. H.
*4476 „ Hawkins, R.
135 „ Haworth, J. E.
1293 Cpl Hayden, E. J.
1157 Pte Hayden, E. A.
3072 „ Hayden, V.
*1970 „ Hayes, C.
5681 „ Hayes, F.
4488 „ Hayes, G.
7008 „ Hayes, P.
7736 „ Hayes, S.
1752 „ Hayes, T.
7252 „ Hayley, A. L.
2608 „ Haylings, F. L.
7009 „ Hayman, E.
1127 „ Hayman, S. A.
7 Sgt Haynes, A.
5104 L/Cpl Haynes, G.
 (M.M.)
3902 Pte Hayward, B.
5102 „ Hayward, G.
1540 „ Haywood, A. T.
4639 „ Haywood, S.
*4102 Sgt Hazel, A. C.
3542 Cpl Hazelwood, A. J.
*1133 Pte Head, J.
3312 „ Healey, J. S.
3071 „ Healey, M. W. R.
2611 „ Healey, W. C.
1562 „ Healy, S. S.
59520 „ Heap, A. A.
338 „ Heap, T. E.
7484 „ Heard, J.
7375 Sgt Heath, K. L. E.
*2148 Cpl Heath, T. L.
*734 L/Cpl Heathcote, A. W.
 (M.M.)
7006 Pte Heber, A. J.
2351 „ Heber, L. P.
579 Sgt Heddell, C.
1559 Pte Heddrick, T. S.
2837 „ Hein, H.
6609 „ Heinjus, W. L.

NOMINAL ROLL

300	„	Heitman, H.
882	Sgt	Henderson, G. A.
6147	C.Q.M.S.	Henderson, G. A.
6041	Pte	Henderson, J.
2968	„	Henderson, R. L.
3103	„	Hendry, H. G.
7485	„	Heney, H. R.
1840	„	Hennings, T. B.
938	Cpl	Henry, E. R.
6043	Pte	Henry, F. A.
6514	Sgt	Henry, F. T.
566	Pte	Henry, H.
2421	„	Henry, J.
7490	„	Henry, L.
*937	„	Henry, W. G.
2674	Sgt	Henrys, I. R.
5682	Pte	Henwood, A. R.
7002	„	Hepworth, A.
3803	„	Herbert, A. R.
3787	Sgt	Herbert, C. L.
*3802	Pte	Herbert, F. R.
*3096	„	Herford, J. H.
3095	„	Herford, R. F.
*1128	„	Heron, J.
6763	„	Heron, T.
*1753	Sgt	Heron, W.
*939	Pte	Herring, E. E.
*5109	„	Hession, C. V.
7486	„	Hewson, G.
4478	„	Hewison, A. W.
134	„	Hewitt, S. D.
165	W.O.	Hewland, W. J.
*5103	Pte	Hewson, C.
*1338	„	Heylem, W. J.
7729	Dvr	Hickey, D.
*130	Pte	Hickey, J.
2472	„	Hickey, J. J.
7491	„	Hickey, J. W.
6401	„	Hickey, S. A.
*3786	„	Hickin, A.
*3785	„	Hicks, G.
2429	„	Hicks, W. J. C.
1342	„	Hickson, E. H.
*2149	„	Hide, W. A.
7262	„	Higginbottom, S.
6030	„	Higgins, J. T.
5104	„	Higginson, J.
1048	„	Highes, F. W.
*6062	L/Cpl	Higlett, W. M.
*1285	Pte	Hignett, E. L.
4484	Cpl	Hill, A. R. J.
3655	Pte	Hill, J. H.
2660	„	Hill, C. A.
2352	„	Hill, E. F.
2661	„	Hill, E. M.
*2146	„	Hill, F. W.
136	Sgt	Hill, H.
*4477	Pte	Hill, J. D. F.
737	„	Hill, W.
5700	„	Hill, W.
2264	„	Hill, W. E.
6515	„	Hill, W. E. A.
133	„	Hill, W. J.
*7357	„	Hillam, A. E.
*2255	„	Hillier, A.
1539	„	Hillier, J. H.
1372	„	Hillin, E.
3065	„	Hillyer, D. R.
*1014	„	Hilton, J.
1541	Sgt	Hilton, J. K.
*299	Pte	Hinchcliffe, N. A.
2847	„	Hincks, W. R.
3066	„	Hind, J.
1754	„	Hinde, C. H.
7007	Pte	Hines, A. P.
6284	„	Hines, J. G.
6040	„	Hines, W. H.
516	L/Cpl	Hinton, H. H.
5109	Cpl	Hirons, J.
2839	„	Hirsch, C. H.
65761	Pte	Hitchcock, M. G.
1131	„	Hitchener, W. A.
794	„	Hitchcock, R. J.
2715	„	Hitchin, R.
*6850	„	Hoad, J. R.
1130	„	Hobbs, J. P.
6037	„	Hobden, P. W.
2151	„	Hobourne, A.
735	„	Hockey, E.
*2794	„	Hockey, T.
1344	„	Hocking, A. A.
2443	„	Hocking, A. C.

2609	,,	Hocking, F. A. W.	2656	Sgt	Hooker, P.
*6517	,,	Hodge, G. H.	1132	Pte	Hooper, E. L.
*6516	,,	Hodge, J. B.	*1366	,,	Hopkins, C.
7013	,,	Hodges, A.	5108	,,	Hopkins, C. B.
5685	,,	Hodges, F.	*3086	,,	Hopkins, J.
3753	,,	Hodges, S. C.	2668	Sgt	Hopson, F. R. (M.M.)
4439	,,	Hodgess, J. H.	7001	Pte	Hopson, W. H.
1369	,,	Hodgson, J. J.	2353	,,	Hoptroff, S. F.
*6760	,,	Hogan, G. H.	*941	,,	Horan, C. T.
6762	,,	Hogan, H. A.	7256	,,	Hord, W. C.
5105	,,	Hogan, J.	4482	,,	Horder, A. J. L.
*6039	,,	Hogan, J.	59525	,,	Hore, T. B.
*7479	,,	Hogan, J. F.	2200	,,	Hornby, G. C. A.
*1341	,,	Hogan, M. J.	1555	,,	Horne, E. J.
6761	,,	Hogan, T. A.	2666	,,	Horne, T.
2330	,,	Hogbin, W. C.	*4604	,,	Horner, J. J.
*1288	Cpl	Holbut, T. J.	2711	,,	Horniman, R. G.
*482	Sgt	Holdaway, W. J.	1125	,,	Horsfield, E.
2848	Pte	Holden, E.	3082	,,	Horsman, G.
90	,,	Holden, F.	3069	,,	Horsnell, J.
2393	,,	Holder, F.	5216	,,	Horswell, H. R.
6282	,,	Holder, F. M.	*2841	,,	Horton, F. C.
6407	,,	Holder, H.	3549	L/Cpl	Hosford, F. B.
*2986	L/Cpl	Holdsworth, C.	3799	Pte	Hoskin, F. W.
4820	,,	Holl, H. R.	*2663	Cpl	Hoskins, H.
303	Pte	Holl, R. R.	*940	Pte	Hoskins, T. G.
*2840	,,	Holland, W. V.	*4486	,,	Hotchkiss, A. D.
2662	,,	Hollibon, E.	3798	,,	Hough, M.
7003	,,	Hollis, L. J.	1755	,,	Houghton, J. W.
1961	,,	Holloway, F. E.	4481	,,	House, T.
5383	,,	Hollywood, P.	*2672	,,	Hovenden, F.
6038	,,	Holman, A.	*5685	,,	Howard, F. R.
2147	,,	Holman, S. J.	2445	,,	Howard, H. G.
3099	,,	Holmes, A. P.	1544	,,	Howard, J.
1339	,,	Holmesby, L. G.	5683	,,	Howard, W. R.
6026	,,	Holt, R. A. (M.M.)	135	,,	Howarth, J. E. (M.M.)
1538	,,	Home, A.	1561	,,	Howden, G.
7010	,,	Homer, W. J.	6512	,,	Howe, R. E.
5107	,,	Homewood, E. J.	132	,,	Howell, F. W.
7358	,,	Honeysett, C. M.	1082	Sgt	Howes, H. G.
3324	,,	Hood, G.	730	Pte	Howitt, W. A.
7488	Sgt	Hook, R. A.	3062	,,	Howlett, R. A.
3793	Cpl	Hooke, A. H.	6035	,,	Hoxby, G. H.
3094	Pte	Hooke, W. H.	7261	,,	Hoy, A.
2568	,,	Hooker, J. K.	5431	,,	Hoy, G.

1134	„	Hoy, H.	1969	„	Hunt, F.
1368	„	Hoyle, G.	2613	„	Hunter, A. F.
*3327	„	Hubbard, E. A.	65759	„	Hunter, J. B.
2849	„	Hubbard, F. J.	*739	„	Hunter, W.
2723	L/Cpl	Hubbard, H.	5782	„	Huntington, G. T.
2607	„	Hudson, A. (D.C.M.)	77	„	Huntsman, F.
			6801	„	Hupton, W.
7259	Pte	Hudson, E. A.	*2143	„	Husk, H. H.
1495	„	Hudson, E.	4603	„	Hutchinson, J. W.
1965	„	Hudson, F. W.			
*1756	„	Hudson, H. T.	2612	„	Hutchison, J.
2606	„	Hudson, J. W.	6519	„	Hutchison, S. G.
*7263	„	Hudson, R. W.	*1127	„	Hutchison, W.
5801	„	Hufton, H.	1129	„	Hutton, C. H.
5802	„	Hufton, P.	3805	„	Hutton, C. R.
3797	„	Hughan, A. W.	*1155	„	Hutton, R. A.
6028	„	Hughan, R.	2145	„	Hynes, A. E.
1129	A/Sgt	Huggins, J.	2738	„	Hynes, A. R.
1048	Pte	Hughes, F. W.	*4036	„	Hyslop, E. J.
2833	„	Hughes, F. R.			
1542	„	Hughes, G.	2488	„	Ide, A.
868	„	Hughes, G. E.	2476	„	Illingworth, A. H.
*1545	„	Hughes, J.	*6523	„	Inch, A. G.
7258	„	Hughes, J.	3105	„	Ind, H. J.
3796	„	Hughes, J. S.	59529	„	Ingal, R. E.
887	Sgt	Hughes, P. I.	2616	„	Ingall, E.
732	Pte	Hugman, G.	2852	„	Ingham, F.
1968	„	Hugo, A. V.	1757	Cpl	Ingham, P. W.
65758	„	Hugo, C. A.	138	Pte	Inglis, W. G.
*1336	„	Huia, A. C.	4492	„	Ingram, J. C.
5111	„	Hull, J. K.	*4640	„	Ingram, J. H.
*1370	„	Hulme, A. L.	2354	„	Ingram, W. L.
1293	„	Humberstone, R. (D.C.M.)	3360	„	Inman, R.
			6768	„	Innes, T. B.
3067	„	Hume, F. D.	2985	„	Ipkendanz, E.
7257	„	Hume, J. W.	*4041	„	Ireland, F. H.
7004	„	Humphrey, F. J.	*4491	„	Ireland, J. A.
*1126	„	Humphrys, R. A.	1135	„	Ireland, W.
6518	„	Humphrey, R. C. V.	5688	„	Irvin, A.
			5686	L/Cpl	Irvin, J. (C. DE G.)
2144	„	Humphreys, W. J.			
			5687	Pte	Irwin, L.
2259	„	Humphries, A.	*288	Cpl	Irvine, E. N.
2673	„	Humphries, H.	*339	Sgt	Irvine, S. C.
2561	„	Humphries, H.	2094	L/Cpl	Irving, G.
*3068	„	Hunia, W.	1971	Pte	Irving, H. H.
1364	„	Hunnikin, G. W.	5114	„	Irving, T. G.

*6293	„	Irwin, J. J.	1973	„ Janvrin, P. A. D.
59530	„	Ison, G. F.	3109	„ Jaques, M. C.
*1565	Cpl	Ison, J. B.	*1781	„ Jarrett, T. J.
3074	Pte	Ives, W. J.	1301	„ Jarvis, W. F.
			6295	„ Jay, P.
599	„	Jackman, A. E.	1972	„ Jeffes, F. C.
2693	„	Jackson, C. T.	*5123	Sgt Jeffery, J.
3077	„	Jackson, A.	65773	Pte Jeffkins, S. R.
7496	„	Jackson, A.	4641	„ Jeffery, W.
*1976	„	Jackson, A. W. P.	7018	„ Jeffreys, E. J.
			7267	„ Jeffreys, L. D.
*2396	„	Jackson, C. T.	2854	„ Jeffries, J.
*1134	„	Jackson, D. J.	4668	„ Jenkin, K. E.
1378	„	Jackson, E.	33	„ Jenkins, A.
3807	„	Jackson, F.	2823	„ Jenkins, A.
1373	„	Jackson, H. P.	1977	„ Jenkins, B. E.
1375	„	Jackson, J.	*2622	„ Jenkins, E.
1546	„	Jackson, J.	575	„ Jenkins, F.
*141	Cpl	Jackson, K. H.	2620	„ Jenkins, G. A.
2945	Pte	Jackson, L. J. A.	*3116	„ Jenkins, H. E.
1113	„	Jackson, N.	2058	„ Jenkins, T.
3108	„	Jackson, R. E.	*544	„ Jennings, T.
1975	„	Jackson, R. S.	2955	„ Jensen, F. C.
7017	„	Jackson, S. E.	581	„ Jensen, R. P.
742	„	Jackson, W. H.	*1569	„ Jepsen, F. I.
1346	„	Jackson, W. H.	6772	„ Jernberg, A. A.
65770	„	Jacobs, J. R.	1760	„ Jerome, D. K.
3078	„	Jacques, A. H.	7250	„ Jessing, A.
6393	„	Jacques, W. A.	743	„ Jewell, F. G.
*340	Cpl	Jagoe, J. J.	4218	L/Cpl Job, G. C.
5767	Pte	James, B.	3111	Pte Jobson, J.
1453	„	James, C. J.	2507	„ John, C. A.
*5217	L/Cpl	James, F. R.	2061	„ John, E.
3808	Pte	James, G.	*5690	„ Johns, J. A.
2737	L/Cpl	James, H. F.	2619	„ Johns, W. T.
5796	Pte	James, H. C.	*1347	„ Johnson, A. G.
5813	„	James, J.	1380	„ Johnson, A. N.
1138	L/Cpl	James, P.	*3153	„ Johnson, A. O.
5689	Pte	James, R. W.	5691	„ Johnson, A. W.
5768	„	James, T. G.	6155	„ Johnson, C. E.
5117	„	James, W.	5804	„ Johnson, C. G.
3076	„	James, W. J.	6769	„ Johnson, C. G.
*3810	„	Jamison, H. A.	6603	Dvr Johnson, E. H.
945	Sgt	Jamieson, J.	1566	Pte Johnson, E. S.
3808	Pte	Jamieson, J.	946	„ Johnson, F. B.
581	„	Jansen, R.	7368	„ Johnson, J. L. O.
6523	„	Janson, V. L.	*5118	„ Johnson, J.

LIEUT. R. L. BULKELEY, M.C. Killed in action.   CAPTAIN R. R. AGNEW, M.C.   CAPTAIN C. HOWIE, M.C.

CAPTAIN J. G. TYSON, M.C. Killed in action.   LIEUT. C. G. PRESCOTT, M.C.

CAPTAIN L. F. KEMMIS, M.C.   CAPTAIN C. F. ELIOTT, M.C.   LIEUT. ERIC SHELLEY, M.C.

LIEUT. H. S. DARE, M.M.   SGT. J. L. ROBERTS, D.C.M., M.M.   CPL. P. TURVEY, D.C.M., M.M.

CAPTAIN E. W. G. WREN, *Croix de Guerre*   SIG. SGT. A. S. McKENZIE, *Croix de Guerre*

LIEUT. F. J. MURN, M.M.   LIEUT. C. H. D. CHAMPION, Killed in action.   MAJOR J. W. B. BEAN

NOMINAL ROLL 369

1568	,,	Johnson, J. W.
2733	,,	Johnson, P. A.
2152	W.O.	Johnson, R.
*1759	Pte	Johnson, R.
931	Sgt	Johnson, S. A.
7269	Pte	Johnson, W. A.
3082	,,	Johnson, W. J.
1376	,,	Johnson, A. T.
1974	,,	Johnson, J.
59532	,,	Johnston, O. B.
*139	,,	Johnston, R. V.
3361	,,	Johnston, T. A.
*3114	,,	Johnston, V. St C.
3361	,,	Johnstone, T. A.
*3814	,,	Jones, A.
2153	,,	Jones, D.
65769	,,	Jones, D.
2155	,,	Jones, E.
1374	,,	Jones, E. W.
7270	,,	Jones, F. B.
*1132	,,	Jones, G. J.
6879	,,	Jones, H. G.
3075	,,	Jones, J. E. C.
1377	,,	Jones, J. T.
2716	Cpl	Jones, L.
*6431	Pte	Jones, L. A.
1133	,,	Jones, L. T.
*1379	,,	Jones, P.
2154	,,	Jones, R.
4493	,,	Jones, R.
2066	,,	Jones, R. A. H.
*1283	Sgt	Jones, R. D.
*3112	Pte	Jones, R. T.
*740	,,	Jones, S.
2468	,,	Jones, S.
*1567	,,	Jones, S. H.
4045	,,	Jones, T.
*6294	,,	Jones, T.
*5692	,,	Jones, W. A. L.
1978	Cpl	Jones, W. C.
7268	Pte	Jones, W. C.
6432	,,	Jones, W. E.
3305	,,	Jordon, J. J.
1446	,,	Jopsen, W. J.
3110	Sgt	Joubert, A.
1136	Pte	Joyce, D.
2095	,,	Joyce, H.
1199	,,	Joyner, A. E.
3113	Cpl	Joynes, R.
4495	Pte	Judd, A. G.
1139	,,	Judd, H. J.
*2866	,,	Jude, S.
	,,	Judson, F. J.
2657	,,	Julien, A.
2659	,,	Julien, W.
6044	,,	Jury, F
745	L/Cpl	Kahle, C. G.
*525	Pte	Kannar, D.
59540	,,	Kannar, W. W.
*2699	,,	Kay, C. C.
2700	,,	Kay, C. L.
1353	,,	Kay, G.
65774	,,	Kay, L. W.
3963	,,	Kay, T. H.
4046	,,	Keane, G. F.
7370	Sgt	Keane, T. M.
2157	Pte	Kearney, T. B.
4498	,,	Kearns, J. T. (M.M.)
*7500	,,	Keary, D. McM.
2267	,,	Keating, T.
2856	,,	Keatinge, E. P.
7501	,,	Keefe, W. P.
1512	,,	Keen, F.
1550	,,	Keenan, J. L.
4501	,,	Keevers, A. R.
1861	L/Cpl	Kegg, N. E. C.
59541	Pte	Keiser, H. A.
1482	Sgt	Kelaher, C. R.
*2686	Pte	Kelaher, J. M.
1383	,,	Kelso, G. W.
5122	,,	Kelvin, W. T. (M.M.)
*5487	,,	Kelley, D.
*1647	,,	Kelly, A.
2375	,,	Kelly, D. G.
*749	,,	Kelly, F.
7273	,,	Kelly, J.
*6774	,,	Kelly, J. E.
2859	,,	Kelly, J. J.
*1382	,,	Kelly, P.
1980	,,	Kelly, P. F.

z

2698	„	Kelly, R. S.	*6298	„	King, H. S.
3124	„	Kelly, R. S.	2626	„	King, C. J.
2997	„	Kelly, W. E.	*6298	„	King, H. S.
3123	„	Kelly, W. J. R.	1499	„	King, J.
1619	„	Kemble, V.	1577	„	King, J.
144	„	Kemp, H.	1381	„	King, O. D.
*147	„	Kendal, V. H.	5694	„	King, V. C.
*6300	„	Kennaugh, F. J.	1384	„	King, W.
747	„	Kennedy, J. A.	1764	„	King, W. H. A.
1328	„	Kennedy, J. A.	7502	„	King, W. S.
7504	„	Kennedy, J. F.	2355	„	Kinsella, G.
*3125	„	Kennedy, L. G.	6854	„	Kirby, T. E.
6301	„	Kennedy, M.	2857	„	Kirby, E.
2690	„	Kennedy, P.	3357	„	Kirby, J.
*4047	„	Kennedy, R. J.	2957	„	Kirby, T. A.
1352	„	Kennedy, S. J.	4314	„	Kirby, W. C.
1140	„	Kennedy, T.	*7499	„	Kirk, T. A.
1979	„	Kennedy, T.	*3079	„	Kirkby, F. J.
744	„	Kennewell, F. G.	1981	„	Kirkham, E.
*2701	„	Kenny, R. C.	*7019	„	Kirkpatrick, S.
7272	„	Kent, H.	3668	„	Kirkpatrick, D.
2693	Cpl	Kent, T. J.	1549	Cpl	Kirkwood, A.
*1762	Pte	Keogh, C. B.	3818	„	Kirnan, T. W.
3121	„	Kerr, R. W.	2158	Pte	Kirton, C. F.
5693	„	Kerr, W. S.	*2624	„	Kirton, F. A.
1576	„	Kerrison, S. G.	1570	„	Kirwan, S.
1763	„	Kerry, R. A.	*2356	„	Kitchen, T. H.
3080	„	Kershaler, W. G.	6299	„	Kitley, C. J.
*1140	„	Kershaw, E. A.	7398	„	Kiviselg, A.
*1141	„	Kevin, D. H.	7020	„	Klein, E. H.
5122	„	Kevin, W. T. (M.M.)	6045	„	Kleinke, T. A.
			2937	„	Klemm, F.
2695	Cpl	Kew, W. (M.M.)	2858	„	Klemm, M. G.
146	Pte	Key, M. D.	1548	„	Klincke, A.
1136	„	Key, T. G.	59538	„	Klump, L.
1139	„	Keys, L. N.	746	„	Kluth, W. F.
745	„	Khale, T. T.	1547	„	Knell, E.
59537	„	Kieley, P.	1620	„	Knight, F.
*3118	„	Kieley, T.	3667	„	Knight, F. J.
2625	„	Kiernan, W. P.	4642	„	Knight, H. W.
1137	„	Killen, R.	2156	„	Knoppe, W. E.
2969	„	Kilty, J.	1138	„	Knott, H.
4497	„	Kime, J.	7503	„	Knott, H.
*2875	„	Kinchington, G. E.	2717	L/Cpl	Knowles, A. L.
			4500	Pte	Knutson, O. G.
6823	„	Kinchington, V.	1350	„	Kohne, W. C.

143	„	Kurtz, H. H.
*7497	„	Kyle, A. R.
1118	„	Kyle, D. S.
953	Pte	Laffan, W.
*1401	„	Laidlaw, J.
117	Sgt	Laidlaw, G.
2512	Pte	Laing, D.
*5803	„	Laing, J. W.
3351	„	Laing, H.
2973	„	Laing, W. L.
*6857	„	Laing, W.
952	„	Lake, S. J.
*1768	„	Lakey, E. T.
3670	„	Lamb, W. P.
5695	„	Lamb, D. A.
5696	„	Lamb, J. R. D.
4513	„	Lambert, C. S.
5123	„	Lambert, N. C.
*993	„	Lambert, R. K.
1142	„	Lambert, T. B. J.
1689	„	Lambie, A. M.
2165	„	Lambkin, O.
1131	„	Lamble, S.
1296	„	Lancaster, A. S.
*1765	„	Lancaster, W. H.
2161	„	Lancken, C. E.
1490	L/Cpl	Lane, A. L.
1982	Sgt	Lane, B. J. A.
6761	Pte	Lane, F. A. J.
3820	„	Lane, W.
*3343	„	Lane, W. C.
491	„	Laner, A.
6309	„	Lang, E. G. (M.M.)
*5697	„	Langham, S. W.
*2053	„	Langston, A. C.
4505	„	Laraghy, C. R.
*4507	„	Laraghy, J. F.
*3821	„	Lardeaux, S. E.
2343	„	Larkin, J. A.
3522	„	Larkin, M. J.
*1387	„	Larking, C. F.
4503	„	Laritt, J.
2631	„	Larsen, A. W.
7505	„	Larster, G. F.
7754	„	Larter, J. A.
151	„	Lathorpe, E. R.
3134	„	Latimer, N. C.
5783	„	Latter, A. C.
*1571	„	Launder, J.
5124	„	Lavender, W. H.
1575	„	Lavings, J. T.
6526	„	Law, A.
6307	„	Law, P.
6775	„	Lawless, J.
3345	„	Lawless, J. W.
5125	L/Cpl	Lawrence, C. W.
1385	Pte	Lawrence, J. E.
6527	„	Lawrence, W. J.
65779	„	Lawson, C. G.
6528	„	Lawson, F. C.
3822	„	Lawson, H. K.
2630	„	Lawson, J. H.
*949	Cpl	Lawson, R.
4103	Pte	Lawson, R. G.
*2452	„	Lax, F.
7510	„	Lay, J. H.
5218	„	Lazonby, J. G.
4605	„	Lazonby, P. A.
750	„	Leach, W.
*5698	L/Cpl	Leal, A. S.
2954	Pte	Leane, A. C.
2060	„	Lear, T.
3136	Cpl	Leary, G. T.
1552	„	Leary, T.
5126	Pte	Leathley, D. F.
*2361	„	Le Clerc, H. O.
3029	„	Lee, D.
2216	„	Lee, G.
4511	„	Lee, G. F.
1389	„	Lee, H.
3344	„	Lee, H.
*2629	Cpl	Lee, N. (M.M.)
2679	Pte	Lee, N.
*4512	„	Lee, R. E.
1573	„	Legg, H. J.
*2162	„	Leggett, D. M.
*341	„	Leighton, F.
6529	Cpl	Lemon, F.
*2171	Pte	Lennon, V. D. A.
*3133	„	Leo, J.
3085	„	Leonard, A. T.

5794	„	Leonard, P. J.		*4506	L/Cpl	Littlefair, J. H.
6777	„	Lerve, H. R.		2473	Pte	Livingstone, C.
2588	„	Leslie, B. L.		3135	„	Livingstone, D. G.
4509	„	Leslie, R. J.				
518	„	Lester, G.		508	Cpl	Livingstone, S. P.
7508	„	Levell, A.		552	Pte	Livermore, E. L.
*1553	„	Levelle, M.		6776	„	Livermore, J.
7512	„	Leverington, H.		*7025	„	Livermore, W.
18892	Cpl	Levy, D. A.		87	Cpl	Llewellyn, J. J.
1399	Pte	Levy, H.		6613	Pte	Lloyd, C. M.
1141	„	Levy, L.		*6530	„	**Lloyd, G. H.**
2633	„	Levy, S.		1315	„	Lloyd, L.
5699	„	Lew, W. C.		52479	„	Lloyd, R.
7274	„	Lewin, W. J.		*1574	„	Lloydworth, F. J.
*2159	„	Lewis, A. D.		1547	„	Llynn, J. T.
4824	„	Lewis, A. C.		1142	„	Loader, G.
*7277	„	Lewis, A. H.		3934	„	Lobley, T.
*490	„	Lewis, G.		2166	„	Lockie, G. E.
4501	„	Lewis, G.		4504	„	Locchi, J.
*2164	„	Lewis, J.		3130	„	Locke, A. F.
2998	„	Lewis, J.		3129	L/Cpl	Locke, G. E.
7507	„	Lewis, J. E.		65778	Pte	Locke, L. J.
3224	„	Lewis, S. D.		3131	„	Lockett, T. W.
3824	„	Lewis, S. D.		*4049	„	Lockhart, J. T.
2998	„	Lewis, W.		3084	„	Lockyer, S.
6046	„	Lewis, W. J.		1295	„	Lockyer, T. J.
*1386	„	Lewis, W. T.		*950	„	Logan, F. W.
59542	„	Ley, W.		*3127	„	Lohan, V. C.
7276	„	Leys, G. O.		*5131	„	Lohse, J. H.
*3823	„	Leyshon, B.		5132	„	Lohse, W. J.
3087	„	Liddell, G.		*6424	„	Lonergan, S.
3962	„	Liddle, F. J.		1455	„	Long, E. E.
2362	„	Lilley, E. W.		1388	„	Long, G. F.
343	„	Lilley, H. W.		2486	„	Long, R. A.
149	A/Sgt	Lincoln, W. D.		752	W.O.	Longworth, R. E.
4050	Pte	Lindfield, A.				
2634	„	Linderup, T. C. R.		6531	Pte	Loopy, J.
				6134	„	Loonam, E.
4515	„	Lindsay, W.		4502	Sgt	Lott, F.
65777	„	Lindsell, R. P.		7586	Pte	Lottomer, W.
2704	„	Ling, A.		6304	„	Lougher, L.
2363	„	Lines, F. A.		*3826	„	Loughery, J.
951	L/Cpl	Linn, R.		*1176	„	Loughery, R. S.
948	Cpl	Lipman, L. B.		*4661	T/Sgt	Love, D. F.
3089	Pte	Lithgow, P. F.		7506	Pte	Loveday, F.
504	„	Litt, J. T.		2635	„	Lovell, A. G.
*751	„	Little, A. J.		7023	„	Loveridge, F. C.

7024	„	Loveridge, W. J.	*1481	C.Q.M.S.	MacGregor, D. N.
2171	„	Lowcock, E.			
1392	„	Low, W.	1588	Pte	MacGregor, J.
1391	„	Lowe, A. S.	2713	„	Machon, A. A. N.
2628	„	Lowe, C.	*2256	„	Mackay, C. P.
2860	„	Lowe, J.	*2257	„	MacKenzie, D. R.
*295	„	Lowe, J. S.	3093	„	Mackenzie, F. B.
2431	„	Lowrey, A.	6534	„	Mackenzie, H. S.
*6880	„	Lucas, A. D. A.	6318	„	Mackenzie, T. W.
7583	„	Lucas, T.	4645	„	Mackey, R.
6305	„	Luff, J. D.	7525	„	Mackie, A.
753	„	Lukeman, W.	3147	„	Mackie, C. J.
6131	„	Lumsden, R. D.	5706	„	Mackie, D. H.
3827	„	Lumby, P. A.	3096	„	Mackinnon, D.
947	Cpl	Lush, A. B.	1589	„	MacLennan, W. S.
7509	Pte	Lush, J. F.	2487	„	MacNamara, D.
2637	„	Lutton, V. W.	1590	„	MacNamara, W. A.
2160	„	Luxton, W. H.			
	Cpl	Lycett, E. P.	*1407	„	MacPherson, A. R.
7511	Pte	Lye, J.			
6049	„	Lyman, F. F.	*5708	L/Cpl	MacPherson, S. G.
3088	„	Lymbery, F. H. W.			
			2176	Pte	MacRea, S.
2467	„	Lynch, A. W.	2656	„	McAllister, J.
698	„	Lynch, F. J.	2885	„	McAlpine, M. D.
3828	Cpl	Lynch, F. W.	1585	„	McAleer, F.
2724	Pte	Lynch, J.	1406	„	McAnnulty, C.
2466	„	Lynch, N.	*1803	„	McAnnulty, C. A.
100	„	Lynch, N. C.	3162	„	McAuley, H. C.
*6050	„	Lyne, C. J.	6072	„	McBride, J.
2861	„	Lyons, G.	3284	„	McBride, P. R.
*150	„	Lyons, J.	6806	„	McCabe, F. L.
2096	„	Lyons, T. V.	6862	„	McCallum, N. A.
1985	„	Lyons, W. J. C.	1587	„	McCallam, J.
50991	„	Lyttle, H. V.	6608	„	McCallam, D. E.
2788	„	Lyttleton, C. E.	*7528	„	McCann, O. E.
			962	L/Cpl	McCann, W. V.
*1365	Pte	Macaulay, S.	1991	Pte	McCarthy, A. J.
*10	Sgt	MacCallum, L. S.	35	„	McCarthy, F.
5705	Pte	Macdonald, J. C.	1581	„	McCarthy, F.
560	Sgt	MacDonald, R. V. Y.	3097	„	McCarthy, F.
			1175	„	McCarthy, R. J.
959	Pte	MacFayden, H. G.	2878	„	McCartney, H.
			3856	„	McClelland, A. A.
2400	„	MacFarlane, A. R.	*82	Sgt	McClelland, R. J.
534	„	MacFarlane, R.	6071	L/Cpl	McClosky, B.

*2169	Pte	McClure, S. R. Le M.	1999	,,	McEvoy, J.
*157	,,	MacClure, V. M.	7040	,,	McEwen, J. A.
*155	,,	McConnell, S.	2673	,,	McFadgyn, L.
4608	,,	McConnell, W.	*6544	,,	McFarlane, D.
344	,,	McConville, T. J.	*1154	,,	McFarlane, F.
6864	,,	McCormack, D.	6795	,,	McFarlane, S. A. J.
65800	,,	McCormack, J.	3317	,,	McFawn, A. A.
6541	,,	McCormack, T. B.	2073	,,	McFayden, L. D. W.
3521	,,	McCormack, W.	4610	L/Cpl	McGarrigle, R.
1485	,,	McCouat, D.	6798	Pte	McGee, R. G.
2413	,,	McCredie, A. C. G.	*1398	Sgt	McGee, S. (M.M.)
			*6858	Pte	McGeorge, C. F.
2659	,,	McCrory, J.	1155	Cpl	McGill, S. C.
3852	,,	McCullagh, —.	3531	Pte	McGinley, J.
2367	,,	McCulloch, G.	6151	,,	McGlashan, A.
346	,,	McCulloch, S. A.	*590	,,	McGlynn, J.
6797	,,	McCulloch, W. J.	7529	,,	McGovern, W. E.
1778	L/Cpl	McDermott, F.	*3165	,,	McGown, A. C.
61662	Pte	McDermott, F. F.	7521	,,	McGrane, J. A.
2658	,,	McDonald, A.	6066	,,	McGrath, F. E.
4053	,,	McDonald, A.	*1149	Cpl	McGrath, H. T. J.
2246	Cpl	McDonald, A. L.	800	Pte	McGrath, J.
2846	Pte	McDonald, C.	6323	,,	McGrath, J. E.
6800	,,	McDonald, D. (M.M.)	1364	,,	McGraths, M. M.
			6067	,,	McGrath, P. A.
484	Cpl	McDonald, D. C.	5147	,,	McGrath, P. V.
2177	Pte	McDonald, E.	*5148	,,	McGrath, W.
2055	,,	McDonald, G. C.	6807	,,	McGrath, W. J.
3098	,,	McDonald, J.	2065	,,	McGregor, D.
6543	,,	McDonald, J.	*1859	,,	McGregor, J.
6065	Sgt	McDonald, J. R.	2642	,,	McGregor, J.
7038	Pte	McDonald, N.	1156	,,	McGregor, R.
1144	,,	McDonald, O. M.	*4056	Cpl	McGregor, R. F.
*587	Sgt	McDonald, R.	3858	Pte	McGuigan, E. T.
*6540	Pte	McDonald, R. G.	3161	Cpl	McGuire, J.
1147	,,	McDonald, W.	2836	Pte	McGuire, M. J.
*6070	,,	McDonnell, F. V.	6805	,,	McHugh, A. P.
*7284	,,	McDonnell, J. H.	3167	,,	McInerney, T. A.
1556	,,	McDonough, W. McL.	1774	,,	McInnes, E. J. R.
			7526	,,	McIntosh, A. S.
2739	,,	McDougal, W.	*3370	,,	McIntosh, H. McD.
*6883	,,	McDougall, D.			
6799	,,	McDougall, D. R.	6142	,,	McIntosh, H. Y.
986	,,	McElroy, J.	1404	,,	McIntosh, W.
1143	,,	McErlean, P.	1362	,,	McIver, G.

1670	,,	McIvor, J.
961	,,	McKay, A.
1318	,,	McKay, J. S.
1304	Cpl	McKay, W. A.
2467	Pte	McKean, W. A.
65785	,,	McKeane, H.
2726	,,	McKeevers, J. R.
6548	,,	McKell, W.
2497	,,	McKenna, E. F.
*1486	Sgt	McKennon, A. W.
294	Sgt	McKenzie, A. S.
1183	Pte	McKenzie, E.
*1396	,,	McKenzie, D.
2171	,,	McKenzie, T.
*6322	,,	McKenzie, W. H.
3099	,,	McKeown, W.
*5144	,,	McKerihan, W. J.
4366	Sgt	McKersie, A.
7037	Pte	McKinnon, S. V. W.
6546	,,	McKinstry, J. B.
*3340	,,	McKnight, C.
1146	,,	McKnight, J. R.
*1583	Cpl	McLachlan, J.
5146	Pte	McLachlan, J. A.
7039	,,	McLaren, F. R.
*5415	,,	McLaughlin, W.
2880	,,	McLaws, R. C.
6803	,,	McLaws, W. J.
*1363	,,	McLean, A. R.
4522	,,	McLean, C. E.
6796	Cpl	McLean, C. N.
4521	Pte	McLean, C. W.
54011	,,	McLean, H. R.
7281	,,	McLean, J.
*4520	,,	McLean, T. R.
741	,,	McLennan, J. A.
3166	,,	McLeod, G.
*2737	,,	McLeod, N. R.
59560	,,	McLeod, P. W.
1381	L/Sgt	McLintock, R. T.
2703	Pte	McLoughlin, C. D.
*4533	,,	McLoughlin, T.
6804	,,	McMahon, J.
6547	,,	McManus, J. J.
5434	,,	McMaster, A. J.
59534	,,	McMasters, N. G.
6974	,,	McMillan, J. A.
*594	,,	McMillan, N. H.
*1184	,,	McMillan, R. A.
354	,,	MacMillan, W. H.
1403	,,	McMillan, J.
2097	Sgt	McMillan, T. (D.C.M.)
38	Pte	McNamara, C. M. P.
960	,,	McNamara, M.
1558	,,	McNamara, P.
6115	,,	McNamara, R.
2727	,,	McNaughton, E. J.
503	,,	McNeill, A.
2920	,,	McNeven, R. J.
2397	L/Cpl	McCrae, J. C.
2432	Pte	McNulty, R. J.
7527	,,	McPhail, C. R.
*3989	,,	McPhee, F.
3098	,,	McPhee, J. A.
*1777	,,	McPhee, K. M.
*302	,,	McPherson, D.
1776	,,	McPherson, G. H.
*5219	,,	McPherson, G. H.
*1555	,,	McPherson, J.
1395	Cpl	McQuirk, A.
*911	Pte	McQuirk, T. A.
1207	,,	McRae, A. G.
7041	,,	McRae, J. W.
1146	,,	McRitchie, W.
1397	,,	McRea, J. C.
1586	,,	McSweeney, E. J.
6860	,,	McVicar, H. W.
3157	L/Cpl	McWilliams, L. J.
6794	Pte	McAndrew, L. D.
*2168	,,	Madden, C. N.
7520	,,	Madden, H. W.
158	,,	Madden, P. S.
2740	,,	Madelena, J.

*2364 „ Madell, H. D.
6052 „ Maddison, H.
7516 „ Maddison, W.
2836 „ Maguire, A. J.
1356 „ Maher, W. N.
*5141 „ Mahoney, C. D.
7518 „ Mahoney, J.
159 „ Maine, K. D.
2358 „ Mair, J. A.
65784 „ Maitland, D. C.
65782 „ Major, C. J.
354 Cpl Malone, J. B.
351 Pte Malone, R. B.
760 „ Maltby, C. E.
3830 „ Manewell, A.
7283 L/Cpl Mangall, J. L.
7033 Pte Mankin, R.
353 „ Manna, E. S.
2365 Sgt Mann, P. A.
(M.S.M.)
*1294 L/Cpl Mann, W.
*3143 Pte Mannell, E. J.
888 Cpl Manning, J.
2744 Pte Manns, C. W.
*2170 „ Manson, A.
59632 „ Manson, D.
1554 „ Mantle, W. J.
1559 „ Maplesden, J. R.
1150 L/Cpl Mapp, S. H.
2652 Pte Mapstone, G. A.
1394 „ Maquard, —
*553 Sgt Mara, R. S.
*1557 Pte March, A. J.
1612 „ Marchant, E.
*2713 „ Mariner, J.
156 Cpl Mark, J.
350 Pte Markowicz, A. J. de T.
1580 „ Marriatt, F.
6783 „ Marshall, A. R.
3159 „ Marshall, G. J.
*1505 Cpl Marshall, J.
2720 „ Marshall, J.
2489 Pte Marshall, J. J.
345 „ Marshall, S. W.
7769 „ Marshall, W.

*164 Cpl Marshall, W. A.
(D.C.M)
*161 Pte Marshall, W. G.
3156 „ Marshall, W. R.
*501 „ Marsden, S. S.
2644 „ Marsden, T. S.
5704 „ Marsden, W.
*69 „ Marston, J.
*1151 „ Martin, B. J.
3138 „ Martin, C. R.
*6425 „ Martin, F. H.
392 „ Martin, G.
3143 „ Martin, H. A.
2649 „ Martin, H. L.
7034 „ Martin, W. L.
1658 „ Martin, O. P.
65865 „ Martin, R.
1992 „ Martin, S.
2078 „ Martin, T. J.
3376 „ Martin, S. S.
284 Sgt Martyn, A. K.
*7043 L/Cpl Martyn, J.
1990 Pte Mason, A. F.
3831 „ Mason, A. H. J.
2716 „ Mason, F.
6785 „ Mason, G.
785 „ Mason, J. H.
7029 „ Mason, K. H.
1153 „ Mason, S. M. V.
2872 „ Mason, W. A.
5404 „ Masters, W. H.
1305 „ Masterton, C.
*2167 Sgt Maston, H. W.
(M.M.)
1355 Pte Masurier, H.
*1579 „ Matchett, H. W.
2172 „ Matchett, J.
13 Cpl Mather, A. E.
152 Pte Mathers, A.
5134 „ Matheson, W. D.
*352 Sgt Matheson, F. H.
153 „ Mathews, A. R.
1672 Pte Mathieson, S.
*4519 Cpl Matich, G.
5135 Sgt Mathews, A. E.
*3313 Pte Mathews, A. G.
2863 „ Mathews, C. H.

3151	„	Mathews, C. J.
759	Cpl	Mathews, F. W.
5136	„	Mathews, G. S. A. (D.C.M.)
2478	Pte	Mathews, G. W. R.
2479	„	Mathews, J. B. J.
3157	„	Mathews, R.
3158	„	Mathews, S. F.
2639	„	Maughan, H.
*1634	„	Maughan, H. W.
1353	„	Maund, E. S.
2847	„	Maunder, P.
*1307	Cpl	Maunsell, A. R. L.
2648	Pte	Maurer, G. P.
*2650	„	Maurer, L. J.
7030	„	Mavelle, B.
*1360	„	Maxwell, A.
*2202	„	Maxwell, E.
390	Sgt	Maxwell, G.
1154	Cpl	Maxwell, W. M.
5707	Pte	May, H.
7519	„	May, W.
6055	„	Maybury, G. A. McD.
2067	„	Mayer, A. L.
2873	„	Mayer, H.
*7026	„	Maynard, H. G.
1394	„	Maynard, J.
*162	Cpl	Mayo, R. S.
5064	Pte	Mazoudier, F. A.
*5711	„	Meade, L. F.
2749	Sgt	Meaker, R.
2750	Pte	Meaker, H. (D.C.M.)
*296	„	Meakins, A. J.
*2646	Sgt	Meaney, E.
6793	Pte	Meanwell, G. M.
6056	„	Measurier, H.
5712	„	Medhurst, J.
3839	„	Medlicott, A. R.
*1148	„	Meech, R. A.
59555	„	Meehan, J. L.
6062	„	Meers, C.
3151	Cpl	Meers, C. J. (D.C.M.)
6060	Pte	Meers, S. C. M.
7059	„	Meers, T. J.
*761	„	Meggy, A. E.
*2951	„	Meggy, D. A.
*2643	„	Meigan, R.
6057	„	Melton, P.
3838	„	Melvin, P. H.
757	„	Memorey, L. W.
2742	Cpl	Menzies, J. W. S.
*3273	Pte	Menzies, R.
*2056	„	Mercer, A. V.
3103	„	Mercer, J. J.
*2718	L/Cpl	Meredith, H.
2864	Pte	Merritt, H. A.
1770	„	Merton, J.
7044	„	Messner, H. V.
2191	„	Meurant, F. F.
7028	„	Meyn, H. J.
4646	„	Michelson, M.
*1462	„	Middleton, T. E.
2508	„	Middleton, W. F.
1993	„	Middleton, W. S.
7031	„	Mildenhall, F. G.
*1560	„	Miles, C. J.
*4528	„	Milford, H.
6314	„	Mill, A. H.
2865	„	Millar, A. R.
6537	„	Millar, R.
1401	„	Miller, A.
5137	„	Miller, A. G.
4518	„	Miller, E. C.
6778	„	Miller, E. L.
*1153	„	Miller, G.
7787	„	Miller, G. T.
3156	„	Miller, H.
2640	„	Miller, I. G.
2949	Cpl	Miller, J. C. McK.
2655	Pte	Miller, L.
3102	„	Miller, L.
*1354	„	Miller, L. W.
*1771	„	Miller, T.
547	„	Miller, W.
3100	„	Miller, W. N.
3104	„	Millett, C. J.
3321	„	Milliard, E.
1191	Sgt	Milliard, J. W. (M.M.)

6784 Pte Milliken, R.
5220 „ Mills, A.
2745 „ Mills, C. F.
*1582 „ Mills, F.
3316 L/Cpl Mills, G.
4606 Pte Mills, H. H.
2483 L/Cpl Mills, J. A. C.
*4104 Pte Mills, R. G.
1402 „ Mills, S. R.
2648 L/Cpl Milner, G.
(M.M.)
2950 Pte Minehan, W. H.
5769 „ Minnett, E.
73 „ Minns, C. A.
355 „ Minter, H. W.
4529 „ Mitchell, C. E.
6536 „ Mitchell, E. A.
1308 Cpl Mitchell, F. J.
3148 Pte Mitchell, H.
577 „ Mitchell, H. C.
2843 „ Mitchell, H. J.
4607 „ Mitchell, J.
571 „ Mitchell, P. T.
2903 „ Mitchell, V. W.
2366 „ Mitchell, W.
*6535 „ Mitchell, W.
*7515 „ Mitten, S. H.
1997 „ Mobbs, A.
*2844 „ Mogan, M. J.
4234 „ Mogg, G. F.
1400 „ Moggach, J.
3834 „ Moir, E. G.
*1150 „ Moir, R. W.
2866 „ Moller, L. F. M.
7278 „ Molloy, P. E.
1399 „ Moloney, J. F.
154 Sgt Monk, A. J. D.
1772 Cpl Monks, L. T.
59556 Pte Monro, A. F.
2732 „ Monro, J. N.
7042 L/Cpl Montague, J.
65785 Pte Montgomery, A. C.
1584 „ Montgomery, H. H.
59558 „ Mooney, A.
1500 Sgt Moore, A. D.

6538 Pte Moore, A. H.
1186 L/Cpl Moore, C. M.
2874 Cpl Moore, C. V.
*1393 Pte Moore, E. A.
2641 „ Moore, E. A.
*3845 „ Moore, F. J.
6313 „ Moore, G.
2867 „ Moore, G. A.
2175 „ Moore, H. J.
7782 „ Moore, L. F. J.
*2399 Cpl Moore, L. P.
357 Pte Moore, F.
3160 „ Moore, S. T.
*6311 „ Moore, T.
6059 „ Moore, T. J.
3101 „ Moorefield, R.
6058 „ Moran, H. E.
59544 „ Morey, C. T.
902 „ Morgan, A.
59557 „ Morgan, A. L.
954 „ Morgan, C. E.
3105 „ Morgan, E. J.
2842 „ Morgan, G. W.
2722 Sgt Morgan, H. R.
6781 Pte Morgan, J. H.
2173 „ Morton, K.
*1460 „ Morgan, P.
*2174 „ Morgan, P.
2651 „ Morgan, R. S.
*2730 Cpl Morgan, T.
3372 Pte Morn, J. N.
*957 „ Morrice, W. J.
1562 „ Morris, B. G.
*160 „ Morris, C. W.
72 „ Morris, E.
*1501 „ Morris, E. O. W.
1205 „ Morris, F.
2944 „ Morris, F. W.
4526 „ Morris, F. W.
*1149 C.S.M. Morris, G. A.
(M.C.)
6539 Pte Morris, H. L.
*3837 „ Morris, J.
758 „ Morris, J. C.
2179 „ Morris, J. R.
7523 „ Morris, L. A. R.
1358 „ Morris, R. A.

3352	„	Morris, R. R.
2180	„	Morris, T. D. P.
3836	„	Morris, W.
3835	„	Morris, W. L.
*2247	Cpl	Morrison, A. E. L.
2381	Pte	Morrison, C. S.
1988	„	Morrison, E. H.
*2734	„	Morrison, G.
956	Cpl	Morrison, J. A. (M.S.M.)
5060	A/Sgt	Morrison, J. A.
*2645	Cpl	Morrison, J. D.
4517	Pte	Morrison, J. W.
*7517	„	Morrison, S.
163	„	Morrison, W.
1152	„	Morrison, W.
3359	Sgt	Morrison, J. S.
3844	Pte	Morrow, S. L.
1577	„	Morton, G.
2173	L/Cpl	Morton, K.
6792	Pte	Morton, W. R.
3090	„	Moses, A. G.
2706	„	Moston, A.
*1359	Sgt	Mott, J. H.
3380	Pte	Mottershead, R. C.
65781	„	Mottram, G.
4525	„	Mould, E.
3350	„	Moylan, J.
3315	„	Moylan, J. J.
3141	„	Moylan, T.
3139	„	Moyle, R.
3106	„	Muddell, C.
*347	„	Mudge, E. F.
3846	„	Muir, A. W.
*3137	„	Muir, R. J.
*6054	„	Muirhead, L.
*955	„	Mulcahy, M. M.
6861	„	Mulholland, R. G.
6782	„	Mullholland, R. T.
1206	„	Mullens, F. H.
2647	„	Mullens, J.
3847	„	Mulligan, W.
*995	„	Mullin, A.
7027	„	Mulvany, V. H.
7514	„	Mulveney, R.
59548	„	Mumby, C. L.
6320	„	Mumford, H.
356	C.Q.M.S.	Mumford, R.
*349	Pte	Muncton, R.
2098	„	Munday, T. J.
*2245	„	Mundy, G. A.
1152	„	Munn, V.
*1357	„	Munro, J. G.
2732	„	Munro, J. N.
1143	Sgt	Munro, S.
3314	„	Munt, F. H.
7282	Pte	Munton, T. P.
1148	Cpl	Murdock, A.
1159	L/Cpl	Murn, J.
1994	Pte	Murtagh, A. J.
6881	„	Murphie, A.
6791	„	Murphie, J.
6882	„	Murphie, T.
2731	„	Murphy, J.
2909	„	Murphy, J. E.
1361	„	Murphy, P.
7035	„	Murphy, P.
*3363	„	Murphy, T.
7280	„	Murphy, T. S. P.
*4523	„	Murphy, W. B.
5142	„	Murphy, W. T.
2851	„	Murray, A. S.
*583	„	Murray, C.
4055	„	Murray, F. L.
2877	„	Murray, H. M.
4532	„	Murray, J.
1998	Sgt	Murray, J. A. (M.M.)
*1661	Pte	Murray, J. J.
*2850	„	Murray, J. N.
*4844	„	Murray, J. S.
*1147	L/Cpl	Murray, N. (M.M. AND BAR)
*2085	Pte	Murray, N. L.
*7032	„	Murray, P.
381	Sgt	Murray, P. V.
1159	Pte	Murray, S. (M.M.)
3161	„	Murray, S.
*1145	L/Cpl	Murray, S. W.

5709	Pte	Murray, W.		*928	„	Newell, V. T.
5143	„	Murray, W. J.		*2000	„	Newland, H.
4516	„	Murray, W. A.		5714	„	Newland, N. G.
6786	„	Murray, W. R.		165	R.S.M.	Newland, W. J. (D.C.M.)
1108	„	Murray-Cowper, J. S.		4058	Pte	Newlands, R. B.
5324	„	Murray-Cowper, N. D.		4537	„	Newman, J.
				3863	„	Newman, R. A.
*1408	„	Musgrove, A.		6549	„	Newson, E. H.
4853	„	Mussett, G. H.		7045	„	Newth, W. S.
7036	„	Myers, D.		7531	„	Newton, A. H.
*3153	„	Mylecharane, W.		358	Cpl	Newton, B. M.
				*2485	Sgt	Newton, C.
2185	Sgt	Nagle, F. W. J.		4611	Pte	Newton, G.
*5717	Pte	Nagle, W. E.		6362	L/Cpl	Newton, N.
2885	„	Nalty, E.		7530	Pte	Niall, C. J.
3640	„	Nangle, W. F.		3867	„	Nichalls, C. V.
2420	„	Napthali, W. H.		6324	„	Nicholas, N. H.
1561	„	Nash, A.		3866	„	Nicholls, E. M.
6426	„	Nash, H. V.		1592	„	Nicholls, F. J.
*963	„	Naughton, J. F.		756	Sgt	Nicholls, W.
*5149	„	Nay, M. J.		2757	Pte	Nicholls, W. E. H.
2712	Cpl	Naylor, J.				
2158	Pte	Neal, E. A.		2186	„	Nichols, J.
5150	„	Neal, V. H. J.		5716	L/Cpl	Nicholson, D. M.
3171	„	Neal, W. J.				
5223	„	Neave, D.		1409	Pte	Nicholson, H. J.
6073	„	Neeson, W.		4538	„	Nicholson, W. H.
2758	„	Neil, H.		2707	„	Nicol, F. J.
3862	„	Neillings, W.		4105	„	Nicol, T.
4859	„	Nell, H.		3331	„	Nissen, T. B.
1564	„	Nelson, C.		2203	Sgt	Nixon, H. J. G.
1668	„	Nelson, H.		*6551	Pte	Nixon, W. F.
3318	„	Nelson, H.		3762	„	Noad, W. H.
2661	„	Neilson, N.		3174	„	Noake, C. S.
3107	„	Nelson, J. McD.		494	„	Noakes, T.
5713	„	Nelson, M. A.		357	Cpl	Noble, V.
4648	L/Cpl	Nelson, R. J.		2509	Pte	Nolan, J.
4671	Pte	Neville, G.		6326	„	Nolan, R. L.
6075	„	Neville, P. A.		1594	„	Norcott, A. J.
59567	„	Nevin, W. G.		*1155	„	Norman, E.
*5715	„	Newberry, H. J.		7834	„	Norman, R.
*1593	„	Newberry, P. N.		*1156	„	Norris, F.
1410	„	Newbold, W.		*498	„	Norris, T.
*755	„	Newbury, W. H.		1565	„	Northill, W. R.
7046	„	Newby, A.		2752	„	Northrop, R.
2852	„	Newby, T.		7589	„	Norton, J. H. C.

NOMINAL ROLL

3171	,,	Norton, W. B.
2188	,,	Norwood, H.
2754	,,	Nott, J. D.
6865	,,	Nowell, J.
14	,,	Nowlan, E. J.
2756	C.Q.M.S.	Nunn, J W.
2662	Sgt	Nurse, C. (M.M.)
65840	Pte	Oakes, C.
2764	,,	Oakes, E. E. H.
*3176	Sgt	Oakford, H. J.
1710	L/Sgt	Oakman, T.
*930	Pte	Oates, J. H.
*12	Sgt	Oates, W. A.
*1158	Pte	O'Brien, B. C. J.
764	,,	O'Brien, C. J.
2080	,,	O'Brien, E. A.
765	,,	O'Brien, E. J.
1411	,,	O'Brien, F.
2887	,,	O'Brien, H. J.
*1159	,,	O'Brien, P. J.
7533	,,	O'Brien, S. W.
*2206	,,	O'Brien, T. L.
2761	,,	O'Brien, W. G.
2205	,,	O'Byrne, E.
6368	,,	O'Connell, T.
5126	,,	O'Connor, E.
7581	,,	O'Connor, F. P.
*359	,,	O'Connor, J.
4650	,,	O'Connor, J.
6327	,,	O'Connor, J.
2456	,,	O'Connor, J. L.
4822	,,	O'Connor, M. G.
*931	,,	Odell, J. F.
3177	,,	Odliff, I. F.
6802	,,	O'Donnell, F. B. (M.M.)
2888	,,	O'Donnell, H. H.
3181	,,	O'Donoghue, W.
6328	,,	Ogilvie, A. J.
2664	,,	Ogilvie, R. O.
1781	,,	Ogle, C. J.
1872	,,	Ogle, C. J.
5151	,,	Ogle, R. J.
1412	,,	Oglesby, S. J.
454	,,	O'Hea, F.
2665	,,	Ohlsson, M. A. C.
59639	,,	O'Keefe, H. J.
*1566	,,	Olds, C.
2181	,,	Olive, A. H.
*7532	,,	Olive, R. J.
5718	,,	Oliver, C. R.
767	Sgt	Oliver, F.
*2496	Pte	Oliver, J. C.
*2943	T/Cpl	Oliver, T. G.
2760	Pte	Oliver, W. H.
*2002	,,	Olliffe, J. J.
*2057	,,	O'Louglin, B. C.
*7048	,,	O'Loughlin, P. J.
3369	,,	O'Neil, J. B.
*2204	,,	O'Neill, J.
*6553	,,	O'Neill, M.
2735	,,	O'Neill, T. E.
2209	,,	Orchard, A.
*1221	,,	Orchard, D.
1596	,,	O'Regan, C. L.
7362	,,	Organ, J.
63890	,,	O'Rierdan, G.
*1801	,,	Orphin, E. T.
*1597	,,	Orr, P.
2663	,,	Osborn, J. W.
1158	,,	Osborne, A. T.
2114	,,	Osborne, R. F.
*7049	,,	Osborne, H. B.
*6554	,,	Osborne, J.
4059	,,	Osborne, J. C.
*3178	,,	Osborne, R. L.
*2208	,,	O'Shea, V. C.
531	,,	Osmond, C.
*766	,,	O'Sullivan, D.
4258	,,	O'Sullivan, V. D. (M.M.)
4259	,,	O'Sullivan, W. J.
*4867	,,	Oswin, H. J.
*1655	,,	Otes, E. G.
6555	,,	Ottoway, P. J.
7050	,,	Outram, G.
165	,,	Outridge, A.
*5719	,,	Overend, V. E. T.
*2003	,,	Owen, J. H.
7534	,,	Owen, O. S.
*559	,,	Owens, J.

1161	Pte	Pack, C.		2890	„	Pascoe, R.
3319	„	Packer, A. McL.		2984	„	Pascoe, S.
7351	„	Packer, C. W.		*2212	„	Pascoe, V. H.
3318	„	Packer, R. B.		*7558	„	Pascoe, W. R.
*1166	Cpl	Page, C. G. (M.M.)		2374	„	Passfield, A. J.
				2402	„	Paterson, C. T.
*5152	Pte	Page, H.		*6331	„	Paton, J.
*542	Bglr	Page, T. A.		2722	„	Patterson, G.
1162	L/Cpl	Paget, I.		1604	„	Patterson, J.
2161	Pte	Paget, I.		*6079	„	Patterson, J. E.
364	„	Paine, E. G.		2768	„	Patterson, S. D.
*5720	„	Pakes, R. P.		6078	„	Patterson, W. H.
3879	„	Palfreeman, C.		1606	„	Pattinson, R. (M.M.)
2213	„	Pallister, G. M.				
1783	„	Palmer, A.		*771	„	Patton, E. W.
2420	„	Palmer, A.		7854	„	Patton, J. A.
2380	„	Palmer, C. B.		6160	„	Paul, J.
3184	„	Palmer, G.		1183	Sgt	Paul, O. H.
7795	„	Palmer, G.		5722	Pte	Paul, R. J.
1789	„	Palmer, H.		3876	„	Paull, J.
2005	„	Palmer, H.		1159	„	Paulson, J. W.
5155	„	Palmer, H.		*535	„	Pavey, H. G.
*7293	„	Palmer, J. C.		3113	„	Payne, C.
*4543	„	Palmer, R. C.		3881	„	Payne, C.
1416	„	Pankhurst, J.		*1420	„	Payne, R.
*1414	Cpl	Parker, C. S.		65809	„	Payne, W. J.
4542	Pte	Parker, E. W.		7054	„	Peacock, N. H.
6081	„	Parker, C. H.		2457	„	Peacock, R. C.
65814	„	Parker, F.		5724	„	Peake, G. H.
548	Sgt	Parker, H.		*5772	„	Peake, W. L.
3109	Pte	Parker, H. L.		6810	„	Pearce, A. S.
496	„	Parker, J.		2004	„	Pearce, E. H.
933	L/Cpl	Parker, F. E.		1163	C.Q.M.S.	Pearce, J. F.
7538	Pte	Parkes, R. G.		18	L/Cpl	Pearce, R. T.
2009	„	Parlett, A. E.		292	Pte	Pearce, S. T.
361	„	Parmenter, L. C.		3370	„	Pearce, W.
4061	„	Parnell, H.		7535	„	Pearce, W.
2368	„	Parr, R. J.		*2010	„	Pearce, W. E.
2140	„	Parry, R. A. (M.M.)		2183	„	Pearce, W. J. H.
				59575	„	Pearn, S. V.
*1784	„	Parsons, G. E.		6811	„	Pearsall, F. G. L.
6885	„	Parsons, J.		6812	„	Peasely, F. W.
5153	„	Parsons, L.		7052	„	Pearson, A. H.
*6867	„	Parsons, R.		1329	Sgt	Pearson, D. E. T.
5723	„	Parsons, W.		*1785	Pte	Pearson, J. B.
5154	„	Partridge, A. E.		*2369	Cpl	Peck, F. A.
7294	„	Pascoe, A. J. F.		*7057	Pte	Peck, E. G.

*769	Cpl	Peile, A. V.
1161	Pte	Pender, T.
2668	,,	Penfold, N.
3112	,,	Penketh, C. V.
6077	,,	Pennell, A.
7058	,,	Pennie, F. R.
2415	,,	Penny, A. G.
770	,,	Penny, L.
*2210	,,	Penty, B.
*787	L/Cpl	Perkins, F.
772	Pte	Perkins, V. B.
3114	,,	Perkins, W. H. G.
*966	,,	Perkins, W. J.
2477	,,	Perrott, F.
2858	,,	Perry, A. M.
4351	,,	Perry, C. W.
*1164	L/Cpl	Perry, F. D.
65813	Pte	Pertzell, E. A.
*1603	,,	Peters, D.
65896	,,	Peterson, A.
7775	,,	Petersen, C. G.
2263	,,	Peterson, E.
1313	,,	Petrie, F.
*7296	,,	Pettersen, G. S.
167	,,	Petts, W.
1530	,,	Phelps, J. H.
7059	,,	Philip, P. A.
*965	,,	Phillips, A. W. F.
5157	,,	Phillips, E. H.
5384	Sgt	Phillips, H. J.
65808	Pte	Phillips, J.
1600	,,	Phillips, J. W.
*1615	,,	Phillips, L. R.
1567	,,	Phillips, T.
2776	Sgt	Phillips, T. M.
1568	Pte	Phillipson, R.
3188	,,	Philp, L.
2770	,,	Philpot, E. A.
1601	,,	Philpot, J. C.
7350	,,	Pickard, W.
65806	,,	Pickard, W. R.
*3192	,,	Pickering, F. H.
5158	L/Cpl	Pickering, G.
*3883	Pte	Pickering, R. T.
3111	,,	Pickering, T. W.
2867	,,	Picton, A.
2870	,,	Picton, A. M.
7291	,,	Picton, C. H. E.
1371	,,	Piccick, W. J.
5159	,,	Pike, C.
*2007	,,	Pike, H. A.
935	,,	Pillar, T.
166	,,	Pinkerton, J.
*964	Pte	Pinkstone, V. J.
2772	,,	Pinson, N. A.
6566	,,	Piper, R. E.
7537	,,	Pitman, J. T.
7539	,,	Pitt, F. J.
3116	,,	Pittard, F. C. W.
3115	,,	Pittard, J. W.
5156	,,	Player, L. M.
*7060	,,	Plummer, W. L.
7298	,,	Plunkett, E. G.
4613	,,	Pobjoy, C. J.
3166	,,	Pogson, F. S.
2370	,,	Polin, V. S.
1162	,,	Pollard, L. B.
1415	,,	Pollitt, F.
*1160	,,	Pollock, W.
*7053	,,	Polson, E. G.
7297	,,	Polson, J. A.
1413	,,	Poole, A.
*6332	,,	Poole, F.
1786	,,	Poole, F. T.
*3187	,,	Pooley, E.
1787	,,	Poore, F. W.
1418	,,	Pope, T. H.
*1599	,,	Popoff, A.
*2182	,,	Popplewell, J.
5760	,,	Popplewell, J. L.
1164	,,	Potiels, J. E.
4064	,,	Porteils, W.
*4547	,,	Porter, A. E.
4544	,,	Porter, C. H.
665	,,	Porter, C.
4546	,,	Porter, S. G.
3117	,,	Porter, W. C.
363	,,	Potter, F.
1788	,,	Powe, N. V.
7536	,,	Powell, A.
4865	,,	Powell, A. R.

168	,,	Powell, E.		6399	,,	Quigley, C. J.
362	,,	Powell, J. H. (M.S.M.)		1790	,,	Quinlan, E. J.
				*1372	,,	Quinn, J.
65805	,,	Power, A.		1791	,,	Quinn, J.
1289	Sgt	Power, S.		5163	,,	Quinlan, J. F.
3183	,,	Power, T.		*2894	,,	Quinn, J. M.
*1569	Pte	Power, W. J.		3975	,,	Quinn, L.
1165	,,	Powys, A. G.		5725	,,	Quinn, W. Y.
5721	,,	Pratt, A. J.		*2574	,,	Quirk, W.
*1166	,,	Pratt, F. C.		6559	,,	Quirk, W. J.
2859	,,	Pratt, J. A.				
2970	,,	Preece, W. E.		2215	Sgt	Rabbidge, E. P.
7051	,,	Prendergast, J.		5164	Pte	Radcliffe, O.
*365	,,	Preston, G.		*7061	,,	Radford, E. G.
2774	Cpl	Preston, W. G.		*175	,,	Radford, J. E.
*798	,,	Price, A.		*170	,,	Rados, P.
59577	Pte	Price, E. J. H.		7544	,,	Rae, J.
5162	,,	Price, R.		2895	,,	Raftry, A.
*1368	,,	Price, S.		1607	,,	Raines, R. J.
*1169	,,	Prideau, G. R.		*2012	,,	Raistick, H.
*2775	,,	Prideaux, M. H.		3972	,,	Ralph, L. A.
3190	,,	Primmer, L. G.		2896	,,	Ralph, V.
1370	,,	Prince, J.		7301	,,	Ralphs, S. W. B.
1419	,,	Prince, E.		2670	,,	Ramsbottom, J.
*2666	,,	Prior, J. A.		*1421	,,	Ramsbottom, J. A.
3111	,,	Prieston, R. J.				
967	L/Cpl	Pritchard, C. A.		1292	,,	Rand, D. C.
*1369	Pte	Prutton, F.		2897	,,	Ranken, G. A.
60	,,	Pryce, D.		2673	,,	Rankin, E.
1163	,,	Pryke, C. A.		1618	,,	Rankine, W. H.
3182	,,	Pryor, G. S.		4284	,,	Ranson, A. W.
3189	,,	Pryor, J. H.		*1664	,,	Ratcliffe, J. P.
3887	L/Cpl	Pugh, A.		*1170	,,	Rathie, A. A.
4959	Pte	Pullen, C.		3125	,,	Ratley, L. C.
1167	,,	Pullen, G. A. R.		16	C.S.M.	Ravell, D. (M.M.)
1417	,,	Purcell, T.				
1602	,,	Purdon, A. A.		*6340	Pte	Raven, A. C.
7797	,,	Purdon, A. H.		6606	,,	Raven, H. V.
6334	,,	Purdue, L. E.		1428	,,	Raven, M.
5725	,,	Purser, H.		*2731	,,	Ravoline, D. S.
5726	L/Cpl	Putre, J. (M.M.)		5728	,,	Rawnsley, A. E.
				6088	,,	Rawnsley, T. W.
*1201	Pte	Putt, A. S.		775	,,	Ray, S. N.
169	,,	Pyman, W. S. J.		4283	,,	Raymone, C.
2005	,,	Pyke, —		31	,,	Raymond, H. T.
875	,,	Pyne, J. J.			,,	Raymond, M. J.
				2995	,,	Raymond, W. E.

SGT. A. H. SECCOMBE,
D.C.M.

PTE G. A. E GILBERT,
M.M. AND BAR

PTE C. CLUTTERBUCK,
D.C.M., M.M.

CPL. R. W. DRUERY,
D.C.M.

PTE P. H. WARD,
D.C.M., M.M.

SGT. J. H. THOMPSON,
D.C.M.

PTE G. ABRAHAM,
D.C.M.

PTE A. FARMER, D.C.M.

14 IN. GUN CAPTURED BY 3RD BATTALION AT ARCY WOOD

Photo: *Aust. War Memorial Museum.*

1607	„	Raynes, R. J.	5167	„	Ries, C.
3212	„	Rayner, E.	*5731	„	Richards, C.
2981	„	Read, A.	562	L/Cpl	Richards, G.
1075	„	Read, A. G.	*6560	Pte	Richards, H.
1617	„	Read, C. S.	*6342	„	Richards, H. M.
1083	Sgt	Read, J.	3120	W.O.	Richards, J. W.
6561	Pte	Reardon, P. W.	65822	Pte	Richards, W. W.
*4614	„	Reckless, H. W.	624	„	Richardson, E. J.
*1425	„	Reece, E.	290	C.Q.M.S.	Richardson, E. L.
7062	„	Reece, S. R.			
*2220	„	Reedy, A. A.	*171	Pte	Richardson, F.
5167	„	Rees, C.	2372	„	Richardson, J. H.
7364	„	Rees, G.			
7306	„	Rees, J. P.	65821	„	Rickard, H.
2739	„	Reeves, D. F.	2861	„	Ricketts, A. J.
551	„	Reeves, G. W. H.	*1373	„	Riddle, G.
1292	„	Reeves, L. J.	4553	„	Riddle, L.
7303	„	Redden, C. H.	1426	Sgt	Riddell, R. C.
2784	„	Redden, G. F.	*7302	Pte	Ridley, A. G.
2014	„	Redfearn, M.	2673	„	Rieson, J. H.
1803	„	Redfern, W.	2903	„	Rigby, N.
6562	„	Redman, C. W.	2893	„	Riley, D.
2218	W.O.	Regan, C. A. (M.S.M.)	*2785	„	Riley, F.
			*2221	„	Riley, J.
65878	Pte	Regan, K. F.	3889	„	Riley, L. R.
6815	„	Regan, R. G.	*1619	„	Rilot, J. C.
1172	„	Reid, A. W.	6394	„	Rinkin, C. C.
7300	„	Reid, R.	177	„	Ritchards, B. R.
*1862	„	Reid, G. T.	176	Sgt	Ritchie, F. E. L. (M.M.)
3123	„	Reid, J. A.			
6084	Sgt	Reid, M. D.	*1793	Cpl	Ritchie, L. G. (M.M.)
*3201	Pte	Reid, W. F.			
3274	„	Rendall, J. C.	2864	Pte	Ritchie, S. G.
174	„	Renehan, M. J.	*5169	„	Rivers, G. T.
6563	„	Rennick, R. J.	368	„	Rix, J. C.
1575	Cpl	Rennie, T.	5168	„	Rixon, J. O. M.
1574	Pte	Rennie, T. C.	*513	„	Rixon, W. K.
5165	„	Retmock, W. T.	7543	„	Rizzo, C.
*1422	„	Reynolds, A.	7064	„	Roach, C. H.
*2207	„	Reynolds, E.	*2458	„	Roach, J. A.
*1171	„	Reynolds, F.	*2781	„	Roach, J. H.
1804	„	Reynalds, J. A.	7546	„	Roach, J. H.
*367	„	Reynolds, J. D.	1172	„	Roach, W. H.
1792	„	Reynolds, L. G.	2416	„	Robbie, N. W. J.
*369	L/Cpl	Rhodes, J.	3158	„	Robens, E. N.
3115	Pte	Rhodes, T. R.	65817	„	Robert, F. L.
1572	„	Rice, W.	774	„	Roberts, F. C. P.

AA

4065	„	Roberts, H.		*4549	Sgt	Robinson, S.
83	Sgt	Roberts, J.		1424	Pte	Robinson, T.
3290	„	Roberts, J. L.		2214	Sgt	Robinson, W. E.
		(D.C.M., M.M.)		6092	Pte	Robson, D. C.
*968	Pte	Roberts, J. M.		2422	„	Robson, E. A.
*4554	„	Roberts, J. T.		7371	„	Roche, J. C.
*570	Cpl	Roberts, N.		1610	„	Rochester, F.
1423	Pte	Roberts, P. J.		2772	„	Rochrig, J. P.
773	„	Roberts, R.		1376	„	Rodgers, A.
2792	„	Roberts, R.		4653	„	Rodgers, E.
*4555	„	Roberts, R. H.		2898	„	Rodgers, E. B.
*3973	„	Roberts, R. O.		4569	„	Rodgers, G.
*1796	Sgt	Roberts, S. A.		*3200	„	Rodgers, W.
1169	Pte	Roberts, S. V.		6427	„	Roe, C.
2184	„	Roberts, T.		4224	„	Rogan, G. F.
6344	„	Roberts, V. G.		*4278	„	Rogers, R. C.
6814	„	Roberts, W. A.		2987	„	Rogers, W.
3119	„	Roberts, W. J.		7304	„	Rogers, W. J.
*2403	„	Robertson, A.		2902	Cpl	Rogerson, A. G.
1168	„	Robertson, A. C		*6083	Pte	Rohan, J. C.
5429	„	Robertson, A. H.		*1613	„	Rolbin, H.
*7365	„	Robertson, H.		1273	„	Rolfe, S. E.
2100	„	Robertson, H. G.		*1173	„	Rollins, E.
3199	„	Robertson, J. C.		5172	„	Rome, G.
*803	Cpl	Robertson, K.		2989	„	Rootes, H. L.
*5774	Pte	Robertson, R. H.		6133	„	Roper, V. M.
397	„	Robertson, T. G.		*4552	„	Roper, W.
2217	„	Robertson, W.		2901	„	Roscoe, S.
2778	Cpl	Robertson, W.		392	„	Rose, A. J.
*173	Pte	Robertson, W. J.		*1797	„	Rose, O.
7807	„	Robins, W. E. J.		1087	Cpl	Rose, W. H. C.
4280	„	Robinson, A. E.		2102	Pte	Rosengard,
7299	„	Robinson, A. E.				J. C. E.
1427	„	Robinson, A. W.				
4066	„	Robinson, C.		2782	„	Rosengren, H.
111	Sgt	Robinson, G.		2015	„	Rosengren, S.
3124	Pte	Robinson, H.		5812	„	Ross, A. B.
1614	„	Robinson, J.		7366	„	Ross, A. C.
2262	„	Robinson, J.		553	Sgt	Ross, D.
5730	„	Robinson, J.		162	„	Ross, F. T.
*1077	„	Robinson, J. A.		1504	Pte	Ross, G.
3424	Cpl	Robinson,		1609	„	Ross, G.
		J. A. R.		3118	„	Ross, H.
7547	Pte	Robinson,		5775	L/Cpl	Ross, H. H.
		J. A. L.		*1170	Pte	Ross, J.
2959	„	Robinson, J. S.		6090	„	Ross, K. H.
1573	„	Robinson, L.		1794	„	Ross, W. P. A.

*1089	Sgt	Rosser, R. W.		5174	L/Cpl	Sackley, E.
1611	Pte	Rossiter, J. R.		5175	Pte	Sackley, J. T.
*1171	,,	Rotton, G. H. E.		*5176	,,	Sackley, W. J.
2868	,,	Roughley, H. M.		*1078	,,	Sale, H. M.
*1795	,,	Rout, C. E.		975	,,	Salisbury, C.
*1798	,,	Rowen, D.		2018	,,	Salisbury, J. C.
2759	,,	Rowan, E.		89	Sgt	Salisbury, W. M.
3410	,,	Rowe, A. R.		*3894	Pte	Salmon, C.
1575	,,	Rowe, G.		*1182	,,	Sames, A. A.
*6086	,,	Rowell, T.		4067	,,	Sams, J. W.
4004	,,	Rowlandson, C.		1434	,,	Samuel, W.
*4001	,,	Rowley, H. T.		2103	,,	Samuels, C. J.
7065	,,	Roy, W.		*1429	,,	Sanders, A.
5729	,,	Rudgley, E.		1623	,,	Sanders, R. L.
2862	,,	Ruff, H. T. I.		*6566	,,	Sanderson, I. E.
2904	,,	Rundle, S.		*6565	,,	Sanderson, J. J.
623	,,	Rush, T. G.		6567	,,	Sanderson, T.
*7545	,,	Russel, J.		705	,,	Sands, J. P.
1374	,,	Russel, W.		4556	,,	Santley, P.
1811	,,	Russell, W. H.		3895	,,	Sargent, B.
*2219	,,	Ruthven, S.		2787	,,	Saturley, C. T.
1800	,,	Rutland, C.		*1252	,,	Saunders, A. G.
2783	Sgt	Rutledge, D. G.		2803	,,	Savell, W. E.
7066	Pte	Rutledge, E. S.		4071	,,	Sawle, E. H.
1235	Cpl	Rutledge, J. W.		4615	,,	Sawyer, A. L.
2669	Pte	Rutter, C. L.		6568	,,	Sawyer, N. G.
1578	,,	Ruttle, T.		5543	Cpl	Saxby, E. J.
3121	,,	Ryall, W. P.				(D.C.M.)
*2671	,,	Ryan, A.		*5533	Pte	Saxby, K. K.
2672	,,	Ryan, A. B		506	,,	Say, L.
1802	,,	Ryan, A. J.		4070	,,	Sayer, T. W. F.
1571	,,	Ryan, D. L.		6100	,,	Scaler, V. N. B.
6091	,,	Ryan, E		7317	,,	Scally, C. S.
*2865	,,	Ryan, H. R. V.		7560	,,	Scaysbrook, E. S.
*2216	,,	Ryan, J. B.		2242	,,	Seader, W.
6150	,,	Ryan, J. J.		*2228	,,	Schadel, E. J.
7542	,,	Ryan, J. W.		*383	C.S.M.	Schaffer, W. B.
3371	,,	Ryan, M.		4561	Pte	Schillabeer, E. G.
6564	,,	Ryan, M.		7067	,,	Schneider, W. H
7063	,,	Ryan, M.		*7597	,,	Schofield, W. E.
2373	,,	Ryan, P.		1386	Cpl	Schomberg, J. H.
131	,,	Ryan, T.		2438	Sgt	Schoder, C. G.
4551	,,	Ryan, T. F.		3127	Pte	Schroder, J. D.
2726	,,	Ryan, T. V.		*4557	,,	Schumutter, C. V.
366	,,	Ryan, W. J.		3136	,,	Scotson, J.
1616	,,	Ryan, W. J.				

493	„	Scott, A.
*1174	L/Cpl	Scott, C.
977	Pte	Scott, C. C.
5739	A/Sgt	Scott, C. O.
178	Pte	Scott, H. J.
3269	„	Scott, J. (M.M.)
3899	„	Scott, J.
7318	„	Scott, J. S.
1580	„	Scott, J. R. B.
1665	L/Cpl	Scott, J. T.
1311	Pte	Scott, L. W.
336	„	Scott, P.
1631	„	Scott, R.
1866	„	Scott, R.
2866	„	Scott, R.
1160	„	Scott, S. J.
7310	„	Scott, T.
4564	„	Scott, W. A. A.
4559	„	Scott, W. H.
*1821	„	Scott, W. P.
2682	„	Scown, A. T.
*6874	„	Scudds, R. H.
*5740	„	Scullin, J. P.
4075	„	Scully, M. B.
370	Bglr	Seach, P. C.
*3223	Pte	Seale, S.
2924	„	Seaman, G. A.
3222	„	Searle, H.
3214	„	Searle, H.
3213	„	Searle, R.
6100	„	Seater, P. N. B.
7560	„	Seazbrook, E. S.
6818	„	Seckold, A. T.
3209	„	See, D.
1579	Sgt	Seccombe, A. H. (D.C.M.)
*485	Sgt	Sedman, R. H.
142	Pte	Seidel, A.
6093	„	Sellars, A.
5177	„	Sellars, J.
6098	„	Selmes, H.
6095	„	Selmes, R. J. G.
7811	„	Selmes, W. J.
59591	„	Semple, A. B.
*2224	Sgt	Senior, S. G.
971	Pte	Seukup, F. H.
5178	„	Sevenoaks, H.
3217	„	Sewell, G.
7813	„	Sewell, G. E.
6819	„	Sexton, J. V.
*529	„	Sexton, N.
7321	„	Seymour, H.
1820	„	Seymour, J.
1867	„	Seymour, T.
7557	„	Shakespear, A. J.
*2790	„	Shanahan, A.
1671	„	Shannon, F. P.
*2020	„	Sharmen, H. J.
2069	„	Sharwood, F. C.
5179	„	Sharp, C. R.
*557	„	Sharp, F.
298	„	Sharp, G. R.
59587	„	Sharpe, A. W.
1806	„	Sharpe, B.
*1306	Cpl	Sharpe, C. H.
2374	Pte	Sharpe, E.
7554	„	Sharpe, G. A.
298	„	Sharpe, G. R.
*1385	„	Sharpe, J.
2806	„	Sharpe, J.
2063	„	Sharpe, S. F.
3900	„	Shaw, E. F.
2919	„	Shaw, F.
2907	„	Shaw, J. A.
7561	„	Shaw, R.
2906	„	Shaw, R. M.
*970	„	Shaw, W. J.
2223	„	Sheaff, R.
3212	„	Shearer, F.
7555	„	Shearman, J.
7588	„	Sheedy, A. T.
2923	„	Sheedy, C. J.
*2396	„	Sheldon, J. E.
5734	„	Sheldon, L. J.
*2791	„	Shelley, J. E.
3131	„	Shelley, M. R.
2908	Dvr	Shepherd, C.
3202	Pte	Shepherd, H.
179	„	Shepherd, L.
*2677	„	Shepherd, P. W.
495	„	Shepherd, R.
4654	„	Shepherd, S. H.
3901	„	Shepherd, R. H.
7314	„	Shepherd, T.

6817	,,	Sherer, A.	186	,,	Sindeeff, N.
*7309	,,	Sheridan, J.	7068	,,	Singe, J. C.
3445	Cpl	Sheridan, N. L. C.	1404	,,	Singh, G.
			6571	,,	Sippel, H. C.
3903	Pte	Sheridan, R. F.	6570	,,	Sippel, L. C.
*969	,,	Sherman, F. P.	976	,,	Sirl, J. A.
1180	,,	Sherwood, J.	3321	,,	Sivyer, G. W.
59593	,,	Sherwood, W. E.	2460	,,	Skeen, J. R.
6569	,,	Shields, R.	5241	,,	Skeen, P. J.
*6345	,,	Shiels, E. M.	*6357	,,	Skelton, W.
7322	,,	Shiner, W. H. A.	*777	,,	Skinner, J. R.
*289	Cpl	Shipp, A. N.	2100	,,	Skinner, W.
7069	Pte	Shoobert, J. B.	7548	,,	Skou, J. C.
699	,,	Shoobridge, E.	2678	,,	Slaney, J.
*682	Sgt	Shooter, H.	6572	,,	Sleaman, T. W. A.
*1628	Pte	Shore, P. P.			
2988	,,	Shorey, G. R.	2809	,,	Sleeper, W.
2679	,,	Short, A.	1379	,,	Sloan, A. H.
3310	,,	Schultz, E. H.	1378	,,	Sloan, J. S.
1182	Cpl	Shurmer, J. W.	3137	,,	Sly, R.
2227	Pte	Siddins, N. M.	2910	,,	Small, H.
1632	,,	Siddins, B. L.	65826	,,	Small, T.
2686	,,	Siggers, C. H.	*975	,,	Smalley, E. J.
1178	,,	Silver, E. A.	6573	,,	Smart, E.
5181	,,	Simcox, F. W.	549	,,	Smart, H. E.
5180	,,	Simmonds, F. G.	1496	,,	Smillie, J. C.
3465	,,	Simmonds, H. J.	3201	,,	Smith, A.
6102	,,	Simmonds, L. H.	4667	,,	Smith, A. A.
3126	,,	Simmons, M.	5737	,,	Smith, A. C.
7047	,,	Simms, E. N.	6348	,,	Smith, A. H.
120	,,	Simpkins, F. G.	*3978	Cpl	Smith, A. J.
780	,,	Simpkins, F. G.	*373	L/Cpl	Smith, A. J. St C.
983	,,	Simon, W. H.			
*1383	,,	Simons, R. C.	2557	Pte	Smith, A. W.
1456	,,	Simpson, A.	7584	,,	Smith, A. W.
4655	,,	Simpson, A. H.	1583	,,	Smith, B. C.
6580	,,	Simpson, J.	3374	,,	Smith, C.
1176	,,	Simpson, J. R.	6575	,,	Smith, C. E.
*1178	,,	Simpson, S. J	3135	,,	Smith, C. L.
*1082	,,	Simpson, W.	4074	,,	Smith, C. R.
2459	,,	Sims, H.	3937	,,	Smith, C. R.
7559	,,	Simson, E. G.	2680	Cpl	Smith, C. S.
4666	,,	Sinclair, E.	3937	Pte	Smith, C. S.
*4299	,,	Sinclair, N. R. J.	50948	,,	Smith, C. S.
2909	,,	Sinclair, T. C.	*183	,,	Smith, C. W.
4616	,,	Sinclair, W.	7319	,,	Smith, D.
2054	,,	Sinclair, G.	*2953	,,	Smith, D. A.

1305	,,	Smith, E. C.	1430	,,	Smith, R.
6360	,,	Smith, E. C.	*3910	L/Cpl	Smith, R.
*5227	,,	Smith, E. J.	4558	Pte	Smith, R.
*5184	L/Cpl	Smith, E. K.	*5445	,,	Smith, R. C.
*2719	Pte	Smith, E. S.	1808	,,	Smith, R. H.
*1085	,,	Smith, F.	6886	,,	Smith, R. J.
1809	,,	Smith, F.	1864	,,	Smith, R. L.
*3132	,,	Smith, F.	*371	,,	Smith, R. W.
1380	,,	Smith, F. E.	*3221	,,	Smith, S. C.
*2815	,,	Smith, F. L.	*7558	,,	Smith, S. E.
3912	,,	Smith, F. W. C.	1433	,,	Smith, S. H.
182	,,	Smith, G. T.	5800	,,	Smith, S. L.
982	,,	Smith, H.	2912	,,	Smith, T. B.
4617	,,	Smith, H.	1627	,,	Smith, T. C.
*5738	,,	Smith, H.	7312	,,	Smith, W.
4000	,,	Smith, H. C.	6096	,,	Smith, W. C.
2913	,,	Smith, H. J.	7311	,,	Smith, W. D.
*6358	,,	Smith, H. J.	2720	,,	Smith, W. F.
6574	,,	Smith, H. C.	*3908	,,	Smith, W. L.
1181	,,	Smith, H. S.	*1625	,,	Smith, W. R.
*6871	,,	Smith, H. S.	6396	,,	Smithers, G.
*3909	,,	Smith, H. T.	3220	,,	Smithson, J. W.
1450	,,	Smith, J.	*7562	,,	Smyth, H. T.
*2022	,,	Smith, J.	2676	,,	Smyth, E. G.
*2186	,,	Smith, J.	*1175	Cpl	Smythe, H. A.
*6352	,,	Smith, J.	2461	Pte	Smythe, P.
7553	,,	Smith, J.	59586	,,	Snell, D.
2226	,,	Smith, J.	*1246	L/Cpl	Sneyd, A. W.
181	,,	Smith, J. A.	5185	Cpl	Snipe, G. T.
*127	,,	Smith, J. E.	*2800	Pte	Snook, A. W.
2019	,,	Smith, J. F.	3717	,,	Snow, H. W.
1179	,,	Smith, J. H.	395	,,	Solomon, M. L.
5761	,,	Smith, J. H. S.	2375	,,	Solomon, S.
3977	,,	Smith, J. J. M.	3357	,,	Solomon, S.
7074	,,	Smith, J. T.	*1087	,,	Solton, H. H. F.
6103	,,	Smith, J. V. L.	2099	,,	Sommers, T. W.
180	,,	Smith, L.	6577	,,	Sone, J. W.
6576	,,	Smith, L.	*5187	,,	Sorenson, H. L.
3134	,,	Smith, L. C.	2807	,,	Souter, A. S.
2446	,,	Smith, M.	778	,,	Souter, D. H.
7324	,,	Smith, O.	1874	,,	South, C. G.
6581	,,	Smith, O. I.	732	,,	South, D.
*1929	,,	Smith, P.	*4069	,,	Southall, A. E.
2244	,,	Smith, P.	6578	,,	Southee, R. R.
*2629	,,	Smith, P.	*7070	,,	Sowerby, J. S.
2675	,,	Smith, P. C.	782	,,	Spalding, J.
1177	,,	Smith, R.	7549	,,	Sparks, E. A.

1811	„	Spedding, J.
6136	„	Speight, A.
*1870	Sgt	Speller, H.
*6099	Cpl	Spence, O.
*891	L/Cpl	Spencer, J. N.
556	Sgt	Spicer, W. H.
7075	Pte	Spilsbury, C. A.
2222	„	Spink, S. N.
59596	„	Spinks, J. W.
376	Cpl	Spratt, H.
3205	Pte	Spriggs, L.
59592	„	Spring, P. G.
*1812	„	Squire, J. C.
1173	„	Squires, J.
*4077	„	Squires, S.
1432	„	Squires, W. T.
3270	„	Stabler, C.
7551	„	Stagg, A. W.
1621	„	Stain, R. A.
6105	„	Stammers, W. E.
7313	Pte	Stanmore, S. F.
*2964	„	Stannard, C. M.
1585	Cpl	Stanwell, F.
2024	Pte	Stanworth, J. A.
*5188	„	Stapleton, J. F.
7071	„	Staub, C.
*539	C.S.M.	Stead, H. F.
*4068	Pte	Steel, J.
3204	„	Steer, G. E.
2810	„	Steinbeck, G. E.
1814	Sgt	Stenson, P. E.
6353	Pte	Stephen, C. A.
1548	„	Stephenson, H. F.
1581	„	Stephenson, J.
3218	„	Stevens, A. H.
3916	„	Stevens, D.
*1813	„	Stevens, E. E.
6129	„	Stevens, F. J.
2916	„	Stevens, E. W.
7316	„	Stevens, G. C.
2917	L/Cpl	Stevens, W. J.
*377	Pte	Stevens, H.
6097	„	Stevenson, E. W.
1582	„	Stevenson, G. A.
*5735	„	Stevenson, J.
974	„	Stevenson, J. F.
293	„	Stevenson, J. G.
7072	„	Stevenson, R. A.
6356	„	Stewart, C.
1301	„	Stewart, C. C.
1622	„	Stewart, C. H.
4080	L/Cpl	Stewart, E. E. L.
3224	Pte	Stewart, L. A. (M.M.)
1085	Sgt	Stewart, M. H.
22	Dvr	Stewart, L. R.
*23	„	Stewart, B.
141	Pte	Stewart, R.
1534	Cpl	Stewart, R.
*2226	Pte	Stewart, R. A.
7552	„	Stewart, R. J.
2225	„	Stewart, R. M.
4563	Cpl	Stewart, T.
1815	Pte	Stewart, W.
7556	„	Stewart, W.
3226	„	Stewart, W. McG.
1816	„	Stick, N. A.
6626	„	Stillwell, A. J.
5189	Cpl	Stinson, J.
*2944	L/Sgt	Stinson, J. B.
*1435	Cpl	Stitt, L. A.
2225	Pte	Stockdale, W. H.
3917	Cpl	Stocker, F. N.
65702	Pte	Stockley, W. J.
3129	„	Stokeld, G.
580	„	Stoker, J.
7076	„	Stokes, E. J.
5736	„	Stokes, L. E.
*1176	„	Stone, R.
*2226	„	Stoneham, P. R.
526	„	Storemont, R. L.
5466	„	Strachan, F. W.
2023	„	Streader, W.
6349	„	Street, J. L.
*1626	„	Streeter, R. C.
*1093	„	Stringfellow, C. W.
6347	„	Stringfellow, E. W.

973	,,	Strong, V.	7328	,, Tagg, W. A.
*6355	,,	Stuart, H. A.	2032	,, Tait, J. J.
2105	,,	Stuart, J.	5743	,, Tait, J. S.
*7550	,,	Stuart, S. F.	188	,, Talbot, W.
1177	,,	Stubbins, W.	*1387	,, Tamblyn, F.
*374	,,	Stubbs, H. R.	5746	,, Tamplin, E. J.
6873	,,	Stubbs, J.	*7329	,, Tanswell, L. V.
*4565	,,	Studdert, J.	*393	Sgt Tanner, A. S.
1436	,,	Studman, W.	1835	Pte Tanner, A. B.
7073	,,	Sturton, E. P.	6366	,, Tanner, B.
2920	,,	Sullivan, A.	1822	,, Taplin, C. J.
1855	,,	Sullivan, C. J.	2440	,, Tapscott, F.
3128	,,	Sullivan, H.	2231	,, Tarling, G. S.
*1584	,,	Sullivan, J. P.	2235	,, Tarling, J. V.
6816	,,	Sullivan, J. R. (M.M.)	2925	,, Tarn, J. T.
			3233	,, Tasker, C. R.
*1817	,,	Sullivan, R. L.	2029	,, Tasker, J.
*3211	,,	Sullivan, W. B.	*2027	,, Tassell, F. E.
7815	,,	Summerell, A.	1391	Sgt Taubman, F.
2889	,,	Summers, P. S.	1633	Pte Taverner, H.
1382	,,	Summersell, F.	2232	,, Taylor, A. C.
59598	,,	Sutherland, L. McG.	4910	,, Taylor, A. H.
			379	,, Taylor, C.
776	,,	Swain, A. J.	509	,, Taylor, C.
1405	Dvr	Swain, A. J.	*1836	,, Taylor, C.
*5742	Pte	Swain, J. W.	59601	,, Taylor, D.
2922	L/Cpl	Swallow, R. C. R.	*2229	,, Taylor, D. W. K.
			1825	,, Taylor, E. C.
6094	Pte	Swan, A.	1899	,, Taylor, E. J.
6354	,,	Swan, F. K.	3188	,, Taylor, E. J.
3133	,,	Swanborough, J. H. E.	1440	,, Taylor, F.
			1507	Cpl Taylor, H. C.
*3206	,,	Swanson, E. J.	*576	Pte Taylor, J.
1819	,,	Sweeney, G.	1097	,, Taylor, J.
7580	,,	Sweeney, J. C.	1185	,, Taylor, J.
6579	,,	Sweeney, J. T.	2510	,, Taylor, J.
4645	,,	Sweeney, L. J.	3141	,, Taylor, J.
4656	,,	Sweeney, L. G.	*1824	,, Taylor, J. A.
185	,,	Sweeney, P.	6586	,, Taylor, L. W.
*1180	,,	Sweeney, T. T.	*6428	,, Taylor, P.
6101	,,	Sweet, A.	105	,, Taylor, R.
2811	,,	Swingler, B. T.	74	,, Taylor, S. A.
184	,,	Sykes, H. A.	2691	Cpl Taylor, V. J.
375	,,	Sykes, H. G.	*1536	Pte Taylor, W.
65825	,,	Sykes, P. J.	2234	,, Taylor, W.
*2812	,,	Sykes, R. P.	6108	,, Taylor, W.
6384	,,	Symonds, D. T.	7077	,, Taylor, W. C.

1089	,,	Taylor, W. H.		2926	Pte	Thompson, S.
1186	,,	Teague, E.		690	,,	Thompson, W.
6824	Cpl	Teague, E.		3138	,,	Thompson, W. E.
6582	Pte	Teale, A. J.				
1125	,,	Teer, E.		785	,,	Thompson, W. E. H. R.
3139	,,	Templeton, A. E.				
*783	,,	Templeton, S. C.		*1185	,,	Thompson, W. H.
1589	,,	Terry, G.		5806	Cpl	Thompson, W. J.
718	Cpl	Tessmer, M. J.		7585	Pte	Thompson, W. L.
*5467	Pte	Thatcher, B.		2824	,,	Thompson, W. W.
*1388	,,	Thew, J. G.				
*1439	,,	Thomas, E. E.		7563	,,	Thorborn, A. D.
*1390	,,	Thomas, E.		*3343	,,	Thorborn, E. R.
*3227	,,	Thomas, F.		5744	L/Cpl	Thorley, E. C.
3231	,,	Thomas, F. G.		3256	Pte	Thorley, L. A.
1635	,,	Thomas, G.		3142	,,	Thorn, W.
*1587	,,	Thomas, J.		6583	,,	Thorne, H. B.
2881	Cpl	Thomas, J. H. (M.M.)		2462	,,	Thornewaite, E.
				2820	,,	Thornton, G. S.
4570	L/Cpl	Thomas, L. (M.M.)		*2030	,,	Thornton, J. H.
				*91	Bglr	Thornton, M. F.
1657	Cpl	Thomas, P. (M.S.M)		1839	Pte	Thorpe, C.
				187	,,	Thorpe, E. W.
3238	Pte	Thomas, R. J.		2817	,,	Thorpe, J.
5777	,,	Thomas, S. G.		*978	,,	Thorpe, R.
7564	,,	Thomas, W.		6363	,,	Thrall, W.
4618	,,	Thomas, W. J.		59540	,,	Thuell, F. J.
*2765	,,	Thomas, W. J.		59641	,,	Thuell, P. J.
3236	,,	Thompson, A. A.		1202	,,	Thurgood, F.
*4908	,,	Thompson, C.		*3459	,,	Thwaite, J. R. L.
1826	Sgt	Thompson, E.				
3140	Pte	Thompson, E. C.		3240	,,	Tighe, F.
2493	,,	Thompson, E. J.		*6107	,,	Tight, M. G.
*6368	,,	Thompson, G.		*2979	Cpl	Tilbrook, W. C.
6365	,,	Thompson, G.		6367	Pte	Tink, R.
2236	,,	Thompson, H.		2825	,,	Tinman, S.
7565	,,	Thompson, J.		*1437	,,	Tipper, R.
*1187	,,	Thompson, J. H.		2826	,,	Titley, T.
748	Sgt	Thompson, J. H. (D.C.M.)		2740	,,	Todd, H. L.
				1830	,,	Tomlinson, J. H. E.
1827	Pte	Thompson, J. S.				
786	Sgt	Thompson, J. W.		1834	,,	Towell, W. M.
4568	Pte	Thompson, J. W.		1586	,,	Towers, J.
65842	,,	Thompson, J. W. H.		2690	Cpl	Townend, C. H.
				2821	Pte	Townend, S. A.
6736	L/Cpl	Thompson, N. B.		2031	,,	Townsend, W. S.
				583	,,	Tracey, V. G.

*5745 ,, Travers, A. L. G.
6409 ,, Travers, N. J.
*976 Cpl Traynor, J. C.
(M.M.)
1099 Pte Treacy, E. J.
*2233 ,, Treffone, H. M.
*1186 C.S.M. Trelease, W. I.
6823 Pte Trewin, W. J.
1389 ,, Trim, H. C.
6137 ,, Trinder, A. C.
5192 ,, Tripp, C.
305 ,, Trotman, G.
304 Cpl Trott, D.
6821 Pte Trotter, A. C.
1100 ,, Truman, R. W.
65837 ,, Tucker, J.
59639 ,, Tuckerman, L. N.
6585 ,, Tubby, H. J.
*980 ,, Tudenham, G. F.
3492 ,, Tull, A.
3232 Cpl Tupper, B. J.
3925 Dvr Turk, I.
6397 Pte Turley, F. W. J.
59642 ,, Turnbull, E.
*5747 ,, Turnbull, E. S.
3927 ,, Turnbull, H.
*2819 ,, Turner, A. A.
*907 Cpl Turner, A. E.
1183 Pte Turner, A. G.
6109 ,, Turner, C.
884 C.S.M. Turner, C. C.
1438 Pte Turner, E.
3455 ,, Turner, H.
5191 ,, Turner, H. J.
*1588 ,, Turner, J. J.
2965 ,, Turner, R. H. M.
1184 ,, Turner, S. C.
2376 Sgt Turner, T. A.
1832 Pte Turner, W.
*1831 ,, Turner, W.
5189 ,, Turner, W.
6111 ,, Turner, W. H.
6584 ,, Turner, W. J.
1503 Cpl Turnham, H. J.

1833 Pte Turpin, F. H.
2693 Sgt Turvey, P.
(D.C.M., M.M.)
Sgt Tutill, T. D. C.
3928 Pte Twopenny, T. N.
2226 ,, Twyman, C.
65838 ,, Tyas, A. E.
1101 ,, Tyler, R. W.
1096 ,, Tymms, F.
3234 ,, Tyson, A. G.

59609 ,, Uebell, C. C.
5453 ,, Ulherr, C. F. F.
2694 ,, Urquhart, W.
4248 ,, Urquhart, R.
4571 L/Cpl Usher, L. N. J.
(M.M.)
380 Pte Upton, W.
4316 ,, Upright, N. J.
*1270 ,, Unverham, H. H.

1382 ,, Vagg, S. P.
6371 ,, Valentine, W. A.
*4572 ,, Vandenbergh, B.
2828 ,, Vandenbergh, W. C.
*789 ,, Varcoe, A. E.
7567 ,, Vaschini, C. H.
2469 ,, Vass, D.
6113 ,, Vaughan, F. T. G.
2033 ,, Vaughan, J. H.
1839 ,, Vaughn, J. W.
1461 ,, Veale, V.
7330 ,, Verge, W. G.
*5193 ,, Vial, E.
1189 ,, Vidler, T.
6876 ,, Vieira, F.
*738 ,, Vile, A. E.
*788 ,, Vile, P.
*1188 ,, Viles, W. J.
4619 ,, Vines, C. R. R.
2695 ,, Vincent, G.
*1837 Cpl Vincent, J.
*189 Pte Vincent, J. H.
1838 ,, Vogt, P. C.

6587	,,	Vokes, B.
*1187	,,	Voss, J. W.
59603	,,	Voysey, L. P.
2932	,,	Wackett, C. W.
*6423	,,	Wade, G. M.
*2439	,,	Wade, T.
2696	,,	Wade, W. G.
1194	,,	Wadie, C. R.
5194	,,	Wainwright, J. A.
*4620	,,	Wait, J. F.
3931	,,	Wakeman, A.
*1444	,,	Wakfer, G. F.
2042	L/Cpl	Walden, G. H.
7063	Pte	Walden, S. E.
5454	,,	Waldock, W.
3148	,,	Waldon, H. V.
575	,,	Waldron, J.
1643	,,	Walford, A. V.
1193	,,	Walker, A. H.
59615	,,	Walker, A. H.
5195	,,	Walker, B.
*569	,,	Walker, C.
1595	,,	Walker, D.
1842	,,	Walker, F.
*1645	,,	Walker, G. H.
*2038	,,	Walker, H.
1102	,,	Walker, H. W.
4574	,,	Walker, J.
*2238	Cpl	Walker, J. M.
3245	Pte	Walker, J. W.
*3832	,,	Walker, L. F.
972	,,	Walker, L. P.
4586	,,	Walker, R. G.
4087	,,	Walker, S. B.
2703	,,	Walker, W. E.
3929	,,	Wall, P. J.
1636	,,	Wallace, A.
3156	,,	Wallace, M.
59644	,,	Wallace, F. H.
4576	,,	Wallace, R. E.
*2848	,,	Wallace, W. J. (M.M.)
3243	,,	Wallis, G. W.
*958	,,	Walls, I.
7339	,,	Walpole, J.
7346	,,	Walpole, L.
1840	,,	Walpole, W.
6375	,,	Walsh, B.
*6384	,,	Walsh, G. F.
797	Cpl	Walsh, L. A.
*3477	Sgt	Walsh, S. N.
1103	Pte	Walsh, R.
7080	,,	Walsh, R. G.
1190	Cpl	Walsh, T. M.
*3930	Pte	Walsh, V. H.
4584	,,	Walsh, W.
4565	L/Cpl	Walsh, W. J.
65844	Pte	Walsh, W. R.
6125	,,	Walter, A. E.
*1295	Cpl	Walter, C. W.
3266	Pte	Walters, C. V.
5751	,,	Walters, T. A.
992	,,	Walton, C. A.
2347	,,	Walton, J.
7595	,,	Warfield, W. O.
4581	,,	Wanless, P. S.
7570	,,	Wann, J. T.
1536	,,	Ward, A. E.
2041	,,	Ward, C.
6588	,,	Ward, E. J.
*7374	,,	Ward, G.
65853	,,	Ward, G. A.
3933	,,	Ward, J.
6589	,,	Ward, J.
7081	,,	Ward, J.
*1592	,,	Ward, J. C.
*1393	,,	Ward, J. H.
3932	,,	Ward, P.
1843	Sgt	Ward, P. H. (D.C.M., M.M.)
567	Pte	Ward, S.
988	,,	Ward, W.
7369	,,	Wardrop, R.
6410	,,	Ware, J. A.
7086	,,	Warham, W. H.
3934	L/Cpl	Warn, R. G.
3378	Pte	Warren, C. T.
3144	,,	Warren, F.
*7093	,,	Warren, H. R.
6832	,,	Warren, J. D.
6117	,,	Wasson, J. J.
*1400	,,	Wasson, R. J.

*2049 „ Wasson, W. T.
59607 „ Waterford, R. K.
*3261 „ Waterhouse, C.
*3153 „ Waters, A. E.
1844 „ Waters, J.
2699 L/Cpl Waters, O. C.
3268 Sgt Watkins, J. W.
(M.M.)
793 „ Watsford, S. L.
*1191 Cpl Watson, A. G.
3242 „ Watson, A. W.
790 Pte Watson, L. A.
58604 „ Watson, O. B.
2490 „ Watson, R.
3935 Cpl Watson, R. E.
981 Pte Watson, T.
6381 „ Watt, A. A.
3255 „ Watt, J. G.
*1660 „ Watt, R. A.
*385 „ Watt, S. A.
6372 „ Watts, E. J.
5748 „ Watts, S. C. M.
*24 Dvr Watterson, J. W.
6826 Pte Wattson, W. J.
7090 „ Wayman, W.
3154 „ Wearne, H. S.
6833 „ Weatherley, C. J.
2701 Cpl Weaver, H. J.
2931 Pte Weaver, T. G.
2050 „ Webb, A. M.
1195 „ Webb, C.
2189 „ Webb, G.
7734 „ Webb
2463 „ Webb, H. W.
*1639 „ Webb, L.
193 „ Webb, W.
2994 „ Webb, V. E.
3936 „ Webb, W. C.
5755 „ Webber, T. F.
*1845 „ Webster, A. W.
1646 „ Webster, H. V.
*3937 Cpl Webster, R.
3254 Pte Webster, W.
3938 „ Weeden, H.
*3262 „ Weeding, A. G.
6590 „ Weeks, H. W.
2188 „ Weeks, W. E.

2101 Sgt Weger, E. C.
(D.C.M.)
1402 Pte Weir, A. E.
2303 „ Weir, D. C.
*3939 „ Weir, G. E.
*7089 „ Weldon, J.
2705 „ Weitzel, F.
382 „ Welch, H.
7084 „ Wellings, A.
527 „ Wells, J.
75 „ Wells, T. B.
1137 Sgt Wells, W. E.
(C. DE G.)
3246 Pte Welsh, F. C.
6593 „ Wenke, D.
792 „ Wennerbom,
E. C.
*6592 „ Werner, E. W.
*6591 „ Werner, N. H.
7342 „ West, A.
12744 „ West, A. E.
3150 „ West, F. H.
*6144 „ West, H. J.
2037 „ West S. H. J.
2700 „ West, W. D.
2934 „ Westerberg,
V. W.
4582 „ Westhead, W. B.
2378 „ Westlake, H. B.
7273 „ Whalan, A. M.
*2043 „ Whaley, P.
1447 „ Whatmough,
W. J.
1593 „ Wheatley,
W. H. K.
4089 L/Cpl Whichelo, A. G.
786 Pte Whitt, R. P.
4930 „ Whit, R. P.
5807 „ White, A. N.
1497 „ White, A.
3377 „ White, B. G.
6594 „ White, B.
2035 „ White, B. A.
987 Cpl White, C. R.
1644 Pte White, D.
1543 Bglr White, F. C.
3320 Sgt White, G. B.

NOMINAL ROLL

7087	Pte	White, H. E.
5808	,,	White, I.
1193	,,	White, J.
7341	,,	White, J. C.
795	,,	White, M. H.
6282	,,	White, P. A.
890	,,	White, S. H. V.
*985	,,	White, W. J.
5795	,,	Whitby, D. D.
4088	,,	Whitby, G. E.
*6398	,,	Whitburn, S.
3155	,,	Whitehead, W. J.
7345	,,	Whiteman, A. C.
4657	,,	Whiteman, E. H.
7572	,,	Whitfield, K. R.
3941	,,	Whiting, E.
*3943	,,	Whiting, H.
*3942	,,	Whiting, W. L.
6121	,,	Whitmore, J.
990	,,	Whittaker, E.
2320	,,	Whittaker, A. T.
3152	,,	Whittingham, F. J.
3349	,,	Whittley, W.
*3272	,,	Whittle, D.
3263	,,	Whittell, R. V.
1192	Cpl	Whitten, H. C.
3151	Pte	Whitney, M.
3944	,,	Whitworth, G. H.
*3259	,,	Whyborn, A. L.
7085	,,	Whyte, V. L.
2464	,,	Wickham, A.
7846	Sgt	Wickham, A. G.
702	Pte	Wicks, J. B.
5234	,,	Wicks, A. W. K.
2494	,,	Wienrabe, L. B.
*1941	,,	Wiggins, A. G.
7078	,,	Wiles, H.
*7082	,,	Wiles, N. J.
2237	,,	Wiles, W.
191	,,	Wilkin, A.
192	,,	Wilkins, A.
1758	,,	Wilkins, P.
2265	,,	Wilkins, W. B.
4072	,,	Wilkinson, E. C.
984	,,	Wilkinson, E. J.
7331	,,	Wilkinson, H. J.
59606	,,	Wilkinson, H. J.
*1196	,,	Wilkinson, J.
2040	L/Cpl	Wilkinson, J.
2702	Pte	Wilkinson, W. R.
*3244	,,	Wilkinson, W. J. H.
2671	Dvr	Willacy, C.
1195	Pte	Willcock, L. B.
*7571	,,	Williams, A.
1194	Cpl	Williams, A. G.
723	Pte	Williams, C. H.
5753	,,	Williams, E.
3149	,,	Williams, E. A.
287	Cpl	Williams, E. R.
198	Pte	Williams, E. T.
7344	,,	Williams, F.
190	,,	Williams, F. C.
387	,,	Williams, G.
1448	,,	Williams, G.
7575	,,	Williams, G. L.
6612	,,	Williams, G. S.
6112	,,	Williams, G. S.
154	,,	Williams, G. J.
4084	,,	Williams, H.
7091	,,	Williams, H. A.
3920	,,	Williams, H. H.
4086	Sgt	Williams, H. W.
2233	Pte	Williams, J.
3157	,,	Williams, J.
*7578	,,	Williams, J. H. P.
2721	,,	Williams, J. N.
2845	,,	Williams, J. W.
4083	,,	Williams, J. W.
6595	,,	Williams, N. V.
1156	Cpl	Williams, R. (D.C.M.)
1188	Pte	Williams, R.
*904	,,	Williams, R.
2482	,,	Williams, R. A.
3380	,,	Williams, R. J.
1445	,,	Williams, S.
383	,,	Williams, T. J.
6126	,,	Williams, T.
*1197	,,	Williamson, A. J. R.
*6596	,,	Williamson, F.
*1594	,,	Williamson, H.

2463	,, Williamson, H.	1637	,, Wilson, R. E.
5465	,, Williamson, W. M.	1441	,, Wilson, S.
		1190	,, Wilson, S. W.
521	,, Williamson, T.	2190	,, Wilson, T.
2671	,, Willicey, C.	*76	,, Wilson, T.
*77	,, Willis, A. J.	2704	,, Wilson, V.
906	,, Willis, C.	7568	,, Wilson, W. J.
*3267	,, Wills, H.	5199	,, Wilson, W.
3976	,, Wills, W.	2192	,, Wilton, R.
1846	,, Willis, J. H.	*991	,, Winch, H. F. C.
546	,, Willis, S. J.	3252	,, Winchester, B.
3846	,, Willis, W.	*1852	,, Winder, S. H.
5197	,, Wilmot, A. E. H.	*1189	,, Winslett, H.
*32716	,, Wilmot, C.	4085	,, Winsor, A.
*1847	,, Wilson, A.	4583	,, Winsor, H.
2239	,, Wilson, A.	6598	,, Wise, C.
2847	L/Cpl Wilson, —.	*2511	,, Wise, G. A. N.
4659	Pte Wilson, A.	6599	,, Wiltshire, R.
6827	,, Wilson, C. H.	*2971	,, Wiseman, V. M.
65848	,, Wilson, A. W.	1106	,, Wishhart, H. W.
7574	,, Wilson, C.	2	O.R. Sgt Witworth, S. N.
*2191	,, Wilson, C. P.		
1192	L/Cpl Wilson, C. W.	*6120	Pte Wisted, G. F.
1850	Pte Wilson, E. A.	804	L/Sgt Wolsey, E. J.
*794	,, Wilson, E. R.	3147	Pte Womsley, V. O.
2404	,, Wilson, F.	3145	,, Wood, A. J.
3159	,, Wilson, F.	19	Sgt Wood, A. W. (M.M.)
3921	,, Wilson, F. J.		
2935	,, Wilson, F. O.	7576	Pte Wood, E. C. S.
2262	,, Wilson, H.	2039	,, Wood, H.
*6597	,, Wilson, J.	194	,, Wood, L. C.
6114	,, Wilson, J.	3248	,, Wood, W.
5198	,, Wilson, J.	7340	,, Woods, A. E.
4326	,, Wilson, J.	*2831	,, Woods, C. H.
1849	,, Wilson, J.	*6379	,, Woods, F. M.
1851	,, Wilson, J.	59608	,, Woods, H.
1442	,, Wilson, J.	*4585	,, Woods, L.
1395	,, Wilson, J.	*2442	C.S.M. Woods, W.
2083	,, Wilson, J.	5072	Pte Woods, W. H.
*3	S/Dmr Wilson, J.	1446	,, Woodberry, T. F.
3260	Pte Wilson, J. H.	124	Cpl Woodbridge, T. F.
1654	,, Wilson, L. E.		
6383	,, Wilson, M.	7569	Pte Woodcroft, G. C.
6122	,, Wilson, M.	59614	,, Woodcock, A. L.
3250	L/Cpl Wilson, N. E. D.	3850	,, Woodgate, W.
		65855	,, Woodland, W. J.
*2068	Pte Wilson, R. H. L.	989	,, Woodruff, H.
		2240	,, Woodward, W.

*2838	,,	Woodward, W. J.	1394	,,	Wycherly, R.
7088	,,	Woofinden, J. E.	5779	,,	Wyer, L. I.
7079	,,	Woollett, A. E. A.	*4580	,,	Wylie, J.
			1637	,,	Wyllie, C.
5200	,,	Woollett, L. R.	2237	,,	Wyles, W.
59612	,,	Woolley, K.	59605	,,	Wynne, D. L.
2836	,,	Wooten, W. A.			
4648	,,	Worboys, P. P.	7095	Pte	Yabsley, J. J.
*4577	,,	Worley, R.	7348	,,	Yanz, F.
1591	,,	Worth, W.	6388	L/Cpl	Yanz, J. L.
*1590	,,	Worthington, R. V.	2242	Pte	Yard, R. P.
			*2243	,,	Yates, T. R.
7337	,,	Wortley, G. T.	7094	,,	Yeo, D. H.
*1107	,,	Wrench, W. G.	*1396	Sgt	York, F. (M.M.)
2697	,,	Wright, A. J.	195	L/Cpl	York, J.
*6119	,,	Wright, A. J.	3952	Pte	Young, C. E.
1854	,,	Wright, C.	*1196	,,	Young, D.
1498	,,	Wright, C. S.	4660	,,	Young, D.
2036	,,	Wright, E. A.	1198	,,	Young, D. H.
*1853	,,	Wright, G. E.	2713	,,	Young, E. I. C.
3265	,,	Wright, H. F.	*1596	,,	Young, H.
65852	,,	Wright, H. V. R.	2706	,,	Young, H.
1443	,,	Wright, J.	7579	,,	Young, J. D.
6378	,,	Wright, J. D.	65858	,,	Young, H. V. G.
2980	,,	Wright, J. K.	540	Cpl	Young, R. G.
386	,,	Wright, L. D.	*6386	Pte	Younger, C. A.
*4578	,,	Wright, P.	6387	,,	Younger, E. O. P.
*384	,,	Wright, R. C.	63885	,,	Younger, L. R.
6600	,,	Wright, R. O.			

APPENDIX

Facing page 65.—The long building on the left is the well-equipped cinema and vaudeville theatre which was greatly patronized by the troops camped at Mena.

Facing page 96.—Lieut-Col Owen, who has just finished his final and inspiring address to his men, can be seen with papers in his hands, at the top of the gangway leading down to the well deck.

Facing page 112.—The rear man of the party was badly hit by shrapnel before reaching the end of the short pier.

Facing page 118.—These stretcher-bearers are carrying wounded down from the trenches at the top of Shrapnel Gully. Between six and seven o'clock on many evenings in July, the enemy's guns at Chanak, on the Asiatic side, used to shell the head of the gully with Jack Johnson's, and casualties were regularly suffered. On the left may be seen a man carrying up filled water bottles from the New Zealand water taps, or from the water carts on the beach.

Facing page 129.—A few tufts of green bush at the top of the trench made this spot more picturesque than was usual in the trenches. With traffic moving along one side of the trenches, soldiers rested and slept on the other side.

Facing page 144.—Nearly opposite the New Zealand water taps was a grave marked, "To an unknown British sailor," one of the tars, who, at the landing, snatched up a rifle and bayonet from a fallen Anzac, and joined the attack.

Facing page 145.—Sgt. Jones fell, with most of his platoon, on the ridges at Gallipoli. The grave, being under direct enemy observation, had to be dug by men as they lay flat upon the ground.

Halstead Printing Company Limited,
Arnold Place, Sydney

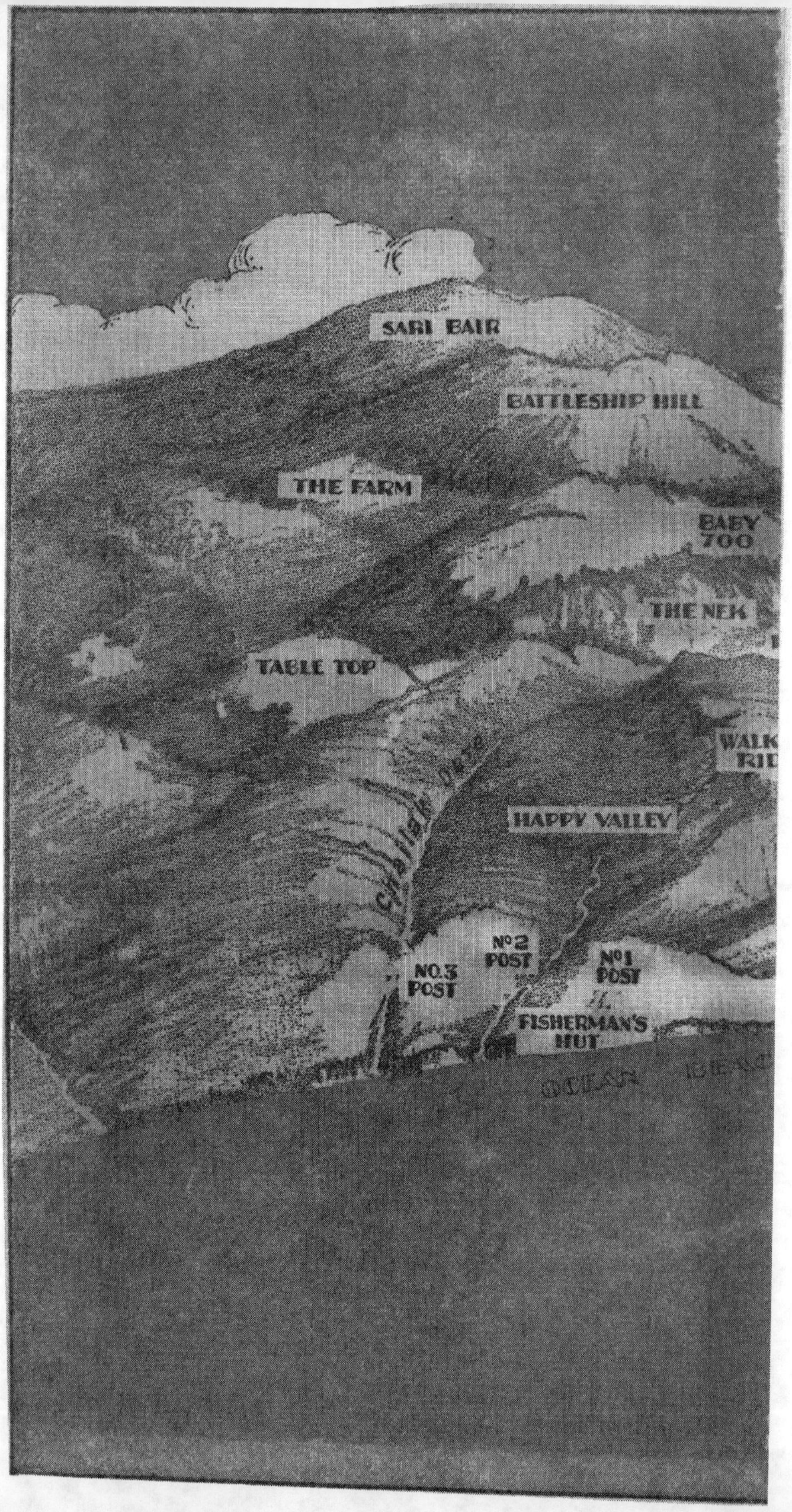
SARI BAIR
BATTLESHIP HILL
THE FARM
BABY 700
THE NEK
TABLE TOP
HAPPY VALLEY
No.2 POST
No.1 POST
NO.3 POST
FISHERMAN'S HUT

CHANAK KALE
KOJO DERE
DARDANELLES
MAIDOS
QUINN'S POST
STEEL'S POST
JOHNSTONE'S JOLLY
LONE PINE
MONASH GULLY
RAZORBACK
VICTORIA GULLY
MACLAGAN'S RIDGE
WHITE'S VALLEY
McCAY'S HILL
SHRAPNEL GULLY
BRIGHTON BEACH
ANZAC COVE
HELL SPIT

www.ingramcontent.com/pod-product-compliance
Lightning Source LLC
Chambersburg PA
CBHW052053300426
44117CB00013B/2104